This book, drawn from the Global Trade Analysis Project (GTAP), aims to help readers conduct quantitative analysis of international trade issues in an economy-wide framework. In addition to providing a succinct introduction to the GTAP modeling framework and data base, this book contains seven of the most refined GTAP applications undertaken to date, covering topics ranging from trade policy to the global implications of environmental policies, factor accumulation, and technological change. The authors of the applications are representative of the broader group of GTAP users. Some are academics, while others are professional economists in national and international agencies. All of their studies can be independently replicated by the reader through accessing software and files via the Internet Readers can also explore the sensitivity of results to varying assumptions and use the applications to launch independent research projects.

# Global Trade Analysis

# Global Trade Analysis
## Modeling and applications

Editor

THOMAS W. HERTEL
*Purdue University*

CAMBRIDGE
UNIVERSITY PRESS

Published by the Press Syndicate of the University of Cambridge
The Pitt Building, Trumpington Street, Cambridge CB2 1RP
40 West 20th Street, New York, NY 10011–4211, USA
10 Stamford Road, Oakleigh, Melbourne 3166, Australia

First published 1997

Printed in the United States of America

*Library of Congress Cataloging-in-Publication Data*
Global trade analysis : modeling and applications / edited by Thomas W. Hertel.
  p.  cm.
Based on the work from the Global Trade Analysis Project (GTAP).
ISBN 0-521-56134-5
1. International trade – Mathematical models.  2. International economic relations –
Mathematical models.  3. Global Trade Analysis Project.  I. Hertel, Thomas W.
(Thomas Warren), 1953–  .  II. Global Trade Analysis Project.
HF1008.G58   1996
382 – dc20                                          95–46688
                                                   CIP

A catalog record for this book is available from the British Library.

ISBN 0-521-56134-5

*I dedicate this book to my wife, Adriela, whose enthusiastic support of this effort has been essential to its success, and to my children, Alexander and Sarah, who have generously shared their father's time with a third child, named GTAP.*

# Contents

# Acknowledgments

As the most visible manifestation of the first years of the Global Trade Analysis Project (GTAP), this book owes its existence to many helping hands. At the top of this list comes Judy Conner, who has played many different roles during the inception of GTAP including: overseeing the day-to-day flow of paper and people; organizing travel, receptions, dinners, and short course logistics; as well as preparing this manuscript. She has offered generous hospitality as well as moral support to the project's staff and visitors, and this has been an important ingredient in keeping things going through the difficult times.

Inspiration for GTAP derived from my 1990–1991 sabbatical year with the Impact Project in Melbourne, Australia. Our stay in Melbourne was hosted by Alan Powell and Ken Pearson, who were most generous with their time and support. Alan's work with Impact demonstrated to me that applied general equilibrium analysis could indeed have a lasting effect on public policy. His guidance in getting GTAP off on the right foot was invaluable. The collaborative relationship with Ken Pearson that emerged from this sabbatical has proven most fruitful, forming the basis for operationalizing the GTAP model. Ken has proven to be an essential ingredient in the highly successful short courses.

While the Impact Project provided the inspiration for GTAP, the idea would not have gotten off the ground without a firm foundation upon which to build. The Australian Industry Commission's SALTER Project provided this starting point. Through the support of Philippa Dee and John Zeitsch, we were able to avoid duplicating the most costly components of that project. Robert McDougall, who provided much of the technical direction for the SALTER Project, became an informal advisor and offered critical advice and guidance along the way. Without his input we would have been in deep trouble. Indeed, his work has proven so valuable that we have hired him as GTAP's deputy director.

Other agencies also stepped in and provided critical support for GTAP in its early stages. The USDA's Economic Research Service has devoted considerable resources to development of the bilateral trade data base underpinning GTAP. In this regard, the continuing support and encouragement of Jerry Sharples and Mathew Shane, as well as many of their colleagues, are greatly appreciated. The staff of the International Economics Division of the World Bank, in particular Will Martin, David Tarr, and Alan Winters, have provided timely support to GTAP.

I also thank Wally Tyner, and the Department of Agricultural Economics at Purdue University, for having the vision and confidence to support GTAP when it was merely a concept. The department has proven to be an excellent environment for developing this project. The current GTAP staff, including Martina Brockmeier, Betina Dimaranan, Karen Huff, Elena Ianchovichina, Jennifer Stevens, and Padma Swaminathan, as well as students in my graduate course, have done an outstanding job of replicating the applications in this book. Their suggestions have considerably improved the end-product. The index to this volume was prepared by Elena Ianchovichina, with special assistance from Prashant Dave.

Finally, I extend a general thank you to members of the network of GTAP users who have given unselfishly of their data, ideas, time, and energies in order to make this idea a reality.

# Contributors

George B. Frisvold
ERS/USDA
Washington, DC
USA

Mark Gehlhar
ERS/USDA
Washington, DC
USA

Denice Gray
ERS/USDA
Washington, DC
USA

Kevin Hanslow
ABARE
Canberra
Australia

Thomas W. Hertel, Director
Global Trade Analysis Project
Purdue University
West Lafayette, IN
USA

Karen M. Huff
Purdue University
West Lafayette, IN
USA

Elena Ianchovichina
Purdue University
West Lafayette, IN
USA

Betsey Kuhn
ERS/USDA
Washington, DC
USA

D. Kent Lanclos
Department of Agricultural
    Economics
University of Idaho
Moscow, ID
USA

Donald MacLaren
The University of Melbourne
Melbourne
Australia

Bradley J. McDonald
GATT
Geneva
Switzerland

Robert McDougall
Deputy Director
Global Trade Analysis Project
West Lafayette, IN
USA

Will Martin
International Economics Division
The World Bank
Washington, DC
USA

Kenneth R. Pearson
Centre of Policy Studies and
  Impact Project
Monash University
Clayton, Victoria
Australia

Carlo Perroni
Department of Economics
University of Western Ontario
London, Ontario
Canada

Alan A. Powell
Department of Econometrics
Monash University
Director (1975–1993) of Impact
  Project
Clayton, Victoria
Australia

Padma V. Swaminathan
Purdue University
West Lafayette, IN
USA

Marinos E. Tsigas
ERS/USDA
Washington, DC
USA

Rod Tyers
Department of Economics
Australian National University
Canberra
Australia

Randall Wigle
Department of Economics
Wilfrid Laurier University
Waterloo, Ontario
Canada

Koji Yanagishima
International Economics Division
The World Bank
Washington, DC
USA

Yongzheng Yang
National Center for Development
  Studies
Australian National University
Canberra
Australia

Linda M. Young
Department of Economics
Montana State University
Bozeman, MT
USA

# Foreword

Economics, perhaps more than any other area of social inquiry, aspires to the status of a science. Like astronomers, we economists acknowledge that our inability to conduct controlled experiments puts us at a disadvantage. But instead of minimizing this disability, all too often we have accentuated it by failing to implement those straightforward measures that are taken as routine in the physical sciences. In particular – and as was forcefully pointed out by Dewald, Thursby, and Anderson in the *American Economic Review* (AER) for September 1986 – we have not even taken the standard precautions needed to ensure that our work can be replicated independently by others.

What is required to ensure replicability? The editors of the AER, in the issue referred to above, announced that it was their policy to "publish papers only where the data used in the analysis are clearly and precisely documented, are readily available to any researcher for purposes of replication, and where details of the computations sufficient to permit replication are provided" (p. v). In the case of applied general equilibrium (AGE) work, this can amount to a tall order.

To take just one well-known example – the Australian ORANI model – a listing of the model's data base and parameter file runs to 646 pages (Kenderes and Strzelecki 1991). The equations of the model itself, their interpretation and illustrative simulations are documented in a 372-page monograph (Dixon, Parmenter, Sutton, and Vincent 1982), and in a journal literature too voluminous to cite here.

Given that a practical AGE model involves a very heavy investment of intellectual effort and data-garnering, it would be amazing if economists did not recognize the potential for economies of scale and scope. The realization of such economies requires the proprietor of a model building effort to see most of the model's core ingredients – such as its standard or default equation listing, data base, and parameter file – as public goods. Around such publicly (or semipublicly) available tools we would expect a community of modelers to develop. Yet such has tended to be the exception rather than the rule.

The Global Trade Analysis Project (GTAP) is such an exceptional venture. At the outset of the project, its founder and director, Tom Hertel, decided that the issues involved in global trade are too important, and the resources available to support research too few, for current opportunities to be squandered by engaging in the wrong sort of replication while failing to attend to the prerequisites listed above for the right sort of replication. By the "wrong" sort of replication I mean unnecessary duplication: that is, two or more individuals or groups making separate demands on research resources to produce essentially the same product, be it a data base, a parameter file, or a core model.

Most of the resistance to sharing resources in AGE modeling can be traced to just two sources: (1) funding difficulties and (2) the academic imperative. If a common, open-access research facility is to be created, how does one elicit enough cooperation among the potential clientele to ensure that attempted free-riding does not sink the initiative? If academic recognition, promotion, and tenure seem to be more available to "loners" who keep their research cards very close to their vests, how can a community of modelers develop around a common modeling resource base? The answer to the first question clearly is that all putative members of a research consortium must recognize that without cooperation all are likely to be worse off. Having faced up to this, they must then agree to behave as responsible members of the modeling community. This implies meeting a share of the funding where possible, and agreeing that modeling infrastructure developed in-house will be shared by all.

The academic imperative will remain an obstacle as long as promotion and tenure committees – not to mention referees and editors of journals in applied economics – continue to reward novelty at the expense of the usefulness of research outputs. Over time I believe we are seeing more and more AGE researchers in academia realize that a quality piece of applied analysis that builds on an existing core model and data base offers better professional opportunities than implementing some new twist for its own sake on a toy model with data of doubtful provenance and relevance to any real-world problem. The chapters in this volume give grounds for hope that I am right about this.

The Australian community of AGE-oriented policy modelers was largely created at the Impact Project. Many key figures of the community either participated in some way in the development of the ORANI model under Peter Dixon and associates (1982) or else attended training courses organized by the project. Similar short courses are now being offered by the Global Trade Analysis Project. Such courses

- Give quick access to the core model, data base, and computing system
- Establish contact with a network of researchers having overlapping interests
- Give hands-on experience with manipulating a state-of-the-art model for policy analysis
- Serendipitously achieve many of the aims of refresher courses in economic theory and policy analysis

The story of the success of the family of ORANI-based models has been described at length in Powell and Lawson (1990), Vincent (1990), Powell and Snape (1992), and Dee (1994). It is an understatement to say that the utility of the approach was not immediately obvious to all players. The turning point in gaining acceptance by officials in policy agencies came when they realized that the AGE approach was not a straitjacket, but offered them enormous flexibility to apply their own insights into particular problems within a consistent economywide framework. This would not have been possible without generic software allowing modelers routinely to modify those parts of the ORANI theory that were not adequate to the task in hand, to eliminate unnecessary detail by aggregating over sectors/agents not currently under focus, and to amplify sectors of current interest by adding equations and data. The GEMPACK software suite developed by Ken Pearson and associates (see Harrison and Pearson 1994) put all this on a routine basis.

Apart from the importance of modeling flexibility to the clientele, and of human capital formation through training courses, other "lessons" gleaned from Impact's two decades of experience [as summarized by Powell and Lawson (1990) and Powell and Snape (1992)] suggest that a project that aims to provide the infrastructure for a focused modeling community should

1. Not be run entirely within a university or entirely within the client policy agencies
2. Be accompanied by full public documentation of data, methods, and results
3. Have detailed involvement of the policy clientele in the design stage of model building
4. Be at full arm's length from executive government

Recommendation 4 involves putting some space between the practitioner who is supplying the tools and the practitioner who is crafting the policy advice. The credibility of the tools should not be left too vulnerable to misjudgments by policy analysts or to the political popularity of particular policy recommendations based on them. Item 3, on the other hand, emphasizes that a policy-oriented model will be of limited use if no policy adviser uses it with enthusiasm.

As noted in the list above, item 2 is simply a criterion for scientific work: results must be capable of replication. Where conflicting interests are at stake, it is unreasonable to expect opponents to accept the reasonableness of assumptions or the internal consistency of simulations without full documentation; moreover, they can be relied upon to invest considerable resources into unearthing any shoddy work. In any event, abiding by best scientific practice is the assurance of quality control. Item 1 recognizes complementarities between the discipline of a civil service environment, which encourages working to a preannounced research program, and the creativity of the academic environment, which does not.

Finally, sponsors need to be convinced that a computable general equilibrium (CGE) model, including its data base/parameter life and computer systems, like any capital good, is subject to both depreciation and obsolescence. An ongoing resource commitment is necessary for updating and refurbishment. Although the institutional setting and subject matter differ from Impact's, I suspect that these insights may be useful in guiding GTAP through its formative years. I would be less than honest, however, if I did not record my pleasure that GTAP's director sees the development of his own project (perhaps somewhat hyperbolically) as "taking Impact abroad" (Hertel 1994).

The research agenda ahead of GTAP will be driven by the energy and vision of its director, and by the research imperatives of all those who use the GTAP framework. The start is impressive, the fundamentals are right. Where policy advisers have vision and are prepared to back that vision by cooperating in the development of a common research infrastructure, the results can be spectacular (as I believe the Australian experience shows). Hardheaded (or at least shrewd) decision makers will not let bureaucratic or academic imperatives encumber the development and use of powerful tools in the crucial task of sharpening the debate about world trading arrangements.

*Alan A. Powell*

REFERENCES

Dee, P. (1994) "General Equilibrium Models and Policy Advice in Australia," paper presented at the IFAC Workshop on Computing in Economics and Finance, Amsterdam, June 8–10.

Dewald, W. G., J. G. Thursby, and R. G. Anderson (1986) "Replication in Empirical Economics," *The American Economic Review* 76:587–603.

Dixon, P. B., B. R. Parameter, J. Sutton, and D. P. Vincent (1982) *Orani: A Multisectoral Model of the Australian Economy.* New York: North Holland.

Harrison, J., and K. R. Pearson (1994) GEMPACK 5.1 Documentation, The IMPACT Project, Monash University.

Hertel, T. W. (1994) "Taking IMPACT Abroad: The Global Trade Analysis Project," paper presented at the IFAC Workshop on Computing in Economics and Finance, Amsterdam, June 8–10.

Kenderes, M., and A. Strzelecki (1991) "Listing the 1986–87 ORANI Database," Industry Commission Research Memorandum No. OA-569, Belconnen, Australia. December.

Powell, A. A., and T. Lawson (1990) "A Decade of Applied General Equilibrium Modelling for Policy Work." In L. Bergman, D. Jorgenson, and E. Zalai (eds.), *General Equilibrium Modeling and Economic Policy Analysis.* Cambridge, MA: Blackwell.

Powell, A. A., and R. Snape (1992) "The Contribution of Applied General Equilibrium Analysis to Policy Reform in Australia," IMPACT Project General Paper No. G-98, Monash University, Melbourne, Australia.

Vincent, D. (1990) "Applied General Equilibrium Modelling in the Australian Industries Assistance Commission: Perspectives of a Policy Analyst." In L. Bergman, D. Jorgenson, and E. Zalai (eds.), *General Equilibrium Modeling and Economic Policy Analysis.* Cambridge, MA: Blackwell.

PART I

INTRODUCTION AND OVERVIEW

# CHAPTER 1

# Introduction

*Thomas W. Hertel*

## What is GTAP?

The Global Trade Analysis Project (GTAP) was established in 1992, with the objective of lowering the cost of entry for those seeking to conduct quantitative analyses of international economic issues in an economywide framework. The project consists of several components:

- A fully documented, publicly available, global data base
- A standard modeling framework
- Software for manipulating the data and implementing the standard model
- A global network of researchers, linked through the Internet, with a common interest in multiregion analysis of trade and resource issues
- A World Wide Web site for distributing software, data, and other project-related items of interest
- A consortium of national and international agencies providing leadership and a base level of support

Part II of this book documents the GTAP model structure, data base, and software. Part III contains seven applications of the model. These are all available through GTAP's Web site, and the interested reader will have the opportunity to access, replicate, and extend these applications using the software described in Chapter 6.

## Motivation for GTAP

As the world economy becomes more integrated, there is an increasing demand for quantitative analyses of policy issues on a global basis. One example is provided by the Uruguay Round negotiations, which took place under the auspices of the General Agreement on Tariffs and Trade (GATT). There has

3

been great interest in estimates of the impact of this agreement on individual countries, international trade, and worldwide welfare. Sector-by-sector analyses are a valuable input into this process. However, by its very nature, the GATT affects all sectors and most regions of the world, so there is no way to avoid employing a data base that is exhaustive in its coverage of commodities and countries. A similar problem exists when one wishes to analyze the economic implications of climate change, economic growth, or any one of a number of issues affecting the world as a whole. GTAP aims to facilitate such multicountry, economywide analyses.

### GTAP data base

The central ingredient in GTAP's success to date has been the global data base, described in detail in Chapters 3 and 4. This data base contains bilateral trade, transport, and protection data characterizing economic linkages among regions, together with individual-country input–output data bases that account for intersectoral linkages within each region. (See Chapter 3, Table 3.1, for a complete list of regions and commodities in version 2 of the GTAP data base.) The construction and maintenance of this data base adheres to the following principles:

**Public availability.** The data base is made available to anyone requesting it, at cost. This prevents needless duplication of effort in creating this public good. In particular, existing aggregations of the data base are provided for free, via anonymous FTP on the internet. New aggregations can be ordered, for a nominal fee, and are then added to the FTP site. Finally, the full data base may be purchased, along with documentation and software, by those interested in performing their own aggregations.

**Annual upgrades.** The data base is upgraded annually. Typically, this involves adding more regions as well as improving the quality of the data base for existing regions. Periodically we update the base year and in the future, the commodity aggregation may change. The data base used in this book is the second release (version 2) of the GTAP data base.

**Broad participation.** The network of GTAP users represents an excellent resource for scrutiny and improvement of the data base. Those who identify areas for improvement or extension of the data base are encouraged to contact the GTAP staff with their ideas so that they may be considered for incorporation into the next year's data base. The operational concept is, "If you don't like it, help fix it!"

**Comparative advantage.** By making the full data base available, and by incorporating improvements offered by members of the network, each individual is able to work to his or her comparative advantage, while capitalizing on the contributions of others.

**Documentation and replicability.** The data base is fully documented. One requirement for new contributions to the GTAP data base is that the sources and procedures used to create them be provided along with the data. In addition, the GTAP software is designed to permit applications to be readily replicated by others (including the readers of this book). Together these two features are designed to enhance the credibility and comparability of global trade analyses.

*Model and software*

In order to operationalize this large data base, a standard modeling framework has been developed. The theory of this multiregion, applied general equilibrium model is developed in Chapter 2. Distinguishing features include: the treatment of private household behavior, international trade and transport activity, and global savings/investment relationships. Also, a number of auxiliary variables have been introduced in order to facilitate alternative closures, including *partial equilibrium* specifications aimed at facilitating comparisons with other models.

The standard GTAP model is implemented using Release 5.1 of the GEM-PACK software suite, developed at the IMPACT Project, Monash University, under the direction of Kenneth Pearson, with the support of the Australian Industry Commission. The software described in this book, and available at no cost from the FTP site, is referred to as the *GTAP Book Version of GEMPACK*. This permits the reader to conduct *nonlinear* simulations of the standard model in which changes in policy, technology, population, and factor endowments are examined. The user specifies the split between exogenous and endogenous variables (i.e., model closure). Behavioral parameters may also be altered. Outputs include a complete matrix of bilateral trade, activity flows (and percentage changes) by sector and region, private and government consumption, regional welfare, and a variety of summary variables. Users with access to a source-code version of GEMPACK may also modify the theory of the model.

At the time of publication of this book, literally dozens of applications of the standard GTAP framework were under way, worldwide. These are aimed at addressing a great variety of issues including: trade policy reform, regional integration, energy policy, global climate change, technological progress, and historical analysis of economic growth and trade. Seven of these applications have been selected for inclusion in this book. They are intended to be representative of some of the types of work for which GTAP is currently being used.

These applications can be accomplished using the standard GTAP model, the software for which is on the FTP site.

### Short course in Global Trade Analysis

Use of this framework has spread quickly around the globe. Only two years into its existence, the framework was being used on five continents, by a wide variety of researchers in academia, public agencies, and even the private sector. A great deal of credit for this must be attributed to the annual Short Course in Global Trade Analysis. This was an innovation adopted from the Impact Project that introduced such a course 20 years ago to encourage use of the ORANI model (see the Foreword, by Alan Powell). The course is offered each summer on the campus of Purdue University and offers participants a hands-on introduction to the material in this book. Periodically, overseas versions of the course are also undertaken. Current developments in the GTAP data base and recent applications are explored and each participant has the experience of replicating/extending one such application during the course.

### Overview of the book

This book is divided into four parts, of which this chapter is the first. Part II develops fundamental components of the GTAP data base and modeling framework. It begins with a thorough exposition of the standard GTAP model structure, including derivations and motivations as well as a complete listing of equations and variables. Chapters 3 and 4 cover the data and parameters in version 2 of the GTAP data base. All the applications in this book build on aggregations of this information. Chapter 5 discusses the method of aggregation. It also demonstrates how the theory, data, and parameters interact to determine *equilibrium elasticities* in the context of a 3x3 aggregation. Part II of the book concludes with Chapter 6, which describes how to access and use the *GTAP Book Version of GEMPACK*. It also contains an example of how to replicate results from an application in Part III. This chapter is accompanied by a "Hands-On" document, which may be obtained from the GTAP Web site.

Having covered the basics behind the GTAP, Part III of the book contains seven applications of the standard model. These are grouped by topic and examine issues such as: economic growth and trade, trade policy, resources, technology, and the environment. The first of these applications, Chapter 7, is authored by McDougall and Tyers; it focuses on the effects of economic growth on factor markets. In particular, they examine the impact that factor accumulation and increased openness in the rapidly developing economies (RDEs) of East Asia has had on factor markets in the older industrialized economies (OIEs). This represents a new, innovative use of applied general equilibrium analysis. McDougall and Tyers find that growth and openness in the RDEs have indeed depressed the demand for unskilled labor in the OIEs, but the effect is quite modest. This leads the authors to side with those arguing that the significant decline in relative wages for the unskilled in recent decades is more likely due to biased technical change in the OIEs themselves.

The next three applications, Chapters 8–10, address various dimensions of trade policy liberalization. This is more familiar turf for AGE modelers. In Chapter 8, MacLaren provides an *ex post* analysis of the Cairns Group strategies for negotiation in the Uruguay Round. In particular, he estimates the benefits, to selected member countries, from alternative unilateral agricultural liberalization scenarios. These are compared to their negotiating positions. He concludes that there *is* an empirical economic basis for the differing political stances that Australia and Canada adopted during the GATT negotiations.

Whereas the MacLaren application focuses on unilateral liberalization in agriculture, the Young–Huff application in Chapter 9 examines the impact of multiregion, across-the-board cuts in protection. In particular, the authors compare two alternative approaches to free trade in the Asia-Pacific region: preferential versus nonpreferential (MFN). The question of which approach to take is currently being debated among Asia-Pacific Economic Cooperation (APEC) members. Some commentators have argued that the customary approach of only reducing intraregional trade barriers is too limiting in the dynamic Asia-Pacific region. Young and Huff shed some light on this issue with a carefully constructed set of experiments that highlight the importance of reciprocity on the part of non-APEC members, when liberalization is conducted on an MFN basis. Without such reciprocity, they find that liberalization on an MFN basis shifts a significant share of the global benefits to non-APEC members.

The final trade policy liberalization application is that of Yongzheng, Martin, and Yanagishima, in Chapter 10. These authors exploit the recent addition to the GTAP data base of bilateral quota rents associated with the Multifibre Arrangement (MFA). They examine the implications of reforming the MFA – or not – in the context of the broader set of Uruguay Round reforms. Failure to relax this system of bilateral quotas in conjunction with the other elements of a Uruguay Round package results in quotas that become *even more binding*. That is, the associated rents increase. The authors find that reform of the MFA comprises a large part of the global welfare gains to be had from the full Uruguay Round package, and the interaction between these bilateral quotas with non-MFA reforms is significant.

The last three applications in Part III of the book are drawn from the rapidly growing body of AGE-based work relating to resources, technology, and the environment. In Chapter 11, Tsigas, Frisvold, and Kuhn use the GTAP framework to examine the implications of climate change for global patterns of production, consumption, and trade. Their emphasis is on agriculture, which is one of the industries most affected by global changes in temperature and precipitation. They survey the scientific literature in this area and specify a set of crop-specific productivity shocks. Simulation of the GTAP model permits them to examine the consequences of the distribution of global food production, consumption, and welfare. They are also able to evaluate the sensitivity of their results to a key scientific uncertainty, namely the potential impact of $CO_2$ fertilization. The authors demonstrate that the latter effect is capable of ameliorating many of the adverse effects of climate change on global food production. However, significant regional shifts in production and welfare remain. Finally, the authors utilize the *partial equilibrium* (PE) closures available in GTAP in order to assess the likely degree of error in earlier PE studies of climate change.

In Chapter 12, Perroni and Wigle show how the standard GTAP model can be supplemented by a set of side calculations in order to permit the user to conduct a more complete analysis of environmental policies. Particular features of the problem that their results address include: the presence of abatement technologies, and the benefits of abatement. Their approach is innovative, drawing on more specialized modeling work they have published elsewhere. The beauty of this chapter is that it shows how to incorporate these very important issues into this standard modeling framework, thereby facilitating combined analyses of resources, trade policy, and the environment.

In the final application, Chapter 13, Frisvold offers a readily accessible analysis of the intersectoral, multiregion effects of technological change in agriculture, using the GTAP framework. The results are used to place in perspective the existing literature on this topic and to shed new light on the question of who gains and who loses from different patterns of innovation and adoption of new technologies. In particular, Frisvold shows how the benefits of technological change depend on: (1) the extent of international spillovers associated with this innovation; (2) the trade position of the innovating country; (3) the stage of production where the innovation occurs; and (4) the factor bias involved.

Part IV of the book offers an evaluation of the GTAP framework, including performance of the standard model and quality of the data base and parameters. It begins with an attempt to evaluate the model's performance in a "backcasting" exercise that focuses on changes in export shares in the Pacific Rim over the decade of the 1980s. This was a period of dramatic change for many East Asian economies. The Newly Industrialized Economies (NIEs) such as Korea and Taiwan shifted their exports from labor-intensive manufactures to knowledge-intensive products, as the "new NIEs" such as Thailand took over exports of the former items. Is GTAP capable of generating these types of changes, based solely on observed changes in factor endowments and population? This is the question Gehlhar asks in Chapter 14. In so doing, he employs both the standard GTAP model, and a slightly modified variant that incorporates a distinction between raw labor and human capital. The latter is shown to improve significantly the predictive power of the model, and this leads him to recommend further development of the data base in this direction. Finally, Chapter 15 provides an overall evaluation of the effort to date, as well as some observations about the future course of global trade analysis using the GTAP framework.

### *Reader's guide*

The appropriate strategy for tackling this book depends on the objectives of the reader. For those who wish to master all the material, the most efficient approach is to read it chronologically–beginning with the model structure, reading about the data base and parameters, accessing the software from the Web site, mastering the 3x3 example, pursuing the applications, and, finally, turning to an evaluation of the GTAP framework. However, many readers will open this book with a specific question in mind. This suggests an alternative approach.

A very natural way to become familiar with GTAP is through a particular application. For example, if you have a specific interest in assessing the impacts of technological change you might wish to begin with Chapter 13. Having read this chapter, you discover the importance of specifying the precise form of technological change under consideration: is it Hicks-neutral – or perhaps labor-augmenting? To understand how these concepts are implemented in the standard GTAP model, you need to backtrack to Chapter 2 and examine the section on producer behavior.

Frisvold's technological change application also highlights the importance of a country's initial trade position and the general equilibrium demand elasticities that face its producers. You might then undertake a selective overview of Chapters 3 and 4, on data and parameters. You might also want to review Chapter 5 in some detail, as it is crucial in understanding the origin and interpretation of the general equilibrium demand elasticities that Frisvold uses in his analysis.

At this point, the reader with an interest in technical change is in a position to replicate the results. Chapter 6 offers a guide to accessing and running the software that accompanies this book. Not only can you replicate the results in Chapter 13, you can also examine their sensitivity to the author's assumptions about parameters and closure of the model. For example, how is the regional distribution of benefits from technical change in a single region affected by increasing the size of the trade elasticities? What happens when some economies attempt to insulate producers from declining world prices?

It is also possible to use this aggregation as a starting point for an entirely different experiment, perhaps involving trade policy liberalization.

Whatever strategy you choose to pursue in reading this book, I hope you will find the combination of theory, data documentation, computing, and applications to be rewarding. We maintain a discussion list and a bibliography of GTAP-based applications to which you are invited to contribute. The discussion list offers a vehicle for GTAP users, worldwide, to communicate with one another. Because GTAP is an ongoing project, we hope you will share your reactions, feedback, and questions with us via electronic mail sent to: *GTAP@FTP.PURDUE.EDU*. You may also wish to join gtap-l, the mailing list for those interested in GTAP, by sending the one-line message "subscribe gtap-l Jean Doe" to: <listserv@vm.cc.purdue.edu>, where Jean Doe is replaced by your name. GTAP also has a Web site with up-to-date information at:

*http://www.agecon.purdue.edu/centers/gtap/*

PART II

STRUCTURE OF GTAP FRAMEWORK

CHAPTER 2

# Structure of GTAP

*Thomas W. Hertel and Marinos E. Tsigas*

## I    Introduction and overview

The purpose of this chapter is to develop the basic notation, equations, and intuition behind the GTAP model of global trade. The computer program documenting the basic model, GTAP94.TAB, is available in electronic form via the Internet (see Chapter 6). It provides complete documentation of the theory behind the model, and when converted to executable files using the GEMPACK software suite (Harrison and Pearson 1994), it forms the basis for implementing the applications outlined in Part III of this book.

The organization of this chapter is as follows. We begin with an overview of the Global Trade Analysis Project (GTAP) model. Next, we develop the basic accounting relationships underpinning the data base and model. This involves tracking value flows through the global data base, from production and sales to intermediate and final demands. Careful attention is paid to the prices at which each of these flows is evaluated, and the presence of distortions (in the form of taxes and subsidies). The relationship between these accounting relationships and equilibrium conditions in the model is then developed. This leads naturally into a discussion of the implications of alternative "partial equilibrium" closures whereby these equations are selectively omitted and the associated complementary variables are fixed. The chapter then turns to the linearized representation of these accounting relations. This is the form in which they are implemented in GEMPACK, which solves the nonlinear equilibrium problem via successive updates and relinearizations.

Section VI of this documentation turns its attention to the equations underpinning economic behavior in the model. We deal in turn with production, consumption, global savings, and investment. There is also a special discussion of macroeconomic closure in the GTAP model. This material is reinforced in the closing section of the chapter by means of a numerical example using a three-region, three-commodity aggregation, in which there is a shock to a single bilateral protection rate.

## II      Overview of the model[1]

### *Closed economy without taxes*

Figure 2.1 offers an overview of economic activity in a simplified version of the GTAP model [see Brockmeier (1996) for a more comprehensive, graphical

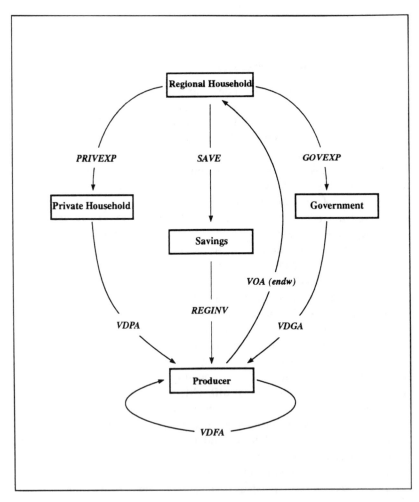

**Figure 2.1.** One-region closed economy without government intervention.

overview]. In this first figure, there is only one region, so there is no trade. There is also no depreciation, and no taxes or subsidies are present. At the top of this figure is the regional household. Expenditures by this household are governed by an aggregate utility function that allocates expenditure across three broad categories: private, government, and savings expenditures.[2] The model user has some discretion over the allocation of expenditures across these types of final demand. In the standard closure, the regional household's Cobb–Douglas utility function assures constant budget shares are devoted to each category. However, real government purchases and savings can also be dictated exogenously (i.e., fixed or shocked), in which case private household expenditure will adjust to satisfy the regional household's budget constraint.

This formulation for regional expenditure has some distinct advantages, as well as some disadvantages. Perhaps the most significant drawback is the failure to link government expenditures to tax revenues. Cutting taxes by no means implies a reduction in government expenditures in the GTAP model. Indeed, to the extent that these tax cuts lead to a reduction in excess burden, regional real income will increase and real government expenditure will likely also rise. This lack of fiscal integrity is dictated by the fact that the GTAP data have incomplete coverage of regional tax instruments. Therefore the model cannot accurately predict what will happen to total tax revenue, and the user who is interested in focusing on government expenditure effects would be required to make some exogenous assumptions in any case.

The greatest advantage of the formulation of regional expenditure displayed in Figure 2.1 is the unambiguous indicator of welfare offered by the regional utility function. A particular simulation might lead to lower relative prices for savings and the composite of government purchases, and higher prices for the private household's commodity bundle. If real private purchases fall, while savings and government consumption rise, is the regional household better off? Without a regional utility function we cannot answer this question.

An alternative approach to this problem of welfare measurement involves fixing the level of real savings and government purchases, and focusing solely on private household consumption as an indicator of welfare. However, private consumption is only slightly more than 50% of final demand in some regions. Forcing all the adjustment in the regional economy's final demand into private consumption seems rather extreme. We believe that the assumption of fixed expenditure shares dictated by the Cobb–Douglas regional expenditure function is more acceptable empirically. That is, a rise in income implies an increase in savings and government expenditures, as well as private consumption.

Since Figure 2.1 assumes the absence of taxes, the only source of income for regional households is from the "sale" of endowment commodities to firms. This income flow is represented by *VOA(endw)* which denotes *Value of Output at Agents' prices* of endowment commodities. (A complete glossary of GTAP notation is provided at the end of this book.) Firms combine these endowment commodities with intermediate goods (*VDFA = Value of Domestic purchases by Firms at Agents' prices*) in order to produce goods for final demand. This involves sales to private households (*VDPA = Value of Domestic purchases by Private households at Agents' prices*), government households (*VDGA = Value of Domestic purchases by Government household at Agents, prices*), and the sale of investment goods to satisfy the regional household's demand for savings (*REGINV*). This completes the circular flow of income, expenditure, and production in a closed economy without taxes.

### *Open economy without taxes*

Figure 2.2 [also taken from Brockmeier (1996)] introduces international trade by adding another region, *Rest of the World* (ROW), at the bottom of the figure. This region is identical in structure to the domestic economy, but details are suppressed in Figure 2.2. It is the source of imports into the regional economy, as well as the destination for exports (*VXMD = Value of eXports at Market prices by Destination*). It is important to note that imports are traced to specific agents in the domestic economy, resulting in distinct import payments to ROW from private households (*VIPA*), government households (*VIGA*), and firms (*VIFA*). This innovation departs from most models of global trade, and was adopted from the SALTER model (Jomini et al. 1991). It is especially important for the analysis of trade policy in regions where import intensities for the same commodity vary widely across uses.

   In moving from a closed to an open economy, we also require the introduction of two global sectors, one of which is displayed in Figure 2.2. The *global bank*, shown in the center of this figure, intermediates between global savings and regional investment. As will be discussed in more detail below, it assembles a portfolio of regional investment goods, and sells shares in this portfolio to regional households in order to satisfy their demand for savings.

   The second global sector (not shown in Figure 2.2) accounts for international trade and transport activity. It assembles regional exports of trade, transport, and insurance services and produces a composite good used to move merchandise trade among regions. The value of these services precisely exhausts the differences between global *fob* exports, and global imports, evaluated on a *cif* basis.

### III     Accounting relationships in the "levels"

#### *Distribution of sales to regional markets*

The basic accounting relationships in the data base/model are best understood in the context of a flow chart. For example, Table 2.1 portrays the sources of

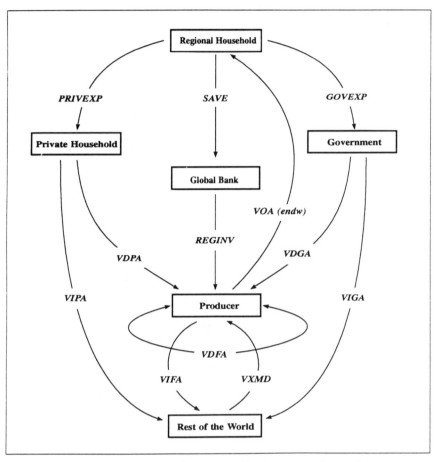

**Figure 2.2.** Multiregion open economy without government intervention.

sectoral receipts in the global data base. (In the data and the model all sectors produce a single output. Thus there is a one-to-one relationship between producing sectors and commodities.) At the top of the figure, *VOA(i,r)* refers to the *Value of Output at Agents' Prices.* (The general explanation for this choice of notation is as follows: value / type of transaction / type of price. See the appendix to this book for an exhaustive listing of variables used in the model and their description.) *VOA(i,r)* represents the payments received by the firms in industry *i* of region *r*. As we will see, these payments must be precisely exhausted on costs, under the zero pure profits assumption. The terms *PS(i,r)* and *QO(i,r)* to the right of *VOA* represent the price and quantity indices that make up *VOA*. They will be discussed in more detail below.

**Table 2.1.** *Distribution of Sales to Regional Markets (i ∈ TRAD)*

| | | | |
|---|---|---|---|
| Domestic market $r$ | | $VOA(i,r)$ <br> $+PTAX(i,r)$ <br> $=VOM(i,r)$ | : $PS(i,r) * QO(i,r)$ <br><br> : $PM(i,r) * QO(i,r)$ |
| | $VDM(i,r)$ | | $VST(i,r)$ |
| | | $VXMD(i,r,s)$ <br> $+XTAXD(i,r,s)$ | :$PM(i,r) * QXS(i,r,s)$ |
| World market | | $=VXWD(i,r,s)$ <br> $+VTWR(i,r,s)$ <br> $=VIWS(i,r,s)$ | : $PFOB(i,r,s) * QXS(i,r,s)$ <br><br> : $PCIF(i,r,s) * QXS(i,r,s)$ |
| | | $+MTAX(i,r,s)$ <br> $=VIMS(i,r,s)$ | : $PMS(i,r,s) * QXS(i,r,s)$ |
| | | $VIM(i,s)$ | : $PIM(i,s) * QIM(i,s)$ |
| Domestic market $s$ | | $=VIPM(i,s)$ <br> $+VIGM(i,s)$ | : $PIM(i,s) * QPM(i,s)$ <br> : $PIM(i,s) * QGM(i,s)$ |
| | $+\sum\limits_{j \in PROD}$ | $VIFM(i,j,s)$ | : $PIM(i,s) * QFM(i,j,s)$ |
| **Where:** | $VDM(i,r)$ | $=VDPM(i,r)$ <br> $+VDGM(i,r)$ | : $PM(i,r) * QPD(i,r)$ <br> : $PM(i,r) * QGD(i,r)$ |
| | $+\sum\limits_{j \in PROD\_COMM}$ | $VDFM(i,j,r)$ | : $PM(i,r) * QFD(i,j,r)$ |

If one adds back the producer tax (or deducts the subsidy) denoted by $PTAX(i,r)$, then we arrive at the *Value of Output at Market prices, VOM(i,r)*. This may be seen to be the sum of the *Value of Domestic sales at Market prices, VDM(i,r)*, and the exports to all destinations, denoted as *Value of eXports of i from r evaluated at domestic Market prices (in r), and Destined for s, VXMD(i,r,s)*. In addition, we must take account of possible sales to the international transport sector, denoted *VST(i,r)*. These sales are designed to cover the international transport margins. They are evaluated at market prices and face no further (border) taxes. Similarly, since domestic sales do not cross a border, they do not face such taxes either.

In order to convert exports to *fob* values, it is necessary to add the export tax, denoted $XTAX(i,r,s)$. Note that these taxes are written in a form that is destination-specific. The data base exhibits destination/source-specific trade policy measures at the level of *disaggregated* regions and commodities (this varies by type of policy intervention). Once the data base has been aggregated over either commodities or regions, bilateral rates of taxation will vary due to compositional differences. Therefore, it is important to maintain this bilateral detail in the modeling framework. Once the export taxes are added in, we obtain the *Value of eXports at World prices by Destination, VXWD(i,r,s)*. The difference between this and the *cif*-based *Value of Imports at World prices by Source, VIWS(i,r,s)*, is the international transportation margin: $VTWR(i,r,s)$ refers to the *Value of Transportation at World prices by Route* for commodity $i$, shipped from $r$ to $s$.

At this point we have taken commodity $i$ from its sector of origin in region $r$ to its export destination in region $s$. In order to evaluate these sales at internal domestic prices in $s$, it is necessary to add import taxes, $MTAX(i,r,s)$ to get $VIMS(i,r,s)$, the *Value of Imports at Market prices by Source*. These imports from alternative sources may then be combined into a single composite, $VIM(i,s)$, the *Value of Imports of i into s at Market prices*. Just as sales in the $r$th market had to be distributed across various destinations, so composite imports of $i$ into $s$ must be distributed across sectors and households in the $s$th market. Possible uses of imports include: $VIPM(i,s)$ – the *Value of Imports by Private households, evaluated at Market prices; VIGM(i,s)* – the *Value of Imports by the Government, evaluated at Market prices*; and $VIFM(i,j,s)$ – the *Value of Imports by Firms in industry j, at Market price*. In a similar fashion, domestic sales, denoted $VDM(i,r)$, must be distributed across private household, government, and firms' uses, as shown at the bottom of Table 2.1.

### Sources of household purchases

Having distributed sales across various markets and taken full account of intervening taxes and transport margins, we are now in a position to consider household and firms' purchases within each of these individual markets. Table 2.2 outlines the distribution of household purchases of tradeable commodities. The top half of this figure pertains to private household purchases, denoted $VPA(i,s)$, to represent the *Value of Private household purchases at Agents' prices*. This represents the sum of expenditures on domestically produced goods, $VDPA(i,s)$, and composite imports, evaluated at agents' prices, $VIPA(i,s)$. Once private household commodity taxes, $IPTAX(i,s)$, are deducted, this brings us to the *Value of Imports by the Private household at Market*

**Table 2.2.** *Sources of Household Purchases* ($i \epsilon$ *TRAD*)

Private household

| | | | |
|---|---|---|---|
| | $VPA(i,s)$ | | $: PP(i,s) * QP(i,s)$ |
| $VDPA(i,s)$ | $: PPD(i,s) * QPD(i,s)$ | $VIPA(i,s)$ | $: PPM(i,s) * QPM(i,s)$ |
| -$\underline{DPTAX(i,s)}$ | | -$\underline{IPTAX(i,s)}$ | |
| $= VDPM(i,s)$ | $: PM(i,s) * QPD(i,s)$ | $= VIPM(i,s)$ | $: PIM(i,s) * QPM(i,s)$ |

--------------------

Government household

| | | | |
|---|---|---|---|
| | $VGA(i,s)$ | | $: PG(i,s) * QG(i,s)$ |
| $VDGA(i,s)$ | $: PGD(i,s) * QGD(i,s)$ | $VIGA(i,s)$ | $: PGM(i,s) * QGM(i,s)$ |
| -$\underline{DGTAX(i,s)}$ | | -$IGTAX(i,s)$ | |
| $= VDGM(i,s)$ | $: PM(i,s) * QGD(i,s)$ | $= VIGM(i,s)$ | $: PIM(i,s) * QGM(i,s)$ |

*prices*, $VIPM(i,s)$, which is the point where we left Table 2.1. Similarly, deducting domestic commodity taxes, $DPTAX(i,s)$, from $VDPA(i,s)$ yields $VDPM(i,s)$, the *Value of Domestic purchases by the Private household, at Market prices*. Thus we have completed the link between industry sales at agents' prices (top of Table 2.1) and private household purchases at agents' prices (top of Table 2.2). The bottom half of Table 2.2 is completely analogous; only $P$ is replaced by $G$ in order to represent purchases by the government household.

### Sources of firms' purchases and household factor income

Next, turn to firms' purchases of intermediate and primary factors of production. The top of Table 2.3 tackles the intermediate inputs, starting with the *Value of Firms' purchases of i, by sector j, in region s at Agents' prices,*

**Table 2.3.** *Sources of Firms' Purchases* *(j ∈ PROD)*

*i ∈ TRAD*: Intermediate inputs

$$VFA(i,j,s) \qquad : PF(i,j,s) * QF(i,j,s)$$

$$VDFA(i,j,s) \quad : PFD(i,j,s) * QFD(i,j,s) \qquad VIFA(i,j,s) \qquad : PFM(i,j,s) * QFM(i,j,s)$$

$$-\underline{DFTAX(i,j,s)} \qquad\qquad\qquad\qquad\qquad -\underline{IFTAX(i,j,s)}$$

$$= VDFM(i,j,s): PM(i,s) * QFD(i,j,s) \qquad = VIFM(i,j,s) \qquad : PIM(i,s) * QFM(i,j,s)$$

*i ∈ ENDW*: Primary factor services

$$VFA(i,j,s) \qquad : PFE(i,j,s) * QFE(i,j,s)$$

$$-\underline{ETAX(i,j,s)}$$

$$= VFM(i,j,s) \qquad : PM(i,s) * QFE(i,j,s)$$

**Zero pure profits**

$$VOA(j,s) = \sum_{i \in TRAD} VFA(i,j,s) + \sum_{i \in ENDW} VFA(i,j,s)$$

$VFA(i,j,s)$. This may be broken into the domestic and imported components, $VDFA(i,j,s)$ and $VIFA(i,j,s)$. Deducting intermediate input taxes, $DFTAX(i,j,s)$ and $IFTAX(i,j,s)$, reduces these values to market prices, $VDFM(i,j,s)$ and $VIFM(i,j,s)$, which are the same as the values reported at the bottom of Table 2.1.

Firms also purchase services of nontradeable commodities, which in this model are termed *endowment commodities*. (In the current data base, these include: agricultural land, labor, and capital.) The next part of Table 2.3 traces the value flows from the firms employing these factors of production, back to the households supplying them. Note that by deducting taxes on endowment

**Table 2.4.** *Sources of Household Factor Service Income*

---

*i ∈ ENDWM*: Mobile endowments

$$\sum_{j \in PROD} VFM(i,j,s) \quad = VOM(i,s) \qquad : PM(i,s) * QO(i,s)$$

$$\quad - \underline{HTAX(i,s)}$$

$$\quad = VOA(i,s) \qquad : PS(i,s) * QO(i,s)$$

*i ∈ ENDWS*: Sluggish endowments

$$VFM(i,j,s) \qquad : PMES(i,j,s) * QOES(i,j,s)$$

$$VOM(i,s) \qquad : PM(i,s) * QO(i,s)$$

$$- \underline{HTAX(i,s)}$$

$$= VOA(i,s) \qquad : PS(i,s) * QO(i,s)$$

---

$i$ used in industry $j$, $ETAX(i,j,s)$, we can move from the *Value of Firms' purchases at Agents' prices, VFA(i,j,s)*, to the *Value of Firms' purchases at Market prices, VFM(i,j,s)*. The final section of Table 2.3 makes the link between firms' receipts [i.e., $VOA(j,s)$], as developed in Table 2.1, and firms' expenditures [i.e., $VFA(i,j,s)$], as shown in Table 2.3. Zero pure economic profits means that revenues must be exhausted on expenditures, once accounting for all tradeable (i.e., intermediate) inputs and endowment (i.e., primary) factors of production.

Table 2.4 details the sources of household factor income. Here, it is necessary to distinguish between endowment commodities that are perfectly mobile, and therefore earn the same market return (*ENDWM_COMM*), and those that are sluggish to adjust and that therefore sustain differential returns in equilibrium (*ENDWS_COMM*). In the former case, we may simply sum over all usage of the factor – since market prices are equal – thereupon deducting the tax on households' supply of primary factor $i$ in region $s$, $HTAX(i,s)$, in order to obtain the *Value of this endowment's "Output" at Agents' prices* (*VOA*). The latter is the amount actually received by the private household supplying the factor in question.

In the case of the sluggish endowment commodities (e.g., land), shocks to the model will introduce differential price changes across sectors. This is reflected in the presence of an industry index $(j)$, in the price component of $VFM(i,j,s)$. These differential prices are then combined into a composite return to the sluggish endowment, at market prices, via a unit revenue function. The resulting *Value of endowment Output at Market prices, VOM(i,s)*, is then handled in the same way as for mobile commodities, deducting household income taxes to arrive at the $VOA(i,s)$.

### Disposition and sources of regional income

When taxes are present, the computation of disposable income for the regional household in Figures 2.1 and 2.2 becomes much more complex. At the top of Table 2.5, we have the condition that expenditures on private, government, and savings commodities must precisely exhaust regional income. This is followed by the expression that decomposes income by source. We begin by adding up endowment income (recall Figures 2.1 and 2.2). Note that all such income earned within a region accrues to households in that same region. From this, we must deduct depreciation expenses required to maintain the integrity of the initial capital stock, $VDEP(r)$, thereupon adding net tax receipts and rents associated with any quantitative restrictions.

Rather than keeping track of individual tax/subsidy flows in the model, the approach taken here is to compare the value of a given transaction, evaluated at agents', market, or world prices. If there is a discrepancy between what households receive for their labor supply and the value of this supply at market prices, then the difference must equal $HTAX(i,r)$, as shown in Table 2.4. Alternatively, this tax revenue could be rewritten in terms of an explicit *ad valorem* tax rate, $\tau(i,r)$, by noting that the household's supply price of endowment $i$ is given by:

$$PS(i,r) = (1 - \tau(i,r))PM(i,r) = TO(i,r)PM(i,r),$$

where $TO(i,r)$ is referred to as the *power* of the *ad valorem* tax. Therefore:

$$VOM(i,r) - VOA(i,r) = (1 - TO(i,r))PM(i,r)QO(i,r)$$
$$= \tau(i,r)PM(i,r)QO(i,r).$$

Thus, the fiscal implications of all tax/subsidy programs may be captured by comparison of the value of a given transaction at agents' versus market (or market versus world) prices. We assume that *taxes levied in region r always accrue to households in region r.*

The remaining terms in the income expression given in Table 2.5 account for all the other possible sources of tax revenues/subsidy expenditures in each

Table 2.5. *Disposition and Sources of Regional Income*

$$\text{EXPENDITURE}(r) = \sum_{i\in TRAD} [VPA(i,r) + VGA(i,r)] + SAVE(r) =$$

$$\text{INCOME }(r) \quad = \qquad\qquad \sum_{i\in ENDW} VOA(i,r) - VDEP(r)$$

$$+ \qquad\qquad \sum_{i\in NSAV} VOM(i,r) - VOA(i,r)$$

$$+ \qquad \sum_{j\in PROD}\sum_{i\in ENDW} VFA(i,j,r) - VFM(i,j,r)$$

$$+ \qquad\qquad \sum_{i\in TRAD} VIPA(i,r) - VIPM(i,r)$$

$$+ \qquad\qquad \sum_{i\in TRAD} VDPA(i,r) - VDPM(i,r)$$

$$+ \qquad\qquad \sum_{i\in TRAD} VIGA(i,r) - VIGM(i,r)$$

$$+ \qquad\qquad \sum_{i\in TRAD} VDGA(i,r) - VDGM(i,r)$$

$$+ \qquad \sum_{j\in PROD}\sum_{i\in TRAD} VIFA(i,j,r) - VIFM(i,j,r)$$

$$+ \qquad \sum_{j\in PROD}\sum_{i\in TRAD} VDFA(i,j,r) - VDFM(i,j,r)$$

$$+ \qquad \sum_{i\in TRAD}\sum_{s\in REG} VXWD(i,r,s) - VXMD(i,r,s)$$

$$+ \qquad \sum_{i\in TRAD}\sum_{s\in REG} VIWS(i,s,r) - VIMS(i,s,r)$$

regional economy. These include: primary factor taxes on firms, commodity taxes on households', and firms' purchases of tradeable goods and trade taxes.[3]

Figures 2.3 and 2.4, taken from Brockmeier (1996), offer graphical depictions of border interventions in GTAP. The two panels in Figure 2.3 refer to the case of export interventions. (Because there are many export destinations, we can interpret the supply curve as representing supply, net of sales to domestic uses, and other export markets.) In the first panel, the domestic price exceeds the world price $(PM(i,r) > PFOB(i,r,s))$, indicating the presence of a subsidy, so that $XTAX(i,r,s) = VXWD(i,r,s) - VXMD(i,r,s) < 0$. In the second panel, the opposite case is presented. Here, the world price is above the market

## Export Subsidy

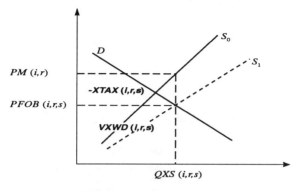

$$VXWD\ (i,r,s)\ =\ VXMD\ (i,r,s)\ -\ XTAX\ (i,r,s)$$

## Export Tax

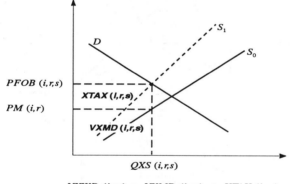

$$VXWD\ (i,r,s)\ =\ VXMD\ (i,r,s)\ +\ XTAX\ (i,r,s)$$

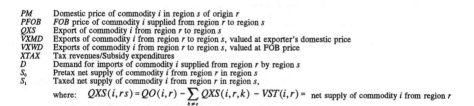

| | |
|---|---|
| *PM* | Domestic price of commodity $i$ in region $s$ of origin $r$ |
| *PFOB* | FOB price of commodity $i$ supplied from region $r$ to region $s$ |
| *QXS* | Export of commodity $i$ from region $r$ to region $s$ |
| *VXMD* | Exports of commodity $i$ from region $r$ to region $s$, valued at exporter's domestic price |
| *VXWD* | Exports of commodity $i$ from region $r$ to region $s$, valued at FOB price |
| *XTAX* | Tax revenues/Subsidy expenditures |
| *D* | Demand for imports of commodity $i$ supplied from region $r$ by region $s$ |
| $S_0$ | Pretax net supply of commodity $i$ from region $r$ in region $s$ |
| $S_1$ | Taxed net supply of commodity $i$ from region $r$ in region $s$, |

where:   $QXS(i,rs) = QO(i,r) - \sum_{k \neq s} QXS(i,r,k) - VST(i,r) =$ net supply of commodity $i$ from region $r$

**Figure 2.3.** Export subsidy or tax in region $r$ on sales to region $s$.

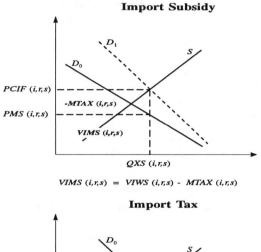

## Import Subsidy

$$VIMS\ (i,r,s)\ =\ VIWS\ (i,r,s)\ -\ MTAX\ (i,r,s)$$

## Import Tax

$$VIMS\ (i,r,s)\ =\ VIWS\ (i,r,s)\ +\ MTAX\ (i,r,s)$$

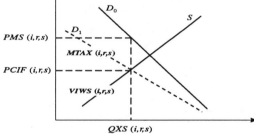

| | |
|---|---|
| PMS | Importer's domestic price of commodity $i$ supplied from region $r$ to region $s$ |
| PCIF | CIF price of commodity $i$ supplied from region $r$ to region $s$ |
| QXS | Exports of commodity $i$ from region $r$ to region $s$ |
| VIMS | Imports of commodity $i$ from region $r$ to region $s$, valued at importer's domestic price |
| VIWS | Imports of commodity $i$ from region $r$ to region $s$, valued at CIF price |
| MTAX | Tax revenues/Subsidy expenditures |
| $D_0$ | Pretax demand for differentiated imports of commodity $i$ from region $r$ in regions |
| $S_1$ | Net supply of commodity $i$ from region $r$ in region $s$ |

where: $QXS(i,rs) = QO(i,r) - \sum_{k \neq s} QXS(i,r,k) - VST(i,r) =$ net supply of commodity $i$ from region $r$

**Figure 2.4.** Import subsidy or tax in region $s$ on purchases from region $r$.

price and their difference contributes positively to regional income. This will be the case regardless of the source of discrepancy in *VXWD* and *VXMD*. For example, if this difference arises due to export restraints, as opposed to taxation, then the resulting income flow is due to quota rents. Nevertheless, it still accrues to the region of origin ($r$).

The two panels in Figure 2.4 refer to the income consequences of import interventions. Because GTAP adopts the Armington approach to import demand, differentiating products by origin, there is no domestic supply of the imported good. Therefore the demand schedule in these panels is conditional on aggregate demand for commodity $i$ in region $s$, as well as the prices of competing imports and the domestic market price of $i$ in region $s$. The excess supply schedule for imports of $i$ from $r$ to $s$ depends on supply conditions in $r$ as well as demand for this commodity in region $s$.

When the market price exceeds the world price, $PMS(i,r,s) > PCIF(i,r,s)$, then $MTAX(i,r,s) > 0$ and this term contributes positively to regional income. This can arise if there is a tariff on imports, *or* it could be due to an import quota. In the case of a binding quota on imports of $i$ into $s$ from $r$:

$$VIMS(i,r,s) - VIWS(i,r,s)$$
$$= (TMS(i,r,s) - 1)PCIF(i,r,s)QXS(i,r,s) > 0$$

represents the associated quota rents. In this instance, the closure must be modified so that $QXS(i,r,s)$ is *exogenous* and the tax equivalent, $TMS(i,r,s)$, is *endogenous*. Again, these quota rents are assumed to accrue to the region administering the quota.

### Global sectors

In order to complete the model, it is necessary to introduce two global sectors. The global transportation sector provides the services that account for the difference between *fob* and *cif* values for a particular commodity shipped along a specific route: $VTWR(i,r,s) = VIWS(i,r,s) - VXWD(i,r,s)$. Summing over all routes and commodities gives the total demand for international transport services shown at the top of Table 2.6. The supply of these services is provided by individual regional economies, which export them to the global transport sector [$VST(i,r)$]. We do not have information that would permit us to associate regional transport services exports with particular commodities and routes. Therefore, all demand is met from the same pool of services, the price of which is a blend of the price of all transport services exports.

The other required global sector is the global banking sector. This intermediates between global savings and investment, as described in Table 2.7. It creates a composite investment good (*GLOBINV*), based on a portfolio of net regional investment (gross investment less depreciation), and offers this to

**Table 2.6.** *The International Transport Sector*

|  |  |  |
|---|---|---|
|  | $VT$ | $: PT * QT$ |
| $= \sum\limits_{ieTRAD} \sum\limits_{reREG} \sum\limits_{seREG}$ | $VTWR(i,r,s)$ | $: PT * QS(i,rs)$ |
| $= \sum\limits_{ieTRAD} \sum\limits_{reREG}$ | $VST(i,r)$ | $: PM(i,r) * QST(i,r)$ |

**Table 2.7.** *Demand for Regional Investment Goods*

|  |  |
|---|---|
| $\sum\limits_{reREG} [REGINV(r)$ | $: PCGDS(r) * QCGDS(r)$ |
| $- \underline{VDEP(r)}]$ | $: PCGDS(r) * KB(r)$ |
| $= GLOBINV$ | $: PSAVE * GLOBALCGDS$ |
| $= \sum\limits_{reREG} SAVE(r)$ | $: PSAVE * QSAVE(r)$ |

**Capital Stocks**

|  |  |
|---|---|
| $VKB(r)$ | $: PCGDS(r) * KB(r)$ |
| $+ REGINV(r)$ | $: PCGDS(r) * QCGDS(r)$ |
| $- \underline{VDEP(r)}$ | $: PCGDS(r) * KB(r)$ |
| $= VKE(r)$ |  |

regional households in order to satisfy their savings demand. Therefore, all savers face a common price for this savings commodity (*PSAVE*). A consistency check on the accounting relationships described up to this point involves separately computing the supply of the composite investment good and the demand for aggregate savings. If (1) all other markets are in equilibrium,

(2) all firms earn zero profits (including the global transport sector), and (3) all households are on their budget constraint, then global investment must equal global savings by virtue of Walras' Law.

Finally, the value of the beginning of period capital stock, $VKB(r)$, is updated by regional investment, $REGINV(r)$, less depreciation, $VDEP(r)$. This yields the value of ending capital stocks, $VKE(r)$. This relationship is shown at the bottom of Table 2.7.

## IV    Equilibrium conditions and partial equilibrium closures

Thus far, we have said nothing about the behavior of individual firms and households. Neoclassical restrictions on such behavior are not necessary to obtain full general equilibrium closure. Rather, it is the exhaustive accounting relationships outlined above that make our model general equilibrium in nature. If any one of them is not enforced, Walras' Law will fail to hold. Since most economists are accustomed to seeing equilibrium conditions written in terms of quantities, not values, it is useful to demonstrate that the accounting relationships provided above do indeed embody the customary general equilibrium relationships. Consider, for example, the market clearing condition for tradeable commodity supplies:

$$VOM(i,r) = VDM(i,r) + VST(i,r) + \sum_{s \in REG} VXMD(i,r,s). \qquad (2.1)$$

This may be rewritten in terms of quantities and a common domestic market price for $i$ in region $r$:

$$\begin{aligned} PM(i,r) * QO(i,r) = \\ PM(i,r) * [QDS(i,r) + QST(i,r) + \sum_{s \in REG} QXS(i,r,s)]. \end{aligned} \qquad (2.2)$$

Upon dividing by $PM(i,r)$ we obtain the usual form of the tradeable commodity market clearing condition:

$$QO(i,r) = QDS(i,r) + QST(i,r) + \sum_{s \in REG} QXS(i,r,s). \qquad (2.3)$$

A similar exercise may be applied to the market clearing conditions for nontradeable commodities. In sum, any market clearing condition can be converted to value terms by multiplying by a *common* price. In so doing, we circumvent the need to partition value flows into prices and quantities. This has the added benefit of vastly simplifying the problem of model calibration, as we will see below.

Having verified that the accounting relationships embody all the necessary general equilibrium conditions, we turn to the problem of creating special closures in which some of these conditions are dropped. This, in turn, permits one to fix certain variables exogenously, as is done *implicitly* in partial equilibrium analysis. The problem lies in ascertaining which variables are associated with which equilibrium conditions. This is akin to identifying the complementary slackness conditions associated with the general equilibrium model.

Perhaps the most obvious complementarity is that between prices and market clearing conditions. Clearly if the latter are to hold, prices must be free to adjust to resolve any imbalance between supply and demand. Therefore, if we fix the price of a tradeable commodity, we must eliminate the associated market clearing condition, equation (2.3). A common partial equilibrium closure for the analysis of farm and food issues involves fixing the prices of all nonfood commodities. In order to implement this closure in our model, all nonfood market clearing conditions must be dropped. (The "dropping" of individual equations is achieved by endogenizing slack variables in the equations to be eliminated. We must always retain equal numbers of endogenous variables and equations if the model is to provide a unique equilibrium solution.)

It is also common in partial equilibrium analyses to assume that the opportunity cost of nonspecific factors is exogenous. For example, in the case of agriculture, one might assume that the labor wage and capital rental rates are fixed. If this is to be done, then the associated regional market clearing conditions for these nontradeable primary factors must be dropped. Similarly, income may be fixed, provided the income computation equation is eliminated.

But what about quantities? Should any of them be fixed? Having fixed the price of nonfood commodities, for example, it hardly makes sense to permit their supplies to be determined endogenously. Any sector experiencing a rise in costs would be driven out of business altogether under such circumstances. For this reason it makes sense to fix nonfood output levels and drop the associated zero profit conditions. These partial equilibrium assumptions, for the example of a food policy shock, may be summarized as follows:

- *Nonfood output levels and prices are exogenous.*
- *Income is exogenous.*
- *Nonspecific primary factor rental rates are exogenous.*

## V      Linearized representation of accounting equations

**Solution via a linearized representation.** While the accounting relationships detailed in Figures 2.1 and 2.2 and Tables 2.1–2.5 are most conveniently expressed in value terms, it is attractive to write the behavioral component of the model in terms of *percentage changes* in prices and quantities.[4] Indeed, we are usually most interested in these percentage changes, as opposed to their levels values. Expressing this nonlinear model in percentage changes

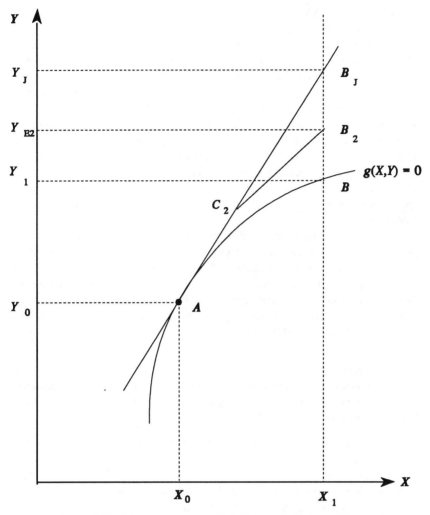

**Figure 2.5.** Solving a nonlinear model via its linearized representation.

does not preclude solution of the true nonlinear problem. Solution of nonlinear AGE models via a *linearized representation* (Pearson 1991)[5] involves successively updating the value-based coefficients via the formula:

$$dV/V = d(PQ)/PQ = p + q,$$

where the lowercase $p$ and $q$ denote proportional changes in price and quantity.

Figure 2.5 provides a graphical exposition of one method of solving a nonlinear model via its linearized representation. For simplicity, the entire model is given by a single equation $g(X,Y) = 0$, where $X$ is exogenous and $Y$ is endogenous. The initial equilibrium is represented by the point $(X_0, Y_0)$. Our counterfactual experiment involves shocking the exogenous variable to $X_1$, and computing the resulting endogenous outcome $Y_1$. If we simply evaluated the linearized representation of the model at $(X_0, Y_0)$ the equations would predict the outcome $B_J = (X_1, Y_J)$. This is the *Johansen approach*, and it is clearly in error, since $Y_J \gg Y_1$. This type of error has led to criticism of the individuals using linearized computable general equilibrium (CGE) models.

However, note that the accuracy of the linearized model can be considerably enhanced by breaking the shock to $X$ into two parts and updating the equilibrium after the first shock. This approach takes us from point $A$ to $C_2$ to $B_2$. It is termed *Euler's method* of solution via linearized representation. By increasing the number of steps, one obtains an increasingly accurate solution of the nonlinear model.

Since Euler's contribution, this approach of relinearizing the model has been considerably refined to yield more rapid convergence to $(X_1, Y_1)$. [See Harrison and Pearson (1994), section 2.5, for more details.] The default method used for solving the GTAP model is *Gragg's method*, with extrapolation. In this case the model is solved several times, each time with a successively finer grid. An extrapolated solution is formed based on these results. As illustrated in Harrison and Pearson (1994, pp. 2–24ff.), this yields good results.

**Form of accounting equations.** Linearization of the accounting equations involves total differentiation so they appear as a linear combination of appropriately weighted price and quantity changes. For example, the tradeable market clearing condition [equation (2.3)] becomes:

$$QO(i,r)qo(i,r) = QDS(i,r)qds(i,r) + QST(i,r)qst(i,r)$$
$$+ \sum_{s \in REG} QXS(i,r,s)qxs(i,r,s), \qquad (2.4)$$

where the lowercase variables are again percentage changes. Multiplying both sides by the common price $PM(i,r)$ yields equation (1) in Table 2.8. Here the coefficients are now in *value* terms. [It is never necessary actually to compute price and quantity *levels* ($P$ and $Q$) under this approach, although this can be done if one chooses to define initial units by choosing, for example, $PM(i,r) = 1$.] Also, note that a slack variable has been introduced into this equation in Table 2.8. It is indexed over all tradeable commodities and regions. By endogenizing selected components of this variable (which appear only in this equation), we are able to eliminate selectively market clearing for individual products. In this case, with the associated tradeable price fixed exogenously $(pm(i,r) = 0)$, the endogenous change in *tradslack(i,r)* accounts for the excess

Table 2.8. *"Accounting" Relationships in the Model*

---

(1)  $VOM(i,r) * qo(i,r) =$  $VieTRAD$
$VreREG$

$$VDM(i,r) * qds(i,r) + VST(i,r) * qst(i,r) + \sum_{seREG} VXMD(i,r,s) * qxs(i,r,s)$$
$$+ VOM(i,r) * tradslack(i,r)$$

(2)  $VIM(i,r) * qim(i,r) =$  $VieTRAD$
$VreREG$

$$\sum_{jePROD} VIFM(i,j,r) * qfm(i,j,r) + VIPM(i,r) * qpm(i,r) + VIGM(i,r) * qgm(i,r)$$

(3)  $VDM(i,r) * qds(i,r) =$  $VieTRAD$
$VreREG$

$$\sum_{jePROD} VDFM(i,j,r) * qfd(i,j,r) + VDPM(i,r) * qpd(i,r) + VDGM(i,r) * qgd(i,r)$$

(4)  $VOM(i,r) * qo(i,r) =$  $VieENDWM$
$VreREG$

$$\sum_{jePROD} VFM(i,j,r) * qfe(i,j,r) + VOM(i,r) * endwslack(i,r)$$

(5)  $qoes(i,j,r) = qfe(i,j,r)$  $VieENDWS$
$VjePROD$
$VreREG$

(6)  $VOA(j,r) * ps(j,r) =$  $ViePROD$
$VreREG$

$$\sum_{ieENDW} VFA(i,j,r) * pfe(i,j,r) + \sum_{IeTRAD} VFA(i,j,r) * pf(i,j,r) + VOA(j,r) * profitslack(j,r)$$

(7)  $VT * pt = \sum_{ieTRAD\_COMM} \sum_{reREG} VST(i,r) * pm(i,r)$

(8)  $PRIVEXP(r) * yp(r) =$  $VreREG$

$$INCOME(r) * y(r) - SAVE(r) * [psave + qsave(r)] - \sum_{ieTRAD} VGA(i,r) * [pg(i,r) + qg(i,r)]$$

---

of supply over demand in the new equilibrium (as a percentage of output in the initial equilibrium).

The next two equations in Table 2.8 enforce equilibrium in the *domestic market* for tradeable commodities, either that which is imported from region *r* in the case of equation (2) or that which is produced domestically in the case of equation (3). Therefore, the common price is once again a domestic market price. We do not include slack variables in these equations, since they refer to the same commodity treated in equation (1). To achieve a partial equilibrium closure, it is sufficient to fix the price of this good at one place in the model.

Table 2.8. *(Cont) "Accounting" Relationships in the Model*

(9)    $INCOME(r) * y(r) =$                                                                                    $\forall r \epsilon REG$

$\quad \sum_{i \epsilon ENDW} VOA(i,r)[ps(i,r) + qo(i,r)] - VDEP(r) * [pcgds(r) + kb(r)]$

$\quad + \sum_{i \epsilon NSAV} VOM(i,r) * [pm(i,r) + qo(i,r)] - VOA(i,r) * [ps(i,r) + qo(i,r)]$

$\quad + \sum_{i \epsilon ENDWM} \sum_{j \epsilon PROD} VFA(i,j,r)[pfe(i,j,r) + qfe(i,j,r)] - VFM(i,j,r) * [pm(i,r) + qfe(i,j,r)]$

$\quad + \sum_{j \epsilon ENDWS} \sum_{i \epsilon PROD} VFA(i,j,r)[pfe(i,j,r) + qfe(i,j,r)] - VFM(i,j,r) * [pmes(i,j,r) + qfe(i,j,r)]$

$\quad + \sum_{j \epsilon PROD} \sum_{i \epsilon TRAD} VIFA(i,j,r) * [pfm(i,j,r) + qfm(i,j,r)] - VIFM(i,j,r) * [pim(i,r) + qfm(i,j,r)]$

$\quad + \sum_{j \epsilon PROD} \sum_{i \epsilon TRAD} VDFA(i,j,r) * [pfd(i,j,r,) + qfd(i,j,r)] - VDFM(i,j,r) * [pm(i,r) + qfd(i,j,r)]$

$\quad + \sum_{i \epsilon TRAD} VIPA(i,r) * [ppm(i,r) + qpm(i,r)] - VIPM(i,r) * [pim(i,r) + qpm(i,r)]$

$\quad + \sum_{i \epsilon TRAD} VDPA(i,r) * [ppd(i,r) + qpd(i,r)] - VDPM(i,r) * [pm(i,r) + qpd(i,r)]$

$\quad + \sum_{i \epsilon TRAD} VIGA(i,r) * [pgm(i,r) + qgm(i,r)] - VIGM(i,r) * [pim(i,r) + qgm(i,r)]$

$\quad + \sum_{i \epsilon TRAD} VDGA(i,r) * [pgd(i,r) + qgd(i,r)] - VDGM(i,r) * [pm(i,r) + qgd(i,r)]$

$\quad + \sum_{i \epsilon TRAD} \sum_{s \epsilon REG} VXWD(i,r,s) * [pfob(i,r,s) + qxs(i,r,s)] - VXMD(i,r,s) * [pm(i,r) + qxs(i,r,s)]$

$\quad + \sum_{i \epsilon TRAD} \sum_{s \epsilon REG} VIMS(i,s,r) * [pms(i,s,r) + qxs(i,s,r)] - VIWS(i,s,r) * [pcif(i,s,r) + qxs(i,s,r)]$

$\quad + INCOME(r) * incomeslack(r)$

(10)    $ke(r) = INVKERATIO(r) * qcgds(r) + [1.0 - INVKERATIO(r)] * kb(r)$                      $\forall r \epsilon REG$

(11)    $globalcgds = \sum_{r \epsilon REG} [REGINV(r)/GLOBINV] * qcgds(r) - [VDEP(r)/GLOBINV(r)] * kb(r)$

(12)    $walras\_sup = globalcgds$

(13)    $GLOBINV * walras\_dem = \sum_{r \epsilon REG} SAVE(r) * qsave(r)$

(14)    $walras\_sup = walras\_dem + walraslack$

Equations (4) and (5) in Table 2.8 refer to market clearing for the nontradeable, endowment commodities. As noted above, the model distinguishes between primary factors that are perfectly mobile across sectors, and those which are "sluggish" in their adjustment. The latter class of endowment commodities can exhibit differential equilibrium rental rates across uses. In the case of mobile endowments, equation (4), the presence of a common market price permits the equilibrium relationship to be written in terms of values at domestic market prices. A slack variable is introduced to permit us selectively to eliminate the market clearing equations and fix rental rates on the respective endowment commodities. In the case of sluggish commodities, no such common price exists and sectoral demands are equated to sectoral supplies. The latter are generated from a constant elasticity of transformation (CET) revenue function, which transforms one use of the endowment into another.

Equation (6) in Table 2.8 is the zero pure profit condition. Since firms are assumed to maximize profits, the quantity changes drop out when the expression at the bottom of Table 2.3 is totally differentiated in the neighborhood of an optimum (e.g., Varian 1978, p. 267). This leaves an equation relating input prices to output prices, where these percentage changes are weighted by values at *agent's* prices. For computational convenience we use different variables to refer to firms' prices for composite intermediate inputs (*pf*) and endowment commodities (*pfe*). The presence of *profitslack(j,r)* permits us to fix output and eliminate the zero profit condition for any sector *j* in any region *r*. In a similar fashion, equation (7) is the zero profit condition for the international transport sector. Here, the total value of transport services (*VT*) is constrained to equal the total value of services exports to this sector/use (*VST*), as described in Table 2.6.

Equation (8) in Table 2.8 assures the complete disposition of regional income (recall Table 2.5). This is done by first deducting savings and government spending (each of which *may* be exogenously specified under some closures) from disposable regional income, thereupon allocating the remainder to private household expenditures *PRIVEXP(r)*. It is followed by equation (9), which generates available income in each region. This is the most complicated equation in the model. It must take account of changes in the value of regional endowments, as well as changes in the net fiscal revenues owing to the *ad valorem* taxes/subsidies. Even if these tax rates do not change, revenues will change due to changes in market prices and quantities. Therefore, in differential form, each of the values must be postmultiplied by the percentage change in both the price and quantity components of the value flow.

Note that in Table 2.8 the quantity change is common for each of the transactions taxes in equation (9). For example, in the case of the tax on firms' use of primary factors, the percentage change in firms' derived demands, *qfe(i,j,r)*, enters both terms. This is simply a reflection of the fact that the tax refers to a particular transaction in quantities. In contrast, the prices faced by firms are: (1) potentially different from market prices, and (2) free to change at different rates when the tax rate dividing them is changed. This is reflected by the fact that *VFA(i,j,r)* is postmultiplied by *pfe(i,j,r)*, while *VFM(i,j,r)* changes according to *pm(i,r)*.

Before going through Table 2.8 equation (9) in more detail it is useful to consider explicitly the taxes associated with each of these price differences. These are revealed in the price linkage equations given in Table 2.9; for example, equation (15) shows the role of income/output taxes that drive a wedge between *VOM(i,r)* and *VOA(i,r)*. The *power of the ad valorem tax* in this case is given by $TO(i,r) = VOA(i,r)/VOM(i,r)$. Therefore, when $TO(i,r) > 1$, firms/households are actually receiving a *subsidy* on the commodity supplied. Similarly, if $dTO(i,r)/TO(i,r) = to(i,r) > 0$ then the subsidy is increased. This choice of notation may seem odd, but it gives rise to a useful pattern across tax instruments. In particular, we adopt the rule that tax rates are always

**Table 2.9.** *Price Linkage Equations*

| | | |
|---|---|---|
| (15) | $ps(i,r) = to(i,r) + pm(i,r)$ | $\forall i \epsilon NSAVE$ <br> $\forall r \epsilon REG$ |
| (16) | $pfe(i,j,r) = tf(i,j,r) + pm(i,r)$ | $\forall i \epsilon ENDWM$ <br> $\forall j \epsilon PROD$ <br> $\forall r \epsilon REG$ |
| (17) | $pfe(i,j,r) = tf(i,j,r) + pmes(i,j,r)$ | $\forall i \epsilon ENDWS$ <br> $\forall j \epsilon PROD$ <br> $\forall r \epsilon REG$ |
| (18) | $ppd(i,r) = tpd(i,r) + pm(i,r)$ | $\forall i \epsilon TRAD$ <br> $\forall r \epsilon REG$ |
| (19) | $pgd(i,r) = tgd(i,r) + pm(i,r)$ | $\forall i \epsilon TRAD$ <br> $\forall r \epsilon REG$ |
| (20) | $pfd(i,j,r) = tfd(i,j,r) + pm(i,r)$ | $\forall i \epsilon TRAD$ <br> $\forall j \epsilon PROD$ <br> $\forall r \epsilon REG$ |
| (21) | $ppm(i,r) = tpm(i,r) + pim(i,r)$ | $\forall i \epsilon TRAD$ <br> $\forall r \epsilon REG$ |
| (22) | $pgm(i,r) = tgm(i,r) + pim(i,r)$ | $\forall i \epsilon TRAD$ <br> $\forall r \epsilon REG$ |
| (23) | $pfm(i,j,r) = tfm(i,j,r) + pim(i,r)$ | $\forall i \epsilon TRAD$ <br> $\forall j \epsilon PROD$ <br> $\forall r \epsilon REG$ |
| (24) | $pms(i,r,s) = tm(i,s) + tms(i,r,s) + pcif(i,r,s)$ | $\forall i \epsilon TRAD$ <br> $\forall r \epsilon REG$ <br> $\forall s \epsilon REG$ |
| (25) | $pr(i,s) = pm(i,s) - pim(i,s)$ | $\forall i \epsilon TRAD$ <br> $\forall s \epsilon REG$ |
| (26) | $pcif(i,r,s) = FOBSHR(i,r,s) * pfob(i,r,s) + TRNSHR(i,r,s) * pt$ | $\forall i \epsilon TRAD$ <br> $\forall r \epsilon REG$ <br> $\forall s \epsilon REG$ |
| (27) | $pfob(i,r,s) = pm(i,r) - tx(i,r) - txs(i,r,s)$ | $\forall i \epsilon TRAD$ <br> $\forall r \epsilon REG$ <br> $\forall s \epsilon REG$ |

defined as the ratio of agent's prices to market prices (or market prices to world prices in the case of border taxes).

Turning to the next price linkage relationship, equation (16) in Table 2.9, we note that an increase in $TF(i,j,r)$, that is, $tf(i,j,r) > 0$, will cause an *increase* in tax revenues. This is because in this case the firms in sector $j$ of region $r$ purchasing mobile endowment commodity $i$ will be forced to pay more, relative to the market price, that is, $pfe(i,j,r) > pm(i,r)$. Owing to the fact that there is not a unique market price for the sluggish endowment commodities purchased by firms, we require a separate price linkage, equation (17) in this case.

Equations (18)–(20) in Table 2.9 describe the linkages between domestic market prices and agents purchasing *domestically produced,* tradeable commodities. These commodity transaction taxes can potentially vary not only across commodities and regions, but also across firms and households in each region. Similarly, equations (21)–(23) describe the linkage between the domestic market price of imports of $i$, by source $r$, and diverse agents in region $s$.

Equation (24) in Table 2.9 establishes the percentage change in the domestic market price for tradeable commodity $i$ in region $s$, based on the change in the border price of that product, $pcif(i,r,s)$ as well as two types of border interventions. Both are *ad valorem* import tariffs. The first, $tms(i,r,s)$, is bilateral in nature, while the second, $tm(i,s)$, is source-generic. The latter may be used to insulate the domestic economy from world price changes. This is done by endogenizing $tm(i,s)$ and establishing some domestic price target. In this model, we choose to fix the ratio of the domestic market price for $i$ to the price of the import composite. This is conveniently defined in the next price linkage, equation (25). In the normal closure, $tm(i,s)$ is exogenous and $pr(i,s)$ is endogenous. However, we imitate the European Union's variable import levy on food products by permitting $tm(i,s)$ to vary so as to fix $pr(i,s)$. In this circumstance, domestic consumers have no incentive to substitute imports for domestic food.

Equation (26) in Table 2.9 links $pcif(i,r,s)$ and $pfob(i,r,s)$. Its derivation is based on the assumption that revenues must cover costs on all *individual* routes, for all commodities. Thus the change in the *cif* price is a weighted combination of the change in the *fob* price and the change in a general transport cost index, $pt$, where the weights refer to the shares of *fob* costs [$FOBSHR(i,r,s)$] and transport costs [$TRNSHR(i,r,s)$] in *cif* costs. To the extent that firms engage in cross-subsidization or the costs of transport services on different routes move independently, this equation will be inaccurate. It is also important to note the implications of equation (26) for price transmission across markets. The greater the transport margin along a given route (i.e., $TRNSHR(i,r,s)$ larger), the weaker the link between a change in the price of $i$ in the export market $r$ and the corresponding change in destination market $s$.

Equation (27) completes the "circle" of price linkages in Table 2.9 by connecting $pfob(i,r,s)$ and domestic market price, $pm(i,r)$. As was the case on the import side, there are two types of export taxes. The first, $txs(i,r,s)$, is destination-specific, while the second, $tx(i,r)$, is destination-generic. The latter may be "swapped" with the normally endogenous change in sectoral output, in order to insulate domestic producers from the vagaries of world markets. For example, this variable export tax / subsidy has been used in modeling the European Union's (EU's) common agricultural policy. Note that since these export taxes refer to the ratio of domestic market prices to world prices, an increase in $TXS(i,r,s)$ results in a fiscal outflow, that is, a subsidy on exports.

Having established the linkage between prices in this model, we are in a position to return to the income computation equation (9) in Table 2.8. In particular, consider the effect of omitting some component of this complicated equation, say, income taxes. How will this affect, for example, a welfare analysis of trade policy reform? Given the presence of income taxes in the initial equilibrium data base, $VOM(i,r) > VOA(i,r)$, if the experiment in question does not alter the *rate* of income taxation, then $to(i,r) = 0$ and $\alpha = ps(i,r) = pm(i,r)$ $\forall i \varepsilon ENDW$. This means the two terms in square brackets [*] change at the same rate. If this change is positive, then omission of this term will lead to an *understatement* of income tax revenues and a subsequent *understatement* of disposable income and household welfare in the new equilibrium. In sum, even when distortions are not affected by a given policy experiment it is important to acknowledge their presence in the economy if an accurate welfare analysis is to be provided.

The final group of accounting equations in Table 2.8 refer to global savings and investment. Because this is a comparative static model, current investment does not augment the productive stock of capital available to firms. The latter is constrained by beginning-of-period capital stock which is exogenous. Therefore, there is only a limited role for investment in our simulations. When investment (and savings) is specified exogenously it will facilitate accumulation of the targeted end-of-period capital stock [see equation (10)]. When investment is endogenous it adjusts in order to accommodate the global demand for savings. (More discussion of these macroeconomic closure issues is provided below.) Equation (11) aggregates regional *gross* investment into global net investment. Equation (13) aggregates regional savings, and equations (12) and (14) permit us either to force the two to be equal (*walraslack* is exogenous) or verify Walras' Law (*walraslack* is endogenous and should be found equal to zero in the solution).

## VI    Behavioral equations

### Firm Behavior

**The "technology tree."** Figure 2.6 provides a visual display of the assumed technology for firms in each of the industries in the model. This kind of a production "tree" is a convenient way of representing separable, constant returns-to-scale technologies. At the bottom of the inverted tree are the individual inputs demanded by the firm. For example, the primary factors of production are: land, labor, and capital. Their quantities are denoted $QFE(i,j,s)$, or,

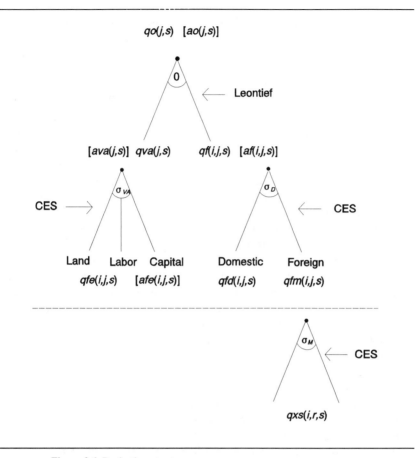

**Figure 2.6.** Production structure.

in percentage change form, $qfe(i,j,s)$. (For the time being, please ignore the terms in brackets [ ] in Figure 2.6. They refer to rates of technical change, to which we will turn momentarily.) Firms also purchase intermediate inputs, some of which are produced domestically, $qfd(i,j,s)$, and some of which are imported, $qfm(i,j,s)$. In the case of imports, the intermediate inputs must be "sourced" from particular exporters, $qxs(i,r,s)$. Recall from Figure 2.1 that this sourcing occurs at the border, since information on the composition of imports by sector is unavailable; hence the dashed line between the firms' production tree and the *constant elasticity of substitution* (CES) nest combining bilateral imports.

The manner in which the firm combines individual inputs to produce its output, $QO(i,s)$, depends largely on the assumptions that we make about *separability* in production. For example, we assume that firms choose their optimal mix of primary factors *independently* of the prices of intermediate inputs. Since the level of output is also irrelevant, owing to our assumption of constant returns to scale, this leaves only the relative prices of land, labor, and capital as arguments in the firms' conditional demand equations for components of value-added. By assuming this type of separability, we impose the restriction that the elasticity of substitution between any individual primary factor, on the one hand, and intermediate inputs, on the other, is equal. This is what permits us to draw the production tree, for it is this common elasticity of substitution that enters the fork in the inverted tree at which the intermediate and primary factors of production are joined. It also represents a significant reduction in the number of parameters that need to be provided in order to operationalize the model.

Within the primary factor branch of the production tree, substitution possibilities are also restricted to one parameter. This CES assumption is quite general in those sectors that employ only two inputs: capital and labor. However, in agriculture, where a third input, land, enters the production function, we are forced to assume that all pairwise elasticities of substitution are equal. This is surely not true, but we do not have enough information to calibrate a more general specification at this point.

In general, the behavioral parameters at each level in the production tree can be specified by the user of the model. However, as will be seen below when we turn to the specific form of the equations used to represent firm behavior, we impose the restriction of nonsubstitution between composite intermediates and primary factors. The fact that this is a very common specification in applied general equilibrium (AGE) models is a poor justification for incorporating it into the GTAP model. Indeed, there is evidence of significant substitutability between some intermediate inputs and primary factors. For example, during the energy price shocks of the 1970s firms demonstrated considerable potential for conserving fuel via the purchase of new, more energy-efficient equipment. Similarly, farmers have shown considerable potential for altering the rate of chemical fertilizer applications in response to changes in the relative price of fertilizer to land. However, these substitution possibilities are not characteristic of *all* intermediate inputs, and their proper treatment requires a more flexible production function than that portrayed in Figure 2.6.[6]

Turning to the intermediate input side of the production tree in Figure 2.6, it can be seen that the separability is symmetric, that is, the mix of intermediate inputs is also independent of the prices of primary factors. Furthermore, imported intermediates are assumed to be separable from domestically produced intermediate inputs. That is, firms first decide on the sourcing of their imports; then, based on the resulting composite import price, they determine the optimal mix of imported and domestic goods. This specification was first proposed by Paul Armington in 1969 and has since become known as the "Armington approach" to modeling import demand. However, it has been widely criticized in the literature. For example, Winters (1984), and Alston et al. (1990) argue that the functional form is too restrictive and that the nonhomothetic, AIDS specification is preferable. Although we agree that more flexible functional forms are preferable, this critique could apply just as well to every other behavioral relationship in the model. The question is: can it be estimated/calibrated and operationalized in the context of a disaggregated global model? At this point the answer is "no," although progress has been made in the context of one-region models (e.g., Robinson et al. 1993).

A more fundamental critique of the Armington approach is provided by the literature on industrial organization, imperfect competition, and trade. Here, product differentiation is *endogenous* and it is associated with individual firms' attempts to carve out a market niche for themselves. Early work along these lines is offered by Spence (1976), and Dixit and Stiglitz (1979). It is now the preferred approach for introducing imperfect competition into AGE models (e.g., Brown and Stern 1989), and it can have significant implications for the effects of trade policy liberalization (Hertel and Lanclos 1994). Also, Feenstra (1994) shows that the failure to account for endogenous product differentiation may be part of the reason import demands appear to be nonhomothetic. This is due to the correlation of income increases with the entry of new exporters and the subsequent increase in import varieties. Even at constant prices, this would dictate an increasing market share for imports.

In sum, although we are not particularly happy with the Armington specification, it *does* permit us to explain cross-hauling of similar products and to track bilateral trade flows. We believe that, in many sectors, an imperfect competition/endogenous product differentiation approach would be preferable. However, those models require additional information on industry concentration (firm numbers) as well as scale economies (or fixed costs), which is not readily available on a global basis. Clearly this is an important area for future work. Indeed, a number of authors have used aggregated versions of the GTAP data base to implement models with imperfect competition (Harrison, Rutherford, and Tarr 1995; Hertel and Lanclos 1994, Francois, McDonald, and Nordstrom 1995).

**Behavioral equations.** The equations describing the firm behavior portrayed in Figure 2.6 are provided in Tables 2.10 and 2.11. Each group of equations refers to one of the "nests" or branches in the technology tree discussed above. For each nest there are two types of equations. The first describes substitution among inputs within the nest. Its form follows directly from the CES form of the production function for that branch. (Details are provided later in this

**Table 2.10.** *Composite Imports Nest*

(28) $pim(i,s) = \sum\limits_{k \in REG} MSHRS(i,k,s) * pms(i,k,s)$

$\forall i \in TRAD$
$\forall s \in REG$

(29) $qxs(i,r,s) = qim(i,s) - \sigma_M(i) * [pms(i,r,s) - pim(i,s)]$

$\forall i \in TRAD$
$\forall r \in REG$
$\forall s \in REG$

**Table 2.11.** *Behavioral Equations for Producers*

**Composite intermediates nest:**

(30) $pf(i,j,r) = FMSHR(i,j,r) * pfm(i,j,r) + [1 - FMSHR(i,j,r)] * pfd(i,j,r)$

$\forall i \in TRAD$
$\forall j \in PROD$
$\forall r \in REG$

(31) $qfm(i,j,s) = qf(i,j,s) - \sigma_D(i) * [pfm(i,j,s) - pf(i,j,s)]$

$\forall i \in TRAD$
$\forall j \in PROD$
$\forall s \in REG$

(32) $qfd(i,j,s) = qf(i,j,s) - \sigma_D(i) * [pfd(i,j,s) - pf(i,j,s)]$

$\forall i \in TRAD$
$\forall j \in PROD$
$\forall s \in REG$

**Value-added nest:**

(33) $pva(j,r) = \sum\limits_{k \in ENDW} SVA(k,j,r) * [pfe(k,j,r) - afe\,k,j,r)]$

$\forall j \in PROD$
$\forall r \in REG$

(34) $qfe(i,j,r) + afe\ (i,j,r) = qva(j,r) - \sigma_{VA}(j)$

$\quad\quad\quad * [pfe(i,j,r) - afe(i,j,r) - pva(j,r)]$

$\forall i \in ENDW$
$\forall j \in PROD$
$\forall r \in REG$

**Total output nest:**

(35) $qva(j,r) + ava\ (j,r) = qo(j,r) - ao(j,r)$

$\forall j \in PROD$
$\forall r \in REG$

(36) $qf(i,j,r) + af\ (i,j,r) = qo(j,r) - ao(j,r)$

$\forall i \in TRAD$
$\forall j \in PROD$
$\forall r \in REG$

**Zero profits (revised):**

(6') $VOA(j,r) * [ps(j,r) + ao(j,r)] =$

$\quad \sum\limits_{i \in ENDW\_COMM} VFA(i,j,r) * [pfe(i,j,r) - afe(i,j,r) - ava(j,r)]$

$\forall j \in PROD$
$\forall r \in REG$

$+ \sum\limits_{i \in TRAD\_COMM} VFA(i,j,r) * [pf(i,j,r) - af(i,j,r)] + VOA(j,r) * profitslack(j,r)$

section.) The second type of equation is the composite price equation that determines the unit cost for the composite good produced by that branch (e.g., composite imports). (It takes the same form as the sectoral zero profit condition given in Table 2.8.) The composite price then enters the next higher nest in order to determine the demand for this composite.

There are several approaches to obtaining the CES-derived demand equations. Here, we opt for an intuitive exposition that begins with the definition of the elasticity of substitution. Indeed, this is the way the CES functional form was invented (Arrow et al. 1961). Consider the two input-case, where the elasticity of substitution is defined as the percentage change in the ratio of the two cost minimizing input demands, given a 1 percent change in the inverse of their price ratio:

$$\sigma \equiv (Q_1 \hat{/} Q_2)/(P_2 \hat{/} P_1). \tag{2.5}$$

(Here, the "hats" denote percentage changes.) A familiar benchmark is the Cobb–Douglas case, whereby $\sigma$ equals 1. In this case cost shares are invariant to price changes. For larger values of $\sigma$, the rate of change in the quantity ratio exceeds the rate of change in the price ratio and the cost share of the input that becomes more expensive actually falls. Expressing equation (2.5) in percentage change form (lowercase letters), we obtain:

$$(q_1 - q_2) = \sigma(p_2 - p_1). \tag{2.6}$$

In order to obtain the form of demand equation used in Table 2.10, several substitutions are necessary. First, note that total differentiation of the production function, and use of the fact that firms' pay factors their marginal value product, gives the following relationship between inputs and output (i.e., the composite good):

$$q = \theta_1 q_1 + (1 - \theta_1)q_2, \tag{2.7}$$

where $\theta_1$ is the cost share of input 1 and $(1 - \theta_1)$ is the cost share of input 2. Solving for $q_2$ gives:

$$q_2 = (q - \theta_1 q_1)/(1 - \theta_1), \tag{2.8}$$

which may be substituted into (2.6) to yield:

$$q_1 = \sigma(p_2 - p_1) + [q - \theta_1 q_1]/(1 - \theta_1). \tag{2.9}$$

This simplifies to the following derived demand equation for the first input:

$$q_1 = (1 - \theta_1)\sigma(p_2 - p_1) + q. \tag{2.10}$$

Note that this conditional demand equation is homogeneous of degree zero in prices, and the compensated cross-price elasticity of demand is equal to $(1 - \theta_1) * \sigma$.

The final substitution required to obtain the CES demand equation intro-duces the percentage change in the composite price:

$$p = \theta_1 p_1 + (1 - \theta_1)p_2. \tag{2.11}$$

As noted above, this is identical to the zero profit condition (6) in Table 2.8, only we have divided both sides by the value of output at agents' prices. Since revenue is exhausted on costs, the resulting coefficients weighting input prices are the respective cost shares. From here, we proceed in an manner analogous to that explored above, first solving for $p_2$ as a function of $p_1$ and $p$, then substituting this into (2.10) to obtain:

$$q_1 = (1 - \theta_1)\sigma\{[p - \theta_1 p_1]/(1 - \theta_1) - p_1\} + q. \tag{2.12}$$

This simplifies to the following, final form of the derived demand equation for the first input in this CES composite:

$$q_1 = \sigma(p - p_1) + q. \tag{2.13}$$

The beauty of equation (2.13) is the intuition it offers, and the fact that *its form is unchanged when the number of inputs increases beyond two*. This equation decomposes the change in a firm's derived demand, $q_1$, into two parts. The first is the substitution effect. It is the product of the (constant) elasticity of substitution and the percentage change in the ratio of the composite price to the price of input 1. The second component is the expansion effect. Owing to constant returns to scale, this is simply an equiproportionate relation-ship between output and input.

We are now in a position to return to Tables 2.10 and 2.11 and consider the individual equations more closely. As noted above, each CES "nest" in Figure 2.6 contains two types of equations: a composite price equation and the set of conditional demand equations. For example, equation (28), at the top of Table 2.10, explains the percentage change in the composite price of imports $pim(i,s)$. In contrast to the sectoral price equation (6) in Table 2.8, we use a cost share, $MSHRS(i,k,s)$ which is the share of imports of $i$ from region $k$ in the composite imports of $i$ in region $s$ (recall that this composite is the same for all uses in the region). The next equation determines the sourcing of imports, according to their individual market prices, $pms(i,r,s)$, relative to the price of composite imports, $pim(i,s)$.

The first set of equations in Table 2.11 describes the composite intermediate inputs nest. This is specific to the individual sector in question. Here, $FMSHR(i,j,r)$ refers to the share of imports in firms' composite tradeable commodity $i$ in sector $j$ of region $r$. Note that our choice of notation requires separate conditional demand equations for imported [equation (31)] and do-mestic [equation (32)] goods. Otherwise, the structure of these demands fol-lows the usual format.

Equations (33) and (34) in Table 2.11 describe the value-added nest of the producers' technology tree. In particular, they explain changes in the price of composite value-added ($pva$) and the conditional demands ($qfe$) for endowment commodities in each sector. Here, the coefficient $SVA(i,j,r)$ refers to the share of endowment commodity $i$ in the total cost of value-added in sector $j$ of $r$. In addition to the price variables, $pfe(i,j,r)$, these equations include variables governing the rate of primary factor-augmenting technical change, $afe(i,j,r)$. More specifically, this is the rate of change in the variable $AFE(i,j,r)$, where $AFE(i,j,r)*QFE(i,j,r)$ equals the *effective* input of primary factor $i$ in sector $j$ of region $r$. Therefore, a value of $afe(i,j,r) > 0$ results in a decline in the effective price of primary factor $i$. For this reason it enters the equations as a deduction from $pfe(i,j,r)$. This has the effect of: (1) encouraging substitution of factor $i$ for other primary inputs via the right-hand side of equation (34), (2) diminishing the demand (at constant effective prices) for $i$ via the left-hand side of equation (34), and (3) lowering the cost of the value-added composite via equation (33) – thereby encouraging an expansion in the use of all primary factors.

Finally, we have the top-level nest, which generates the demand for composite value-added and intermediate inputs. Since we have assumed no substitutability between intermediates and value-added, the relative price component of these conditional demands drops out, and we are left with only the expansion effect. Furthermore, there are three types of technical change introduced in this nest. The variables $ava(j,r)$ and $af(i,j,r)$ refer to input augmenting technical-change in composite value-added and intermediates, respectively. The variable $ao(j,r)$ refers to Hicks-neutral technical change. It uniformly reduces the input requirements associated with producing a given level of output. Finally, we have restated the zero profits condition ($6'$), which serves to determine the price of output in this sector. This revised equation reflects the effect of technical change on the composite output price for commodity $j$ produced in region $r$.

**Implications for tariff reform.** At this point it is useful to employ the linearized representation of producer behavior provided in Table 2.11 to think through the effects of a trade policy shock. Consider, for example, a reduction of the bilateral tariff on imports of $i$ from $r$ into $s$, $tms(i,r,s)$. This lowers $pms(i,r,s)$ via price linkage equation (24) in Table 2.9. Domestic users immediately substitute away from competing imports according to equation (29) in Table 2.10. Also, the composite price of imports facing sector $j$ falls via equations (28) and (23), thereby increasing the aggregate demand for imports through equation (31) in Table 2.11. Cheaper imports serve to lower the composite price of intermediates through equation (30), which causes excess profits at current prices, via equation (6). This in turn induces output to expand, which in turn generates an expansion effect via equations (35) and (36) in Table 2.11. (Of course, in a partial equilibrium model whereby nonfood sectors' activity levels are exogenous, the latter effect will be present only when $j$ refers to a food sector.)

The expansion effect induces increased demands for primary factors of production via equation (34) in Table 2.11. In a partial equilibrium closure, labor and capital might be assumed forthcoming in perfectly elastic supply from the nonfood sectors, so $pfe(i,j,r)$ is unchanged for $i$ = labor, capital. However, in the general equilibrium model, this expansion generates an excess demand via the mobile endowment market clearing condition equation (4), thereby bidding up the prices of these factors, and transmitting the shock to other sectors in the liberalizing region.

Now turn to region $r$, which produces the goods for which $tms(i,r,s)$ is reduced. Equation (29) in Table 2.10 may be used to determine the implications for total sales of $i$ from $r$ to $s$, given the responses of agents in region $s$ to the tariff shock. Equation (1) dictates the subsequent implications for total output: $qo(i,r)$ (unless this market clearing condition has been eliminated, and $pm(i,r)$ fixed, under a particular PE closure). At this point, the equations in Table 2.11 again come into play, with equations (35) and (36) transmitting the expansion effect back to intermediate demands and to region $r$'s factor markets.

### Household behavior

**Theory.** As shown in Figures 2.1 and 2.2, regional household behavior is governed by an aggregate utility function, specified over composite private consumption, composite government purchases, and savings. The motivation for including savings in this static utility function derives from the work of Howe (1975), who showed that the intertemporal, extended linear expenditure system (ELES) could be derived from an equivalent, atemporal maximization problem, in which savings enters the utility function. Specifically, he begins with a Stone–Geary utility function, thereupon imposing the restriction that the subsistence budget share for savings is zero. This gives rise to a set of expenditure equations for current consumption that are equivalent to those flowing from Lluch's (1973) intertemporal optimization problem.[7] In the GTAP model we employ a special case of the Stone–Geary utility function, whereby *all* subsistence shares are equal to zero. Therefore, Howe's result, linking this specification with a well-defined intertemporal maximization problem, is applicable.

The other feature of our regional household utility function requiring some explanation is the use of an index of current government expenditure to proxy the welfare derived from the government's provision of public goods and

Table 2.12. *Household Behavior*

Aggregate utility

(37) $INCOME(r) * u(r) = PRIVEXP(r) * up(r)$
$\quad\quad\quad + GOVEXP(r) * [ug(r) - pop(r)] + SAVE(r) * [qsave(r) - pop(r)]$ $\quad\quad\forall reREG$

Regional savings:

(38) $qsave(r) = y(r) - psave + saveslack(r)$ $\quad\quad\forall reREG$

Government purchases:

(39) $ug(r) = y(r) - pgov(r) + govslack(r)$ $\quad\quad\forall reREG$

Demand for composite goods:

(40) $pgov(r) = \sum\limits_{i \in TRAD\_COMM} (VGA(i,r)/GOVEXP(r)) * pg(i,r)$ $\quad\quad\forall reREG$

(41) $qg(i,r) = ug(r) - [pg(i,r) - pgov(r)]$ $\quad\quad\forall ieTRAD$
$\quad\quad\forall reREG$

Composite tradeables:

(42) $pg(i,s) = GMSHR(i,s) * pgm(i,s) + [1 - GMSHR(i,s)] * pgd(i,s)$ $\quad\quad\forall ieTRAD$
$\quad\quad\forall seREG$

(43) $qgm(i,s) = qg(i,s) + \sigma_D(i) * [pg(i,s) - pgm(i,s)]$ $\quad\quad\forall ieTRAD$
$\quad\quad\forall seREG$

(44) $qgd(i,s) = qg(i,s) + \sigma_D(i) * [pg(i,s) - pgd(i,s)]$ $\quad\quad\forall ieTRAD$
$\quad\quad\forall seREG$

services to private households in the region. Here, we draw on the work of
Keller (1980, chap. 8), who demonstrates that if (1) preferences for public
goods are separable from preferences for private goods, and (2) the utility
function for public goods is identical across households within the regional
economy, then we can derive a public utility function. The aggregation of
this index with private utility in order to make inferences about regional
welfare requires the further assumption that the level of public goods provided
in the initial equilibrium is optimal. Users who do not wish to invoke this
assumption can fix the level of aggregate government utility, letting private
consumption adjust accordingly.

**Equations.** The behavioral equations for regional households in the model
are laid out in Table 2.12. As previously noted, this household disposes of
total regional income according to a Cobb–Douglas per capita utility function
specified over the three forms of final demand: private household expenditures,
government expenditures, and savings [equation (37)]. Thus in the standard
closure, the claims of each of these areas represent a constant share of total
income. This may be seen from equations (38) and (39), which determine the

Table 2.12. *(Cont)  Household Behavior*

Private Household demands:

$$(45) \quad yp(r) = \sum_{i \in TRAD} [CONSHR(i,r) * pp(i,r)] \qquad \forall reREG$$

$$+ \sum_{i \in TRAD} [CONSHR(i,r) * INCPAR(i,r)] * up(r)$$

$$+ pop(r)$$

Composite demands:

$$(46) \quad qp(i,r) = \sum_{k \in TRAD} EP(i,k,r) * pp(k,r) + EY(i,r) * [yp(r) - pop(r)] + pop(r) \qquad \begin{matrix} \forall ie TRAD \\ \forall reREG \end{matrix}$$

Composite tradeables:

$$(47) \quad pp(i,s) = PMSHR,(i,s) * ppm(i,s) + [1 - PMSHR(i,s)] * ppd(i,s) \qquad \begin{matrix} \forall ie TRAD \\ \forall se REG \end{matrix}$$

$$(48) \quad qpd(i,s) = qp(i,s) + \sigma_D(i,) * [pp(i,s) - ppd(i,s)] \qquad \begin{matrix} \forall ie TRAD \\ \forall se REG \end{matrix}$$

$$(49) \quad qpm(i,s) = qp(i,s) + \sigma_D(i) * [pp(i,s) - ppm(i,s)] \qquad \begin{matrix} \forall ie TRAD \\ \forall se REG \end{matrix}$$

changes in real expenditures on savings and government activities as a function of regional income and prices. These equations also include slack variables that may be swapped with the quantities of savings and government composites, *qsave* and *ug*, if the user wishes to specify the latter variables exogenously. In order to assure the exhaustion of total regional income under these closures, equation (8) computes the change in private household spending as a residual. Both private and government demands are composite goods that require further elaboration. We turn first to the disaggregate government demands.

**Government demands.** Once the percentage change in real government spending has been determined, the next task is to allocate this spending across composite goods. Here, the Cobb–Douglas assumption of constant budget shares is once again applied. This is implemented via equations (40) and (41) in Table 2.12. In the first of these equations an aggregate price index for all government purchases, $pgov(r)$, is established. This in turn provides the basis for deriving the conditional demands for composite tradeable goods, $qg(i,r)$. Note the similarity between equation (41) and the CES production nests in Table 2.11. [Since we restrict the elasticity of substitution among composite products in the government's utility function to be unitary, this parameter does not appear in equation (41).]

Once aggregate demand for the composite is established, the remainder of the government's utility "tree" is completely analogous to that of the firms represented in Figure 2.6 and Table 2.11. First, a price index is established, equation (42), then composite demand is allocated between imports and domestically produced goods. Finally, the sourcing of imports occurs at the border, via the equations in Table 2.10. Due to the lack of use-specific Armington substitution parameters, $\sigma_D$ is also assumed to be equal across all uses, that is, across all firms and households. Therefore, the only thing that distinguishes firms' and households' import demands are the differing import shares. However, this is not an insignificant difference. Some sectors/households are more intensive in their use of imports. Consequently, they will be more directly affected by a change in, for example, a tariff on the imported goods. This is why the effort expended to establish the detailed mapping of imports to sectors is warranted.

**Private demands.** The nonhomothetic nature of private household demands necessitates a somewhat different treatment. First of all, the computation of the utility of private household consumption must now take explicit account of the rate of population growth. Therefore the percentage change in private utility, $up(r)$, is defined on a per capita basis. The particular method for calculating the percentage change in the utility of private consumption is dictated by the assumed form of private household preferences. For practical reasons, we have chosen to employ the constant difference of elasticities (CDE) functional form, first proposed by Hanoch (1975). It lies midway between the nonhomothetic CES on the one hand, and the fully flexible functional forms on the other. For our purposes, its main virtue is the ease with which it may be calibrated to existing information on income and own-price elasticities of demand. (For an exhaustive treatment of the calibration and use of the CDE functional form in AGE models, see Hertel et al. 1991.)

The CDE implicit expenditure function is given by (2.14):

$$\sum_{i \in TRAD} B(i,r) * UP(r)^{\beta(i,r)\gamma(i,r)} * [PP(i,r) / E(PP(r), UP(r))]^{\beta(i,r)} \equiv 1. \quad (2.14)$$

Here, $E(\cdot)$ represents the minimum expenditure required to attain a prespecified level of private household utility, $UP(r)$, given the vector of private household prices, $PP(r)$. Minimum expenditure is used to normalize individual prices. These scaled prices are then raised to the power $\beta(i,r)$ and combined in an *additive* form. Unless $\beta$ is common across all commodities in a given region, minimum expenditure cannot be factored out of the left-hand side expression and (2.14) is an *implicitly additive* expenditure function. The calibration problem involves choosing the values of $\beta$ to replicate the desired compensated, own-price elasticities of demand, then choosing the $\gamma$'s to replicate the targeted income elasticities of demand. (The shift term $B(i,r)$ is a scale factor embodied in the budget share, CONSHR($i,r$), in the linearized representation of these preferences.)

Total differentiation of (2.14) and use of Shephard's lemma permits us to derive the relationship between minimum expenditure, utility, and prices that is given in equation (45) of Table 2.12 (see also Hertel, Horridge, and Pearson 1992). Equation (46) determines per capita private household demands for the tradeable composite commodities: $qp(i,r) - pop(r)$. As long as $EY(i,r)$ departs from unity, the $pop(r)$ term does not cancel out, as it did in the case of homothetic government and savings demands. Finally, in Table 2.12 we have a block of equations that develop the mix of composite consumption of tradeable commodities, based on domestic and composite imported goods.

As noted in the previous paragraph, the parameters of the CDE function are initially selected (i.e., calibrated) to replicate a prespecified vector of own-price and income elasticities of demand. However, with the exception of some special cases of the CDE (e.g., the Cobb–Douglas), these elasticities are not constants. Rather, they vary with expenditure shares / relative prices. [See Hertel et al. (1991) for derivations and more detailed discussion of these formulas. Chapter 4 also provides illustrations of how the income elasticities of demand vary over expenditure levels.] For this reason we need some supplementary formulas describing how the elasticities are updated with each iteration of the nonlinear solution procedure.

The formulas for the uncompensated price and income elasticities of demand, $EP(i,k,r)$ and $EY(i,r)$, are reported in Table 2.13. (These are not assigned equation numbers, as they are merely used to compute parameter values to be used in the system of equations representing the model. Therefore, they are given the prefix "F.") The first of these simply defines a parameter, $\alpha$, that is equal to one minus the CDE substitution parameter. (This simplifies some of the other formulas.) Formulas (F2) and (F3) compute the own- and cross-price Allen partial elasticities of substitution in consumption. (The latter are symmetric.) These are simply a function of $\alpha$ and the consumption shares. It may be seen that when $\beta(i,r) = \beta \; \forall i$, then the cross-price elasticities of substitution are all equal to $1 - \beta = \alpha$ and the CDE simplifies to a CES function. Furthermore, when $\beta = 1$, there is no substitution in consumption and when $\beta = 0$, preferences are Cobb–Douglas. When premultiplied by CONSHR($i,r$), formula (F3) yields the compensated, own-price elasticity of demand for commodity $i$. Once these have been specified, this linear system of equations may be solved for the "calibrated" values of $\alpha$, and hence $\beta$, via (F1). (See Chapter 4 for a more extensive discussion of calibration procedures.)

Formula (F4) shows how the income elasticities of demand are computed as a function of consumption shares, the income expansion parameters, $\gamma$'s, and the $\alpha$'s. Because of this, calibration of the own-price elasticities of demand

**Table 2.13.** *Formulas for Private Households' Elasticities of Demand in the Presence of CDE Preferences*

(F1) $\alpha(i,r) = [1 - \beta(i,r)]$

$\forall ieTRAD$
$\forall reREG$

(F2) $APE(i,k,r) = \alpha(i,r) + \alpha(k,r) - \sum_{meTRAD} [CONSHR(m,r) * \alpha(m,r)]$

$\forall i \neq keTRAD$
$\forall reREG$

(F3) $APE(i,i,r) = 2.0 * \alpha(i,r) - \sum_{meTRAD} [CONSHR(m,r) * \alpha(m,r)]$
$\qquad - \alpha(i,r)/CONSHR(i,r)$

$\forall ieTRAD$
$\forall reREG$

(F4) $EY(i,r) = [\sum_{meTRAD} CONSHR(m,r) * \gamma(m,r)]^{-1} * \gamma(m,r) * [1.0 - \alpha(i,r)]$
$\qquad + \sum_{meTRAD} CONSHR(m,r) * \gamma(m,r) * \alpha(m,r)$
$\qquad + \{\alpha(i,r) - \sum_{meTRAD} [CONSHR(m,r) * \alpha(m,r)]\}$

$\forall ieTRAD$
$\forall reREG$

(F5) $EP(i,k,r) = [APE(i,k,r) - EY(i,r)] * CONSHR(k,r)$

$\forall ieTRAD$
$\forall keTRAD$
$\forall reREG$

**Table 2.14.** *Supply of Sluggish Endowments*

(50) $pm(i,r) = \sum_{kePROD\_COMM} REVSHR(i,k,r) * pmes(i,k,r)$

$\forall ieENDWS$
$\forall reREG$

(51) $qoes(i,j,r) = qo(i,r) - endwslack(i,r) + \sigma_T(i) * [pm(i,r) - pmes(i,j,r)]$

$\forall ieENDWS$
$\forall jePROD$
$\forall reREG$

must precede calibration of the income elasticities. Finally, the two may be combined to yield the uncompensated, own-price elasticities of demand reported in (F5).

### Imperfect factor mobility

The two equations in Table 2.14 describe the responsiveness of imperfectly mobile factors of production to changes in the rental rates associated with those sectors in which these sluggish factors are employed. The mobility of these endowments is described with a CET revenue function (Powell and Gruen 1968), which is completely analogous to the CES cost functions used above, except the revenue function is *convex in prices*. Thus the elasticity of transformation is nonpositive, $\sigma_T < 0$. As $\sigma_T$ becomes larger in absolute value, the degree of sluggishness diminishes and there is a tendency for rental rates across alternative uses to move together. As with the CES nests discussed above, the first equation (50) introduces a price index and the second equation (51) determines the transformation relationships. Note also that equation (51) is where we introduce the slack variable, to be used in those cases where the user wishes to fix the market price of a sluggish endowment commodity.

### Macroeconomic closure

Having described the structure of final demand, as well as factor market closure in the GTAP model, it remains to discuss the determination of aggregate investment. Like most comparative static AGE models, GTAP does not account for macroeconomic policies and monetary phenomena, which are the usual factors explaining aggregate investment. Rather, we are concerned with simulating the effects of trade policy and resource-related shocks on the medium-term patterns of global production and trade. Because this model is neither an intertemporal model (e.g., McKibbin and Sachs 1991), nor sequenced through time to obtain a series of temporary equilibria (e.g., Burniaux and van der Mensbrugghe 1991), investment does not come "on-line" next period to affect the productive capacity of industries/regions in the model. However, a reallocation of investment across regions *will* affect production and trade through its effects on the profile of final demand. Therefore, it is important to give this some attention. Also, a proper treatment of the savings–investment link is necessary in order to complete the global economic system, thereby assuring consistency in our accounting.

Because there is no intertemporal mechanism for determination of investment, we face what Sen (1963) defined as a problem of *macroeconomic closure* [see also Taylor and Lysy (1979)]. Following Dewatripont and Michel (1987), we note that there are four popular solutions to the fundamental indeterminacy of investment in comparative static models. The first three are nonneoclassical closures in which investment is simply fixed and another source of adjustment is permitted. In the fourth closure investment is permitted to adjust; however, rather than including an independent investment relationship, it simply accommodates any change in savings.

In addition to adopting a closure rule with respect to investment, it is necessary to come to grips with potential changes in the current account. Many multiregion trade models have evolved as a set of single-region models that are linked via bilateral merchandise trade flows [e.g., early versions of the SALTER model, which evolved from the ORANI model of Australia; see also Lewis, Robinson, and Wang (1995)]. These models have no *global closure* with respect to savings and investment, but instead impose the macroeconomic closure at the regional level. Here it is common to force domestic savings and investment to move in tandem, by fixing the current account balance. To understand this, it is useful to recall the following accounting identity (e.g., Dornbusch 1980), which follows from equating national expenditure from the sources and uses sides:

$$S - I \equiv X + R - M, \tag{2.15}$$

which states that the national savings ($S$) minus investment ($I$) is identically equal to the current account surplus, where $R$ is international transfer receipts. (In the GTAP data base we do not have observations on $R$, so it is set equal to zero and $S$ is derived as a residual, which reflects national savings, net of the unobserved transfers.) By fixing the right-hand side of identity (2.15) one also fixes the difference between national savings (including government savings) and investment. This may be accomplished in the GTAP framework by fixing the trade balance [DTBAL($r$) = 0, see equation (98) in Table 2.18] and freeing up either national savings [endogenize *saveslack*($r$) in equation (38)] or investment [endogenize *cgdslack*($r$) in equation (11′)].

If global savings equals global investment in the initial equilibrium, then the summation over the left-hand side of equation (2.15) equals zero and the sum of all current account balances must initially be zero (provided *cif/fob* margins are accounted for in national exports). Furthermore, by fixing the right-hand side of (2.15) on a regional basis, each region's share in the global pool of net savings is fixed. In this way, equality of global savings and investment in the new equilibrium is also assured, in spite of the fact that there is no "global bank" to intermediate formally between savings and investment on a global basis. Finally, since investment is forced to adjust in line with regional changes in savings, this approach clearly falls within the "neoclassical" closure, as identified by Dewatripont and Michel (1987).

The exogeneity of the current account balance embodies the notion that this balance is a macroeconomic, rather than microeconomic, phenomenon: to a great extent, the causality in identity (2.15) runs from the left side to the right side. It also facilitates analysis by forcing all adjustment to external imbalance onto the current account. If savings does not enter the regional utility function (as is the case in most multiregion AGE models outside of GTAP), this is also the right approach to welfare analysis because an arbitrary shift away from savings toward current consumption and increased imports would otherwise permit an increase in utility to be attained, even in the absence of improvements in efficiency or regional terms of trade.

For some types of experiments, however, modelers may wish to endogenize the balances on either side of identity (2.15). For example, some trade policy reforms raise returns to capital and/or lower the price of imported capital goods. In this case, we would expect the increased rate of return on new investment to result in an increase in regional investment and, *ceteris paribus*, a deterioration in the current account. In other cases one might wish to explore the implications of, for example, an *exogenous* increase in foreign direct investment, which would also dictate a deterioration in the current account. Once the left-hand side of (2.15) is permitted to adjust, a mechanism is needed to ensure that the global demand for savings equals the global demand for investment in the postsolution equilibrium. The easiest way to do so is through the use of a "global bank" to assemble savings and disburse investment. This is the approach that we adopt here.

The global bank in the GTAP model uses receipts from the sale of a homogeneous savings commodity to the individual regional households in order to purchase (at price *PSAVE*) shares in a portfolio of regional investment goods. The size of this portfolio adjusts to accommodate changes in global savings. Therefore, the *global closure* in this model is neoclassical. However, on a regional basis, some adjustment in the mix of investment is permitted, thereby adding another dimension to the determination of investment in the model.

### *Fixed capital formation and allocation of investment across regions*

We have incorporated two alternative investment components into the model. The user may choose which "theory" to employ, depending on her or his individual needs and the simulation being conducted. The first investment component enforces a close link between regional rates of return on capital. This component is described in equations (2.16)–(2.26) below. It draws on the formulation used to allocate investment across *sectors* in the ORANI model (Dixon et al. 1982). The second investment component is based on the assumption that the regional composition of global capital stock will be left unaltered in the simulation, and it is described in equations (2.26) and (2.27) below. At the end of this section we incorporate these two alternative investment components into a single set of composite equations, and explain how the user may specify which is to be used.

We begin by assuming that the productive capacity of capital declines geometrically over time, with depreciation rate $DEPR(r)$. As a result the end-of-period capital stock, $KE(r)$, is equal to the beginning-of-period capital stock, $KB(r)$, multiplied by $[1 - DEPR(r)]$ and augmented by gross investment,

*REGINV(r)*. This accounting relationship is shown in the lower part of Table 2.7 and it is reproduced below:

$$KE(r) = KB(r) * [1 - DEPR(r)] + REGINV(r). \qquad (2.16)$$

We differentiate both sides of accounting relationship (2.16) to obtain:

$$dKE(r) = [1 - DEPR(r)] * dKB(r) + dREGINV(r), \qquad (2.17)$$

which may be rewritten in terms of percentage changes as:

$$ke(r) = [1 - DEPR(r)] * [KB(r)/KE(r)] * kb(r) \\ + [REGINV(r)/KE(r)] * reginv(r), \qquad (2.18)$$

where variables in lowercase represent the percentage change of the corresponding level variables in uppercase.

Let us now define the ratio of investment to end-of-period capital stock, *INVKERATIO(r), as:*

$$INVKERATIO(r) = REGINV(r)/KE(r)$$

and note that

$$[1 - DEPR(r)] * [KB(r)/KE(r)] = \{KB(r)[1 - DEPR(r)] \\ + REGINV(r) - REGINV(r)\}/KE(r) \\ = \{KE(r) - REGINV(r)\}/KE(r) \\ = 1 - INVKERATIO(r).$$

We substitute this into (2.18) to obtain the following relation:

$$ke(r) = [1 - INVKERATIO(r)] * kb(r) + INVKERATIO(r) * reginv(r). \\ (2.19)$$

Because GEMPACK is not case-sensitive, we need to provide an alternative name for *reginv(r)*, the percentage change in regional investment, to distinguish it from *REGINV(r)*. For this we use *QCGDS(r)* (see Capital Stocks section of Table 2.7), thereby obtaining equation (10) in Table 2.8.

We then define the current net rate of return on fixed capital in region *r*, *RORC(r)*, as the ratio of the rental for capital services, *RENTAL(r)*, to the purchase price of capital goods, *PCGDS(r)*, less the rate of depreciation, *DEPR(r)*:

$$RORC(r) = RENTAL(r)/PCGDS(r) - DEPR(r). \qquad (2.20)$$

Expressing equation (2.20) in percentage change terms, we obtain:

$$rorc(r) = [RENTAL(r)/(RORC(r) * PCGDS(r))] * [rental(r) - pcgds(r)]. \\ (2.21)$$

**Table 2.15.** *Investment Equations*

**Equations of notational convenience**

(52) $ksvces(r) = \sum_{h \in ENDWC} [VOA(h,r) / \sum_{k \in ENDWC} VOA(k,r)] * qo(h,r)$     $\forall reREG$

(53) $rental(r) = \sum_{h \in ENDWC} [VOA(h,r) / \sum_{k \in ENDWC} VOA(k,r)] * ps(h,r)$     $\forall reREG$

(54) $qcgds(r) = \sum_{h \in CGDS} [VOA(h,r) / REGINV(r)] * qo(h,r)$     $\forall reREG$

(55) $pcgds(r) = \sum_{h \in CGDS} [VOA(h,r) / REGINV(r)] * ps(h,r)$     $\forall reREG$

(56) $kb(r) = ksvces(r)$     $\forall reREG$

**Rate of return equations**

(57) $rorc(r) = GRNETRATIO(r) * [rental(r) - pcgds(r)]$     $\forall reREG$

(58) $rore(r) = rorc(r) - RORFLEX(r) * [ke(r) - kb(r)]$     $\forall reREG$

$RORDELTA * rore(r) + (1 - RORDELTA)$

(11) $* \{[REGINV(r)/NETINV(r)] * qcgds(r) - [VDEP(r)/NETINV(r)] * kb(r)\}$     $\forall reREG$

$= RORDELTA * rorg + (1 - RORDELTA) * globalcgds + cgdslack(r)$

$RORDELTA * globalcgds + (1 - RORDELTA) * rorg =$

(59) $\qquad RORDELTA * \sum_{reREG} \{[REGINV(r)/GLOBINV] * qcgds(r) - [VDEP(r)/GLOBINV] * kb(r)\}$

$+ (1 - RORDELTA) * \sum_{reREG} [NETINV(r)/GLOBINV] * rore(r)$

**Price of Savings**

(60) $psave = \sum_{reREG} NETINV(r)/GLOBINV * pcgds(r)$

We note that

$$RENTAL(r) / [RORC(r) * PCGDS(r)] = [RORC(r) + DEPR(r)] / RORC(r), \tag{2.22}$$

and we define the ratio of gross returns [i.e., $RORC(r) + DEPR(r)$] to net returns as:

$$GRNETRATIO(r) = [RORC(r) + DEPR(r)] / RORC(r). \tag{2.23}$$

We substitute equations (2.22) and (2.23) into equation (2.21) to obtain equation (57) in Table 2.15.

For our rate-of-return investment component, we assume that investors are cautious in assessing the effects of net investment in a region. They behave as if they expect that region's rate of return in the next period, $RORE(r)$, to decline with positive additions to the capital stock. The rate at which this decline is expected is a function of the flexibility parameter $RORFLEX(r)>0$:

$$RORE(r) = RORC(r)[KE(r)/KB(r)]^{-RORFLEX(r)}. \qquad (2.24)$$

Therefore, the elasticity of $RORE(r)$ with respect to $KE(r)$ is equal to minus $RORFLEX(r)$. Equation (2.24) in percentage change terms is given by equation (58) in Table 2.15. We then assume that investors behave in such a way that changes in regional rates of return are equalized across regions:

$$rore(r) = rorg, \qquad (2.25)$$

where $rorg$ is the percentage change in a global rate of return. Thus, the model will distribute a change in global savings across regions in such a way that all *expected* regional rates of return change by the same percentage. A small value for $RORFLEX(r)$, say, $RORFLEX(r) = 0.5$, implies that a 1% increase in $KE(r)$ is expected to reduce the rate of return on capital by 0.5%. (For example, if the current rate of return were 10%, the expected rate of return on a net investment equal to 1% of $KE(r)$ would be 9.995%, i.e., little change.) In this case the supply of new capital goods is *very* sensitive to the expected rate of return. In order to maintain equal changes in $RORE$ across regions, the model will produce large changes in regional investment.

However, a large value for $RORFLEX(r)$, say, $RORFLEX(r) = 50$, implies that a 1% increase in $KE(r)$ is expected to cut the rate of return on capital in half. In this case the supply of new capital goods is not very sensitive to changes in the expected rate of return. Therefore, equal changes in $RORE$ across regions can be accommodated with small changes in regional investment. In other words, if the user believes that the experiment under consideration will not have a great impact on regional investment (or wishes to abstract from such effects) large values of $RORFLEX(r)$ should be chosen.

Relatively high values for the coefficient $RORFLEX(r)$ are supported by the work of Feldstein and Horioka (1980). They correlated the share of gross domestic investment to gross domestic product with the share of gross domestic savings to gross domestic product (see Feldstein and Horioka 1980; Feldstein 1983). They found a close correlation between savings and investment, and they concluded that even between industrialized countries, international capital mobility may be limited.

The second investment component adopts an extreme position in which we assume that the regional composition of capital stocks will not change at all so that regional and global net investment move together:

$$globalcgds = [REGINV(r)/NETINV(r)] * qcgds(r) \qquad (2.26)$$
$$- [VDEP(r)/NETINV(r)] * kb(r),$$

where *globalcgds* is the percentage change in global supply of new capital goods. In this case, the percentage change in the global rate of return on capital variable, *rorg*, is computed as a weighted average of regional variables (the latter being now wholly unrelated):

$$rorg = \sum_{r \in REG} [NETINV(r)/GLOBINV] * rore(r)$$

where

$$NETINV(r) = (REGINV(r) - VDEP(r)). \qquad (2.27)$$

To summarize, under the rate-of-return component, investment behavior is determined by equations (2.25) above and equation (11) in Table 2.8. Under the alternative component, investment behavior is determined by equations (2.26) and (2.27). Both systems are summarized in Table 2.16.

We have combined these two systems in equations (2.28) and (2.29), employing the parameter *RORDELTA*: this is a binary parameter that takes the values 0 and 1. For *RORDELTA*=1 we obtain the rate-of-return model, and for *RORDELTA*=0 we obtain the alternative model.

$$RORDELTA \quad * rore(r) + (1 - RORDELTA) * \{[REGINV(r)/NETINV(r)]$$
$$* qcgds(r) - [VDEP(r)/NETINV(r)] * kb(r)\}$$
$$= RORDELTA * rorg + (1 - RORDELTA) * globalcgds \qquad (2.28)$$

and

$$RORDELTA * globalcgds + (1 - RORDELTA) * rorg$$
$$= RORDELTA * \sum_{r \in REG} \{[REGINV(r)/GLOBINV]$$
$$* qcgds(r) - [VDEP(r)/GLOBINV] * kb(r)\}$$
$$+ (1 - RORDELTA) * \sum_{r \in REG} [NETINV(r)/GLOBINV] * rore(r) \qquad (2.29)$$

Equation (2.28) is shown in Table 2.15 as equation (59), and equation (2.29) is shown in Table 2.15 as equation (11'). It replaces equation (11) in Table 2.8.

Once the level of investment activity in each region has been determined, it remains only to generate the mix of expenditures for domestic and imported inputs used in the production of fixed capital in region *r*: *VDFA(i,"cgds",r)* and *VIFA(i,"cgds",r)*, respectively. This is completely analogous to the production of tradeable commodities. In fact, the same equations are used to generate these derived demands. We assume that a unit of capital for investment in region *r* is created by assembling composite intermediate inputs in fixed proportions [equation (36) in Table 2.11]. The composite intermediate input is, in turn, a CES combination of domestic and foreign imported inputs [equations (31) and (32) in Table 2.11 and equation (29) in Table 2.10]. However, in contrast to the

**Table 2.16. Regional Allocation of Investment Under Alternative Closures**

**Rate-of-return component:**

$$rore(r) = rorg$$

$$globalcgds = \sum_{r \in REG} \{[REGINV(r) / GLOBINV] * qcgds(r) - [VDEP(r) / GLOBINV] * kb(r)\}$$

**Alternative component:**

$$globalcgds = [REGINV(r) / NETINV(r)] * qcgds(r) - [VDEP(r)/NETINV(r)] * kb(r)$$

$$rorg = \sum_{r \in REG} [NETINV(r) / GLOBINV * rore(r))$$

Table 2.17. *The Global Shipping Industry*

$$(7')\ VT * pt = \sum_{i \epsilon TRAD} \sum_{r \epsilon REG} VST(i,r) * pm(i,r)$$

$$(61)\ qst(i,r) = qt + [pt - pm(i,r)]$$ 

$\forall ie TRAD$
$\forall reREG$

$$(62)\ VT * qt = \sum_{i \epsilon TRAD} \sum_{r \epsilon REG} \sum_{s \epsilon REG} VTWR(i,r,s) * [qxs(i,r,s) - atr(i,r,s)]$$

$$(26')\ pcif(i,r,s) = FOBSHR(i,r,s) * pfob(i,r,s) + TRNSHR(i,r,s) * [pt - atr(i,r,s)]$$

$\forall ie TRAD$
$\forall reREG$
$\forall seREG$

production of tradeable commodities, capital creation requires no services of primary factors. This is because it is a fictitious activity that merely assembles goods destined for fixed investment in region r. In other words, the use of land, labor, and capital associated with capital formation is already embodied in the intermediate inputs assembled by this investment sector.

### Global transportation

In addition to the global bank, another global activity is required in this model in order to intermediate between the supply of, and demand for, international transport services. These services are provided via a Cobb–Douglas production function that demands, as inputs, services exports from each region. Lacking the data to link exports of transport services with specific routes, we simply combine these services into a single composite international transport good, the value of which is $VT = QT * PT$. The percentage change equation for the composite price index was given in equation (7) of Table 2.8. For convenience, it is repeated as equation (7') in Table 2.17. Recall that this is akin to a zero profit condition for the aggregate transport sector. The next equation (61) in Table 2.17 derives the conditional demands for the inputs to the shipping services sector, assuming that the share of each region in the global industry is constant, that is, Cobb–Douglas technology. Therefore, this equation includes an expansion effect ($qt$) and a substitution effect, whereby the elasticity of substitution is assumed to be unitary.

The next two equations in Table 2.17 refer to the uses of the composite international shipping service. We assume that this composite is employed in fixed proportions with the volume of a particular good shipped along a particular route, $QXS(i,r,s)$. In other words: $ATR(i,r,s) * QTS(i,r,s) = QXS(i,r,s)$, where $QTS(i,r,s)$ is the amount of the homogeneous product $QT$ used in shipping one unit of commodity $i$ from $r$ to $s$, and $ATR(i,r,s)$ is a technical coefficient. Equilibrium in the global transport services market therefore requires that:

$$\sum_{i \varepsilon TRAD} \sum_{r \varepsilon REG} \sum_{s \varepsilon REG} QTS(i,r,s) = QT. \tag{2.30}$$

Proportionately differentiating this equation gives:

$$\sum_{i \varepsilon TRAD} \sum_{r \varepsilon REG} \sum_{s \varepsilon REG} QTS(i,r,s) * qts(i,r,s) = QT * qt. \tag{2.31}$$

Multiplying both sides by the common price of the composite transport service, and substituting $[qxs(i,r,s) - atr(i,r,s)]$ for $qts(i,r,s)$ gives equation (62) in Table 2.17. The presence of $atr(i,r,s)$ in this formulation permits the user to introduce commodity/route-specific technical change in international transport services. This also requires us to modify the *fob/cif* price linkage equation (26) in Table 2.9 to reflect the fact that an increase in efficiency along a particular route will lower *cif* values, for a given *fob* price. This revision is reported in (26') of Table 2.17.

### *Summary indices*

This section discusses the summary indices computed in the GTAP model. These equations do not play a role in determining the equilibrium solution. Indeed, all these indices *could* be computed after the fact. However, it is convenient to include them in the model so that their rates of change are reported along with the other results. Table 2.18 shows aggregate indices of prices received [$psw(r)$, equation (64)] and prices paid [$pdw(r)$, equation (65)] for products sold and purchased by each region (inclusive of savings and investment, which represent transactions with the global bank). The difference between $psw(r)$ and $pdw(r)$ measures the percentage change in each region's terms of trade, $tot(r)$.

GTAP also computes regional equivalent variation measures, $EV(r)$, which arise due to the simulation under consideration. The values for $EV(r)$ are in 1992 \$US million, and they are computed as:[8]

$$EV(r) = u(r) * INC(r)/100.$$

Since $u(r)$ reports the percent change in per capita welfare, equation (67) in Table 2.18 also includes the rate of change in population on the right-hand side so that the *EV* reported by the model represents total regional welfare. The worldwide equivalent variation (WEV) is then computed as the simple summation of the regional *EV*s, equation (68). This is followed by an equation generating the percentage in the region-specific consumer price index, $ppriv(r)$.

Other useful price and quantity indices included in GTAP refer to trade, regional gross domestic product (GDP), and income magnitudes. To obtain

**Table 2.18.** *Summary Indices*

(64) $VWLDSALES(r) * psw(r) = \sum\limits_{i\in TRAD} \sum\limits_{s\in REG} VXWD(i,r,s) * pfob(i,r,s)$  $\forall r\in REG$

$\qquad + VST(i,r) * pm(i,r) + [REGINV(r) - VDEP(r)] * pcgds(r)$

(65) $VWLDSALES(r) * pdw(r) = \sum\limits_{i\in TRAD} \sum\limits_{k\in REG} VIWS(i,k,r) * pcif(i,k,r)$  $\forall r\in REG$

$\qquad + SAVE(r) * psave$

(66) $tot(r) = psw(r) - pdw(r)$  $\forall r\in REG$

(67) $EV(r) - [INC(r)/100] * [URATIO(r) * POPRATIO(r)] * [u(r) + pop(r)] = 0$  $\forall r\in REG$

(68) $WEV - \sum\limits_{r\in REG} EV(r) = 0$  $\forall r\in REG$

(69) $PRIVEXP(r) * ppriv(r) = \sum\limits_{i\in TRAD} VDA(i,r) * pp(i,r)$  $\forall r\in REG$

(70) $GDP(r)*vgdp(r) = \sum\limits_{i\in TRAD} VGA(i,r)*[pg(i,r)+qg(i,r)]$  $\forall r\in REG$

$\qquad + \sum\limits_{i\in TRAD} VPA(i,r)*[pp(i,r)+qp(i,r)]+REGINV(r)*[pcgds(r)+qcgds(r)]$

$\qquad + \sum\limits_{i\in TRAD} \sum\limits_{s\in REG} VXWD(i,r,s)*[pfob(i,r,s)+qxs(i,r,s)]+ \sum\limits_{i\in TRAD} VST(i,r)*[pm(i,r)+qst(i,r)]$

$\qquad - \sum\limits_{i\in TRAD} \sum\limits_{r\in REG} VIWS(i,r,s)*[pcif(i,r,s)+qxs(i,r,s)]$

(71) $GDP(r)*pgdp(r) = \sum\limits_{i\in TRAD} VGA(i,r)*pg(i,r)$  $\forall r\in REG$

$\qquad + \sum\limits_{i\in TRAD} VPA(i,r)*pp(i,r)+REGINV(r)*pcgds(r)$

$\qquad + \sum\limits_{i\in TRAD} \sum\limits_{s\in REG} VXWD(i,r,s)*pfob(i,r,s)+ \sum\limits_{i\in TRAD} VST(i,r)*pm(i,r)$

$\qquad - \sum\limits_{i\in TRAD} \sum\limits_{r\in REG} VIWS(i,r,s)*pcif(i,r,s)$

(72) $qgdp(r) = vgdp(r) - pgdp(r)$  $\forall r\in REG$

(73) $VXW(i,r) * vxwfob(i,r) = \sum\limits_{s\in REG} VXWD(i,r,s) * [qxs(i,r,s) + pfob(i,r,s)]$  $\forall i\in TRAD$
$\qquad + VST(i,r) * [qst(i,r) + pm(i,r)]$  $\forall r\in REG$

quantity indices, it is necessary to compute the corresponding value and price indices first, because we are aggregating over different commodities. For example, variable $qgdp(r)$, equation (72) of Table 2.18, is a quantity index for domestic product.[9] Table 2.18 shows that we first compute a value index, $vgdp(r)$, in equation (70), which accounts for changes in prices and quantities, and a price index, $pgdp(r)$, in equation (71), which accounts for changes in prices only. The quantity index, $qgdp(r)$, is then computed as the difference between $vgdp(r)$ and $pgdpr(r)$. For simulations of trade and domestic policy

**Table 2.18.** *(cont.)* *Summary Indices*

(74) $VIW(i,s) * viwcif(i,s) = \sum_{r \in REG} VIWS(i,r,s) * [pcif(i,r,s) + qxs(i,r,s)]$     $\forall i \in TRAD$   $\forall s \in REG$

(75) $VXWREGION(r) * vxwreg(r) = \sum_{i \in TRAD} VXW(i,r) * vxwfob(i,r)$     $\forall r \in REG$

(76) $VIWREGION(s) * viwreg(s) = \sum_{i \in TRAD} VIW(i,s) * viwcif(i,s)$     $\forall s \in REG$

(77) $VXWCOMMOD(i) * vxwcom(i) = \sum_{r \in REG} VXW(i,r) * vxwfob(i,r)$     $\forall i \in TRAD$

(78) $VIWCOMMOD(i) * viwcom(i) = \sum_{s \in REG} viw(i,s) * viwcif(i,s)$     $\forall i \in TRAD$

(79) $VXWLD * vxwwld = \sum_{r \in REG} VXWREGION(r) * vxwreg(r)$

(80) $VWOW(i) * valuew(i) = \sum_{r \in REG} VOW(i,r) * [pxw(i,r) + qo(i,r)]$     $\forall i \in TRAD$

(81) $VXW(i,r) * pxw(i,r) = \sum_{s \in REG} VXWD(i,r,s) * pfob(i,r,s) + VST(i,r) * pm(i,r)$     $\forall i \in TRAD$   $\forall r \in REG$

(82) $VIW(i,s) * piw(i,s) = \sum_{r \in reg} VIWS(i,r,s) * pcif(i,r,s)$     $\forall i \in TRAD$   $\forall r \in REG$

(83) $VXWREGION(r) * pxwreg(r) = \sum_{i \in TRAD} VXW(i,r) * pxw(i,r)$     $\forall r \in REG$

(84) $VIWREGION(s) * piwreg(s) = \sum_{i \in TRAD} VIW(i,s) * piw(i,s)$     $\forall s \in REG$

(85) $VXWCOMMOD(i) * pxwcom(i) = \sum_{r \in REG} VXW(i,r) * pxw(i,r)$     $\forall i \in TRAD$

(86) $VIWCOMMOD(i) * piwcom(i) = \sum_{s \in REG} VIW(i,s) * piw(i,s)$     $\forall i \in TRAD$

(87) $VXWLD * pxwwld = \sum_{r \in REG} VXWREGION(r) * pxwreg(r)$

(88) $VWOW(i) * pw(i) = \sum_{r \in REG} VOW(i,r) * pxw(i,r)$     $\forall i \in TRAD$

changes, the solution value for $qgdp(r)$ will typically be small, reflecting only shifts in the economy's production possibilities frontier owing to the improved allocation of a fixed resourcebase. But for simulations of endowment growth, the solution value for $qgdp(r)$ will provide a summary measure of growth for the region.

We next turn to a set of equations defining changes in aggregate trade values, prices, and quantity indices. Equations (73)–(78) compute the percentage change in export and import values: (1) by commodity *and* region, (2) by

Table 2.18. *(cont.)*  *Summary Indices*

| | |
|---|---|
| (89) $qxw(i,r) = vxwfob(i,r) - pxw(i,r)$ | $\forall i \in TRAD$ <br> $\forall r \in REG$ |
| (90) $qiw(i,s) = viwcif(i,s) - piw(i,s)$ | $\forall i \in TRAD$ <br> $\forall s \in REG$ |
| (91) $qxwreg(r) = vxwreg(r) - pxwreg(r)$ | $\forall r \in REG$ |
| (92) $qiwreg(s) = viwreg(s) - piwreg(s)$ | $\forall s \in REG$ |
| (93) $qxwcom(i) = vxwcom(i) - pxwcom(i)$ | $\forall i \in TRAD$ |
| (94) $qiwcom(i) = viwcom(i) - piwcom(i)$ | $\forall i \in TRAD$ |
| (95) $qxwwld = vxwwld - pxwwld$ | |
| (96) $qow(i) = valuew(i) - pw(i)$ | $\forall i \in TRAD$ |
| (97) $DTBALi(i,r) = [VXW(i,r)/100] * vxwfob(i,r) - [VIW(i,r)/100] * viwcif(i,r)$ | $\forall i \in TRAD$ <br> $\forall r \in REG$ |
| (98) $DTBAL(r) = [VXWREGION(r)/100] * vxwreg(r) - [VIWREGION(r)/100] * viwreg(r)$ | $\forall r \in REG$ |

region for all traded commodities, and (3) by commodity for all regions in the world. Equation (79) computes the percentage change in the value of total world trade, and equation (80) computes the percentage in value of world output, by commodity.[10] These are followed by eight analogous equations, (81)–(88), which compute the associated price indices, after which we are able to extract pure volume changes for aggregate trade and output [equations (89)–(96)].

The last two equations in the model are given at the bottom of Table 2.18. They are used to compute the change in trade balance, by commodity and by region. This is a value-based concept, and $DTBAL(r)$, equation (98), refers to the changes in the current account for each region.

## VII    A simple numerical example

Perhaps the best way to understand how this model works is to perform a simple experiment and examine the resulting changes in endogenous variables of interest. (This is example 21 in the Hands-On document, referred to in Chapter 6, and available through the Web site.) In order to keep things simple, we will work with a three-commodity/three-region aggregation of the data base. The three commodities are: food, manufactures, and services. The three regions are: the United States (US), the European Union (EU), and the rest

Table 2.19. *Impact of a 10% Cut in the Power of the Ad Valorem Tariff on EU Imports of US Foods on EU Food Sector in a Standard GE Closure using Johansen Solution Method and Fixed Investment Portfolio (RORDELTA = 0)*

| VARIABLE | PERCENTAGE CHANGE | EQUATION # |
|---|---|---|
| $pm(food, usa) = .140$ | | |
| $pfob(food, usa, eu) = .140$ (tx, txs exogenous) | | (27) |
| $pcif(food, usa, eu) = .124 = (.893) * (.140) + (.107) * (-.008)$ | | (26) |
| $pms(food, usa, eu) = -9.876 = .124 - 10.0$ | | (24) |
| $pim(food, eu) = -1.631 = (.164) * (-9.876) + (.000) * (-.121) + (.836) * (-.016)$ | | (28) |
| $qxs(food, usa, eu) = 41.433 = 3.18 - (4.64) * [-9.876 - (-1.631)]$ | | (29) |
| $pf(food, food, eu) = -.259 = .092 * (-1.631) + .908 * (-.121)$ | | (30) |
| $qfm(food, food, eu) = 3.002 = -.288 - (2.40) * [-1.631 - (-.259)]$ | | (31) |
| $qfd(food, food, eu) = -0.621 = -.288 - (2.40) * [-.121 - (-.259)]$ | | (32) |
| $ps(food, eu) = -0.121$ | | (1) |

* Equation numbers refer to GTAP model equations presented in earlier tables.

of the world (ROW). The experiment involves a bilateral reduction in the level of the EU's import tariff onUS food products. In particular, *tms(food,usa,eu)* = −10%. This implies a cut of 10% in the *power of the ad valorem tariff*, which amounts to a 10% cut in the domestic price of US food exports to the EU, *ceteris paribus*. Furthermore, we begin by performing only the *first step* in a multistep solution of the model developed above. In terms of Figure 2.5, this means we are moving from $(X_0, Y_0)$ to $(X_1, Y_J)$, where $Y_J$ is a Johansen approximation to $Y_1$ (the true solution). This is merely a pedagogical device to facilitate discussion of our example, since in the Johansen solution, the linearized form of the model in Tables 2.8–2.18 will *hold exactly*. For small shocks this may provide a reasonable approximation to the true, nonlinear price and quantity changes. However, *it is a very poor method for assessing welfare changes* [see Hertel, Horridge, and Pearson (1992) for an extensive discussion of these issues]. The reader can observe this approximation error by comparing the Johansen solution with the Gragg outcomes (given in brackets) in Tables 2.20, 2.22, and 2.23.

Tables 2.19 and 2.20 report selected changes in the EU, resulting from the bilateral tariff cut. We begin at the top of the table, with the market price of US food in the US. This market price rises by 0.140% due to increased demand. Since there is no change in the border tax, *pfob* rises by the same amount, via equation (27) in Table 2.9. The *cif* price of US food exports to the EU depends also on changes in the price index of international transport

Table 2.20. *Economywide Effects in EU of a 10% Cut in the Power of the Ad Valorem Tariff on EU Imports of US Food in a Standard GE Closure Using Johansen Solution Method and RORDELTA = 0 (Nonlinear solution in brackets)*

| COMMODITY | VARIABLE (PERCENTAGE CHANGE) | | | | | |
|---|---|---|---|---|---|---|
| | pm(i, eu)[a] | | qo(i, eu) | | qp(i, eu) | |
| Land | -.414 | [-.515][b] | 0.0 | [0] | na | [na] |
| Labor | -.029 | [-.041] | 0.0 | [0] | na | [na] |
| Capital | -.028 | [-.041] | 0.0 | [0] | na | [na] |
| Food | -.121 | [-.154] | -.288 | [-.355] | .036 | [.042] |
| *mnfrs* | -.030 | [-.041] | .064 | [.086] | .012 | [.007] |
| Services | -.030 | [-.042] | .012 | [.012] | .011 | [.007] |
| *cgds* | -.026 | [-.037] | -.003 | [-.004] | na | [na] |

[a] All price changes are relative to the price of the numeraire, which is savings.
[b] Nonlinear solution obtained by applying the Gragg, 2-4-6, method.

services, *pt*. This drops slightly due to the decline in the price of EU transport services [Table 2.19 and equation (7)]. Therefore, *pcif* increases by a slightly smaller amount.

The bilateral tariff instrument, which is the subject of this experimental shock, enters via equation (24) in Table 2.9. Its reduction serves to lower the domestic market price of EU food imports from the US, *pms (food,usa,eu)*, by 9.876%. This price cut has two immediate effects. First, it lowers the price of composite imports by 1.631% [equation (28) in Table 2.10], a value that is roughly equal to the share of US imports in total expenditures on imported food multiplied by -9.876%. The second immediate effect of this price cut is that it encourages agents in the EU to alter their sourcing of food imports in favor of US products [equation (29) in Table 2.10]. The responsiveness of this shift in the model is dictated by the elasticity of substitution among food imports ($\sigma_M$). Its value in the aggregated data base is 4.64. This figure is multiplied by the percentage change in the cost of food imports from the US, relative to composite import costs, or the difference in these two individual percentage changes. This equals 38.26%. If the level of imports *qim* were unchanged, this would be the end of the story. However, the impact of the bilateral cut in protection continues, since the cheaper imports result in a substitution of composite imports for domestic food. This effect varies by sector in this model, due to the differing importance of imports in the composite intermediate good. Since the substitution structure in each of these is very similar, we choose to focus on the EU food industry, which is the largest user, accounting for 52.7% of total food imports in that market. In this industry, aggregate imports increase by 3.18%. Thus the total increase in US food imports by the EU food industry is equal to 41.4%.

The numerical implementations of equations (30) and (31) in Table 2.11 describe the changes at the next level of the production tree (recall Figure

2.3). They account for the 3.0% increase in composite food imports by this sector. However, note from equation (31) that in this case the expansion and substitution effects work in opposite directions, since $qf(food,eu) = qo(food,eu)$ < 0. That is, the food sector as a whole contracts, and with it, there is a decline in the demand for intermediate products, in this case food. Equation (32) shows that the demand for domestically produced intermediates actually falls. Finally, owing to a decline in the total demand for domestically produced food, the price of EU-produced food falls.

Table 2.20 reports selected price and quantity changes for the EU as a whole, owing to this bilateral tariff cut. The price of farmland falls, since this factor has no alternative uses outside of the food sector in our model, and output in that sector has declined. With labor and capital being released from the food sector, the nonfood sectors are able to expand. In general equilibrium, households increase their consumption of all nonsavings commodities due to the lower prices. The demand for savings falls, since its price is determined by a weighted combination of the capital goods prices from all regions, which tend to rise relatively more than other goods prices.

Now turn to the effects of the tariff cut on the US economy, which are reported in Tables 2.21 and 2.22. Equation (1) in Table 2.21 combines the increase in US–EU exports, together with changes in sales to other destinations/uses in order to estimate the change in food sector output in the US. The first figures in parentheses are the shares of sales to various uses. From this, it can be seen that exports to the EU account for only 1.3% of the value of total US food sector output (at domestic market prices). This considerably tempers the impact of the 41.4% increase in sales. Of course the importance of this market for selected, *disaggregated* producer groups can be much larger, and might warrant strategic disaggregation of the data base to capture such effects.

It is not surprising that the bulk of US food sales goes to the domestic market (92.6%). However, it is somewhat surprising that the tariff cut in the EU causes domestic sales of US food to *increase*. More insight into this result may be obtained by considering the numerical implementation of equation (3) in Table 2.21. This shows the changes in composition of domestic sales. As expected, sales to other industries and final demand fall, as US supply prices for food are bid up by the EU users. However, these declines are more than offset by an increase in *intermediate* demands for food in the US food sector. In other words, to meet the increased demand for food in the EU, domestic sales of intermediate goods must also increase.

Table 2.22 describes the economywide effects of the bilateral tariff cut on the US. Here, the land rental rate rises by more than the food price, and labor and capital wages rise by somewhat less, with the relative capital intensity of the food sector favoring capital over labor. Continuing the analogy, we see

**Table 2.21.** *Impact of a 10% Cut in the Power of the Ad Valorem Tariff on EU Imports of US Food on Total Food Sales in the US in a Standard GE Closure Using Johansen Solution Method and RORDELTA = 0*

| VARIABLE | PERCENTAGE CHANGE | EQUATION # |
|---|---|---|

$qo(food, usa) = 0.688$                 (1)[a]

$= SHRODM(food, usa) * qds(food, usa) \rightarrow (.926) * (.207)$
$\quad SHROTM(food, usa) * qst(food, usa) \rightarrow (.000) * (.000)$

$\sum_{j} SHROXMD(food, usa, s) * qxs(food, usa, s)$

$\quad\quad\quad\quad s = usa \rightarrow (.000) * (.-.133)$
$\quad\quad\quad\quad s = eu \rightarrow (.013) * (41.433)$
$\quad\quad\quad\quad s = row \rightarrow (.060) * (-.634)$

where:
$qds(food, usa) = .207$               (3)

$= \sum_{j} SHRDFM(food, j, usa) * qfd(food, j, usa)$

$\quad\quad\quad\quad j = food \rightarrow (.334) * (.662)$
$\quad\quad\quad\quad j = mnfcs \rightarrow (.010) * (-.143)$
$\quad\quad\quad\quad j = svcs \rightarrow (.121) * (-.022)$
$\quad\quad\quad\quad j = egds \rightarrow (.000) * (-.042)$

$+ SHRDPM(food, usa) * qpd(food, usa) \rightarrow (.517) * (-.019)$
$+ SHRDGM(food, usa) * qgd(food, usa) \rightarrow (.018) * (-.031)$

[a] Equation numbers refer to GTAP model equations presented in earlier tables.

**Table 2.22.** *Economywide Effects in the US of a 10% Cut in the Power of the Ad Valorem Tariff on EU Imports of US Food in a Standard GE Closure Using Johansen Solution Method and RORDELTA = 0 (Nonlinear solution in brackets)*

| COMMODITY | VARIABLE (Percentage Change) | | | | | |
|---|---|---|---|---|---|---|
| | pm(i, usa)[a] | | qo(i, usa) | | qp(i, usa) | |
| land | 1.066 | [1.378][b] | 0 | [0] | na | [na] |
| labor | .109 | [ .141] | 0 | [0] | na | [na] |
| capital | .125 | [ .162] | 0 | [0] | na | [na] |
| food | .140 | [ .181] | .688 | [.886] | -.000 | [-.000] |
| mnfrs | .100 | [ .129] | -.120 | [-.155] | .037 | [.048] |
| services | .111 | [ .144] | -.001 | [-.001] | .009 | [.011] |
| cgds | .095 | [ .123] | -.001 | [-.002] | na | [na] |

[a] All price changes are relative to the price of the numeraire, which is savings.
[b] Nonlinear solution obtained by applying the Gragg, 2-4-6, method.

Table 2.23. *Macroeconomic Effects of a 10% Cut in the Power of the Ad Valorem Tariff on EU Imports of US Food in a Standard GE Closure: Fixed (RORDELTA = 0) and Variable (RORDELTA = 1) Portfolios, and Johansen and Nonlinear Solution Methods Compared*

| VARIABLE | | | | | | |
|---|---|---|---|---|---|---|
| | US | | EU | | ROW | |
| | PERCENTAGE CHANGE | | | | | |
| $qxwreg(r)$ | .138 (.057)[a] | [.178][b] | .233 (.263) | [.317] | -.007 (.007) | [-.006] |
| $rorc(v)$ | .045 (.051) | [.059] | -.003 (-.005) | [-.006] | -.003 (-.004) | [-.003] |
| $tot(v)$ | .110 (.128) | [.142] | -.043 (-.049) | [-.060] | -.007 (-.008) | [-.008] |
| $up(r)$ | .013 (.016) | [.017] | .015 (.014) | [.013] | -.003 (-.004) | [-.004] |
| $ug(r)$ | .013 (.015) | [.016] | -0.007 (-.008) | [-.014] | -.005 (-.006) | [-.006] |
| $qsave(r)$ | .118 (.138) | [.153] | -.037 (-.042) | [-.056] | -.006 (-.007) | [-.006] |
| $u(r)$ | .015 (.018) | [.019] | .006 (.004) | [.001] | -.004 (-.005) | [-.004] |
| | *$US Million* | | | | | |
| $EV(r)^c$ | 778 (941) | [1004] | 346 (251) | [62] | -347 (-410) | [-396] |
| $DTBAL(r)$ | -8 (-663) | [-9] | 0 (297) | [-22] | 7 (366) | [31] |

[a] Flexible investment portfolio, *RORDELTA* = 1, and Johansen solution method reported in parentheses.
[b] Fixed investment portfolio, *RORDELTA* = 0, and *nonlinear* solution obtained via Gragg, 2-4-6, method in brackets.
[c] Equivalent variation refers to the Cobb—Douglas, superutility function for region *r*. It is computed in equation (67) of Table 2.18.

that the manufacturing sector must contract in order to make way for expansion of the US food sector. Finally, note that composite consumption of nonfood manufactures and services increases, as households substitute imported for domestic goods.

The final table, Table 2.23, summarizes the macroeconomic effects of the EU's bilateral tariff cut. The increase in demand for US products bids up US prices, relative to the prices of products supplied from the EU and ROW. Since the EU must export more products to pay for the increase in food imports, their export volume increases by .233%, in the case where *RORDELTA* = 0 and a simple Johansen solution is used. (See the top entry in the second column of Table 2.23.) Therefore, the EU supply prices must fall relative to other regions. This results in a terms-of-trade deterioration for the EU, as seen in the third row of Table 2.23. The terms-of-trade for ROW are marginally worsened, due to displacement by US exporters. This translates into a welfare loss for ROW. In the EU, the terms-of-trade decline is more than offset by the improved allocation of domestic resources, and aggregate regional welfare rises by $346 million. The US gains $778 million due to its improved terms-of-trade, following the preferential cut in border taxes on US food exports to the EU.

It is interesting to note that the trade balance hardly changes, $DTBAL$ $(r)$ ≈ 0, in those simulations where $RORDELTA$ = 0. This is a robust outcome that follows from equation (2.15) and the treatment of savings and investment in the model. The demand for savings is tied directly to income, which is little affected in this (and most other) policy reform experiments. Since regional savings doesn't change much, global savings, and hence global investment, are unaltered. Therefore, the only means of altering the left-hand side of (2.15), $(S − I)$, and hence the trade balance, is to alter the regional allocation of investment. When $RORDELTA$ = 0, this is not possible. Therefore, there can be little change in the right-hand side of (2.15), $(X − M)$.

This is no longer true, however, when $RORDELTA$ = 1, and the global bank's allocation of investment across regions is flexible. In the lower (parenthetical) entries of Table 2.23, we report results of the Johansen simulation with $RORFLEX$ = 10 (the default setting for this parameter). Now changes in rate-of-return on investment come into play. From the second row of Table 2.23, we see that $rorc(eu)$ < 0, since the rental rate on capital declines relative to the price of capital goods. Therefore, there is an incentive to divert some investment to other regions. Given $S$, the resulting decline in $I$ requires an increase in $(X − M)$ via identity (2.15). This is achieved by a slightly larger increase in export volume (.263% vs. .233%) from the EU, and a smaller increase in imports. Not surprisingly, this results in a stronger terms-of-trade deterioration and therefore a smaller gain in welfare, as opposed to the case where $RORDELTA$ = 0.[11]

A comparison of the Johansen results with the nonlinear results (reported in brackets in Table 2.23) shows that the Johansen solution yields a poor approximation to the true welfare effects on the EU, even for this relatively small shock. This is because the change in EU utility reflects the difference between two larger changes, one of which is positive (efficiency gains) and one of which is negative (terms-of-trade effect). As can be seen from the third row of Table 2.23, the Johansen solution underestimates the true deterioration in the EU's terms of trade by a third. On the other hand, this solution procedure tends to *overstate* the gains from elimination of a distortion. Therefore, it is not surprising that the gain in EU welfare is *overstated* by more than five times ($346 million vs. the true gain of $62 million, reported in brackets). Indeed, it is not uncommon for such comparisons to yield sign reversals in some regions' welfare. In sum, use of the Johansen one-step solution procedure for purposes of decomposing small changes in prices and quantities (as in Tables 2.19 and 2.21) is very useful. However, *it is not an acceptable procedure for conducting welfare analysis of policy reforms*. For welfare analysis, the nonlinear solution procedures available in GEMPACK must be used.

## VIII    Summary

This completes our summary of the structure of the GTAP model. For your convenience, we have assembled a glossary of notation used in the model. This is provided at the back of this book. As noted, the electronic file, GTAP94.TAB, contains a complete listing of the model code. It is available on the Web site. Access to this site is discussed in Chapter 6. The best way to become familiar with the model is to apply it to a particular problem of interest. After covering the data base, the parameters, aggregation, and computing issues, we will turn to a set of seven diverse applications of this model.

NOTES

1. The authors would like to thank Martina Brockmeier for her development of much of this material. For a more extensive graphical exposition of the GTAP model, see Brockmeier (1996).
2. The motivation for including savings in this atemporal utility function derives from Howe (1975) and is discussed at greater length below.
3. In some cases the initial data base does not include taxation in these markets. However, the possibility of introducing such taxation is available in the model, and it must therefore be accounted for in the computation of regional income.
4. The most natural way to implement this model would be via a *mixed* levels and percentage change representation. Indeed, this is possible in GEMPACK (Harrison and Pearson 1994). However, it is computationally more burdensome. Also, by linearizing the accounting equations some additional insights may be obtained.
5. This type of nonlinear solution procedure is now the default option in GEMPACK. For an exhaustive comparison of the linearized and levels approaches to AGE modeling, the reader is referred to Hertel, Horridge, and Pearson (1992).
6. For the user with an interest in applications for which intermediate–intermediate and intermediate–primary factor substitution is important, it will be necessary to modify the basic model, tailoring it to the specific needs at hand. However, this is not particularly difficult, as will be seen below.
7. Howe (1975) also shows that the savings share parameter in the atemporal utility function can be related to 1 minus the ratio of consumer's rate of time preference to the rate of reproduction of capital.
8. The coefficient $INC(r)$ reports *initial* equilibrium values for regional expenditure (which must equal income).
9. Values for the coefficient gross domestic product, $GDP(r)$, are computed as follows:

$$GDP(r) = \sum_{i \in TRAD}[VGA(i,r) + VPA(i,r)] + VOA(\text{"CGDS"},r)$$
$$+ \sum_{i \in TRAD}\sum_{s \in REG}VXWD(i,r,s) + \sum_{i \in TRAD}VST(i,r) - \sum_{i \in TRAD}\sum_{r \in REG} VIWS(i,r,s).$$

10. The coefficient $VOW(i,r)$ measures the value of regional production at world prices, and its values are computed as follows: $VOW(i,r) = VDM(i,r) * PW\_PM(i,r) + \sum_{s \in REG}VXWD(i,r,s)$. The coefficient $PW\_PM(i,r)$ converts domestic use valued at market prices, $VDM(i,r)$, to world prices, and it is computed as follows: $PW\_PM(i,r) = \sum_{s \in REG}VXWD(i,r,s) / \sum_{s \in REG}VXMD(i,r,s)$.
11. The combination of $RORDELTA = 1$ and the Gragg nonlinear solution procedure actually gives a slight *decline* in EU welfare.

## REFERENCES

Alston, J. M., C. A. Carter, R. Green, and D. Pick (1990) "Whither Armington Trade Models?" *American Journal of Agricultural Economics* 72(2):455–467.

Armington, P. A. (1969) "A Theory of Demand for Products Distinguished by Place of Production," *IMF Staff Papers* 16:159–178.

Arrow, K. J., H. B. Chenery, B. S. Minhas, and R. M. Solow (1961) "Capital-Labor Substitution and Economic Efficiency," *Review of Economics and Statistics* 43:225–250.

Brockmeier, M. (1996) "A Graphical Exposition of the GTAP Model," GTAP Technical Paper, Center for Global Trade Analysis, Purdue University, West Lafayette, IN.

Brown, D. K., and R. M. Stern (1989) "U.S.–Canada Bilateral Tariff Elimination: The Role of Produce Differentiation and Market Structure." In R. C. Feenstra (ed.), *Trade Policies for International Competitiveness*. Chicago: University of Chicago Press.

Burniaux, J. M., and D. van der Mensbrugghe (1991) "Trade Policies in a Global Context: Technical Specification of the Rural/Urban-North/South (RUNS) Applied General Equilibrium Trade Model," Technical Paper No. 48, Paris, OECD, The Development Centre, November.

Dewatripont, M., and G. Michel (1987) "On Closure Rules, Homogeneity and Dynamics in Applied General Equilibrium Models," *Journal of Development Economics* 26:65–76.

Dixit, A. K., and J. E. Stiglitz (1979) "Monopolistic Competition and Optimum Product Diversity," *American Economic Review* 67:297–308.

Dixon, P. B., B. R. Paramenter, J. Sutton, and D. P. Vincent (1982) *Orani: A Multisectoral Model of the Australian Economy*. New York: North Holland.

Dornbusch, R. (1980) *Open Economy Macroeconomics*. New York: Basic Books.

Feenstra, R. C. (1994) "New Product Varieties and the Measurement of International Prices," *American Economic Review* 84:157–177.

Feldstein, M. (1983) "Domestic Savings and International Capital Movements in the Long Run and Short Run," *European Economic Review* 21:129–151.

Feldstein, M., and Charles Horioka (1980) "Domestic Savings and International Capital Flows," *Economic Journal* 90:314–329.

Francois, J., B. McDonald, and H. Nordstrom (1995) "Assessing the Uruguay Round," paper presented at the World Bank Conference on Developing Economies and the Uruguay Round, January.

Hanoch, G. (1975) "Production and Demand Models in Direct or Indirect Implicit Additivity," *Econometrica* 43:395–419.

Harrison, G., T. Rutherford, and D. Tarr (1995) "Quantifying the Uruguay Round," paper presented at the World Bank Conference on Developing Economies and the Uruguay Round, January.

Harrison, W. J., and K. R. Pearson (1994) "Computing Solutions for Large General Equilibrium Models Using GEMPACK," Impact Project Preliminary Working Paper No. IP-64.

Hertel, T. W., J. M. Horridge, and K. R. Pearson (1992) "Mending the Family Tree: A Reconciliation of the Linearization of Levels Schools of Applied General Equilibrium Modeling," *Economic Modelling* 9:385–407.

Hertel, T. W., and D. K. Lanclos (1994) "Trade Policy Reform in the Presence of Product Differentiation and Imperfect Competition: Implications for Food Processing Activity." In M. Hartmann, P. M. Schmitz, and H. von Witzke (eds.),

*Agricultural Trade and Economic Integration in Europe and in North America.* Kiel: Wissenschaftsverlag Vauk Kiel KG.

Hertel, T. W., E. B. Peterson, P. V. Preckel, Y. Surry, and M. E. Tsigas (1991) "Implicit Additivity as a Strategy for Restricting the Parameter Space in CGE Models," *Economic and Financial Computing* 1(1):265–289.

Howe, H. (1975) "Development of the Extended Linear Expenditure System from Simple Saving Assumptions," *European Economic Review* 6:305–310.

Jomini, P., J. F. Zeitsch, R. McDougall, A. Welsh, S. Brown, J. Hambley, and J. Kelly (1991) *SALTER: A General Equilibrium Model of the World Economy,* Vol. 1, "Model Structure, Database and Parameters." Canberra, Australia: Industry Commission.

Keller, W. J. (1980) *Tax Incidence: A General Equilibrium Approach.* Amsterdam: North Holland.

McKibbin, W., and J. Sachs (1991) *Global Linkages: Macroeconomic Interdependence and Cooperation in the World Economy.* Washington, DC: The Brookings Institution.

Lewis, J. D., S. Robinson, and Z. Wang (1995) "Beyond the Uruguay Round: The Implications of an Asian Free Trade Area," *China Economic Review* 6(1)35–90.

Lluch, C. (1973) "The Extended Linear Expenditure System," *European Economic Review* 4:21–32.

Pearson, K. R. (1991) "Solving Nonlinear Economic Models Accurately via a Linear Representation," Impact Project Working Paper No. IP-55.

Powell, A. A., and F. H. Gruen (1968) "The Constant Elasticity of Transformation Frontier and Linear Supply System," *International Economic Review* 9(3):315–328.

Robinson, S., M. E. Burfisher, R. Hinojosa-Ojeda, and K. E. Thierfelder (1993) "Agricultural Policies and Migration in the U.S.-Mexico Free Trade Area: A Computable General Equilibrium Analysis," *Journal of Policy Modeling,* 15(5):673–701.

Sen, A. K. (1963) "Neo-classical and Neo-Keynesian Theories of Distribution," *Economic Record* 39:54–64.

Spence, M. E. (1976) "Product Selection, Fixed Costs and Monopolistic Competition," *Review of Economic Studies* 43:217–236.

Taylor, L., and F. J. Lysy (1979) "Vanishing Income Redistributions: Keynesian Clues about Model Surprises in the Short Run," *Journal of Development Economics* 6:11–29.

Varian, H.R. (1978) *Microeconomic Analysis.* New York: Norton.

Winters, L. A. (1984) "Separability and the Specification of Foreign Trade Functions," *Journal of International Economics* 17:239–263.

CHAPTER 3

# Overview of the GTAP data base

*Mark Gehlhar, Denice Gray, Thomas W. Hertel,*
*Karen M. Huff, Elena Ianchovichina, Bradley J. McDonald,*
*Robert McDougall, Marinos E. Tsigas, and Randall Wigle*


## I   Introduction and overview

The centerpiece of the Global Trade Analysis Project (GTAP) data base consists of bilateral trade, transport, and protection matrices that link 24 country/regional economic data bases. (See Table 3.1 for a complete list of regions and sectors in version 2 of the GTAP data base.[1]) The regional data bases are derived from individual country input–output tables.[2] The purpose of this chapter is to document the sources and procedures used in constructing the disaggregated 37-sector, 24-region data base that forms the basis for subsequent applications.

The next section discusses processing of the international bilateral merchandise trade data, which are published by the Statistical Office of the United Nations. These data are ideal for our purposes, but their reliability is questionable [see, for example, DeWulf (1981); Hiemstra and Mackie (1986); and Tsigas, Hertel, and Binkley (1992)]. Therefore, we discuss a statistical procedure for reconciling discrepant trade statistics and producing balanced bilateral trade and transport matrices for 1992. These bilateralized flows are also used to determine the pattern of trade in nonfactor services.

The third section discusses the support and protection data developed for GTAP. These are expressed in the form of *ad valorem* equivalent, tariff, and nontariff barriers, and they draw heavily on information submitted to the General Agreement on Tariffs and Trade (GATT) in connection with the Uruguay Round negotiations. For this reason, there is not a unique base year. However, these protection data are broadly indicative of the level of support prevailing prior to the Uruguay Round.

We then turn to the basic input–output (IO) data that provide information about the individual regional economies in GTAP. Some of these were obtained from the Australian Industry Commission (IC), while others were contributed

74

Table 3.1. *Regions and Commodities in Version 2 of the GTAP Data Base*[*]

| Listing of regions in the data base | Listing of industries (Cont'd) |
|---|---|
| 1. Australia (AUS) | 6. Other livestock (OLP) |
| 2. New Zealand (NZL) | 7. Forestry (FOR) |
| 3. Canada (CAN) | 8. Fishing (FSH) |
| 4. United States of America (US) | 9. Coal (COL) |
| 5. Japan (JPN) | 10. Oil (OIL) |
| 6. Republic of Korea (KOR) | 11. Gas (GAS) |
| 7. EU-12 (EU) | 12. Other minerals (OMN) |
| 8. Indonesia (IND) | 13. Processed rice (PCR) |
| 9. Malaysia (MYS) | 14. Meat product (MET) |
| 10. Philippines (PHL) | 15. Milk products (MIL) |
| 11. Singapore (SGP) | 16. Other food products (OFP) |
| 12. Thailand (THA) | 17. Beverages and tobacco (BT) |
| 13. People's Republic of China (CHN) | 18. Textiles (TEX) |
| 14. Hong Kong (HKG) | 19. Wearing apparel (WAP) |
| 15. Taiwan (TWN) | 20. Leather, etc. (LEA) |
| 16. Argentina (ARG) | 21. Lumber and wood (LUM) |
| 17. Brazil (BRA) | 22. Pulp, paper, etc. (PPP) |
| 18. Mexico (MEX) | 23. Petroleum and coal products (PC) |
| 19. Rest of Latin America (LAM) | 24. Chemicals, rubber and plastics (CRP) |
| 20. Sub-Saharan Africa (SSA) | 25. Nonmetallic mineral products (NMM) |
| 21. Middle East and North Africa (MNA) | 26. Primary ferrous metals (IS) |
| 22. Eastern Europe and Former Soviet Union (EIT) | 27. Nonferrous metals (NFM) |
| 23. South Asia (SAS) | 28. Fabricated metal products nec. (FMP) |
| 24. Regions not elsewhere classified (ROW) | 29. Transport equipment (TRN) |
| | 30. Machinery and equipment (OME) |
| | 31. Other manufacturing (OMF) |
| Listing of industries/commodities | 32. Electricity, water, and gas (EGW) |
| 1. Paddy rice (PDR) | 33. Construction (CNS) |
| 2. Wheat (WHT) | 34. Trade and transport (TT) |
| 3. Grains (other than rice and wheat: GRO) | 35. Other services (private) (OSP) |
| 4. Nongrain crops (NGC) | 36. Other services (government)(OSG) |
| 5. Wool (WOL) | 37. Ownership of dwellings (DWE) |

[*] See also GTAP mapping file, available on the FTP site.

by members of the GTAP network. In the case of the six composite regions in the data base, no IO information is available, so we use representative combinations of the known tables to obtain estimated IO tables. The procedures for doing so are described in some detail in this section.

Because the IO tables making up the regional data bases refer not to 1992, but rather to the latest available year, they must be updated to conform to the 1992 trade and macroeconomic data. We accomplish this complicated task using the FIT software package (James and McDougall 1993). Once this is done, the trade and regional data bases may be merged. If everything has been done correctly, the data base balances and the sum of all region' savings (income private and public consumption) must, by virtue of Walras' Law, equal global investment. This offers a final consistency check on the GTAP data base.

## II    International trade data

This section covers development of the GTAP bilateral trade data base.[3] We begin with a discussion of the basic source of global bilateral trade data and the problems encountered in using it for analytical purposes. We then turn to some issues of data consistency, followed by a discussion of reconciliation procedures.

### Institutional background

The trade data upon which the GTAP data base is built originate from United Nations D-series trade statistics. COMTRADE (COMmodity TRADE) is the registered name of the data base maintained by the United Nations (UN) Statistical Office. This data base is one of the most complete and exhaustive data bases in terms of commodity and country coverage. It is a daunting task to maintain a data base of this size, with contributions from all the countries of the world, so it is hardly surprising that there are problems of availability, quality, and consistency. In order to address these concerns, the UN established an interagency task force on international trade statistics. This task force has three main goals: (1) improving the flow of data from national authorities to the COMTRADE system, (2) adjusting reported data that do not comply with international guidelines to assure intercountry comparability, and (3) improving the estimation process used to create data files for those countries and periods for which no reported data are available. Thus far, most progress has been made in the area of the first goal.

The UN has made numerous attempts to estimate missing trade values. Traditionally, the UN Statistical Office has used a "gap filling" methodology called the Trade Estimation System (TESSY) to provide trade statistics for nonreported trade. This system employs a matrix balancing algorithm starting with known border sums. It fills in the unknown cells in the bilateral matrix. TESSY was started in 1979 in order to create estimates for all missing values in the UN trade data base and to provide a complete set of data with which to test the LINK project model. In fact, the UN maintains a data base of estimated data separate from the reported data contained in COMTRADE. However, this estimated data base is made available only to selected international agencies on a limited basis.

The disadvantage in using matrix balancing techniques such as TESSY is that there are an infinite number of solutions for a given problem. Therefore, it is difficult to place a particular degree of confidence in the balanced matrix. Responding to this dissatisfaction with existing methods, the Economic Research Service of the United States Department of Agriculture (USDA) has recently developed a new methodology to fill in missing gaps in the UN trade data. This methodology uses a statistical approach requiring time-series data. The statistical approach can yield more reliable estimates; however, it requires time-series data for each country. This limits country coverage to those that report on a reasonably regular basis. Estimates of missing data points with this approach were made at the 4-digit Standard International Trade Classification (SITC) level. The estimates provided by USDA/Economic Research Service (ERS) were merged with the UN COMTRADE data to create a starting point for the development of a GTAP trade data base. From there, the data are aggregated starting from the 4-digit SITC level to the 31 merchandise sectors in the GTAP data base. Once aggregated, specialized reconciliation procedures are employed. We next turn to a discussion of the issues and procedures of data reconciliation.

### Concepts and definitions relevant to reconciliation

There are several perspectives on the meaning of consistency and reliability in trade data. For example, Rozanski and Yeats (1992) developed a method for evaluating UN trade statistics based on a set of consistency tests. These include checks on the consistency across SITC revisions; consistency checks within the SITC hierarchy levels, that is, 3-digit and 4-digit levels, and consistency across international agencies. It is beyond the scope of this project to test reliability or ensure the type of consistency proposed by Rozanski and Yeats. For the GTAP model to be operational there must ultimately be unification of reported export data with reported import data. This involves evaluating the consistency of trade data based on the partner country approach, that is, a country's reported exports (imports) are compared with a partner's reported imports (exports) with the objective of identifying major value differences (Morgenstern 1963; Yeats 1978). Counterpart trade statistics are consistent if: $X_{ij} = M_{ij}$, where $X_{ij}$ is reported exports by the $i$th exporter to $j$th importer, and $M_{ij}$ is reported imports by the $j$th importer from the $i$th exporter. In an overwhelming majority of cases, when two trading partners report the value of their trade to the UN, the export figures and the corresponding import figures disagree. This type of inconsistency is the focus of our reconciliation effort.

### Reconciliation procedures

There is no common method for reconciling differences in counterpart trade statistics. Reconciliation methods vary according to the type of inconsistencies one perceives the need to resolve. Some argue that reported exports are more consistent than reported imports and that imports need to be adjusted in the reconciliation process. Arguments in favor of reported exports make the following points: (1) valuation conventions–export data are free of transportation and insurance charges, thus enhancing comparability across trade flows; and (2) ships do not appear in the import matrix.

Others contend that reported imports are more consistent than reported exports and the latter should be adjusted (Parniczky 1980). Arguments in favor of reported imports include: (1) underreporting of exports by customs authorities, (2) better commodity identification of imports due to closer inspection, and (3) uncertain destination of exports under the conditions created by entrepot trade.

We do not presume that reported exports are better or worse than reported imports. Rather, we examine this issue on a country-by-country, and commodity-by-commodity, basis. We regard countries that regularly under- or overreport trade figures as being "systematically biased." This is a statistical concept that may be formalized as follows. Let $X_{ij}$ represent the observed export value (*fob*) reported by the $i$th country as exported to the $j$th country, and let $X^*_{ij}$ represent the actual value (unobserved). The term $\beta_i$ represents the "exporter bias" coefficient:

$$X_{ij} = \beta_i X^*_{ij}\, e_i. \tag{3.1}$$

The term $\beta_i$ is a systematic component that can be estimated. The error term $e_i$ accounts for the nonsystematic component. Similarly, the reported import value $M_{ij}$ is described as:

$$M_{ij} = \alpha_j M^*_{ij} e_j, \tag{3.2}$$

where $M_{ij}$ represents the observed import value (*cif*) reported by the $j$th country imported from the $i$th country. The term $\alpha_j$ represents the "importer bias" coefficient.

In comparing the difference between the actual value of exports $X^*_{ij}$ and the actual value of imports $M^*_{ij}$ for a given transaction, the import value in general would exceed the value of exports because of the presence of the transportation margin. This relationship can be written as a ratio:

$$\frac{M^*_{ij}}{X^*_{ij}} = 1 + g = \gamma. \tag{3.3}$$

Variable $g$ represents the proportion of the *fob* value of exports that is attributable to transportation costs. The term $\gamma > 1$ is equal to the *cif/fob* ratio. A general price rise has no effect on the *cif/fob* ratio because it is expressed in relative terms. The *cif/fob* ratio is another systematic discrepancy between reported imports and exports; however, unlike reporting biases, which are country-specific, this ratio is commodity-specific.

At this point, we have identified three systematic components of the discrepancy between reported imports and exports: exporter bias, importer bias, and the commodity-specific margin. Now combine equations (3.1)–(3.3) into a single equation that describes the relationship between the ratio of reported trade values and the systematic components:

$$\frac{M_{ij}}{X_{ij}} = \frac{\alpha_j e_j}{\beta_i e_i} \gamma. \tag{3.4}$$

Rewriting (3.4) in natural logarithms yields:

$$\ln\frac{M_{ij}}{X_{ij}} = \ln\alpha_j - \ln\beta_i + \ln\gamma + \ln e_j - \ln e_i. \tag{3.5}$$

From equation (3.5) we may estimate the systematic components: $\alpha_j$, $\beta_i$, and $\gamma$.

We estimate a dummy-variable model that contains specific indicator variables for each importer and each exporter. A commodity-specific dummy variable is used for each commodity. For every country, we estimate an exporter bias $\beta_j$, and an importer bias $\alpha_i$. Also, a commodity-specific margin $\gamma$ is estimated. Biased reporting is estimated in the regression model on a relative basis. For example, underreporting is estimated for a specific country when it consistently underreports relative to other countries with which it trades.

The estimated coefficients are used to adjust reported export and import data so that the reconciled data are on a bias-free, *fob* basis. Consistency is achieved by adjusting trade data so that exports equal imports:

$$X_{ij} = M_{ij}. \tag{3.6}$$

Transactions reported by both exporter and importer are referred to as "two-sided" transactions. These are distinguished from transactions for which there is only one value reported (by either the exporter or importer), which are referred to as "one-sided." We use only two-sided transactions in the regression analysis, since the dependent variable is a ratio of the two values.

Our reconciliation procedure is extended such that multiple bias coefficients are estimated for a given reporter. This is useful given the diversity in reporting behavior across commodities for any one country. Having many traded commodities in our data,[4] we recognize that a country can overreport exports for one commodity and underreport exports of another. It is therefore necessary to estimate multiple bias coefficients for each reporting country.

To obtain these alternative bias measures for each country, we apply the model to several subsets of the data containing unique reporting biases. With little *a priori* information on which countries over- or underreport what commodities, it is only through the regression results that differences in report-ing patterns are revealed. Once the average reporting biases are estimated, the data are transformed by those biases. In those instances in which this transformation worsens the discrepancy between reported imports and exports, we assume that a different type of bias applies. These "nonconforming" obser-vations are separated out, and a different regression model is applied. This process of data segmentation is repeated several times until a satisfactory degree of conformity is obtained.

## Evaluation of the reconciliation of partner statistics

How does reconciliation alter the total value of merchandise trade data? By design, the method adjusts reported values based on "relative" biases for bilateral transactions. This type of adjustment alters the reported totals some-what for individual reporters. Table 3.2 shows the import totals by region as reported by the importer, the importers' partners, and the reconciled total. For almost all the reporting countries there are only slight changes in the total reported values. Of course, there are cases of *severe* underreporting (or nonre-porting) in some countries in the composite regions of Latin America, sub-Saharan Africa, the Middle East and North Africa, and Eastern Europe / Former Soviet Union. In most of these cases, the partners' reported trade was used, after adjusting for the international transport margins.

In the final column of Table 3.2, comparisons are made with International Monetary Fund (IMF) merchandise import totals. Entries report the ratio of the reconciled GTAP value to the IMF value. For the US, Canada, and Austra-lia, the IMF's totals are higher than the GTAP totals. In other individual countries, the GTAP totals are higher than the IMF totals. The largest discrep-ancy is for China, where the GTAP total is 1.222 times greater than the IMF total. In this case, the GTAP total relied heavily on the partners' reporting of China's exports. We presume that this is due to underreporting of trade flows by China, as well as differences in reporting conventions. In the case of Mexico, the large discrepancy (1.148) may be attributed to differences in reporting practices for the manufacturing plants along the US–Mexico border.

Table 3.3 shows the size of world trade, by GTAP commodity. World merchandise trade is weighted heavily toward finished manufactured goods including transportation equipment and machines. Together, these make up over 45% of the total. Oil, and chemicals, rubber, and plastics also constitute a large share (16%) of total merchandise trade. The presence of certain highly disaggregate commodities (e.g., rice and wool) in this data base reflects the special needs of the Australian Industry Commission, which did much of the original data work underpinning GTAP (Jomini et al. 1991).

**Table 3.2.** *Reported and Reconciled Totals of Merchandise Imports by Region*
*(1992 $US million)*

| Region | Reported by Importer | Reported by Partner | Reconciled Value | Reconciled/IMF ratio |
|---|---|---|---|---|
| | (cif value) | (fob value) | (fob value) | (fob basis) |
| AUS | 38,201 | 32,098 | 37,997 | .931 |
| NZL | 8,959 | 6,200 | 8,719 | 1.075 |
| CAN | 116,358 | 106,031 | 113,495 | 0.907 |
| US | 531,381 | 407,887 | 512,032 | 0.955 |
| JPN | 222,922 | 141,873 | 217,564 | 1.096 |
| KOR | 79,934 | 51,840 | 78,125 | 1.010 |
| EU | 568,296 | 412,215 | 558,921 | n.a. |
| IDN | 27,069 | 18,109 | 27,114 | 1.024 |
| MYS | n.a. | 28,271 | 33,594 | 0.927 |
| PHL | 12,769 | 11,406 | 14,865 | 1.024 |
| SGP | 70,784 | 42,981 | 73,088 | 1.100 |
| THA | 39,005 | 28,749 | 40,168 | 1.108 |
| CHN | 75,229 | 46,181 | 78,706 | 1.222 |
| HKG | 122,389 | 95,209 | 120,827 | n.a. |
| TWN | n.a. | 56,965 | 54,545 | n.a. |
| ARG | 14,597 | 12,681 | 14,269 | 1.047 |
| BRA | 22,601 | 16,522 | 24,944 | 1.212 |
| MEX | 47,640 | 53,645 | 55,330 | 1.148 |
| LAM | 43,988 | 72,664 | 71,836 | n.a. |
| SSA | 2,329 | 32,626 | 34,464 | n.a. |
| MNA | 49,583 | 129,395 | 127,816 | n.a. |
| EIT | 20,794 | 39,549 | 69,831 | n.a. |
| SAS | 33,536 | 25,178 | 32,250 | n.a. |
| ROW | 239,709 | 231,673 | 248,502 | n.a. |

*Margins function and estimation*

International transportation margins can pose a barrier to trade much the same as do tariffs. In addition, the presence of transport costs typically means that prices are not fully transmitted across geographically separated markets. Most models of international trade do not include trade margins. As a consequence, analyses of the implications of policy shocks for the pattern of international trade are unlikely to be accurate in cases in which substantial margins are involved. The GTAP model has an explicit role for the export of international

Table 3.3. *Reconciled World Totals of Merchandise Trade by Commodity*
*(1992 $US million)*

| Sector | Reconciled (fob value) | Share of Total% |
|---|---|---|
| PDR | 613 | 0.02 |
| WHT | 12,278 | 0.46 |
| GRO | 11,288 | 0.43 |
| NGC | 57,318 | 2.16 |
| WOL | 4,176 | 0.16 |
| OLP | 12,368 | 0.47 |
| FOR | 7,693 | 0.29 |
| FSH | 26,488 | 1.00 |
| COL | 17,140 | 0.65 |
| OIL | 176,604 | 6.67 |
| GAS | 28,553 | 1.08 |
| OMN | 52,432 | 1.98 |
| PCR | 3,166 | 0.12 |
| MET | 21,082 | 0.80 |
| MIL | 9,139 | 0.34 |
| OFP | 71,072 | 2.68 |
| B&T | 27,763 | 1.05 |
| TEX | 93,936 | 3.55 |
| WAP | 105,610 | 3.99 |
| LEA | 54,849 | 2.07 |
| LUM | 56,237 | 2.12 |
| PPP | 71,811 | 2.71 |
| P&C | 53,650 | 2.03 |
| CRP | 251,252 | 9.48 |
| NMM | 28,961 | 1.09 |
| I&S | 76,664 | 2.89 |
| NFM | 52,426 | 1.98 |
| FMP | 57,192 | 2.1 |
| TRN | 320,245 | 12.09 |
| OME | 781,253 | 29.49 |
| OMF | 105,742 | 3.99 |
| TOTAL | 2,649,002 | 100.00% |

transportation services, and for their use in the bilateral movement of merchandise between regions.

International trade margins vary widely across traded commodities and across routes. Agricultural goods generally have a low value per ton compared to nonagricultural or manufactured goods, thus leading to a higher trade margin. Within the food sector, margins tend to be lower for high-value processed food products and higher for low-value bulk commodities (Gehlhar,

Binkley, and Hertel 1991). Variation in margins by route are also caused by differences in the volume shipped and differences in port efficiency. Small ports with lower trade volumes tend to have fewer mechanized facilities, thereby increasing the time for loading and unloading. Therefore, the *fob–cif* margin can vary substantially across ports.

Although it is technically possible to estimate transportation margins based on *fob–cif* values by commodity and route, such data are often reported inconsistently. It is not uncommon to find that the export value reported on an *fob* basis exceeds the corresponding reported import value on a *cif* basis. For this reason, it is useful to estimate a general "margins function" that can be used to produce margins estimates, even when *fob–cif* comparisons are not possible.

For practical reasons, the estimation of a margins function is done independently of the reconciliation phase. However, we use a similar statistical technique. Like the model developed from equation (3.5), the dependent variable is the ratio of the two values (*cif/fob*). Furthermore, we wish to control for reporting biases by individual countries, so the same dummy variables are used to measure reporting biases. However, we also need to add explanatory variables specific to the trade margin. For example, as world freight rates rise, relative to other prices, we would expect a corresponding rise in the trade margin. The variable used for world freight rates is a dry-cargo freight index based on tramp voyage rates for 28 routes (OECD 1964–1987, in *Maritime Transport*). This is an annual freight index constructed to give worldwide coverage. Because this index was published in nominal values, it was deflated by the US consumer price index (CPI) to reflect real changes in freight cost.

Distance in miles also enters our margins function. We expect larger trade margins for longer routes. A Mercator's projection map giving the mileage for various water routes is used to determine the shortest distances from port to port. We also add variables designed to deal with port-specific effects. Estimates of port capacity, by country, would have been ideal; however, this information was unavailable. Furthermore, because countries have multiple ports, and because we do not know where trade leaves/enters the country, we are not able to address this component in our regression model. However, we do have estimates of the volume of trade along specific routes, and we use it as an explanatory variable in the margins function. We expect that the margin will be a decreasing function of the total volume of trade along a given route. Since our trade flows are expressed in value terms (current $US), we deflate the flows in order to obtain a proxy for trade volume.

Recall the relationship between the trade data and the margin:

$$\frac{M^*_{kijt}}{X^*_{kijt}} = 1 + g = \gamma. \tag{3.7}$$

The terms $X^*_{kijt}$ and $M^*_{kijt}$ represent bias-free reported export and import values from exporter $i$ to importer $j$, for commodity $k$, in time period $t$. We choose the Cobb–Douglas functional form to represent the relationship between this ratio and its arguments:

$$\gamma_{kijt} = \gamma_k D_{ij}^{\theta_D} F_t^{\theta_F} V_{ijt}^{\theta_V}, \tag{3.8}$$

where $\gamma_{kijt}$ represents the *cif/fob* ratio for commodity $k$, shipped from $i$ to $j$ in time period $t$. The $\gamma_k$ term represents the general ratio over all routes and time periods for commodity $k$. The variables $D_{ij}$, $F_t$, and $V_{ijt}$ represent distance from $i$ to $j$, world freight rate in time $t$, and volume of total trade from $i$ to $j$ in time $t$, respectively. The coefficients $\theta_D$, $\theta_F$, and $\theta_V$ are estimated in natural logarithmic forms, yielding:

$$ln\left(\frac{M^*_{kijt}}{X^*_{kijt}}\right) = \gamma_k C_k + \theta_D \ln D_{ij} + \theta_F \ln F_t + \theta_V \ln V_{ijt}. \tag{3.9}$$

Here, $C_k$ is a dummy variable identifying the $k$th commodity.

Finally, we must deal with the fact that the data are not free of country-specific reporting biases. We correct for this aspect by using individual dummy variables for each importer and exporter. The final margins model is:

$$Y_s = \mu + \sum_{N-1}^{i=1} \alpha_j \, C_{is1} - \sum_{N-1}^{i=1} \beta_i \, C_{is2} + \sum_{K}^{i=1} \gamma_k \, C_{is3}$$
$$+ \, \theta_D \ln D_{ij} + \theta_F \ln F_t + \theta_{VT} \ln \, V_{ijt} + e_s. \tag{3.10}$$

(The notation is simplified by letting $Y_s = \ln (M_{kijt}/X_{kijt})$, where $S = 1 \ldots s$ is an index representing the total number of observations in the entire data set.)

We use the parameter estimates from (3.10) to compute bilateral transportation margins for 1992. In computing margins, we fix the time dimension by holding the world freight rate constant, and we allow distance and traded volumes to change as we move across different routes. The only factor missing from equation (3.8) that must be included is the effect of reporting biases on margins, which we will denote as coefficient $A$. This coefficient can be summarized as follows:

$$A = e^\mu \prod_{i=1}^{N-1} \overline{C}_{i1}^{\alpha_i} \overline{C}_{i2}^{\beta_i}, \tag{3.11}$$

where $\overline{C}_{i1}$ and $\overline{C}_{i2}$ are the samplewide means of the dummy variables, $\mu$ is the estimated intercept, and $\alpha_i$ and $\beta_i$ are the estimated importer and exporter biases. We can now write the bilateral trade margins function as follows:

$$\gamma_{kijt} = \gamma_k A * D_{ij}^{\theta_D} F_t^{\theta_F} V_{ijt}^{\theta_{VT}}]. \tag{3.12}$$

Equation (3.12) is used to generate the *cif/fob* ratio for all commodities and routes.

Table 3.4. *Exports of Nonfactor Services by Region* (*1992 $US billions*)

| Region | Exports[a] | Imports | |
|---|---|---|---|
| | | Nonshipping | Shipping[b] |
| EU[c] | 234.74 | 171.26 | 46.47 |
| [32.08%][d] | (29.49%)[e] | (29.21%) | (22.18%) |
| US | 152.65 | 87.66 | 36.75 |
| [26.49%] | (19.18%) | (14.95%) | (17.53%) |
| Japan | 73.84 | 70.10 | 21.10 |
| [17.81%] | (9.28%) | (11.96%) | (10.07%) |
| Australia | 16.49 | 9.56n | 3.06 |
| [30.57%] | (2.07%) | (1.63%) | (1.46%) |
| Other East Asia | 111.00 | 57.24 | 40.37 |
| [17.35%] | (13.95%) | (9.76%) | (19.27%) |
| Latin America | 37.51 | 33.48 | 12.99 |
| [19.51%] | (4.71%) | (5.71%) | (6.20%) |
| Other regions | 169.70 | 157.08 | 48.82 |
| [20.92%] | (21.33%) | (26.79%) | (23.29%) |
| World | 795.94 | 586.37 | 209.56 |
| [23.10%] | (100.00%) | (100.00%) | (100.00%) |

[a] Includes shipping services.
[b] Shipping services purchased as part of *cif* merchandise imports.
[c] Excludes EU intraregional trade.
[d] Share of total exports comprising services.
[e] Percentage of total services exports.

### Trade in services

Trade in services includes trade in factor services (interest, profits, and dividends) as well as trade in nonfactor services (business, insurance, and financial services). In the GTAP framework we have data only on nonfactor services trade, which is in turn broken into shipping and nonshipping services components. Regional exports of shipping services are available in the UN COMTRADE data base, but trade in nonshipping services is not. Therefore, it must be obtained from alternative sources. The IMF is one of the better sources of this information and was used extensively for obtaining data on trade in services. The 1992 services trade data were assembled on an individual-country basis for total exports and imports. GTAP regional totals were obtained by aggregating individual countries. In doing so, all regional totals of services trade contain intraregional trade, with the exception of the European Union (EU), where it is excluded.[5]

Table 3.4 reports trade in these services, by selected regions. World exports of nonfactor services are reported in the first column. In total, they amount to $795 billion (excluding intra-EU trade). About a third of this (29.49%) comes from the EU. (Parenthetic entries in Table 3.4 refer to the share of each region's nonfactor services exports in the worldwide total.) These exports include both shipping and nonshipping services. The former are obtained from the COMTRADE data base. Since these shipping services exports can be used for transporting goods between any two trading partners, tracking the source and destination of shipping services is not possible. For this reason the GTAP model treats these flows as exports to the "global shipping sector" (see Chapter 2). They are then embodied in the value of merchandise imports *cif* rather than as an individual component of total imports.

Imports of nonfactor services in Table 3.4 are broken into two components: shipping and nonshipping. The shipping component totals $209 billion, and represents the trade margin component of merchandise imports, valued on a *cif* basis. The nonshipping component of nonfactor services amounts to $586 billion. Again, the EU is the dominant trading partner, making up about 29% of this total. Together, the sum of shipping and nonshipping services imports equals total services exports ($795 billion).

Trade in nonshipping, nonfactor services represents a significant component of global trade. The bracketed entries in the left-hand margin of Table 3.4 report the share of these services exports in the regional and world totals. From this, it may be seen that services trade makes up 23.1% of total trade in the GTAP data base, on a worldwide basis. However, this figure is higher for the EU (32%), which supplies a disproportionate share of the world's shipping services.

Having only the totals of nonfactor services trade by individual countries, it was necessary to allocate this total across the six GTAP service sectors (sectors 32–37 in Table 3.1). It would be inappropriate to allocate total services equally across all sectors. Some service sectors are largely "nontradeable" services; naturally, their share of total traded services is small. These sectors electricity, water and gas (32), construction (33), and ownership of dwellings (37). The sectoral shares used to make the allocation were obtained from the original country IO tables. In the case of countries for which the IO data shares were missing, we used the average shares for all reporting countries.

Once the sectoral allocation of nonfactor, nonshipping services was made, these totals were bilateralized among trading partners. The bilateral pattern of services trade is not available on a global basis. We approximate the bilateral trade patterns for services based on bilateral merchandise trade patterns. Solving this problem entails satisfying the sectoral services totals of individual countries (for both imports and exports) while preserving the initial bilateral merchandise share coefficients. This is not possible. Therefore a constrained matrix balancing algorithm was adopted.[6] This minimizes the deviation between the final trade shares and the initial shares while satisfying the sectoral total values. Bilateral trade patterns for all six service sectors were obtained independently by this method. One consequence of this approach is that only countries that trade with one another in merchandise trade will trade in services, and the proportions are roughly the same. Further work is needed in order to establish a more reliable pattern of trade in nonfactor services.

In order to balance world trade, total exports of all goods and services must be equal to total imports of all goods and services. Therefore, the difference between *cif* imports and *fob* exports must equal the value of shipping services. This is summarized as follows:

| Total merchandise imports (*cif*) | Total merchandise exports (*fob*) |
| +Nonshipping services | +Nonshipping services |
| | +Shipping services |
| Total imports | = Total exports |

## III    Support and protection data

This section documents the support and protection data (SPD) in GTAP. Our goal is to make the process followed in developing these data transparent to users of GTAP. This will help users become aware of the advantages and limitations of this part of the data base, thereby informing the choice and implementation of the simulations that are ultimately done.

One of the first points to be made is that the SPD are not comprehensive. Some of the limitations will be addressed in the coming years, but others never will nor could be. While there are gaps in the coverage of industries, and policy types, the only sector that is wholly neglected is the services sector. Protection of and support to the service sector are especially difficult to quantify. This does not mean, of course, that the sector is without distortions or that these distortions are unimportant, as the attention given the sector during the Uruguay Round has suggested.

The best-quality data in the SPD are those relating to tariffs. As will be detailed below, the information is systematically aggregated up from extremely detailed tariff line information, using bilateral import weights. The resulting bilateral rates therefore reflect compositional differences in the tariff/trade structure. Nontariff information is most complete in the cases of agriculture and textiles/wearing apparel. However, antidumping duties are also incorporated for Canada, the EU, and the US. Also, the export restraining effects of EU price undertakings are included.

Other trade measures, despite their importance, are very difficult to quantify in a useful way.[7] Some studies that have focused on particular industries in particular countries have usefully quantified nontariff measures. However, data used in disaggregated multicountry general equilibrium models have not accurately and comprehensively incorporated most other nontariff measures. In developing the SPD it was thought better to do a solid job of incorporating tariff and selected nontariff, information and to leave other policy measures aside for the time being, given the dubious information content of the latter.

Despite the several missing pieces to the protection puzzle mentioned in the above paragraphs, we would not be inclined to use, for a general set of problems, any other existing data base over this one. Although these data are incomplete, others are lacking in important areas or, still worse, are misleading. Given the first-order importance that initial distortions play in any quantitative analysis of trade policies, we welcome an increased focus on trade policy measurement.[8]

### Individual-country tariffs

The tariff data used in the protection data base draw on the original country submissions to the GATT for the Uruguay Round. The data vary by year reported, reporting tariff code, level of aggregation, and number of line items. For each tariff line item in each country file, there are data on (1) the value of total imports, (2) bilateral import values from the 17 other GTAP countries, and (3) three different tariff rates: most favored nation (MFN), generalized system of preferences (GSP), and the tariff rates actually applied. The latter applied rates reflect the tariffs charged at the time of file submission, and may be lower than the ceiling rate at which the tariff is bound (MFN rate).

Tariff rates faced by different exporters may vary for a variety of reasons. Discriminatory rates could result from regional trade agreements, the presence of GSP rates for lower-income countries (usually limited to particular commodities), and an importer's refusal to grant MFN status to a particular exporter. It would be desirable to include discriminatory tariff rates in the protection data. Yet some economists argue that implicit discrimination, operating through the composition of trade in developed countries' tariff schedules, far outweighs in importance such discriminatory tariff practices as the GSP and preferential trading arrangements. In the GTAP data base we have chosen to focus on bilateral variation due to compositional differences in trade.

Tariff schedules for most countries contain between 5,000 and 10,000 tariff lines and product classifications.[9] Empirical trade policy models necessarily incorporate trade policies based on aggregations of these tariff lines. Bilateral tariffs at the GTAP level of aggregation were constructed by aggregating *applied* tariff rates from the tariff lines to the GTAP sectors using bilateral import value weights. As noted above, this can result in significant differences in aggregated tariff rates for the same GTAP commodity imported from different sources. For example, imports from developing countries may be mostly primary or semiprocessed goods, while imports from developed countries may be mostly processed goods. If tariff rates vary with the stage of processing, as they often do, then the average tariff within an aggregate faced by developing countries will differ in a systematic way from that faced by developed countries.

Table 3.5.  *Comparison of Simple Average Tariffs to Weighted Average Tariffs*

| Importer | Indonesia | United States | Australia | New Zealand |
|---|---|---|---|---|
| Industry | Nongrain Crops (4) | Beverages and Tobacco (17) | Textiles (18) | Chemicals, Rubber, and Plastics (24) |
| Simple average | 17.1 | 8.0 | 25.4 | 14.0 |
| Minimum | 0.0 | 0.0 | 0.0 | 0.0 |
| Maximum | 40.0 | 338.0 | 115.0 | 524.0 |
| Std. dev. | 11.7 | 17.4 | 18.1 | 21.8 |
| Trade weighted average | 3.9 | 4.3 | 13.2 | 19.8 |
| **Bilateral Weighted Averages** | | | | |
| Argentina | 2.2 | 5.3 | 14.0 | 5.0 |
| Australia | 0.9 | 2.7 | n.a. | 23.3 |
| Brazil | 3.4 | 15.8 | 4.2 | 22.2 |
| Canada | 24.1 | 2.3 | 26.7 | 11.8 |
| China | 7.8 | 2.6 | 12.3 | 20.0 |
| EU | 10.4 | 4.5 | 16.9 | 18.1 |
| Hong Kong | 3.5 | 5.1 | 12.3 | 24.7 |
| Indonesia | n.a. | 3.1 | 10.3 | 31.8 |
| Japan | 6.3 | 3.2 | 7.6 | 20.2 |
| Korea, S. | 11.4 | 2.4 | 6.9 | 25.4 |
| Malaysia | 12.4 | 1.1 | 13.2 | 36.0 |
| Mexico | 0.0 | 6.8 | 17.0 | 13.5 |
| New Zealand | 10.3 | 0.5 | 23.3 | n.a. |
| Philippines | 5.1 | 2.4 | 29.4 | 12.4 |
| Singapore | 12.0 | 0.8 | 9.4 | 19.8 |
| Taiwan | 3.4 | 4.3 | 12.2 | 27.6 |
| Thailand | 9.8 | 5.2 | 11.2 | 23.3 |
| US | 2.9 | n.a. | 16.9 | 17.1 |
| ROW | 1.7 | 2.5 | 10.5 | 19.1 |

Given the Armington framework (product differentiation by region of origin) adopted in the GTAP, the incorporation of bilateral average tariff rates means that each trade flow can be subject to a unique tariff rate. Table 3.5 gives four examples comparing simple average tariffs and bilateral weighted average tariffs. The bilateral weighted averages can be above or below the simple average tariffs, depending on the composition of imports. In most cases, the simple average overstates the average constructed using total trade weights (compare the first row in Table 3.5 to the fifth row), but the case of chemicals, rubber, and plastics trade in New Zealand illustrates that this generalization does not always hold.

The bottom portion of Table 3.5 reports bilateral, trade-weighted average applied tariffs for these four cases. Differences in these rates reflect the interaction between variation in tariff line rates and bilateral trade flows. In each case, some tariff lines are free of tariffs while others are quite high (524% is the maximum applied rate for chemicals, rubber, and plastics imports in New Zealand). For example, from the first column in Table 3.5 it is clear that these compositional considerations discriminate most heavily against Canadian nongrain crop sales to Indonesia. In contrast, the nongrain crops shipped by Australia to Indonesia face almost no tariffs (on average).

Several steps were involved in calculating GTAP tariff rates.[10] The first step was to create a rest of the world (ROW) import value in order to generate a single trade-weighted tariff for exports from the 6 composite regions in the GTAP data base. The ROW import value is equal to the total import value less the import values from the other 17 countries. This means that there is no bilateral variation in the individual-country GTAP tariffs vis-à-vis the 6 composite regions. Each country file was then aggregated to the GTAP level to create the bilateral trade-weighted average tariffs for each country file.

The first 18 columns of Table 3.6 report the weighted average bilateral tariffs levied by the each of the GTAP regions for all merchandise trade. (The last 6 columns correspond to composite region tariffs that derive from a different source, discussed below.) Just as we observed at the individual commodity level in Table 3.5, Table 3.6 shows that there remains considerable bilateral variation in the applied tariff rates, aggregated over all merchandise trade. Thus the average tariff on *all* merchandise imports into Canada from New Zealand is 2.9%, whereas imports from Hong Kong are subjected to an average tariff of 15.2%. In other words, Hong Kong exports to Canada involve products with relatively high tariff rates. In general, the highest average tariffs in this table are levied by the Philippines, Thailand, China, Argentina, and Brazil.

The last 6 *rows* of these first 18 *columns* in Table 3.6 correspond to imports into the 18 individual GTAP countries from the 6 composite regions. As noted above, these share a common tariff rate at the 37-sector, GTAP level of aggregation, because they are trade-weighted averages using a common, ROW import level. However, once these tariffs are aggregated up from the 37-sector GTAP level, they, too, exhibit significant bilateral variation. For instance, Middle East and North African exports to New Zealand (mostly oil) face an average bilateral tariff of 1.8%, whereas the average tariff on imports from South Asia (much of this, textiles and other light manufactures) is over 20%.

Finally, note that it is possible to use the aggregation methodology outlined above for aggregation of detailed tariff *offers*, such as those submitted under

Table 3.6. *Average Bilateral Applied Tariff Rates for All Merchandise Trade*

| | AUS | NZL | CAN | US | JPN | KOR | EU | IDN |
|---|---|---|---|---|---|---|---|---|
| | (Percentage of cif values) | | | | | | | |
| AUS | 0.0 | 15.0 | 5.3 | 4.3 | 1.7 | 10.5 | 2.5 | 5.3 |
| NZL | 10.7 | 0.0 | 2.9 | 2.3 | 5.1 | 11.8 | 3.8 | 11.3 |
| CAN | 14.3 | 18.4 | 0.0 | 3.2 | 3.1 | 9.9 | 4.8 | 5.5 |
| US | 15.9 | 23.1 | 7.1 | 0.0 | 3.1 | 16.5 | 4.2 | 12.1 |
| JPN | 18.9 | 32.2 | 7.6 | 5.2 | 0.0 | 18.3 | 9.1 | 14.3 |
| KOR | 17.8 | 23.0 | 9.8 | 6.1 | 6.9 | 0.0 | 7.1 | 18.0 |
| EU | 15.4 | 21.8 | 8.9 | 4.5 | 7.1 | 18.0 | 0.0 | 16.2 |
| IDN | 8.9 | 17.3 | 9.2 | 7.5 | 3.2 | 9.3 | 7.9 | 0.0 |
| MYS | 13.8 | 15.6 | 7.6 | 4.4 | 2.6 | 12.2 | 7.1 | 12.3 |
| PHL | 14.8 | 25.7 | 11.9 | 8.7 | 5.1 | 14.1 | 10.0 | 10.8 |
| SGP | 16.1 | 42.3 | 6.3 | 3.8 | 5.2 | 20.1 | 9.7 | 11.0 |
| THA | 8.5 | 13.6 | 9.2 | 6.6 | 6.1 | 15.6 | 8.2 | 9.7 |
| CHN | 19.8 | 35.0 | 12.7 | 6.2 | 7.0 | 14.4 | 5.9 | 11.1 |
| HKG | 17.1 | 34.5 | 15.2 | 11.1 | 6.8 | 20.5 | 10.2 | 18.9 |
| TWN | 15.2 | 28.0 | 8.5 | 5.9 | 8.2 | 19.2 | 7.2 | 18.9 |
| ARG | 9.2 | 6.7 | 8.5 | 5.1 | 4.7 | 21.4 | 10.0 | 3.9 |
| BRA | 15.3 | 19.8 | 8.3 | 5.6 | 3.4 | 13.5 | 6.7 | 10.8 |
| MEX | 10.3 | 12.2 | 6.8 | 4.0 | 1.6 | 12.2 | 2.6 | 11.0 |
| LAM | 10.3 | 5.5 | 3.1 | 4.5 | 2.8 | 7.1 | 6.6 | 4.1 |
| SSA | 4.1 | 3.2 | 1.3 | 1.1 | 3.2 | 6.2 | 3.9 | 5.8 |
| MNA | 5.7 | 1.8 | 1.6 | 2.0 | 0.6 | 5.7 | 2.8 | 1.4 |
| EIT | 13.5 | 20.6 | 6.8 | 5.1 | 3.3 | 14.6 | 5.5 | 8.4 |
| SAS | 10.1 | 20.8 | 16.2 | 10.3 | 3.9 | 12.6 | 8.6 | 6.8 |
| ROW | 19.4 | 24.2 | 5.0 | 4.3 | 3.8 | 13.4 | 5.7 | 10.3 |

the Uruguay Round negotiations. The policy shocks to be implemented in the model may then be derived by differencing the two bilateral tariff matrices. Analyzing policy shocks using two sets of tariffs, both of which have been aggregated up from the original tariff line items, more accurately captures the policy change. This is particularly true when a tariff cutting formula is nonlinear. For instance, early in the Kennedy Round, the European Community proposed a tariff cutting plan under which tariffs on manufactured products would be reduced by 50% of the difference between existing rates and 10%.[11] Current practice in most modeling exercises involves simply applying the formula to a model's aggregated tariffs. However, due to variation in the disaggregated tariffs (see the standard deviations in Table 3.5), it is much

Table 3.6. *Average, Bilateral Applied Tariff Rates for all Merchandise Trade*

| | | | | (Percentage of cif values) | | | | |
|---|---|---|---|---|---|---|---|---|
| | MYS | PHL | SGP | THA | CHN | HKG | TWN | ARG |
| AUS | 3.8 | 17.3 | 1.1 | 21.0 | 24.4 | 0.0 | 3.8 | 15.5 |
| NZL | 3.8 | 16.1 | 0.1 | 27.0 | 16.0 | 0.0 | 8.1 | 19.8 |
| CAN | 6.3 | 18.3 | 0.0 | 25.1 | 12.7 | 0.0 | 3.7 | 23.4 |
| US | 7.2 | 21.7 | 0.1 | 33.1 | 16.4 | 0.0 | 7.8 | 24.5 |
| JPN | 9.6 | 23.8 | 0.2 | 36.9 | 34.3 | 0.0 | 5.9 | 22.0 |
| KOR | 9.1 | 23.6 | 1.6 | 34.9 | 29.9 | 0.0 | 6.7 | 25.7 |
| EU | 9.1 | 26.4 | 0.1 | 35.3 | 38.8 | 0.0 | 8.1 | 17.5 |
| IDN | 9.1 | 23.6 | 0.6 | 34.2 | 22.2 | 0.0 | 3.5 | 26.4 |
| MYS | 0.0 | 22.6 | 1.2 | 38.7 | 29.4 | 0.0 | 4.7 | 16.6 |
| PHL | 10.6 | 0.0 | 0.3 | 41.6 | 26.5 | 0.0 | 4.8 | 26.9 |
| SGP | 8.1 | 22.1 | 0.0 | 27.5 | 28.1 | 0.0 | 7.5 | 30.3 |
| THA | 12.9 | 24.7 | 0.4 | 0.0 | 25.7 | 0.0 | 5.9 | 24.3 |
| CHN | 5.4 | 22.3 | 0.2 | 31.9 | 0.0 | 0.0 | 5.7 | 29.1 |
| HKG | 10.3 | 29.8 | 0.5 | 28.1 | 41.5 | 0.0 | 11.1 | 21.6 |
| TWN | 13.8 | 30.2 | 0.2 | 42.7 | 38.9 | 0.0 | 0.0 | 30.8 |
| ARG | 6.4 | 27.3 | 0.0 | 22.4 | 18.0 | 0.0 | 5.4 | 0.0 |
| BRA | 6.0 | 18.6 | 0.0 | 15.1 | 23.9 | 0.0 | 4.0 | 26.6 |
| MEX | 5.5 | 21.3 | 0.3 | 31.3 | 21.1 | 0.0 | 0.0 | 19.6 |
| LAM | 7.3 | 12.1 | 2.7 | 37.4 | 16.9 | 0.0 | 4.0 | 24.3 |
| SSA | 7.0 | 29.9 | 0.4 | 16.3 | 23.6 | 0.0 | 6.2 | 24.3 |
| MNA | 1.9 | 19.7 | 1.0 | 25.7 | 5.8 | 0.0 | 4.3 | 18.8 |
| EIT | 5.4 | 15.5 | 1.3 | 21.1 | 14.6 | 0.0 | 6.8 | 20.3 |
| SAS | 9.5 | 18.2 | 1.0 | 19.1 | 16.7 | 0.0 | 4.9 | 29.4 |
| ROW | 9.8 | 19.6 | 0.3 | 31.3 | 19.2 | 0.0 | 6.1 | 21.8 |

preferable to apply the formula to the original country tariff submission data and then reaggregate to find the new tariff rates at the 37-sector level of aggregation. This approach was used in a GTAP analysis of the Uruguay Round offers conducted in conjunction with the US International Trade Commission and the World Bank.

## Composite region tariffs

Tariff data for the six composite regions were supplied by the International Economics Division of the World Bank. Due to the large number of countries involved, and the limited data availability for many of these countries, *representative* countries were used for each of the composite regions. The particular

Table 3.6. *Average, Bilateral Applied Tariff Rates for all Merchandise Trade*

| | | | | (Percentage of cif values) | | | | |
|------|------|------|------|------|------|------|------|------|
| | BRA | MEX | LAM | SSA | MNA | EIT | SAS | ROW |
| AUS | 8.1 | 9.3 | 11.0 | 7.4 | 7.4 | 8.5 | 9.2 | 9.3 |
| NZL | 30.7 | 12.6 | 13.4 | 10.9 | 11.9 | 9.8 | 5.8 | 9.3 |
| CAN | 17.7 | 10.7 | 9.7 | 10.4 | 10.0 | 10.7 | 9.9 | 9.5 |
| US | 21.7 | 10.3 | 11.4 | 10.8 | 10.8 | 11.5 | 9.9 | 10.8 |
| JPN | 50.9 | 14.1 | 13.1 | 12.9 | 12.6 | 11.9 | 12.1 | 12.7 |
| KOR | 46.3 | 12.0 | 13.5 | 13.8 | 12.4 | 13.2 | 11.6 | 12.3 |
| EU | 45.8 | 13.1 | 10.7 | 10.8 | 10.6 | 10.7 | 9.6 | 10.6 |
| IDN | 32.6 | 12.4 | 11.2 | 10.2 | 11.5 | 7.4 | 9.4 | 10.0 |
| MYS | 38.6 | 12.9 | 10.8 | 9.6 | 10.1 | 11.8 | 9.2 | 10.8 |
| PHL | 32.4 | 16.0 | 11.3 | 9.1 | 11.7 | 11.4 | 11.9 | 11.6 |
| SGP | 34.2 | 13.7 | 5.2 | 7.2 | 9.6 | 9.1 | 7.0 | 9.0 |
| THA | 25.4 | 14.0 | 11.6 | 11.6 | 11.4 | 11.5 | 11.5 | 11.9 |
| CHN | 18.4 | 13.2 | 11.6 | 11.7 | 11.4 | 10.3 | 11.3 | 10.9 |
| HKG | 45.4 | 16.8 | 16.2 | 16.0 | 15.7 | 15.4 | 15.7 | 14.8 |
| TWN | 38.3 | 6.0 | 14.4 | 13.6 | 13.9 | 14.7 | 12.8 | 14.4 |
| ARG | 39.3 | 8.3 | 11.1 | 12.5 | 12.5 | 11.9 | 11.1 | 11.6 |
| BRA | 0.0 | 13.4 | 10.9 | 11.3 | 11.4 | 11.1 | 11.0 | 10.9 |
| MEX | 23.6 | 0.0 | 9.1 | 10.4 | 4.7 | 11.4 | 10.0 | 8.3 |
| LAM | 19.9 | 10.0 | 12.3 | 11.8 | 12.4 | 11.2 | 10.7 | 11.5 |
| SSA | 2.9 | 12.4 | 10.9 | 8.2 | 7.2 | 8.0 | 8.1 | 9.2 |
| MNA | 4.9 | 9.5 | 5.9 | 5.8 | 6.4 | 3.9 | 3.5 | 3.6 |
| EIT | 24.4 | 9.5 | 11.6 | 8.8 | 9.0 | 6.4 | 6.7 | 7.1 |
| SAS | 45.2 | 11.2 | 12.7 | 11.3 | 11.5 | 12.0 | 10.9 | 13.0 |
| ROW | 33.4 | 11.8 | 10.2 | 10.8 | 10.5 | 10.4 | 10.0 | 10.4 |

countries used are given in Table 3A.1, in the appendix at the end of this chapter. In several cases, tariff data were available, but bilateral import data were not. In the cases of Algeria and Saudi Arabia, bilateral data from similar countries within the region were used. In the case of sub-Saharan Africa (which excludes South Africa), no trade data were available and so a composite of total import data from other developing countries was used to weight the tariffs prior to aggregation.

The composite region tariffs are listed in the last six columns of Table 3.6. These rates fall in the midrange of the full table. They are higher than tariffs in the Canada, US, Japan, and the EU, but not as high as in many of the other developing countries. It should be noted that, since these two sets of tariff data were generated using different procedures, they are not directly comparable. Nevertheless, we feel that including this first approximation to the composite region tariffs is better than simply setting them equal to zero.

### Multifibre arrangement

The Multifibre Arrangement (MFA) is a system of bilateral import quotas restricting textile, leather, and wearing apparel exports from low-cost suppliers into the industrialized markets. Along with agriculture, this is the area of global merchandise trade with some of the largest distortions. The recent Uruguay Round agreement aims to eliminate the MFA by the year 2005. However, there are also a series of safeguard provisions that could result in less than full liberalization. Because the MFA import quotas are bilateral in nature, the degree to which the quotas bind, and the resulting export tax equivalents, vary by country. Furthermore, the quotas do not apply to all textile and wearing apparel exports, although there is the potential for extended coverage, if global quotas are triggered by excess supplies. Finally, as economic conditions change, and countries move from low-skill to higher-skill exports, the value of the country-specific tax equivalents will change. All these factors make it difficult to provide a consistent, quantitative evaluation of the MFA.

Table 3.7 reports the bilateral export tax equivalents for textiles and wearing apparel used in version 2 of the GTAP data base. They are based on two Ph.D. dissertations at the Australian National University (Saad 1993; Yang 1992). These disaggregate analyses were based on market conditions in the mid-1980s, and employed the Hamilton arbitrage method to estimate the tax equivalent value of the MFA quotas. Gotch (1993, table 14) reports East Asian MFA export tax equivalents used in the SALTER model at the Australian Industry Commission, which are derived from these two studies, assuming 100% coverage ratios. We begin with these rates, and modify them to reflect market conditions in the 1990s. In particular, the export tax equivalents from the established exporters (Korea, Hong Kong, and Taiwan) are cut by one-third. However, the tax equivalents from the other exporters are unchanged. (While we believe the MFA has become more restrictive for some of these other markets, we also believe the 100% coverage assumption is too strong.) We then extend the quotas to regions outside East Asia by relating the export tax in each region to that of the most restrictive MFA exporter, namely, China.[12] For example, in Table 3.7 it is assumed that the export tax equivalents for South Asia are the same as for China, those for most of Latin America are half of China's, and so on. These adjustments are very crude, but we believe that they improve the overall value of the protection data base for analyzing reform of the MFA.

Table 3.7. *Ad Valorem Export Tax Equivalents Associated with the Multifibre Arrangement: Top Entry Refers to Textiles, Bottom Entry to Wearing Apparel (percentage of fob values)*

| Source | Destination | | | Source | Destination | | |
| | Canada | US | EU | | Canada | US | EU |
|---|---|---|---|---|---|---|---|
| AUS[a] | 0.00 | 0.00 | 0.00 | CHN[a] | 23.21 | 18.41 | 27.35 |
| | 0.00 | 0.00 | 0.00 | | 42.00 | 40.32 | 36.11 |
| NZL[a] | 0.00 | 0.00 | 0.00 | HKG[a] | 7.63 | 7.67 | 8.10 |
| | 0.00 | 0.00 | 0.00 | | 15.49 | 18.19 | 15.55 |
| CAN[a] | 0.00 | 0.00 | 0.00 | TWN[a] | 9.43 | 8.16 | 11.64 |
| | 0.00 | 0.00 | 0.00 | | 19.15 | 19.35 | 22.35 |
| US[a] | 0.00 | 0.00 | 0.00 | ARG[b] | 0.00 | 0.00 | 0.00 |
| | 0.00 | 0.00 | 0.00 | | 0.00 | 0.00 | 0.00 |
| JPN[a] | 0.00 | 0.0 | 0.00 | BRA[b] | 11.61 | 9.21 | 13.68 |
| | 0.00 | 0.00 | 0.00 | | 21.00 | 20.16 | 18.06 |
| KOR[a] | 9.63 | 9.85 | 10.09 | MEX[b] | 11.61 | 9.21 | 13.68 |
| | 19.54 | 23.33 | 19.37 | | 21.00 | 20.16 | 18.06 |
| EU[a] | 0.00 | 0.00 | 0.00 | LAM[b] | 11.61 | 9.21 | 13.68 |
| | 0.00 | 0.00 | 0.00 | | 21.00 | 20.16 | 18.06 |
| IDN[a] | 17.50 | 11.95 | 17.46 | SSA[b] | 0.00 | 0.00 | 0.00 |
| | 41.13 | 46.74 | 48.37 | | 0.00 | 0.00 | 0.00 |
| MYS[a] | 15.17 | 9.50 | 11.70 | MNA[b] | 5.80 | 4.60 | 6.84 |
| | 35.66 | 37.14 | 32.40 | | 10.50 | 10.08 | 9.03 |
| PHL[a] | 11.52 | 8.57 | 10.03 | EIT[b] | 7.74 | 6.14 | 9.12 |
| | 27.08 | 33.52 | 27.79 | | 14.00 | 13.44 | 12.04 |
| SGP[a] | 11.89 | 7.93 | 10.10 | SAS[b] | 23.21 | 18.41 | 27.35 |
| | 27.94 | 31.01 | 27.98 | | 42.00 | 40.32 | 36.11 |
| THA[a] | 13.71 | 9.07 | 12.85 | ROW[b] | 4.64 | 3.68 | 5.47 |
| | 32.23 | 35.46 | 35.58 | | 8.40 | 8.06 | 7.22 |

[a] Gotch (1993), based on Yang (1992) and Saad (1993).
[b] Inferred from Gotch (1993), based on personal communications with Yang.

### Antidumping duties

The support and protection data include estimated antidumping (AD) duties in three GTAP importing regions: Canada, the EU, and the US. These three regions make up a large share of global AD cases. However, some of the other active users of AD duties, such as Australia, are excluded due to lack of information. While AD actions are on the upswing worldwide, most of the newer users of AD still have a relatively small number of AD duties in force.

Each AD duty or price undertaking[13] was allocated to one GTAP sector. The ratio of the number of tariff lines fully or partially covered by the order to the number of tariff lines in the GTAP sector to which the order was allocated was then calculated; we term this the coverage ratio. The duties were then aggregated to GTAP sectors using the methodology suggested by Magee (1972), which employs the coverage ratio to weight the orders. The

Magee methodology is a simple way of reducing the downward bias that otherwise exists in average tariff calculations.[14] The final step was to aggregate across exporters for those orders affecting exporting countries in the composite GTAP regions, such as the EU.[15] This was calculated as an unweighted average of the duties found using the Magee methodology above.

The Canadian AD duties included in the 1994 GTAP data base are based on 88 AD orders in force as of June 30, 1993.[16] (See Table 3.8.) Each of these orders refers to a particular commodity being exported from a particular country, and AD duties imposed by Canada generally apply to all firms exporting from that country. The estimated average margin of dumping determined by the Canadian authorities for these orders was 33.3%, with some as high as 87%. These orders are found in 13 GTAP sectors and on 15 GTAP regions, and they are weighted by their coverage ratios before aggregation to the GTAP concordance. At the GTAP sector level, the resulting duties are under 10% in most cases. Exceptions include nongrain crops from the US, with a duty of almost 30%, and pulp and paper, for which the AD duties on imports from the 12 GTAP regions covered by orders are between 10 and 20% for most exporters.

United States AD duties are applied on a firm-specific basis. Products of firms from the same exporting country accused of dumping the same product often are assessed different AD duties, and often an "all other firms" rate is introduced that is applied against exports of other firms. This creates special problems in describing the magnitude of AD duties in effect, as firm-specific trade data that could be used to aggregate these duties are not normally available. Therefore, for any one order we calculated the duty as the midpoint of the highest and lowest AD duties assigned the various firms.[17] The AD duties of the US are based on 266 AD orders in effect as of December 31, 1992 (Table 3.8). The average of the estimated duties prior to aggregation is 45%. The US duties cover portions of 15 GTAP sectors and 15 GTAP regions. As in Canada, most of the aggregated duty rates are under 10%. Notable exceptions are chemical, rubber, and plastic imports from Japan (24%), machinery and equipment imports from Japan (31%), and primary ferrous metals imports from Brazil and Taiwan (19% and 12%, respectively).

The AD measures included in the database for the EU include both AD duties and price undertakings resulting from AD cases, based on orders in effect as of December 31, 1992. These orders include 42 undertakings, 85 duties, and 35 orders with both undertakings and duties. The average margin for the 162 AD actions that enter the database is 30%. The orders include AD duties in 9 GTAP sectors and 13 GTAP regions and price undertakings in 10 GTAP sectors and 13 GTAP regions. Price undertakings are incorporated into the database as export tax equivalents so that the economic rents resulting from the undertakings are properly allocated to the exporters. The most

**Table 3.8. Summary of Antidumping Duties**

| Importer | Number of Orders Covered | Date | Estimated Average Margin | Number of GTAP Sectors | Number of GTAP Exporters |
|---|---|---|---|---|---|
| Canada | 88 | June 30, 1993 | 33% | 13 | 15 |
| EU | 162 | December 31, 1992 | 30% | 10 | 13 |
| US | 266 | December 31, 1992 | 45% | 15 | 15 |

frequent occurrences of these actions are in the case of chemicals, rubber, and plastics, followed by machinery and equipment, and textiles. The highest individual values are for machinery and equipment imports from Japan (14% AD duty and 10% price undertaking).

### Agricultural support data

Agricultural policies, although quite complex, have been the topic of many measurement efforts. The Producer and Consumer Subsidy Equivalent (PSEs and CSEs), measures developed by the Organization for Economic Coopera- tion and Development (OECD) and separately by the Economic Research Service (ERS) of the US Department of Agriculture, are solid attempts to quantify nontariff (and tariff) policies for many agricultural products. Com- bined, they give us agricultural support and protection data on most of the individual countries within our regional groups, plus representative members of the six composite regions. (In the case of Mexico, protection data were obtained from Burfisher et al.) Beyond reporting the estimate of the impact of government policies on producer and consumer prices, these two sources give information by type of policy, which can be used to separate the producer and consumer price impacts into border measures and domestic measures.

Measured support for agricultural commodities displays more volatility than that in other sectors. Supply uncertainties (e.g., weather), exchange rate volatility, and price-inelastic demand contribute to world price variability. Further, many agricultural policies (e.g., variable levies) are designed to insu- late domestic producers from this world price variability. Measured support for a commodity then varies with its world price from year to year, even without changes in policies or policy parameters. Because of this situation, we chose to calculate an average of several years' support. This average is designed to be representative of the late 1980s.

Driven by the need to enhance the transparency of these policies in support of international negotiations, the PSE data estimate the overall impact of policies on producers of farm commodities. The information contained in these data allows one to decompose the PSEs into import tariff equivalents, export subsidies, and production subsidies. For purposes of the GTAP data base we use the PSE data base for generating import tariff equivalents and output subsidies (Tables 3.10 and 3.11). Export subsidies are obtained directly from individual-country submissions to the GATT (see Table 3.9). We do not incorporate consumption subsidies.

**Export subsidies.** As part of their Uruguay Round commitments on agricul- tural export subsidies, member countries were required to submit schedules to the GATT in early 1994 detailing their agricultural export subsidies, on a

Table 3.9. *Value of Agricultural Export Subsidies (1992 $US Million)*

| Country | Commodity (GTAP code) | | | | | | | |
|---|---|---|---|---|---|---|---|---|
| | Paddy Rice (1) | Wheat (2) | Other Grains (3) | Nongrain Crops (4) | Meat Products (13) | Milk Products (14) | Other Food (16) | Beverage & Tobacco (17) |
| AUS | | | | 0.4 | | 136.1* | | |
| CAN | | 304.6 | 114.0 | 64.9 | | 123.6 | 7.7 | |
| US | 18.3* | 845.8* | 84.0 | 0.3* | 69.0 | 212.5 | | |
| EU | 84.8 | 2644.2* | 1333.1 | 975.0 | 3136.5 | 4295.9 | 138.1 | |
| IDN | 28.3 | | | | | | | |
| BRA | | | 0.1 | 68.3 | 12.4 | 0.2 | 30.8 | 0.3 |

* Refers to 1991–1992 outlays. All other entries refer to annual averages for the 1986–1990 base period.
Source: GATT country submissions.

Table 3.10. *Combined Tariff and Tariff Equivalent Values for Farm and Food Products (percentage of cif value)*

| | AUS* | NZL* | CAN* | US* | JPN* | KOR* | EU* | IDN* | MYS | PHL | SGP | THA* |
|---|---|---|---|---|---|---|---|---|---|---|---|---|
| Paddy rice | 4 | 0 | 0 | 1 | 353 | 317 | 129 | 0 | 0 | 50 | 0 | 0 |
| Wheat | 0 | 0 | 29 | 10 | 491 | 5 | 51 | 0 | 1 | 10 | 0 | 0 |
| Grains (other than rice and wheat) | 2 | 1 | 15 | 4 | 463 | 403 | 68 | 8 | 0 | 20 | 0 | 19 |
| Nongrain crops | 9 | 5 | 24 | 11 | 96 | 382 | 59 | 67 | 2 | 38 | 0 | 60 |
| Wool | 2 | 0 | 2 | 5 | 0 | 10 | 1 | 5 | 2 | 20 | 0 | 30 |
| Other livestock | 2 | 3 | 22 | 18 | 58 | 49 | 56 | 8 | 2 | 21 | 0 | 11 |
| Processed rice | 4 | 0 | 1 | 5 | 351 | 317 | 129 | 0 | 0 | 0 | 0 | 0 |
| Meat products | 9 | 15 | 22 | 18 | 58 | 50 | 56 | 30 | 1 | 34 | 0 | 54 |
| Milk products | 35 | 11 | 135 | 100 | 344 | 123 | 133 | 28 | 1 | 16 | 0 | 23 |
| Other food products | 4 | 15 | 7 | 7 | 9 | 17 | 13 | 20 | 14 | 22 | 0 | 50 |
| Beverages & tobacco | 9 | 0 | 14 | 6 | 12 | 74 | 18 | 24 | 1 | 45 | 0 | 60 |

* Includes tariff equivalent estimates of nontariff barriers.

Table 3.10. *Combined Tariff and Tariff Equivalent Values for Farm and Food Products (Percentage of cif value)*

| | CHN* | HKG | TWN* | ARG | BRA | MEX* | LAM | SSA | MNA | EIT | SAS | ROW |
|---|---|---|---|---|---|---|---|---|---|---|---|---|
| Paddy rice | 0 | 0 | 81 | 12 | 20 | 10 | 12 | 3 | 2 | 0 | 2 | 3 |
| Wheat | 0 | 0 | 308 | 21 | 0 | 10 | 9 | 6 | 6 | 8 | 8 | 5 |
| Grains (other than rice and wheat) | 10 | 0 | 326 | 15 | 22 | 20 | 13 | 11 | 11 | 11 | 4 | 11 |
| Nongrain crops | 24 | 0 | 73 | 17 | 21 | 2 | 11 | 10 | 10 | 10 | 10 | 9 |
| Wool | 15 | 0 | 0 | 21 | 25 | 3 | 8 | 5 | 6 | 9 | 5 | 7 |
| Other livestock | 35 | 0 | 5 | 18 | 11 | 3 | 9 | 9 | 9 | 10 | 9 | 10 |
| Processed rice | 0 | 0 | 81 | 0 | 20 | 10 | 13 | 12 | 12 | 8 | 11 | 12 |
| Meat products | 45 | 0 | 16 | 12 | 30 | 7 | 14 | 13 | 12 | 12 | 7 | 11 |
| Milk products | 36 | 0 | 72 | 22 | 36 | 8 | 14 | 14 | 14 | 14 | 12 | 14 |
| Other food products | 29 | 0 | 12 | 17 | 49 | 5 | 14 | 13 | 13 | 13 | 12 | 13 |
| Beverages & tobacco | 97 | 0 | 36 | 21 | 31 | 15 | 7 | 6 | 6 | 8 | 3 | 7 |

**Table 3.11.** *Output Subsidies for Farm and Food Sectors (percentage of market values)*

| | AUS | NZL | CAN | US | JPN | KOR | EU | IDN | MYS | PHL | SGP | THA |
|---|---|---|---|---|---|---|---|---|---|---|---|---|
| Paddy rice | 3.7 | 0.0 | 0.0 | 57.3 | 10.1 | 50.5 | 7.2 | 4.7 | 0.0 | -2.1 | 0.0 | 2.3 |
| Wheat | 4.1 | 2.7 | 16.8 | 32.4 | 14.8 | -0.3 | 6.3 | 0.0 | 0.0 | -2.2 | 0.0 | 0.0 |
| Grains (other than rice & wheat) | 3.6 | 1.9 | 7.6 | 30.6 | 16.4 | 8.1 | 2.5 | 10.6 | 0.0 | -2.1 | 0.0 | -0.3 |
| Nongrain crops | 2.2 | -0.8 | 10.3 | 5.2 | 48.9 | 36.7 | 71.0 | 1.9 | 0.0 | -2.4 | -1.8 | 0.4 |
| Wool | 3.3 | 2.0 | 3.5 | 66.0 | 0.0 | -0.1 | 0.4 | 0.0 | 0.0 | -0.8 | 0.0 | 0.0 |
| Other livestock | 1.3 | 1.5 | 4.7 | 3.5 | 0.5 | 14.8 | 9.2 | -0.5 | 0.0 | -1.8 | -2.1 | -0.1 |
| Processed rice | -0.7 | 0.0 | -0.4 | -0.4 | 0.0 | -0.2 | 0.0 | -1.0 | 0.0 | -0.7 | 0.0 | -1.4 |
| Meat products | -0.7 | -0.7 | 21.9 | -0.3 | -1.3 | -1.6 | 0.2 | -0.8 | 0.0 | -2.2 | -1.4 | -0.8 |
| Milk products | -5.7 | 0.8 | 4.5 | 4.3 | 7.2 | 19.9 | -0.4 | -1.1 | 0.0 | -4.4 | -0.6 | -3.1 |
| Other food products | -0.9 | -0.3 | -0.4 | -0.5 | -0.8 | -5.8 | 0.0 | -1.2 | 0.0 | -2.0 | -0.7 | -1.5 |
| Beverages & tobacco | -1.0 | -0.5 | -1.5 | -18.8 | -46.4 | -52.3 | -2.5 | -14.7 | 0.0 | -13.9 | -0.4 | -41.2 |

**Table 3.11.** *Output Subsidies for Farm and Food Sectors (percentage of market values)*

| | CHN | HKG | TWN | ARG | BRA | MEX | LAM | SSA | MNA | EIT | SAS | ROW |
|---|---|---|---|---|---|---|---|---|---|---|---|---|
| Paddy rice | -0.9 | 0.0 | -1.1 | 0.0 | 45.6 | 1.3 | 152.1 | -71.1 | -11.7 | 127.1 | 6.2 | -1.4 |
| Wheat | -1.0 | 0.0 | -0.7 | 0.0 | 24.9 | 2.7 | 47.8 | -7.6 | 145.6 | -14.0 | -4.4 | 12.7 |
| Grains (other than rice & wheat) | -2.5 | 0.0 | 0.0 | 0.0 | 28.1 | 4.2 | 161.3 | -1.9 | 42.7 | 21.3 | -15.5 | 26.1 |
| Nongrain crops | -4.1 | 0.0 | -0.7 | 0.0 | 0.5 | 1.0 | -27.3 | 9.7 | 36.0 | 49.8 | 2.9 | 142.4 |
| Wool | -0.8 | 0.0 | 0.0 | 0.0 | 0.5 | 0.0 | 0.0 | -0.6 | -1.5 | -0.8 | -0.8 | -0.9 |
| Other livestock | -0.9 | 0.0 | -0.1 | 0.0 | 5.9 | -0.1 | 1.0 | -0.8 | -0.7 | 28.6 | 1.0 | -0.4 |
| Processed rice | -4.6 | 0.0 | -0.2 | 0.0 | -0.2 | 3.9 | -1.0 | -3.2 | -0.9 | -0.9 | -4.6 | -0.8 |
| Meat products | -2.5 | 0.0 | -2.1 | 0.0 | 0.0 | -0.1 | -0.8 | -1.9 | -1.1 | -0.2 | -2.5 | -0.6 |
| Milk products | -7.4 | 0.0 | -1.2 | 0.0 | -0.1 | -0.1 | -2.2 | -3.9 | -2.8 | 13.5 | 12.7 | -0.4 |
| Other food products | -3.6 | 0.0 | -1.1 | 0.0 | 0.4 | 3.8 | -1.5 | -2.5 | -2.4 | -0.5 | -3.6 | -0.7 |
| Beverages & tobacco | -23.6 | 0.0 | -54.8 | 0.0 | -0.4 | -21.2 | -31.5 | -20.9 | -36.0 | -19.2 | -23.6 | -33.4 |

detailed commodity basis, for the period 1986–1990. Country submissions were then examined by other Uruguay Round participants for methodology and accuracy prior to completion of the Uruguay Round at Marrakesh in mid-April 1994. This and other such information became public at that time.

The Uruguay Round schedules for the base export subsidy outlays form the basis for the agricultural export subsidies in the GTAP data base. Export subsidies are recorded on the GATT schedules for 6 countries (counting the EU as one), and for as many as 20 agricultural commodities in any one country. These subsidies are reported in Table 3.9, based on GTAP commodity categories. Canada, the US, and the EU are the major users of this form of subsidy, with the EU expending over $10 billion (in 1992 dollars) on exports subsidies for grain, dairy, and meat products.

**Import Nontariff Barriers (NTBs).** Table 3.10 reports import barriers in the data base for the 11 farm and food sectors and the 24 GTAP regions. Asterisks denote wedges that include information from the PSE data base in the form of world/domestic price gaps. Where this information is available, one would assume that the size of this gap exceeds any tariff that may be present. However, we adopt the simple rule of taking the *larger* of the two distortions. Table 3.10 represents the tariff/NTB data base after it is combined in this manner. The most striking entries are for grain imports into Japan and Korea, where quotas have sustained an extremely high level of domestic prices relative to world prices. Dairy products also exhibit a great deal of protection across many of the economies.

**Output subsidies.** As noted above, much of the support for agriculture comes in the form of subsidies on input usage or on output. Both these types of support are combined into a single output subsidy. Of course, in some regions (e.g., sub-Saharan Africa) producers receive less than the market value of their produce, and this is reflected in an output tax. In the case of the composite regions, output subsidies were derived from PSE data for a subset of the countries in each region. Appendix Table 3A.2 lists the countries for which this information was available in each of the six composite regions. Finally, where PSE data are not available, we simply use the indirect tax rate reported in the input–output table.

The GTAP output subsidies for farm and food products are reported in Table 3.11. Entries represent the subsidy (or tax in the case of negative numbers) as a percentage of market values. Note that in some cases (Malaysia and Hong Kong) there is no tax at all. This is because these countries are not represented in the PSE data base and their IO tables do not report indirect taxes for these sectors. The Philippines is not represented in the PSE data base but it does include indirect taxes in its IO table, so all of the sectors experience a small negative subsidy (i.e., a tax). The largest producer subsidies occur for grains in North and South America, and in the economies in transition [Eastern Europe and the Former Soviet Union (FSU)]. In the latter case, these subsidies may well have changed dramatically in recent years. This is a problem that each GTAP user must come to grips with based on its individual needs. For example, it may be appropriate to adjust protection levels prior to proceeding with policy analysis.

**Other commodity taxes.** In some cases the IO tables also include a variety of commodity taxes. We leave these in place, but do not report on them here, as they are generally sparse and quite small as a percent of market value. However, we encourage the GTAP user to examine these tax rates when they receive an aggregation of the data base, as they may play some role in determining second-best outcomes.

**Effective rates of protection.** One useful means of summarizing the profile of combined protection measurers, by region, is the effective rate of protection (ERP), which is obtained by comparing value-added at domestic market and world prices, using the same factor proportions. Stevens (1995) has developed a formula for calculating ERPs in the GTAP data base, based on a composite measure of import and export protection, as follows:

$$TC(i,r) = \gamma(i,r) * TM(i,r) + [1 - \gamma(i,r)] * TX(i,r), \qquad (3.13)$$

where $\gamma(i,r) = VDM(i,r)/[VDM(i,r) + VXM(i,r)]$ is the ratio of domestic sales of merchandise commodity $i$, produced in region $r$, to total (domestic and export) sales, at market prices. $TM(i,r)$ and $TX(i,r)$ are the power of the *ad valorem* rates of import (both tariff and NTB) and export protection, respectively. Therefore, an import tariff ($TM(i,r) > 1$) is represented as supporting the price of domestic sales, but not exports, and vice versa for an export subsidy ($TX(i,r) > 1$).

Stevens applies these composite border support measures to output and intermediate inputs, by sector, to obtain value-added at world prices as follows:

$$VAW(j,r) = VOM(j,r)/TC(j,r) - \sum_{i \in TRAD} VFM(i,j,r)/TC(i,r). \qquad (3.14)$$

Value-added at market prices, $VAM(j,r)$, is computed from (3.14) by setting $TC(i,r) = 1 \ \forall i$. She then computes the sectoral ERP as:

$$ERP(j,r) = [VAM(j,r) - VAW(j,r)]/VAM(j,r). \qquad (3.15)$$

Note that this is not the same formula as that in the literature, where $VAW(j,r)$ appears in the denominator. The conventional formulation causes problems when $VAW(j,r)$ becomes negative, as is the case for some $(j,r)$ pairs in the data base.

Table 3.12. *Effective Rates of Protection for GTAP Data Base by Sector and Region*

|      | AUS   | NZL   | CAN   | USA   | JPN   | KOR   | EU    | IND   |
|------|-------|-------|-------|-------|-------|-------|-------|-------|
| PDR  | 0.03  | -0.02 | -0.01 | -0.34 | 1.02  | 0.95  | 1.00  | 0.00  |
| WHT  | -0.02 | -0.07 | 0.14  | 0.54  | 1.11  | 0.03  | 0.66  | -0.04 |
| GRO  | -0.01 | -0.04 | 0.22  | 0.04  | 1.11  | 1.14  | 0.73  | 0.08  |
| NGC  | 0.07  | -0.01 | 0.31  | 0.13  | 0.84  | 1.06  | 1.24  | 0.40  |
| WOL  | -0.02 | -0.05 | -0.20 | 0.04  | -0.08 | -0.25 | -0.12 | 0.04  |
| OLP  | 0.01  | 0.02  | 0.27  | 0.84  | 1.03  | 1.08  | 0.60  | 0.07  |
| FOR  | -0.01 | -0.01 | 0.00  | -0.02 | -0.01 | 0.04  | -0.13 | 0.14  |
| FSH  | -0.04 | -0.02 | -0.01 | -0.01 | 0.04  | 0.19  | 0.01  | 0.19  |
| COL  | -0.05 | -0.06 | -0.01 | -0.03 | -0.01 | 0.05  | 0.05  | 0.00  |
| OIL  | -0.02 | -0.01 | 0.00  | 0.00  | 0.00  | 0.05  | -0.06 | 0.00  |
| GAS  | 0.01  | -0.01 | 0.03  | -0.01 | 0.05  | 0.04  | -0.05 | 0.01  |
| OMN  | -0.02 | 0.00  | -0.02 | -0.01 | 0.00  | 0.03  | -0.02 | 0.01  |
| PCR  | -0.01 | -0.09 | -0.03 | 0.04  | 2.58  | 1.60  | 1.33  | -0.03 |
| MET  | 0.17  | 0.14  | 1.57  | 0.28  | 0.81  | 0.75  | 0.65  | 0.73  |
| MIL  | 0.84  | -0.08 | 1.93  | 1.88  | 5.52  | 47.16 | 1.02  | -0.14 |
| OFP  | 0.02  | 0.24  | 0.05  | 0.11  | -0.40 | -1.20 | -0.09 | -0.59 |
| B_T  | 0.09  | -0.15 | 0.16  | 0.06  | 0.07  | 0.47  | 0.15  | 0.15  |
| TEX  | 0.25  | 0.32  | 0.20  | 0.16  | -0.01 | -0.67 | 0.11  | 0.20  |
| WAP  | 0.10  | 0.81  | 0.28  | 0.31  | 0.31  | 0.05  | 0.13  | -2.29 |
| LEA  | 0.24  | 0.32  | 0.20  | 0.09  | 0.16  | -0.17 | -0.04 | -0.15 |
| LUM  | 0.25  | 0.40  | 0.09  | 0.04  | 0.09  | 0.41  | 0.02  | 0.12  |
| PPP  | 0.12  | 0.30  | 0.07  | 0.00  | 0.03  | 0.06  | 0.07  | 0.09  |
| P_C  | -0.07 | 0.22  | 0.09  | 0.01  | -0.04 | 0.17  | 0.07  | 0.09  |
| CRP  | 0.23  | 0.19  | 0.12  | 0.22  | 0.09  | 0.10  | 0.17  | -0.01 |
| NMM  | 0.30  | 0.38  | 0.16  | 0.15  | 0.06  | 0.36  | 0.09  | 0.33  |
| I_S  | 0.20  | 0.27  | 0.15  | 0.17  | 0.07  | 0.10  | 0.07  | 0.04  |
| NFM  | 0.13  | 0.10  | 0.05  | 0.05  | 0.01  | 0.29  | 0.01  | 0.07  |
| FMP  | 0.30  | 0.51  | 0.11  | 0.10  | 0.06  | 0.29  | 0.07  | 0.39  |
| TRN  | 0.22  | 0.49  | 0.03  | 0.00  | 0.01  | 0.05  | 0.08  | 0.22  |
| OME  | 0.22  | 0.29  | 0.05  | 0.17  | 0.03  | 0.16  | 0.10  | 0.03  |
| OMF  | 0.10  | 0.12  | 0.10  | 0.07  | 0.00  | -0.09 | 0.04  | 0.27  |

Table 3.12 reports ERPs from version 2 of the GTAP data base, for all 31 merchandise commodities in all 24 regions. Using equations (3.13)–(3.15), these entries summarize *all* border protection in the data base. The highest ERPs are for dairy products (sector 15). With few exceptions, most regions support this sector heavily. In Korea, value-added at *market prices* is very small, and value-added at *world prices* is a very large negative number. This

Table 3.12. *Effective Rates of Protection for GTAP Data Base by Sector and Region*

|       | MYS   | PHL   | SGP   | THA   | CHN   | HKG   | TWN   | ARG   |
|-------|-------|-------|-------|-------|-------|-------|-------|-------|
| PDR   | 0.00  | 0.38  | 0.00  | -0.02 | -0.04 | 0.00  | 0.62  | 0.06  |
| WHT   | 0.01  | 0.08  | 0.00  | -0.11 | -0.04 | 0.00  | 1.00  | 0.12  |
| GRO   | -0.13 | 0.18  | 0.00  | 0.10  | 0.08  | 0.00  | 1.42  | 0.08  |
| NGC   | -0.06 | 0.27  | 0.00  | 0.36  | 0.20  | 0.00  | 0.45  | 0.13  |
| WOL   | 0.01  | 0.18  | 0.00  | -0.05 | 0.15  | 0.00  | -0.06 | 0.13  |
| OLP   | 0.02  | 0.21  | 0.00  | 0.04  | 0.38  | 0.00  | -0.36 | 0.16  |
| FOR   | -0.04 | 0.09  | 0.00  | 0.15  | 0.09  | 0.00  | 0.00  | 0.09  |
| FSH   | 0.05  | 0.15  | 0.00  | 0.23  | 0.29  | 0.00  | 0.06  | 0.04  |
| COL   | -0.05 | 0.29  | 0.00  | 4.36  | 0.12  | 0.00  | -0.01 | 0.11  |
| OIL   | -0.08 | 0.03  | 0.00  | 0.24  | -0.02 | 0.00  | 0.02  | 0.21  |
| GAS   | -0.09 | 0.21  | 0.00  | -0.01 | 0.15  | 0.00  | 0.02  | -0.03 |
| OMN   | -0.01 | 0.03  | 0.00  | 0.04  | 0.12  | 0.00  | -0.02 | 0.18  |
| PCR   | 0.01  | -1.84 | 0.00  | -0.06 | -0.23 | 0.00  | 0.62  | -0.10 |
| MET   | -0.01 | 0.50  | 0.00  | 0.82  | 0.83  | 0.01  | 0.86  | -0.06 |
| MIL   | -0.06 | 0.14  | 0.00  | 0.23  | 0.46  | 0.00  | 1.14  | 0.25  |
| OFP   | 0.18  | 0.16  | 0.00  | 0.40  | 0.82  | 0.00  | -0.60 | 0.14  |
| B_T   | 0.00  | 0.53  | 0.00  | 0.47  | 0.82  | 0.00  | 0.30  | 0.19  |
| TEX   | 0.12  | 0.37  | 0.00  | 0.55  | 0.66  | 0.01  | -0.09 | 0.35  |
| WAP   | -1.17 | -0.78 | -0.69 | 0.39  | -0.13 | -0.84 | -0.08 | 0.34  |
| LEA   | -0.01 | 0.05  | 0.01  | 0.18  | -0.11 | 0.00  | -0.06 | 0.34  |
| LUM   | 0.17  | 0.46  | 0.01  | 0.56  | 0.24  | 0.00  | 0.03  | 0.35  |
| PPP   | 0.08  | 0.26  | 0.00  | 0.22  | 0.27  | 0.00  | 0.02  | 0.26  |
| P_C   | 0.40  | 0.42  | 0.03  | -0.16 | 0.21  | 0.00  | 0.13  | 0.21  |
| CRP   | 0.01  | 0.18  | 0.00  | 0.27  | 0.16  | 0.00  | 0.02  | 0.13  |
| NMM   | 0.37  | 0.36  | 0.00  | 0.64  | 0.50  | 0.00  | 0.07  | 0.34  |
| I_S   | -0.03 | 0.16  | 0.00  | 0.12  | 0.11  | 0.00  | 0.06  | 0.19  |
| NFM   | -0.01 | 0.12  | 0.00  | -0.23 | 0.07  | 0.00  | -0.01 | 0.16  |
| FMP   | 0.21  | 0.60  | 0.00  | 0.45  | 0.49  | 0.00  | 0.13  | 0.39  |
| TRN   | 0.14  | 0.19  | 0.00  | 0.68  | 0.20  | 0.00  | 0.27  | 0.40  |
| OME   | -0.05 | -0.07 | 0.00  | 0.01  | 0.26  | 0.00  | 0.02  | 0.17  |
| OMF   | 0.10  | -0.08 | 0.00  | 0.09  | 0.07  | 0.01  | -0.02 | 0.21  |

results in an ERP of 47.16! Meat products, equation (3.14), are also heavily protected across the board. However, other food products, equation (3.16), show negative ERPs for many of the East Asian economies (e.g., −1.2 in Korea) due to elevated prices for agricultural inputs (see entries in rows 1–6).

Textiles and wearing apparel also show some high rates of protection and taxation, owing to the MFA. Note that since these bilateral quotas are applied

Table 3.12. *Effective Rates of Protection for GTAP Data Base by Sector and Region*

|       | BRA   | MEX   | LAM   | SSA   | MNA   | EIT   | SAS   | ROW  |
|-------|-------|-------|-------|-------|-------|-------|-------|------|
| PDR   | 0.17  | 0.11  | 0.14  | 0.03  | 0.02  | -0.04 | 0.01  | 0.03 |
| WHT   | -0.10 | 0.10  | 0.09  | 0.05  | -0.12 | 0.09  | 0.08  | 0.04 |
| GRO   | 0.19  | 0.20  | 0.24  | 0.11  | 0.14  | 0.15  | 0.03  | 0.15 |
| NGC   | 0.16  | 0.02  | 0.07  | 0.07  | 0.10  | 0.11  | 0.09  | 0.16 |
| WOL   | 0.21  | 0.01  | 0.03  | -0.02 | 0.06  | 0.07  | 0.02  | 0.04 |
| OLP   | 0.06  | -0.01 | 0.09  | 0.12  | 0.10  | 0.12  | 0.10  | 0.12 |
| FOR   | 0.15  | 0.10  | 0.05  | 0.00  | 0.01  | 0.04  | 0.00  | 0.04 |
| FSH   | 0.27  | 0.21  | 0.07  | 0.06  | 0.06  | 0.07  | 0.03  | 0.04 |
| COL   | -0.46 | 0.06  | 0.14  | 0.00  | 0.15  | 0.02  | 0.12  | 0.05 |
| OIL   | -0.14 | 0.00  | 0.01  | -0.01 | 0.00  | 0.00  | 0.01  | 0.00 |
| GAS   | -0.07 | 0.04  | 0.11  | -0.02 | 0.01  | -0.01 | -0.02 | 0.00 |
| OMN   | -0.04 | 0.05  | 0.03  | 0.00  | 0.04  | 0.12  | 0.01  | 0.05 |
| PCR   | 0.59  | 0.10  | 0.20  | 1.07  | 0.88  | 0.29  | 0.36  | 0.91 |
| MET   | 0.62  | 0.24  | 0.24  | 0.29  | 0.22  | 0.21  | 0.02  | 0.18 |
| MIL   | 0.85  | 0.29  | 0.24  | 0.22  | 0.25  | 0.28  | 0.64  | 0.25 |
| OFP   | 0.83  | 0.03  | 0.14  | 0.16  | 0.22  | 0.21  | 0.41  | 0.20 |
| B_T   | 0.28  | 0.17  | 0.06  | 0.05  | 0.05  | 0.07  | 0.00  | 0.06 |
| TEX   | 0.58  | 0.18  | 0.18  | 0.19  | 0.17  | 0.17  | 0.14  | 0.15 |
| WAP   | 0.56  | 0.19  | -0.01 | 0.05  | 0.01  | 0.05  | -0.30 | 0.07 |
| LEA   | 0.55  | 0.20  | 0.10  | 0.11  | 0.14  | 0.12  | 0.08  | 0.13 |
| LUM   | 0.33  | 0.16  | 0.17  | 0.12  | 0.23  | 0.18  | 0.19  | 0.17 |
| PPP   | 0.00  | 0.03  | 0.12  | 0.14  | 0.16  | 0.15  | 0.12  | 0.11 |
| P_C   | 0.01  | 0.46  | 0.09  | 0.07  | 0.11  | 0.16  | 0.05  | 0.18 |
| CRP   | 0.35  | 0.09  | 0.09  | 0.13  | 0.10  | 0.12  | 0.14  | 0.10 |
| NMM   | 0.52  | 0.18  | 0.18  | 0.18  | 0.21  | 0.16  | 0.16  | 0.18 |
| I_S   | 0.41  | 0.06  | 0.11  | 0.12  | 0.15  | 0.11  | 0.12  | 0.12 |
| NFM   | 0.35  | 0.06  | 0.01  | 0.06  | 0.14  | 0.08  | 0.15  | 0.12 |
| FMP   | 0.52  | 0.12  | 0.18  | 0.19  | 0.18  | 0.17  | 0.18  | 0.16 |
| TRN   | 0.15  | 0.12  | 0.15  | 0.12  | 0.17  | 0.15  | 0.16  | 0.12 |
| OME   | 0.38  | -0.02 | 0.12  | 0.13  | 0.12  | 0.12  | 0.14  | 0.09 |
| OMF   | 0.70  | 0.10  | 0.17  | 0.15  | 0.15  | 0.17  | 0.17  | 0.12 |

in the *exporting region*, the ERP measure for the importing region (e.g., textiles in the US) does not reflect this intervention. Despite the presence of these export restraints, it is interesting that most textile ERPs are positive. However, because the tax equivalents tend to be higher for wearing apparel than for textiles, the apparel sector shows some significant negative entries for heavily restricted exporters, despite the importance of textiles as an input (e.g., -2.29 for Indonesia).

In sum, there are many different components of protection in the GTAP data base. Not all of them work in the same direction. Stevens's modified ERP measure provides a useful summary of some of their interactions. However, as she also documents in her thesis, the ERP is an imperfect predictor of the effects of trade policy reform, and therefore does not offer a substitute for well-defined simulation experiments.

## IV    Input–output tables

Input–output tables were obtained for the latest available reference year. (This section covers both work done originally for the SALTER model and new work for the GTAP.[18]) These reference years ranged from 1980 to 1987 (see Table 3.12). We follow Hambley (1993) in adopting the following target format for the IO data:

- An intermediate input matrix for domestic use of domestically produced commodities
- An intermediate input matrix for domestic usage of imports
- Industry payments to land, labor, and capital services
- Final demands for domestically produced commodities by private households and the government, and for gross fixed capital formation,
- Final demands for imported commodities by private households and the government, and for gross fixed capital formation
- Taxes

We begin this stage with a collection of IO tables for various countries, expressed in various currencies and representing different years. The tables come from diverse sources, and differ widely in structure, layout, and sectoral detail. A summary of sources and reference years is provided in Table 3.13. By the end of this stage we have a collection of tables with a consistent structure and sectoral classification, ready to be updated to a common base year.

Besides these formal requirements, we impose some conditions on the content of the tables. We eliminate negative flows, and impose a sectoral balance condition whereby each sector's sales and costs are equal (where profits are counted in with costs). We also make some minor adjustments to avoid technical problems in later processing.

### Data structure

**Import detail.** Following the lead of the SALTER effort, the GTAP data structure provides for full import use information. In other words, it tracks the value of import usage for each individual commodity in each individual use category. In order to appreciate the importance of import-sourcing by use,

**Table 3.13.** *Sources of Input-Output Data*

| Region | Reference Period | Source |
|---|---|---|
| Australia | 1986–87 | Kenderes and Strzelecki (1992) |
| New Zealand | 1986–87 | Department of Statistics (1991), New Zealand |
| Canada | 1986 | Statistics Canada (1987) |
| United States | 1985 | Ministry of International Trade and Industry (1989), Japan |
| Japan | 1985 | Ministry of International Trade and Industry (1989), Japan |
| Korea | 1985 | Bank of Korea (1988) |
| European Union | 1980 | Ryan (1992) |
| Indonesia | 1985 | Central Bureau of Statistics, Indonesia |
| Malaysia | 1983 | Department of Statistics (1988), Malaysia |
| Philippines | 1985 | National Economic and Development Authority (1988), Philippines |
| Singapore | 1983 | Department of Statistics (1987), Singapore |
| Thailand | 1985 | Institute for Developing Economies, Tokyo and Socio Economic Policy and Forecasting Unit, Chulahlongkorn University Social Research Institute, Thailand |
| China (PRC) | 1987 | Department of Balances of National Economy of the State Statistical Bureau and Office of the National Input–Output Survey (1987), China |
| Hong Kong | 1988 | Tormey (1993) |
| Taiwan | 1986 | Directorate General of Budget, Accounting and Statistics (1986), Taiwan |
| Argentina | 1984 | Secretaria de Planificacion (1986), Argentina |
| Brazil | 1980 | Sectretaria de Planejamento e Coordenacao da Presidencia da Republica Fundacao IBGE (1980), Brazil |
| Mexico | 1985 | Secretaria de Pramacion y Presupuesto (1985), Burfisher, Thierfelder, and Hanson (1992) |
| Rest of Latin America | 1992 | Representative composite |
| S-S. Africa | 1992 | Representative composite |
| M.E. and North Africa | 1992 | Representative composite |
| E. Europe and FSU | 1992 | Representative composite |
| South Asia | 1992 | Representative composite |
| Regions not Elsewhere Classified | 1992 | Representative composite |

it is instructive to consider a specific example, taken from version 2 of the data base. Table 3.14 reports the share of imports in composite demand, by commodity and use for the Korean economy.[19] For ease of exposition, the 37 sectors have been aggregated up to 12 sectors/commodities. The information in this table is based on the 1985 Korean IO table (see Table 3.13), updated to 1992 macroeconomic and trade data using the procedures described below.

Examination of Table 3.14 shows clearly that the intensity of imports of any given commodity varies widely by use. For example, the last column shows that 22% (value-based share) of all chemical, rubber, and plastic (CRP) products used in Korea is imported. However, only 3% of private household

Table 3.14. *Share of Imports in Composite Demand at Market Prices, by Use*

| | Intermediate Uses | | | | | | | | | | | | Final Demands | | | Total Uses |
|---|---|---|---|---|---|---|---|---|---|---|---|---|---|---|---|---|
| | crops | othagr | extract | food | textiles | apparel | crp | metals | trnseq | macheq | othmnfc | svces | Inv | Priv | Gov | |
| crops | 0.06 | 0.00 | 0.51 | 0.35 | 0.99 | 0.49 | 0.99 | 0.52 | 0.76 | 0.67 | 0.81 | 0.00 | 0.01 | 0.07 | 0.14 | 0.39 |
| other agr. | 0.10 | 0.79 | 0.54 | 0.08 | 1.00 | 0.99 | 0.36 | 0.72 | 0.86 | 0.09 | 0.57 | 0.13 | 0.90 | 0.31 | 0.77 | 0.25 |
| extraction | 0.00 | 0.00 | 0.51 | 0.21 | 0.03 | 0.03 | 0.48 | 0.40 | 0.20 | 0.27 | 0.21 | 0.10 | 0.01 | 0.06 | 0.08 | 0.28 |
| food | 0.00 | 0.00 | 0.10 | 0.26 | 0.04 | 0.83 | 0.58 | 0.00 | 0.10 | 0.03 | 0.38 | 0.03 | 0.26 | 0.02 | 0.08 | 0.06 |
| textiles | 0.03 | 0.01 | 0.18 | 0.04 | 0.17 | 0.27 | 0.14 | 0.05 | 0.12 | 0.11 | 0.06 | 0.02 | 0.14 | 0.04 | 0.22 | 0.17 |
| apparel | 0.05 | 0.01 | 0.18 | 0.01 | 0.01 | 0.80 | 0.51 | 0.01 | 0.40 | 0.01 | 0.25 | 0.01 | 0.32 | 0.06 | 0.62 | 0.07 |
| crp | 0.05 | 0.00 | 0.24 | 0.15 | 0.14 | 0.17 | 0.39 | 0.18 | 0.31 | 0.23 | 0.23 | 0.07 | 0.08 | 0.03 | 0.09 | 0.22 |
| metals | 0.19 | 0.04 | 0.10 | 0.08 | 0.11 | 0.25 | 0.09 | 0.21 | 0.23 | 0.24 | 0.14 | 0.07 | 0.23 | 0.19 | 0.07 | 0.19 |
| transport eq | 0.00 | 0.00 | 0.09 | 0.00 | 0.00 | 0.00 | 0.01 | 0.04 | 0.42 | 0.20 | 0.17 | 0.35 | 0.17 | 0.01 | 0.15 | 0.22 |
| mach. & eq. | 0.02 | 0.02 | 0.32 | 0.18 | 0.40 | 0.15 | 0.46 | 0.45 | 0.36 | 0.54 | 0.28 | 0.34 | 0.55 | 0.15 | 0.14 | 0.47 |
| other mnfc. | 0.10 | 0.01 | 0.08 | 0.41 | 0.57 | 0.54 | 0.24 | 0.23 | 0.39 | 0.67 | 0.28 | 0.42 | 0.23 | 0.44 | 0.66 | 0.36 |
| services | 0.01 | 0.01 | 0.05 | 0.03 | 0.02 | 0.06 | 0.06 | 0.02 | 0.04 | 0.05 | 0.04 | 0.13 | 0.01 | 0.03 | 0.00 | 0.04 |
| all goods | 0.04 | 0.03 | 0.39 | 0.27 | 0.38 | 0.27 | 0.36 | 0.21 | 0.27 | 0.36 | 0.21 | 0.14 | 0.17 | 0.04 | 0.00 | 0.18 |

Source: GTAP data base, aggregation of version 2.

purchases of CRP products is sourced from abroad, while 39% of the own-intermediate inputs used by the CRP sector is purchased from overseas. This means that a tariff reduction in this sector will have little direct effect on consumer prices. The first-round effect will be predominantly through lower input costs to firms. Furthermore, the intensive use of imported CRP intermediates by the CRP sector itself will somewhat blunt the effect of competition from more competitive imports.

The last row in Table 3.14 reports the average variation in import intensity, by use. Here it can be seen that, on average, the firms use imports relatively more intensively than do households. Indeed, the average import intensity of private household consumption is only 4%. This stands in sharp contrast to many of the productive sectors, where average import intensities across all intermediate purchases is between 35% and 40% in the cases of extractive industries, textiles, CRP, and machinery and equipment. Even investment goods are more heavily import-oriented than are consumer goods, with an average intensity of 17%. All this information is lost in the bulk of the multiregion AGE data bases in which imports are blended at the border. In such cases, the implicit import intensity is equal across all uses, and is given by the entries in the final column of Table 3.14.

While this detailed breakdown of intermediate and final import usage is available in many published IO tables, other source tables provide less than full information: some give imports by commodity but not by use, others by use but not commodity. Those IO tables with less than full import detail present a special problem; we need somehow to transport this partial information into the full information structure.

In those cases where the IO tables do not provide sufficient information on the breakdown of commodity demands, we assume that the commodity-specific import share of composite commodity demand is uniform across use categories. So, for instance, while the import share for oil may differ from the import share for iron and steel, across all the different sectors that use oil, the oil import share is assumed to be the same. This permits us to share out total imports of a given commodity across intermediates and final demands. We consider this assumption more realistic for narrowly defined commodities than for broadly defined commodities. So where the source data are highly disaggregated, we transport the import information from the partial to the full information data structure before aggregating commodities to the GTAP classification.

The uniform import share assumption lets us generate full import information given source statistics for imports by commodity. The source IO tables provide imports by use category; however, we go to an outside source for imports by commodity. The outside source is the GTAP trade data base described above. In these cases, we must employ an iterative matrix balancing algorithm (RAS) to match both the by-commodity and the by-use-category import data.

**Import valuation.** The import valuation problem arises because the GTAP import usage data are duty-inclusive, but some source tables provide duty-exclusive values. These tables also provide data for total duty by use category. We allocate this total across commodities by assuming a uniform duty rate across all commodities in each use category. While this assumption is clearly unrealistic, it does not affect the duty rates in the GTAP data base; these derive from the protection data base described earlier in this chapter.

**Primary factor detail.** With the primary factor detail, the problem arises because the GTAP recognizes capital and agricultural land as separate factors, but the source statistics do not. Furthermore, primary factor payments in agriculture are highly variable due to variability in commodity prices, coupled with a tendency for primary factors to be sector-specific. Therefore we have gone to outside sources for statistical estimates of the primary factor cost shares in agriculture, by region. This information has been obtained for Australia, China, Canada, the EU, Japan, Korea, the Philippines, Taiwan, and the US. In the case of other regions, we have utilized labor payments data from the IO tables, thereafter imposing a simple 50–50 split between capital and land in agricultural industries.

*Material requirements*

The previous paragraphs have discussed requirements relating to the form of the IO tables; we now turn to requirements relating to their contents. These material requirements include a ban on negative flows, and a requirement that total sales should equal total costs in each sector. Besides being necessary restrictions in order to implement the GTAP model, these also act as a useful diagnostic check. Large imbalances may indicate that the source data have been misinterpreted, or that mistakes have been made in implementing the processing procedures.

Some of the source statistics follow conventions that permit negative flows of commodities. In particular, many treat sales by final buyers as negative flows; so for instance, sales of scrap by households to industry may be treated as negative sales by industry to households. While these negative flows are a practical expedient in IO accounting, they are not compatible with the GTAP production structure. The GTAP production functions are defined only over nonnegative input levels.

The other material requirement is that for each sector, total sales should be equal to total costs, where (by convention) costs include profit. This sectoral balance condition applies to square tables using the same sectoral classification for commodities as for industries; therefore, it applies to the GTAP data base. However, it does not apply to all the source data bases. With this convention, the requirement is an accounting identity, but one that some tables violate. Imbalances arise, for instance, in converting a nonsquare table into a square table using an imperfect concordance.

We impose the sectoral balance condition not just for the sake of satisfying accounting identities, but because of the effect of imbalances on model results. If, for instance, a certain sector has total sales 20% higher than total costs, the 20% imbalance acts like a free good, with every dollar's worth of inputs into the sector generating $1.20 worth of output. Policies that assist this sector would therefore tend to appear beneficial; likewise policies assisting sectors with negative imbalances would tend to appear harmful. These outcomes, however, would reflect not real economic mechanisms but defects in the data base.

### Representative IO tables for composite regions

**Overview.** The construction of a global data base presents a challenge. Many of the regions of the world are still not represented in this data base with IO tables. This section discusses how to deal with this problem. It outlines our strategy for creating IO tables for the regions for which we do not have original IO tables. [This approach capitalizes on software documented in Calder, McDougall, and Strzelecki (1993), in a way first proposed by Robert McDougall (1992).] It has the virtue of building on known information from the data base using a very simple and transparent set of assumptions. This assures consistency in applying accounting concepts and sectoral definitions. We mention some of its limitations at the end of this section.

The GTAP data base for 18 regions provides a complete and consistent accounting of domestic economic activity. We use these data bases to construct domestic accounts for the 6 composite regions: Rest of Latin America and Caribbean, Sub-Saharan Africa, Middle East and North Africa, Eastern Europe and Former Soviet Union, South Asia, and Regions not Classified Elsewhere. We do so based on the assumption that the average patterns of production, consumption, and savings in any individual country in these 6 composite regions can be approximated by patterns observed in one of the countries for which we have IO information. In particular, we associate a known GTAP region with each of the member countries in a composite region using a per capita income criterion and a secondary criterion based on the overall structure of production in the economy.

The logic behind the choice of per capita income as a primary criterion is rather simple. Consider, for example, the aggregate private household's budget share spent on food. Gains in per capita income generally increase food demand less than proportionately. Thus, a country with low per capita income is likely to spend a higher portion of income on food. In contrast, a country with high per capita income will spend a much smaller portion of its household income on food. For this reason, we expect countries with similar per capita incomes to have relatively similar budget shares for food. Further refinements could take account of relative food prices in the country, but this requires a very large amount of added information. Demand in nonfood sectors is simply expected to follow patterns based on per capita income levels. We believe that rather than investing a great deal of energy in refining this method, it is preferable to reduce the size of the approximation errors by expanding the individual-country coverage in GTAP.

**Implementation.** We start by establishing correspondences among the countries in each of the six composite regions with known GTAP regions according to per capita GDP, with production structure as a secondary criterion. Table 3.15 reports the correspondences among countries in one of the six composite regions, namely, "Rest of Latin America." The first column in this table reports the GTAP country used as a proxy, and associates this proxy country with particular countries in the region (indented entries). The latter entries therefore provide a summary of the countries included in this particular composite region. As shown in Table 3.15, we associate the three poorest countries in this region with China. Honduras is associated with Indonesia, based on per capita GDP; Bolivia and Peru are linked with the Philippines (Bolivia, based on its production structure–see footnote *b* in Table 3.15), and so on. Brazil, Mexico, and Argentina combined, are associated with quite a number of countries in this region, as might be expected.

The breakdown of this composite region's GDP among the GTAP regions and the resulting six sets of weights assigned to each of these regions are presented in the final three columns of Table 3.15. From the bottom row, one notes that the total GDP for the Rest of Latin America and the Caribbean region is $300,901.60 million. About one quarter of this total ($71,427 million) derives from countries associated with Brazil. Thus, the weight for Brazil is $w_{Brazil} = [71,427/300,901.60] = 0.2374$. This is reported in the last column of Table 3.15. Similarly, the GDP of countries associated with Mexico is $58,149 million. Therefore, the weight for Mexico is $w_{Mexico} = [58,149.40/300,901.60] = 0.1933$. Individual GTAP countries that have not been associated with any country in the Rest of Latin American and the Caribbean region have zero weights.

**Table 3.15.** *Mapping from Regions in the GTAP Data Base to Countries in Composite Region: Rest of Latin America and the Caribbean*

| Country | GDP[a] Per Capita | GDP[a] | Group GDP | GDP Share |
|---|---|---|---|---|
| China group | | | 4940.11 | 0.0164 |
| Guyana | 474.68 | 375.00 | | |
| Haiti | 410.53 | 2717.71 | | |
| Nicaragua | 447.31 | 1847.40 | | |
| Indonesia group | | | 3284.22 | 0.0109 |
| Honduras | 601.51 | 3284.22 | | |
| Philippines group | | | 27370.55 | 0.0910 |
| Bolivia[b] | 673.10 | 5270.35 | | |
| Peru | 984.42 | 22100.20 | | |
| Thailand group | | | 94345.58 | 0.3135 |
| Belize | 1920.00 | 384.00 | | |
| Dominican Rep. | 1034.62 | 7728.59 | | |
| Guatemala | 1071.24 | 10433.90 | | |
| Colombia | 1453.71 | 48583.10 | | |
| Ecuador | 1041.54 | 11186.10 | | |
| El Salvador | 1193.16 | 6443.06 | | |
| Jamaica | 1333.51 | 3293.77 | | |
| Paraguay | 1354.92 | 6124.24 | | |
| Grenada | 1875.72 | 168.82 | | |
| Brazil group | | | 71427.00 | 0.2374 |
| Costa Rica[c] | 2106.45 | 6529.99 | | |
| Panama | 2168.01 | 5441.70 | | |
| St. Lucia | 2799.74 | 391.96 | | |
| St. Vincnt & Grnd. | 2083.84 | 229.22 | | |
| Dominica | 2203.17 | 154.22 | | |
| Venezuela | 2897.77 | 58679.90 | | |
| Mexico group | | | 58149.40 | 0.1933 |
| Chile | 3029.66 | 41203.40 | | |
| Trinidad & Tobago | 4276.11 | 5387.90 | | |
| Argentina group | | | 1856.60 | 0.0062 |
| Suriname | 4641.51 | 1856.60 | | |
| Korea group | | | 36141.59 | 0.1201 |
| Antigua & Barbuda | 6178.83 | 432.52 | | |
| Barbados | 6692.58 | 1740.07 | | |
| Puerto Rico | 6692.58 | 33969.00 | | |
| Australia group | | | | |
| Bahamas | 13025.21 | 3386.55 | 3386.55 | 0.0113 |
| Total | n.a. | 300,901.60 | 300,901.60 | 1.0000 |

[a] The World Bank provided data on GDP and population.
[b] Reallocated based on structure of production.
[c] We have used geographical considerations to group Costa Rica with Brazil.

Once the weights reported in Table 3.13 have been computed for all 6 composite regions, we use the 18 input–output tables to compute the IO parameters for each region using a linear approximation technique. Intuitively, what we do is to calculate the weighted means assigned to the parameters of each composite region. For example, the average propensity to save in each composite region is computed as:

$$s = \sum_r w_r s_r^*, \; = 1, \ldots, 14,$$

where $w_r$ is the weight assigned to the $r$th GTAP region, and $s_r$ is the savings propensity computed for the $r$th GTAP region. Of course $\Sigma_r w_r = 1$.

**Strengths and limitations of the approach.** An important strength of this approach is the ease with which we generate new IO tables for the rest of the world (ROW) using existing programs. It also permits us to generate tables that are inherently consistent with the rest of the data base. Of course, this approach can be refined in many ways. It might be worth trying to establish mappings between GTAP countries and countries in a composite region using other criteria in addition to per capita GDP and its distribution over the three main sectors of an economy. However, any such approach is necessarily arbitrary and there is merit in the simplicity and transparency of the per capita approach. Ultimately the best way to reduce the approximation error in these composite regions is to add more individual countries to the GTAP data base. In this way we reduce the size of the composite regions while simultaneously enhancing the portfolio of countries with which to approximate the remaining countries' unknown IO structures.

## V    Updating the IO tables and balancing the data base

This section discusses procedures for updating the IO information to 1992, based on macroeconomic data from UN, World Bank, IMF, and OECD publications, and balancing it with the trade and protection data discussed above. The vehicle for accomplishing this update is the FIT software developed at the Australian Industry Commission (James and McDougall 1993). FIT is an IO model that allows targeting of economic magnitudes to match conditions in a particular year. These target variables are shocked, and changes in all other variables of the model are computed in response to these shocks. FIT maintains market clearing and zero profit conditions, while fixing primary factor prices and permitting value-added, as well as the intensity of input usage to adjust, subject to a prespecified penalty function. Eight exogenous variables were targeted for the update in each region: (1) exports by commodity, (2) imports by commodity, (3) aggregate household consumption expenditures, (4) aggregate government spending, (5) aggregate expenditures for gross capital formation, (6) import tariffs, (7) export subsidies, and (8) production subsidies/taxes. The updated data represent an internally consistent IO table that can be incorporated into the GTAP data base.

Table 3.16 provides some summary statistics for the 24 regions in the GTAP data base after updating to 1992. The first column reports each region's share in global GDP. From this, it can be seen that the EU and US economies are dominant. Together they account for more than half of the global value of goods and services produced. This is followed by

Table 3.16. *Composition of Final Demand in the Data Base*

| Region | Share of Global GDP, % | Composition of Final Demand (Share of GDP) | | | | | |
|---|---|---|---|---|---|---|---|
| | | Composition | Investment | Government | Exports[a] | Imports[b] | Total |
| AUS | 1.31 | 0.61 | 0.19 | 0.18 | 0.18 | -0.17 | 1.0 |
| NZL | 0.18 | 0.61 | 0.17 | 0.16 | 0.35 | -0.29 | 1.0 |
| CAN | 2.56 | 0.58 | 0.18 | 0.21 | 0.26 | -0.22 | 1.0 |
| US | 25.73 | 0.69 | 0.13 | 0.19 | 0.10 | -0.10 | 1.0 |
| JPN | 15.92 | 0.57 | 0.31 | 0.09 | 0.11 | -0.09 | 1.0 |
| KOR | 1.30 | 0.53 | 0.36 | 0.11 | 0.33 | -0.33 | 1.0 |
| EU | 29.15 | 0.62 | 0.20 | 0.19 | 0.11 | -0.12 | 1.0 |
| IND | 0.57 | 0.52 | 0.34 | 0.09 | 0.30 | -0.25 | 1.0 |
| MYS | 0.30 | 0.44 | 0.29 | 0.11 | 0.72 | -0.57 | 1.0 |
| PHL | 0.24 | 0.70 | 0.20 | 0.09 | 0.31 | -0.31 | 1.0 |
| SGP | 0.15 | 0.59 | 0.55 | 0.13 | 2.31 | -2.59 | 1.0 |
| THA | 0.48 | 0.56 | 0.40 | 0.10 | 0.35 | -0.41 | 1.0 |
| CHN | 2.16 | 0.53 | 0.25 | 0.12 | 0.29 | -0.18 | 1.0 |
| HKG | 0.11 | 2.32 | 1.06 | 0.33 | 2.92 | -5.63 | 1.0 |
| TWN | 1.00 | 0.51 | 0.21 | 0.16 | 0.44 | -0.31 | 1.0 |
| ARG | 1.00 | 0.81 | 0.17 | 0.04 | 0.07 | -0.08 | 1.0 |
| BRA | 1.70 | 0.65 | 0.18 | 0.15 | 0.11 | -0.08 | 1.0 |
| MEX | 1.45 | 0.73 | 0.21 | 0.09 | 0.17 | -0.21 | 1.0 |
| LAM | 1.12 | 0.75 | 0.20 | 0.11 | 0.30 | -0.36 | 1.0 |
| SSA | 0.73 | 0.72 | 0.16 | 0.15 | 0.26 | -0.29 | 1.0 |
| MNA | 2.53 | 0.56 | 0.24 | 0.23 | 0.29 | -0.31 | 1.0 |
| EIT | 3.62 | 0.71 | 0.18 | 0.12 | 0.10 | -0.11 | 1.0 |
| SAS | 1.43 | 0.69 | 0.20 | 0.12 | 0.12 | -0.13 | 1.0 |
| ROW | 5.26 | 0.58 | 0.21 | 0.21 | 0.28 | -0.28 | 1.0 |

[a] Valued at *fob* prices.
[b] Valued at *cif* prices.

Japan, with 15.9% of global GDP. The remaining regions are all much smaller economies.

The next five columns of Table 3.16 break up the individual components of GDP by region. The first reports the share of private consumption in GDP. This is very high for the US (69%) and low for some of the Asian economies, where investment is relatively higher. For example, Korea's share of consumption in regional GDP is only 53%, whereas its investment share is 36% (vs. 13% in the US). The share of government expenditures in GDP is reported in the next column of Table 3.16. This is particularly high in Europe (19%), and much lower in Japan (9%).

The next two columns in the Table 3.16 report the share of exports (*fob* basis) and imports (*cif* basis) in GDP. Note that the largest economies are relatively less reliant on trade, with shares ranging from 9 to 12%. At the other extreme are the small trading economies: Singapore and Hong Kong. Here, trade flows are far larger than GDP. These economies present special problems for the GTAP data base due to the prevalence of reexports. In the case of Hong Kong, asymmetric reporting practices have led to an overstatement of imports (which include imports for reexports), relative to exports (which do not include reexports).[20]

Having updated the individual-region IO tables to conform with 1992 macroeconomic, trade, and policy control totals, we are now in a position to bring all the individual IO tables together to construct a global data base. We check accounting relationships to determine if the data are globally consistent. Also, capital stock and depreciation values, compiled from Nehru and Dhareshwan (1993), are incorporated into the data base. Finally, the bilateral detail from the trade matrix is brought in, along with the international trade and transport margins that account for the difference between *cif* and *fob* values. This completes development of the global data base.


## Appendix: Representative countries used for construction of composite region protection


**Table 3A.1.** *Trade/Tariff Pairs for Construction of Bilateralized Tariffs for Composite Regions*

| Composite Region | Country Tariff schedules (Substituted trade in parentheses, if applicable) |
| --- | --- |
| Rest of Latin America | Bolivia, Chile, Paraguay, Colombia, Ecuador, Peru |
| Sub-Saharan Africa | Kenya, Nigeria (Brazil, Mexico, India, and Tunisia's total imports used for both of these countries) |
| Middle East and North Africa | Tunisia, Algeria (Tunisia), Oman, Saudi Arabia (Oman) |
| Eastern Europe & FSU | Poland, Hungary |
| South Asia | India (with supplementary information from Pakistan and Sri Lanka) |
| Rest of World | Sweden, Norway, Finland, Switzerland, Austria |

**Table 3A.2.** *Composite Region Coverage of PSE Information*

| Rest of Latin America | Sub-Saharan Africa |
|---|---|
| Chile | Kenya |
| Colombia | Nigeria |
| Jamaica | Senegal |
| Venezuela | Zimbabwe |
| **East Europe & Former Soviet Union** | **Middle East & North Africa** |
| Hungary | Algeria |
| Poland | Egypt |
| Former Soviet Union | |
| Yugoslavia | |
| Czechoslovakia | |
| **ROW** | **South Asia** |
| South Africa | Bangladesh |
| Turkey | India |
| | Pakistan |

## NOTES

1. Individuals interested in obtaining an electronic concordance with SITC, International Standard Industrial Classification (ISIC), Harmonized System (HS), or other commodity classifications are referred to the Web site discussed in Chapter 1. The problem of establishing concordances is no easy matter, since the development of a global data base requires drawing data from several sources. The ISIC provides a logical hub for the GTAP IO-based concordance. However, while the ISIC classification provides acceptable coverage of industrial products in GTAP, it lacks detailed coverage of agricultural and certain natural resource–based commodities. Therefore, the GTAP concordances deviate from the ISIC classification in these areas. For example, there are only two ISIC industrial codes that describe primary agriculture: 1110–Agricultural and Livestock Production and 1120–Agricultural Services. GTAP, on the other hand, disaggregates primary agriculture into 6 commodities: 1 paddy rice, 2 wheat, 3 grains (except wheat and rice), 4 nongrain crops, 5 wool, and 6 other livestock products.
2. The design of these 37-sector IO tables, the strategy for processing them, as well as a number of raw tables were inherited from the SALTER Project (Hambley 1993). This project was executed by the Australian Industry Commission, on behalf of the Department of Foreign Affairs and Trade. For this reason, the two data bases are compatible and can share common information. However, the final GTAP and SALTER data bases share no common data, owing to differences in base years as well as differing trade and protection information.
3. Much of the work reported here was conducted in conjunction with ongoing work on improving the quality of international trade statistics at the ERS of the USDA.
4. The data include 24 reporting countries, 31 aggregated commodities for merchandise trade, and 31 years of information (1962–1992).
5. The IO structure of the EU was built such that intraregional trade occurs as a part of other domestic transactions; therefore, it is not observed as intraregional trade.

6. This was accomplished using the Generalized Algebraic Modeling System (GAMS) software (Brooke, Kendrick, and Meeraus 1988), which is designed to solve such problems efficiently. In this case, the objective function minimized the squared deviations between the initial trade share coefficients and final share coefficients such that merchandise trade patterns were imposed on the services trade patterns.

7. The term *useful* here is taken to mean specifically the applicability for inclusion into an economic modeling framework. There exists, for example, a quite comprehensive data base that describes the number and type of nontariff measures by country and industry. Some researchers have, in fact, used the number of nontariff measures in an industry as an indication of the measures' distortionary impact. Readers with an interest in this area should consult Laird and Yeats (1990).

8. It is heartening to learn that the Organization for Economic Cooperation and Development (OECD) is considering undertaking the calculation of effective rates of protection for member countries, rates that would, wherever possible, include the impact of both tariff and nontariff measures.

9. Under the HS, participating countries have harmonized tariff schedules to the first 6 digits. For many products, tariffs are collected based on 8-digit or even 10-digit classifications. The HS contains 5,019 lines at the 6-digit level.

10. Taiwan is an exception to the above process of creating country files. Taiwan gave a tariff file to the GATT for accession purposes, but it was in a format different from GATT member files. The file used for the GTAP data base is based on one created by the US Trade Representatives (USTR) Office from the original Taiwanese file. From this file, it was possible to create bilateral weighted average rates only for the US, Japan, and the EU; all other bilateral rates were filled in with a constructed ROW weighted average rate. About 40 of the tariff line items were blank in the USTR file because specific duties were not converted to *ad valorem* equivalents and were deleted when constructing the weighted averages. The tariff rates reflect those in effect in 1992, although the trade values used were three-year averages from 1989–1991. The rates used were those received by the US–that is, reciprocal rates if they exist, and general rates otherwise.

11. The tariff negotiations of the Kennedy Round are the topic of Baldwin (1965).

12. Personal communication with Yongzheng Yang.

13. Price undertakings require a price increase on the part of the exporter; therefore, price undertakings are reported here as export taxes. For those orders that resulted in both duties and undertakings, half of the resulting margin was allocated as an import duty and half was allocated as an export tax. The aggregation of export taxes resulting form price undertakings was carried out in the same manner as the aggregation of the duties, as explained below.

14. The Magee approach is designed to yield a bias-free welfare loss estimate of a tariff or other duty.

15. Both Canada and the US normally consider EU member states separately for antidumping investigations.

16. Based on GATT, *Trade Policy Review: Canada*, 1995. For information on the operation of the antidumping regimes of Canada, the EU, and the US, consult Finger (1993), Jackson and Vermulst 1989), and the GATT *Trade Policy Review* of each country.

17. At first this appears to be a neutral assumption. However, as there is reason to believe that firms with the largest exports are being assessed the highest duties, we believe this method understates the actual impact of the orders.

18. Brown, Strzelecki, and Watts (1993); Calder, McDougall, and Strzelecki (1993); and Hambley (1993), are important background materials.

19. See Hertel, Ianchovichina, and McDonald (1996) for elaboration of this example. They use a modified version of the GTAP data base to analyze the impact of the Uruguay Round on Korea.
20. This trade imbalance results in a very large negative rate of savings. Therefore, we recommend users aggregate Hong Kong with one or more of its major trading partners in GTAP applications using this version of the data base. We will address this problem in the future data releases.

## REFERENCES

Brooke, A., D. Kendrick, and A. Meeraus (1988) *GAMS: A User's Guide*. San Francisco: The Scientific Press.

Brown, S., A. Strzelecki, and G. Watts (1993) "Matching Input-Output Data to International Trade Data and Assembling a SALTER Data Base." SALTER Working Paper No. 19. Canberra, Australia: Australian Industry Commission.

Calder, W., R. McDougall and A. Strzelecki (1993) "Procedures for Later Stage Processing of Single-Region Input-Output Data for SALTER," SALTER Working Paper No. 18. Canberra, Australia: Australian Industry Commission.

DeWulf, L. (1981) "Statistical Analysis of Under- and Over-invoicing in Imports," *Journal of Developing Economics* 8:303–323.

Finger, J. Michael (1993) *Antidumping: How It Works and Who Gets Hurt*. Ann Arbor: University of Michigan Press.

GATT. *Trade Policy Review* (various countries and issues).

Gehlhar, M. J., J. K. Binkley, and T. W. Hertel (1991) "Estimation of Trade Margins for Food Products: An Application of the UN Bilateral Trade Data," NC-194 Occasional Paper Series OP-24.

General Agreement on Tariffs and Trade (GATT) (1992) *Trade Policy Review: Canada*, Geneva: GATT.

General Agreement on Tariffs and Trade (GATT) (1993) *Trade Policy Review: European Community*, Geneva: GATT.

General Agreement on Tariffs and Trade (GATT) (1994) *Trade Policy Review: United States*, Geneva: GATT.

Gotch, M. (1993) "Industry Assistance Data for SALTER," SALTER Working Paper No. 14. Canberra, Australia: Australian Industry Commission.

Hambley J. (1993) "Early Stage Processing of International Trade and Input-Output Data for SALTER," SALTER Working Paper No. 15. Canberra, Australia: Australian Industry Commission.

Hertel, T. W., E. Ianchovichina, and B. J. McDonald (1996) "Multi-region AGE Modeling Methods for International Trade." In J. Francois (ed.), *Applied Trade Policy Modeling: A Handbook*, forthcoming, Cambridge University Press.

Hiemstra, S. W., and A. B. Mackie (1986) *Methods of Reconciling World Trade Statistics*. Economic Research Service, Foreign Economic Report No. 217.

IMF (1992 and 1994) *International Financial Statistics*, May, Washington, DC: IMF.

Jackson, J. H., and E. A. Vermulst (1989) *Antidumping Law and Practice: A Comparative Study*. Ann Arbor: University of Michigan Press.

James, M., and McDougall, R. (1993) "FIT: An Input-Output Data Update Facility for SALTER," SALTER Working Paper No. 17. Canberra, Australia: Australian Industry Commission.

Jomini, P., J. F. Zeitsch, R. McDougall, A. Welsh, S. Brown, J. Hambley, and J. Kelly (1991) *SALTER: A General Equilibrium Model for the World Economy*, Vol. 1, "Model Structure, Database and Parameters." Canberra, Australia: Australian Industry Commission.

Laird, S., and A. Yeats (1990) *Quantitative Methods for Trade-Barrier Analysis*. New York: New York University Press.

Magee, S. P. (1972) "The Welfare Effects of Restrictions on US Trade," *Brookings Papers on Economic Activity*, Vol. 3.

McDougall, R. (1992) "FIT: An Input-Output Data Update Facility for SALTER," SALTER Working Paper No. 17. Canberra, Australia: Australian Industry Commission.

Morgenstern, O. (1963) *On the Accuracy of Economic Observations*. Princeton, NJ: Princeton University Press.

Nehru, V., and A. Dhareshwar (1993) "A New Database on Physical Capital Stock: Sources, Methodology, and Results," unpublished manuscript, International Economics Department, The World Bank.

OECD (1964–1987) *Maritime Transport*, various issues.

Parniczky, G. (1980) "On the Inconsistency of World Trade Statistics," *1980 International Statistics Review*, pp. 43–48.

Rozanski, J., and A. Yeats (1992) "On the Accuracy of Economic Observations: An Assessment of Trends in Reliability of International Trade Statistics," presented at a Ford Foundation conference *Database of Development Analysis*. New Haven, CT: Yale University, May.

Ryan, C. (1992) "The SALTER Model: Construction of the European Database," SALTER Working Paper No. 10. Canberra, Australia: Australian Industry Commission.

Saad, I. (1993) "Indonesian Manufacturing Exports After the Petroleum Boom: Focusing on Clothing and Textiles," unpublished Ph.D. dissertation. Canberra, Australia: Australian National University.

Secretaria de Pramacion Y Presupuesto (1985) "Matriz de Insumo-Producto de Mexico," unpublished data. Mexico City.

Stevens, J. (1995) "Effective Protection in General Equilibrium: The Case of Korea," unpublished M.S. thesis. Department of Agricultural Economics, Purdue University.

Tormey, J. (1993) "Creating Synthetic Single Region Input-Output Data for SALTER: Hong Kong and the Rest of the World," SALTER Working Paper No. 20, June.

Tsigas, M. E., T. W. Hertel, and J. K. Binkley (1992) "Estimates of Systematic Reporting Biases in Trade Statistics." *Economic Systems Research* 4(4):297–310.

Yang, Y. (1992) "The Impact of Multifibre Arrangement on World Clothing and Textile Markets with Special Reference to China," unpublished Ph.D. dissertation. Canberra, Australia: Australian National University.

Yeats, A. (1978) "On the Accuracy of Partner Country Trade," *Oxford Bulletin of Economics and Statistics* 40(1):341–361.

# CHAPTER 4

# GTAP behavioral parameters

*Karen M. Huff, Kevin Hanslow, Thomas W. Hertel, and Marinos E. Tsigas*

## I    Introduction and overview

This chapter documents the parameters that specify marginal behavior in the Global Trade Analysis Project (GTAP) model. These behavioral parameters, along with the theory of the model as described in Chapter 2 and the composition of the benchmark data (i.e., the value flows described in Chapter 3), will determine simulation results. No individual component can be said to be more important than the others. For some simulations, it is the accounting identities that determine results, whereas the behavioral parameters may play a relatively small role. For other simulations, the specification of certain elasticities is of paramount importance. Documentation of these elasticities is the purpose of this chapter.

In section II, we discuss the behavioral parameters at the disaggregate 37-commodity, 24-region level. Most behavioral parameters in GTAP are based on constant elasticity specifications [e.g., the constant elasticity of substitution (CES) function], which simplify model calibration. However, consumer behavior in GTAP is based on the constant difference elasticity (CDE) function, of which the CES is a special case. Because this has not been widely used in applied general equilibrium (AGE) modeling to date, we provide a brief overview and motivation for the CDE in section III of this chapter. We then discuss the calibration and performance of the CDE demand system.

## II    Disaggregate behavioral parameters

There are four types of behavioral parameters in GTAP: elasticities of substitution (in both consumption and production), transformation elasticities that determine the degree of mobility of primary factors across sectors, the flexibilities of regional investment allocation, and consumer demand elasticities. We begin with the elasticities of substitution that determine the conditional price responsiveness of the nested-CES utility and production functions.

Table 4.1: GTAP Substitution Elasticities

| | Value-Added $(\sigma_{V_A})$ | Domestic/Imported $(\sigma_D)$ | Sourcing of Imports $(\sigma_M)$ |
|---|---|---|---|
| Paddy rice (PDR) | 0.56 | 2.2 | 4.4 |
| Wheat (WHT) | 0.56 | 2.2 | 4.4 |
| Grains (other than rice and wheat: GRO) | 0.56 | 2.2 | 4.4 |
| Nongrain crops (NGC) | 0.56 | 2.2 | 4.4 |
| Wool (WOL) | 0.56 | 2.2 | 4.4 |
| Other livestock (OLP) | 0.56 | 2.8 | 5.6 |
| Forestry (FOR) | 0.56 | 2.8 | 5.6 |
| Fishing (FSH) | 0.56 | 2.8 | 5.6 |
| Coal(COL) | 1.12 | 2.8 | 5.6 |
| Oil (OIL) | 1.12 | 2.8 | 5.6 |
| Gas (GAS) | 1.12 | 2.8 | 5.6 |
| Other minerals (OMN) | 1.12 | 2.8 | 5.6 |
| Processed rice (PCR) | 1.12 | 2.2 | 4.4 |
| Meat products (MET) | 1.12 | 2.2 | 4.4 |
| Milk products (MIL) | 1.12 | 2.2 | 4.4 |
| Other food products (OFP) | 1.12 | 2.2 | 4.4 |
| Beverages and tobacco (BT) | 1.12 | 3.1 | 6.2 |
| Textiles (TEX) | 1.26 | 2.2 | 4.4 |
| Wearing apparel (WAP) | 1.26 | 4.4 | 8.8 |
| Leather, etc. (LEA) | 1.26 | 4.4 | 8.8 |
| Lumber and wood (LUM) | 1.26 | 2.8 | 5.6 |
| Pulp, paper, etc. (PPP) | 1.26 | 1.8 | 3.6 |
| Petroleum and coal products (PC) | 1.26 | 1.9 | 3.8 |
| Chemicals, rubber and plastics (CRP) | 1.26 | 1.9 | 3.8 |
| Nonmetallic mineral products (NMM) | 1.26 | 2.8 | 5.6 |
| Primary ferrous metals (IS) | 1.26 | 2.8 | 5.6 |
| Nonferrous metals (NFM) | 1.26 | 2.8 | 5.6 |
| Fabricated metal products nec. (FMP) | 1.26 | 2.8 | 5.6 |
| Transport Equipment (TRN) | 1.26 | 5.2 | 10.4 |
| Machinery and equipment (OME) | 1.26 | 2.8 | 5.6 |
| Other manufacturing (OMF) | 1.26 | 2.8 | 5.6 |
| Electricity, water, and gas (EGW) | 1.26 | 2.8 | 5.6 |
| Construction (CNS) | 1.4 | 1.9 | 3.8 |
| Trade and transport (TT) | 1.68 | 1.9 | 3.8 |
| Other services (private) (OSP) | 1.26 | 1.9 | 3.8 |
| Other services (government) (OSG) | 1.26 | 1.9 | 3.8 |
| Ownership of dwellings (DWE) | 1.26 | 1.9 | 3.8 |

*Source*: Jomini *et al.*, table 4.3, 1991.

## Elasticities of substitution

The SALTER Project engaged in an extensive review of the literature and some original empirical work to specify values for substitution elasticities on a *commodity-specific, region-generic* basis (Jomini et al. 1991). Because we have adopted the SALTER commodity concordance, it was quite natural also to adopt SALTER substitution elasticity values. Instead of attempting to refine these values further, we have chosen to focus our efforts on other problems. However, estimation and validation of these substitution elasticities is an important priority for future work.

The first column of Table 4.1 reports the elasticities of substitution, $\sigma_{VA}$, in the value-added aggregates for each of the GTAP sectors. The overall elasticity of substitution among primary factors determines the ability of the economy to alter its output mix in response to changes in relative commodity prices. These parameters also play an important role in determining sectoral supply response, in the presence of sector-specific and sluggish factors of production. For example, with the supply of agricultural land fixed in the model, the ability to expand farm output can be directly linked to the ease of substitution of labor and capital for land. Note that the relatively small elasticity of substitution in primary production means that aggregate agricultural supply response is somewhat limited. When capital is treated as a sluggish factor of production, this elasticity of substitution plays the same role in capital using sectors. The greatest degree of substitutability (1.68) arises in the trade and transport sector.

Table 4.1 also reports the elasticities of substitution $\sigma_D$, and $\sigma_M$ for the Armington structure in GTAP. The first value, $\sigma_D$, describes the ease of substitution between the domestic good and the composite import, by commodity. As such, it governs the composite import demand elasticity. The second Armington parameter, $\sigma_M$, determines the case of substitution among imports from different sources. In the SALTER parameter file, this is equal to twice the value of $\sigma_D$. This is an empirical regularity, reported in Jomini et al. (1991), which considerably simplifies the task of parameterizing a multiregion trade model. In the absence of additional information, it probably also makes sense to preserve this relationship when conducting systematic sensitivity analysis on the Armington structure.

### Mobility parameters

The second type of behavioral parameters in GTAP relate to primary factor mobility. Within each region, the model distinguishes between primary factors that are perfectly mobile across productive sectors and those factors that are sluggish (see also Chapter 2). In an experiment with sluggish endowment commodities, it is important to determine *how much of a disparity in relative sectoral returns can be sustained over the simulation period.* This disparity is governed by the elasticity of transformation, $\sigma_T < 0$, for sluggish endowment commodities. If $\sigma_T$ is close to zero, then the allocation of factors across uses is nearly fixed and unresponsive to changes in relative returns. As $\sigma_T$ takes on more negative values, then the supply of factors to various uses becomes more and more responsive to relative returns [see equation (51) in Table 2.14 of Chapter 2]. In the limit, as $\sigma_T \rightarrow -\infty$, this factor is perfectly mobile and no differential return can be sustained over the time horizon envisioned in the simulation. If this is the case, then the factor in question should be reclassified into the set of mobile endowment commodities.

### Flexibilities of regional investment

In addition to the elasticity of transformation for endowment commodities, there is another set of "mobility" parameters that determine the flexibility of regional investment. If the GTAP user chooses to allow the allocation of global investment to regional economies to respond to region-specific rates of return on capital (i.e., parameter *RORDELTA* is 1), then parameter *RORFLEX(r)* > 0 must be properly specified [equation (58) of Table 2.15 in Chapter 2]. The smaller the *RORFLEX(r)*, the greater the responsiveness of international investment to a change in the rate of return in region *r*. Because *RORFLEX(r)* is indexed over regions, it is possible to have some regions where investment is quite sensitive to changing rates of return, and others where this is not the case.

### *Consumer demand elasticities*

The parameters that describe demand behavior in initial equilibrium for the representative private household are *region-specific*. Consumer behavior in GTAP is based on the CDE expenditure function, which is most naturally calibrated to income and own-price elasticities of demand (Hertel et al. 1991). We obtained information on income elasticities of demand from three sources: a world food model recently estimated by the Food and Agriculture Organization (1993), the SALTER model (Jomini et al. 1991), and Theil, Chung, and Seale (1989). Using these income elasticities, we derived own-price demand elasticities based on a linear expenditure system (LES) relationship (Frisch 1959). As discussed in the next section, the CDE is a more flexible functional form than the LES, and we could have used independent information on own-price demand elasticities in this calibration exercise. However, deriving own-price elasticities from the income elasticities and the Frisch parameter provided a useful starting point for establishing consistent own-price effects. In the future, we hope to supplement the elasticities file with cross-country studies of own-price responses. In addition, by using the CDE, GTAP modelers are given the flexibility to adjust commodity-specific substitution effects to conform with outside information on own-price elasticities of demand for key commodities in any particular application.

For agricultural and food commodities we draw upon the Food and Agriculture Organization (FAO) model (FAO 1993), which has excellent country coverage and has proved to be a good source for recent estimates of income elasticities. Some comments on the way we used the FAO income elasticities follow:

- We considered 0.1 as the lower bound for income elasticities because smaller values can cause calibration problems for the CDE.
- For the European Union (EU), we used FAO estimates for Germany because the EU has not been identified as a single region in the FAO model.

- Elasticities for the 6 composite regions were computed in all cases as a weighted sum of elasticities for the 18 individual GTAP regions (see Chapter 3 for a discussion of these weights).
- The region "China" in the FAO model covers both the PRC and Taiwan. We applied the FAO estimates for China to both GTAP regions.
- For "other grains" we used FAO elasticities for maize or other coarse grains (otherwise the lower bound of 0.1 was applied).
- The income elasticities employed for "meat products" were linear averages of the FAO values for beef, pork, chicken, and lamb.
- For "other food products" we computed a linear average of FAO elasticities for butter and oils.
- The elasticity applied to "processed rice" was set equal to twice the value employed for "paddy rice" in each region because processed products typically have higher income elasticities of demand than their raw counterparts.
- The income elasticities employed for "textiles and wearing apparel" have been taken from Theil and colleagues (1989) and then reduced by one half to be applied to "wool and other agricultural products."

For nonagricultural, and nonfood commodities, we used income elasticities from the SALTER model and Theil, Chung, and Seale (1989). In particular, we used SALTER elasticities for the regions common to both GTAP and SALTER. Values for countries in the Association of South East Asian Nations (ASEAN) region of SALTER have been applied to Indonesia, Malaysia, Philippines, Singapore, and Thailand in GTAP. The ASEAN values were also applied to China and Taiwan in the GTAP. For Hong Kong, Argentina, and Brazil we used estimates from Theil and colleagues. Values for Mexico were computed as a linear average of those applied to Argentina and Brazil. Table 4.2 presents income elasticities of demand chosen for the GTAP data. Engel aggregation does not hold for all regional income elasticities in Table 4.2. We impose this condition in the calibration phase by proportionally adjusting all income elasticities.

Values for own-price elasticities of demand were computed following the procedure outlined in Zeitsch et al. (1991) for own-price elasticities of demand (Frisch 1959):

$$\varepsilon_{ii} = -s_i\eta_i\left(1 + \frac{\eta_i}{\omega}\right) + \frac{\eta_i}{\omega}, \qquad (4.1)$$

where $\varepsilon_{ii}$ is the uncompensated own-price demand elasticity for commodity $i$; $\eta_i$ is the income elasticity of demand for commodity $i$, $s_i$ is the expenditure

**Table 4.2. GTAP Income Elasticities of Demand**

| | AUS | NZL | CAN | US | JPN | KOR | EU | IDN | MYS | PHL | SGP | THA |
|---|---|---|---|---|---|---|---|---|---|---|---|---|
| PDR | 0.20 | 0.10 | 0.20 | 0.20 | 0.10 | 0.30 | 0.20 | 0.50 | 0.20 | 0.20 | 0.30 | 0.10 |
| WHT | 0.10 | 0.10 | 0.10 | 0.10 | 0.10 | 0.30 | 0.10 | 1.00 | 0.31 | 0.50 | 0.10 | 0.50 |
| GRO | 0.10 | 0.10 | 0.10 | 0.10 | 0.10 | 0.10 | 0.10 | 0.10 | 0.17 | 0.20 | 0.10 | 0.10 |
| NGC | 0.10 | 0.10 | 0.10 | 0.10 | 0.10 | 0.10 | 0.10 | 0.10 | 0.10 | 0.10 | 0.10 | 0.10 |
| WOL | 0.48 | 0.48 | 0.48 | 0.48 | 0.48 | 0.48 | 0.48 | 0.48 | 0.48 | 0.48 | 0.48 | 0.48 |
| OLP | 0.48 | 0.48 | 0.48 | 0.48 | 0.48 | 0.48 | 0.48 | 0.48 | 0.48 | 0.48 | 0.48 | 0.48 |
| FOR | 1.15 | 1.17 | 1.10 | 1.09 | 1.12 | 1.19 | 1.13 | 1.23 | 1.23 | 1.23 | 1.23 | 1.23 |
| FSH | 1.15 | 1.17 | 1.10 | 1.09 | 1.12 | 1.19 | 1.13 | 1.23 | 1.23 | 1.23 | 1.23 | 1.23 |
| COL | 1.15 | 1.17 | 1.10 | 1.09 | 1.12 | 1.19 | 1.13 | 1.23 | 1.23 | 1.23 | 1.23 | 1.23 |
| OIL | 1.15 | 1.17 | 1.10 | 1.09 | 1.12 | 1.19 | 1.13 | 1.23 | 1.23 | 1.23 | 1.23 | 1.23 |
| GAS | 1.15 | 1.17 | 1.10 | 1.09 | 1.12 | 1.19 | 1.13 | 1.23 | 1.23 | 1.23 | 1.23 | 1.23 |
| OMN | 1.15 | 1.17 | 1.10 | 1.09 | 1.12 | 1.19 | 1.13 | 1.23 | 1.23 | 1.23 | 1.23 | 1.23 |
| PCR | 0.40 | 0.20 | 0.40 | 0.40 | 0.20 | 0.60 | 0.40 | 1.00 | 0.40 | 0.40 | 0.60 | 0.20 |
| MET | 0.30 | 0.11 | 0.27 | 0.13 | 0.70 | 0.78 | 0.33 | 0.86 | 0.36 | 0.66 | 0.56 | 0.40 |
| MIL | 0.10 | 0.10 | 0.10 | 0.10 | 0.50 | 1.07 | 0.10 | 1.34 | 0.38 | 0.50 | 0.40 | 0.54 |
| OFP | 0.20 | 0.25 | 0.17 | 0.15 | 0.75 | 0.83 | 0.17 | 0.97 | 0.74 | 0.92 | 0.58 | 0.93 |
| B_T | 0.94 | 0.96 | 0.90 | 0.89 | 0.89 | 0.86 | 0.90 | 0.83 | 0.83 | 0.83 | 0.83 | 0.83 |
| TEX | 0.96 | 0.96 | 0.96 | 0.96 | 0.96 | 0.96 | 0.96 | 0.96 | 0.96 | 0.96 | 0.96 | 0.96 |
| WAP | 0.96 | 0.96 | 0.96 | 0.96 | 0.96 | 0.96 | 0.96 | 0.96 | 0.96 | 0.96 | 0.96 | 0.96 |
| LEA | 0.96 | 0.96 | 0.96 | 0.96 | 0.96 | 0.96 | 0.96 | 0.96 | 0.96 | 0.96 | 0.96 | 0.96 |
| LUM | 1.15 | 1.17 | 1.10 | 1.09 | 1.12 | 1.19 | 1.13 | 1.23 | 1.23 | 1.23 | 1.23 | 1.23 |

**Table 4.2.** *GTAP Income Elasticities of Demand*

| | AUS | NZL | CAN | US | JPN | KOR | EU | IDN | MYS | PHL | SGP | THA |
|---|---|---|---|---|---|---|---|---|---|---|---|---|
| PPP | 1.15 | 1.17 | 1.10 | 1.09 | 1.12 | 1.19 | 1.13 | 1.23 | 1.23 | 1.23 | 1.23 | 1.23 |
| P_C | 1.15 | 1.17 | 1.10 | 1.09 | 1.12 | 1.19 | 1.13 | 1.23 | 1.23 | 1.23 | 1.23 | 1.23 |
| CRP | 1.15 | 1.17 | 1.10 | 1.09 | 1.12 | 1.19 | 1.13 | 1.23 | 1.23 | 1.23 | 1.23 | 1.23 |
| NMM | 1.15 | 1.17 | 1.10 | 1.09 | 1.12 | 1.19 | 1.13 | 1.23 | 1.23 | 1.23 | 1.23 | 1.23 |
| I_S | 1.15 | 1.17 | 1.10 | 1.09 | 1.12 | 1.19 | 1.13 | 1.23 | 1.23 | 1.23 | 1.23 | 1.23 |
| NFM | 1.15 | 1.17 | 1.10 | 1.09 | 1.12 | 1.19 | 1.13 | 1.23 | 1.23 | 1.23 | 1.23 | 1.23 |
| FMP | 1.15 | 1.17 | 1.10 | 1.09 | 1.12 | 1.19 | 1.13 | 1.23 | 1.23 | 1.23 | 1.23 | 1.23 |
| TRN | 1.07 | 1.09 | 1.03 | 1.01 | 1.03 | 1.03 | 1.04 | 1.01 | 1.01 | 1.01 | 1.01 | 1.01 |
| OME | 1.07 | 1.09 | 1.03 | 1.01 | 1.03 | 1.03 | 1.04 | 1.01 | 1.01 | 1.01 | 1.01 | 1.01 |
| OMF | 1.07 | 1.09 | 1.03 | 1.01 | 1.03 | 1.03 | 1.04 | 1.01 | 1.01 | 1.01 | 1.01 | 1.01 |
| EGW | 1.15 | 1.17 | 1.10 | 1.09 | 1.12 | 1.19 | 1.13 | 1.23 | 1.23 | 1.23 | 1.23 | 1.23 |
| CNS | 1.15 | 1.17 | 1.10 | 1.09 | 1.12 | 1.19 | 1.13 | 1.23 | 1.23 | 1.23 | 1.23 | 1.23 |
| T_T | 1.15 | 1.16 | 1.10 | 1.08 | 1.11 | 1.17 | 1.12 | 1.20 | 1.20 | 1.20 | 1.20 | 1.20 |
| OSP | 1.16 | 1.18 | 1.11 | 1.09 | 1.14 | 1.23 | 1.14 | 1.29 | 1.29 | 1.29 | 1.29 | 1.29 |
| OSG | 1.15 | 1.17 | 1.10 | 1.09 | 1.12 | 1.19 | 1.13 | 1.23 | 1.23 | 1.23 | 1.23 | 1.23 |
| DWE | 1.15 | 1.17 | 1.10 | 1.09 | 1.12 | 1.19 | 1.13 | 1.23 | 1.23 | 1.23 | 1.23 | 1.23 |

**Table 4.2.  GTAP Income Elasticities of Demand**

| | CHN | HKG | TWN | ARG | BRA | MEX | LAM | SSA | MNA | EIT | SAS | ROW |
|---|---|---|---|---|---|---|---|---|---|---|---|---|
| PDR | 0.25 | 0.20 | 0.25 | 0.10 | 0.20 | 0.30 | 0.20 | 0.23 | 0.20 | 0.17 | 0.25 | 0.15 |
| WHT | 0.30 | 0.40 | 0.30 | 0.10 | 0.40 | 0.40 | 0.43 | 0.34 | 0.38 | 0.44 | 0.30 | 0.17 |
| GRO | 0.10 | 0.10 | 0.10 | 0.10 | 0.10 | 0.10 | 0.11 | 0.12 | 0.11 | 0.11 | 0.10 | 0.10 |
| NGC | 0.10 | 0.10 | 0.10 | 0.10 | 0.10 | 0.10 | 0.10 | 0.10 | 0.10 | 0.10 | 0.10 | 0.10 |
| WOL | 0.48 | 0.48 | 0.48 | 0.48 | 0.48 | 0.48 | 0.48 | 0.48 | 0.48 | 0.48 | 0.48 | 0.48 |
| OLP | 0.48 | 0.48 | 0.48 | 0.48 | 0.48 | 0.48 | 0.48 | 0.48 | 0.48 | 0.48 | 0.48 | 0.48 |
| FOR | 1.23 | 1.27 | 1.23 | 1.33 | 1.32 | 1.33 | 1.27 | 1.24 | 1.20 | 1.28 | 1.23 | 1.14 |
| FSH | 1.23 | 1.27 | 1.23 | 1.33 | 1.32 | 1.33 | 1.27 | 1.24 | 1.20 | 1.28 | 1.23 | 1.14 |
| COL | 1.23 | 1.27 | 1.23 | 1.33 | 1.32 | 1.33 | 1.27 | 1.24 | 1.20 | 1.28 | 1.23 | 1.14 |
| OIL | 1.23 | 1.27 | 1.23 | 1.33 | 1.32 | 1.33 | 1.27 | 1.24 | 1.20 | 1.28 | 1.23 | 1.14 |
| GAS | 1.23 | 1.27 | 1.23 | 1.33 | 1.32 | 1.33 | 1.27 | 1.24 | 1.20 | 1.28 | 1.23 | 1.14 |
| OMN | 1.23 | 1.27 | 1.23 | 1.33 | 1.32 | 1.33 | 1.27 | 1.24 | 1.20 | 1.28 | 1.23 | 1.14 |
| PCR | 0.50 | 0.40 | 0.50 | 0.20 | 0.40 | 0.60 | 0.41 | 0.46 | 0.41 | 0.34 | 0.50 | 0.29 |
| MET | 0.67 | 0.38 | 0.67 | 0.18 | 0.55 | 0.41 | 0.51 | 0.64 | 0.49 | 0.49 | 0.67 | 0.47 |
| MIL | 0.75 | 0.54 | 0.75 | 0.10 | 0.40 | 0.47 | 0.56 | 0.66 | 0.60 | 0.46 | 0.75 | 0.35 |
| OFP | 0.85 | 0.58 | 0.85 | 0.54 | 0.82 | 0.79 | 0.85 | 0.85 | 0.72 | 0.86 | 0.85 | 0.56 |
| B_T | 0.83 | 1.02 | 0.83 | 1.02 | 1.02 | 1.02 | 0.92 | 0.85 | 0.86 | 0.93 | 0.83 | 0.90 |
| TEX | 0.96 | 0.96 | 0.96 | 0.96 | 0.96 | 0.96 | 0.96 | 0.96 | 0.96 | 0.96 | 0.96 | 0.96 |
| WAP | 0.96 | 0.96 | 0.96 | 0.96 | 0.96 | 0.96 | 0.96 | 0.96 | 0.96 | 0.96 | 0.96 | 0.96 |
| LEA | 0.96 | 0.96 | 0.96 | 0.96 | 0.96 | 0.96 | 0.96 | 0.96 | 0.96 | 0.96 | 0.96 | 0.96 |

**Table 4.2. *GTAP Income Elasticities of Demand***

| | CHN | HKG | TWN | ARG | BRA | MEX | LAM | SSA | MNA | EIT | SAS | ROW |
|---|---|---|---|---|---|---|---|---|---|---|---|---|
| LUM | 1.23 | 1.27 | 1.23 | 1.33 | 1.32 | 1.33 | 1.27 | 1.24 | 1.20 | 1.28 | 1.23 | 1.14 |
| PPP | 1.23 | 1.27 | 1.23 | 1.33 | 1.32 | 1.33 | 1.27 | 1.24 | 1.20 | 1.28 | 1.23 | 1.14 |
| P_C | 1.23 | 1.27 | 1.23 | 1.33 | 1.32 | 1.33 | 1.27 | 1.24 | 1.20 | 1.28 | 1.23 | 1.14 |
| CRP | 1.23 | 1.27 | 1.23 | 1.33 | 1.32 | 1.33 | 1.27 | 1.24 | 1.20 | 1.28 | 1.23 | 1.14 |
| NMM | 1.23 | 1.27 | 1.23 | 1.33 | 1.32 | 1.33 | 1.27 | 1.24 | 1.20 | 1.28 | 1.23 | 1.14 |
| I_S | 1.23 | 1.27 | 1.23 | 1.33 | 1.32 | 1.33 | 1.27 | 1.24 | 1.20 | 1.28 | 1.23 | 1.14 |
| NFM | 1.23 | 1.27 | 1.23 | 1.33 | 1.32 | 1.33 | 1.27 | 1.24 | 1.20 | 1.28 | 1.23 | 1.14 |
| FMP | 1.23 | 1.27 | 1.23 | 1.33 | 1.32 | 1.33 | 1.27 | 1.24 | 1.20 | 1.28 | 1.23 | 1.14 |
| TRN | 1.01 | 1.26 | 1.01 | 1.31 | 1.31 | 1.31 | 1.14 | 1.03 | 1.03 | 1.17 | 1.01 | 1.05 |
| OME | 1.01 | 1.26 | 1.01 | 1.31 | 1.31 | 1.31 | 1.14 | 1.03 | 1.03 | 1.17 | 1.01 | 1.05 |
| OMF | 1.01 | 1.26 | 1.01 | 1.31 | 1.31 | 1.31 | 1.14 | 1.03 | 1.03 | 1.17 | 1.01 | 1.05 |
| EGW | 1.23 | 1.27 | 1.23 | 1.33 | 1.32 | 1.33 | 1.27 | 1.24 | 1.20 | 1.28 | 1.23 | 1.14 |
| CNS | 1.23 | 1.27 | 1.23 | 1.33 | 1.32 | 1.33 | 1.27 | 1.24 | 1.20 | 1.28 | 1.23 | 1.14 |
| T_T | 1.20 | 1.27 | 1.20 | 1.33 | 1.32 | 1.33 | 1.25 | 1.21 | 1.18 | 1.27 | 1.20 | 1.13 |
| OSP | 1.29 | 1.27 | 1.29 | 1.33 | 1.32 | 1.33 | 1.30 | 1.29 | 1.24 | 1.31 | 1.29 | 1.16 |
| OSG | 1.23 | 1.27 | 1.23 | 1.33 | 1.32 | 1.33 | 1.27 | 1.24 | 1.20 | 1.28 | 1.23 | 1.14 |
| DWE | 1.23 | 1.27 | 1.23 | 1.33 | 1.32 | 1.33 | 1.27 | 1.24 | 1.20 | 1.28 | 1.23 | 1.14 |

share of commodity $i$; and $\omega$ is the Frisch parameter, that is, minus the reciprocal of the marginal utility of income, or the money flexibility.

The values chosen for $\omega$ were taken from Zeitsch et al. (1991) for the SALTER regions in GTAP. For the other regions in GTAP the following values were employed: (1) for China and Taiwan $\omega = -5$; (2) for Hong Kong $\omega = -4$; (3) for Argentina, Brazil, and Mexico $\omega = -3$; and (4) for the six composite regions we used weighted average values of $\omega$ based on known regions in GTAP (see Chapter 3 for the relevant weights). The subsequent values for the uncompensated own price elasticities of demand, based on the GTAP data set, are reported in Table 4.3. To calibrate the CDE expenditure function, we need compensated elasticities, $v_{ii}$, which can be derived as follows:

$$v_{ii} = \varepsilon_{ii} + s_i \eta_i. \tag{4.2}$$

## III    CDE private household preferences

This section discusses the specification of consumption demands for the private household in GTAP. This involves three issues: choosing a functional form for the underlying utility or expenditure function, selecting values for income and price elasticities of demand (discussed in the previous section), and calibrating the model to income and price elasticities. The functional form chosen must satisfy theoretical restrictions and be analytically tractable, and the elasticity values should be consistent with empirical evidence. The first restriction means that we have to choose a functional form from the family of well-known functions: Cobb–Douglas, constant elasticity of substitution (CES), linear expenditure system (LES) (Stone 1954), constant ratios of elasticities homothetic (CRESH) (Hanoch 1971), the translog, and others.

A Cobb–Douglas utility function implies unitary uncompensated own-price and income elasticities. This property is not supported by empirical evidence and it would lead to biased results for many AGE simulations. The CES relaxes the assumption of unitary uncompensated own-price elasticities, but its income elasticities are unitary, since, like the Cobb–Douglas, it is a homothetic utility function. A homothetic utility function implies that average household budget shares spent on various commodities are independent of total expenditures.[1] Such a property is hard to justify given the evidence that, for example, the share of food expenditures tends to decline with total expenditures. For example, the US spends less than 10% on food, and Israel spends about 25% (Putnam and Allshouse 1993, p. 139).

The LES of demand equations is based on the Klein–Rubin utility function (Klein and Rubin 1948–1949), which represents nonhomothetic preferences; therefore, its income elasticities are not unitary. However, its marginal budget shares are constant with respect to the level of expenditure.[2] This property is

**Table 4.3. GTAP Own Price Elasticities of Demand**

| | AUS | NZL | CAN | US | JPN | KOR | EU | IDN | MYS | PHL | SGP | THA |
|---|---|---|---|---|---|---|---|---|---|---|---|---|
| PDR | -0.1370 | -0.0398 | -0.1026 | -0.1081 | -0.0405 | -0.0926 | -0.0966 | -0.0964 | -0.0412 | -0.0381 | -0.0571 | -0.0191 |
| WHT | -0.0685 | -0.0398 | -0.0513 | -0.0541 | -0.0405 | -0.0926 | -0.0484 | -0.2022 | -0.0593 | -0.0953 | -0.0190 | -0.0953 |
| GRO | -0.0685 | -0.0398 | -0.0513 | -0.0541 | -0.0405 | -0.0309 | -0.0484 | -0.0201 | -0.0326 | -0.0385 | -0.0191 | -0.0191 |
| NGC | -0.0695 | -0.0405 | -0.0523 | -0.0546 | -0.0415 | -0.0361 | -0.0489 | -0.0298 | -0.0204 | -0.0233 | -0.0241 | -0.0224 |
| WOL | -0.3288 | -0.1913 | -0.2462 | -0.2595 | -0.1943 | -0.1482 | -0.2319 | -0.0914 | -0.0914 | -0.0914 | -0.0914 | -0.0914 |
| OLP | -0.3306 | -0.1920 | -0.2471 | -0.2600 | -0.1950 | -0.1508 | -0.2353 | -0.0982 | -0.0985 | -0.0969 | -0.1043 | -0.1025 |
| FOR | -0.7877 | -0.4662 | -0.5649 | -0.5894 | -0.4534 | -0.3691 | -0.5464 | -0.2386 | -0.2352 | -0.2363 | -0.2344 | -0.2481 |
| FSH | -0.7882 | -0.4662 | -0.5642 | -0.5893 | -0.4563 | -0.3797 | -0.5467 | -0.2599 | -0.2715 | -0.2971 | -0.2425 | -0.2559 |
| COL | -0.7877 | -0.4663 | -0.5641 | -0.5893 | -0.4534 | -0.3792 | -0.5465 | -0.2343 | -0.2343 | -0.2343 | -0.2343 | -0.2343 |
| OIL | -0.7878 | -0.4662 | -0.5641 | -0.5892 | -0.4535 | -0.3673 | -0.5463 | -0.2343 | -0.2344 | -0.2343 | -0.2359 | -0.2343 |
| GAS | -0.7877 | -0.4662 | -0.5662 | -0.5892 | -0.4535 | -0.3673 | -0.5464 | -0.2348 | -0.2382 | -0.2379 | -0.2343 | -0.2343 |
| OMN | -0.7877 | -0.4662 | -0.5642 | -0.5893 | -0.4534 | -0.3673 | -0.5460 | -0.2343 | -0.2344 | -0.2356 | -0.2344 | -0.2345 |
| PCR | -0.2742 | -0.0797 | -0.2052 | -0.2163 | -0.0830 | -0.2051 | -0.1935 | -0.2875 | -0.0835 | -0.0966 | -0.1159 | -0.0430 |
| MET | -0.2097 | -0.0459 | -0.1425 | -0.0720 | -0.2900 | -0.2586 | -0.1692 | -0.1857 | -0.0776 | -0.1525 | -0.1103 | -0.0981 |
| MIL | -0.0698 | -0.0408 | -0.0528 | -0.0548 | -0.2050 | -0.3385 | -0.0500 | -0.2568 | -0.0792 | -0.1022 | -0.0802 | -0.1064 |
| OFP | -0.1447 | -0.1118 | -0.0937 | -0.0855 | -0.3450 | -0.3232 | -0.0895 | -0.2237 | -0.1761 | -0.2744 | -0.1386 | -0.2191 |
| B_T | -0.6597 | -0.3966 | -0.4722 | -0.4902 | -0.3792 | -0.3003 | -0.4516 | -0.1953 | -0.1874 | -0.1995 | -0.1707 | -0.1922 |
| TEX | -0.6620 | -0.3948 | -0.4960 | -0.5211 | -0.3921 | -0.3042 | -0.4782 | -0.1922 | -0.2072 | -0.1903 | -0.2332 | -0.1972 |
| WAP | -0.6638 | -0.3953 | -0.5067 | -0.5293 | -0.4063 | -0.3168 | -0.4716 | -0.1855 | -0.1953 | -0.1968 | -0.2101 | -0.2419 |
| LEA | -0.6601 | -0.3871 | -0.4957 | -0.5216 | -0.3924 | -0.2992 | -0.4687 | -0.1847 | -0.1841 | -0.1856 | -0.2025 | -0.1920 |
| LUM | -0.7902 | -0.4729 | -0.5690 | -0.5922 | -0.4557 | -0.3702 | -0.5534 | -0.2400 | -0.2408 | -0.2388 | -0.2484 | -0.2399 |

Table 4.3. GTAP Own Price Elasticities of Demand

| | AUS | NZL | CAN | US | JPN | KOR | EU | IDN | MYS | PHL | SGP | THA |
|---|---|---|---|---|---|---|---|---|---|---|---|---|
| PPP | -0.7907 | -0.4775 | -0.5713 | -0.5949 | -0.4576 | -0.3740 | -0.5521 | -0.2373 | -0.2482 | -0.2373 | -0.2478 | -0.2363 |
| P_C | -0.7961 | -0.4787 | -0.5734 | -0.6006 | -0.4566 | -0.3703 | -0.5634 | -0.2562 | -0.2725 | -0.2461 | -0.2655 | -0.2436 |
| CRP | -0.7926 | -0.4836 | -0.5726 | -0.5972 | -0.4673 | -0.3989 | -0.5568 | -0.2550 | -0.2938 | -0.2672 | -0.2683 | -0.2688 |
| NMM | -0.7881 | -0.4674 | -0.5652 | -0.5897 | -0.4546 | -0.3686 | -0.5477 | -0.2353 | -0.2374 | -0.2353 | -0.2355 | -0.2376 |
| I_S | -0.7877 | -0.4662 | -0.5641 | -0.5923 | -0.4535 | -0.3673 | -0.5462 | -0.2343 | -0.2344 | -0.2348 | -0.2344 | -0.2344 |
| NFM | -0.7877 | -0.4663 | -0.5641 | -0.5892 | -0.4544 | -0.3673 | -0.5464 | -0.2343 | -0.2344 | -0.2343 | -0.2394 | -0.2343 |
| FMP | -0.7888 | -0.4689 | -0.5652 | -0.5902 | -0.4549 | -0.3693 | -0.5476 | -0.2365 | -0.2380 | -0.2358 | -0.2391 | -0.2362 |
| TRN | -0.7401 | -0.4544 | -0.5500 | -0.5633 | -0.4260 | -0.3246 | -0.5152 | -0.2041 | -0.2621 | -0.1957 | -0.1965 | -0.2045 |
| OME | -0.7406 | -0.4557 | -0.5428 | -0.5547 | -0.4303 | -0.3402 | -0.5113 | -0.2037 | -0.2920 | -0.2069 | -0.2708 | -0.2180 |
| OMF | -0.7355 | -0.4427 | -0.5331 | -0.5504 | -0.4225 | -0.3242 | -0.5073 | -0.1944 | -0.2040 | -0.1958 | -0.2311 | -0.2044 |
| EGW | -0.7932 | -0.4807 | -0.5786 | -0.6058 | -0.4711 | -0.3806 | -0.5551 | -0.2430 | -0.2544 | -0.2500 | -0.2499 | -0.2453 |
| CNS | -0.7877 | -0.4673 | -0.5645 | -0.5892 | -0.4535 | -0.3673 | -0.5502 | -0.2343 | -0.2343 | -0.2348 | -0.2343 | -0.2371 |
| T_T | -0.8563 | -0.6135 | -0.7065 | -0.7073 | -0.6260 | -0.4946 | -0.6392 | -0.4829 | -0.3916 | -0.4614 | -0.4793 | -0.5117 |
| OSP | -0.8149 | -0.5710 | -0.6311 | -0.7299 | -0.6482 | -0.4960 | -0.6990 | -0.3788 | -0.2992 | -0.3071 | -0.3316 | -0.3723 |
| OSG | -0.8132 | -0.5232 | -0.5800 | -0.6419 | -0.5052 | -0.4236 | -0.5610 | -0.2651 | -0.2546 | -0.2701 | -0.2632 | -0.2602 |
| DWE | -0.8307 | -0.5575 | -0.6580 | -0.5894 | -0.4538 | -0.4235 | -0.6031 | -0.2353 | -0.2966 | -0.3046 | -0.2578 | -0.2348 |

Table 4.3. GTAP Own Price Elasticities of Demand

| | CHN | HKG | TWN | ARG | BRA | MEX | LAM | SSA | MNA | EIT | SAS | ROW |
|---|---|---|---|---|---|---|---|---|---|---|---|---|
| PDR | -0.0619 | -0.0500 | -0.0500 | -0.0333 | -0.0669 | -0.1000 | -0.0512 | -0.0716 | -0.0527 | -0.0423 | -0.0614 | -0.0561 |
| WHT | -0.0660 | -0.1000 | -0.0617 | -0.0333 | -0.1333 | -0.1333 | -0.1077 | -0.0724 | -0.0983 | -0.1102 | -0.0658 | -0.0660 |
| GRO | -0.0254 | -0.0250 | -0.0202 | -0.0334 | -0.0334 | -0.0348 | -0.0275 | -0.0277 | -0.0280 | -0.0268 | -0.0265 | -0.0385 |
| NGC | -0.0310 | -0.0270 | -0.0228 | -0.0363 | -0.0363 | -0.0364 | -0.0305 | -0.0260 | -0.0287 | -0.0257 | -0.0306 | -0.0391 |
| WOL | -0.0968 | -0.1200 | -0.0960 | -0.1600 | -0.1600 | -0.1601 | -0.1207 | -0.0983 | -0.1239 | -0.1193 | -0.0963 | -0.1841 |
| OLP | -0.1413 | -0.1281 | -0.0996 | -0.1615 | -0.1634 | -0.1656 | -0.1274 | -0.1276 | -0.1302 | -0.1217 | -0.1423 | -0.1861 |
| FOR | -0.2481 | -0.3178 | -0.2461 | -0.4434 | -0.4411 | -0.4452 | -0.3237 | -0.2548 | -0.3141 | -0.3182 | -0.2482 | -0.4393 |
| FSH | -0.2658 | -0.3277 | -0.2690 | -0.4435 | -0.4421 | -0.4469 | -0.3308 | -0.2767 | -0.3220 | -0.3201 | -0.2662 | -0.4405 |
| COL | -0.2530 | -0.3200 | -0.2460 | -0.4433 | -0.4400 | -0.4433 | -0.3199 | -0.2565 | -0.3118 | -0.3184 | -0.2532 | -0.4382 |
| OIL | -0.2460 | -0.3181 | -0.2460 | -0.4434 | -0.4400 | -0.4433 | -0.3181 | -0.2534 | -0.3091 | -0.3181 | -0.2460 | -0.4381 |
| GAS | -0.2460 | -0.3176 | -0.2460 | -0.4433 | -0.4421 | -0.4433 | -0.3190 | -0.2535 | -0.3091 | -0.3183 | -0.2460 | -0.4386 |
| OMN | -0.2460 | -0.3180 | -0.2462 | -0.4433 | -0.4400 | -0.4434 | -0.3186 | -0.2540 | -0.3094 | -0.3178 | -0.2460 | -0.4382 |
| PCR | -0.1139 | -0.1009 | -0.1067 | -0.0671 | -0.1366 | -0.2001 | -0.1082 | -0.1295 | -0.1202 | -0.0855 | -0.1138 | -0.1147 |
| MET | -0.1448 | -0.0982 | -0.1609 | -0.0665 | -0.2035 | -0.1606 | -0.1495 | -0.1459 | -0.1450 | -0.1304 | -0.1450 | -0.1865 |
| MIL | -0.1513 | -0.1372 | -0.1544 | -0.0358 | -0.1403 | -0.1605 | -0.1465 | -0.1386 | -0.1613 | -0.1195 | -0.1513 | -0.1385 |
| OFP | -0.2079 | -0.1619 | -0.2292 | -0.2187 | -0.3127 | -0.3105 | -0.2620 | -0.2233 | -0.2216 | -0.2466 | -0.2108 | -0.2395 |
| B_T | -0.2186 | -0.2834 | -0.2125 | -0.3703 | -0.3642 | -0.3687 | -0.2627 | -0.2152 | -0.2530 | -0.2543 | -0.2178 | -0.3616 |
| TEX | -0.2387 | -0.3119 | -0.1933 | -0.3473 | -0.3331 | -0.3318 | -0.2530 | -0.2208 | -0.2587 | -0.2511 | -0.2350 | -0.3738 |
| WAP | -0.2128 | -0.3433 | -0.2153 | -0.3413 | -0.3466 | -0.3386 | -0.2845 | -0.2124 | -0.2797 | -0.2544 | -0.2118 | -0.3938 |
| LEA | -0.1977 | -0.3255 | -0.1976 | -0.3284 | -0.3303 | -0.3296 | -0.2485 | -0.2012 | -0.2532 | -0.2452 | -0.1974 | -0.3747 |
| LUM | -0.2519 | -0.3278 | -0.2501 | -0.4502 | -0.4553 | -0.4523 | -0.3261 | -0.2581 | -0.3144 | -0.3262 | -0.2516 | -0.4432 |

Table 4.3. GTAP Own Price Elasticities of Demand

| | CHN | HKG | TWN | ARG | BRA | MEX | LAM | SSA | MNA | EIT | SAS | ROW |
|---|---|---|---|---|---|---|---|---|---|---|---|---|
| PPP | -0.2538 | -0.3270 | -0.2584 | -0.4530 | -0.4467 | -0.4489 | -0.3228 | -0.2585 | -0.3143 | -0.3277 | -0.2536 | -0.4442 |
| P_C | -0.2501 | -0.3331 | -0.2576 | -0.4813 | -0.4679 | -0.4452 | -0.3324 | -0.2615 | -0.3198 | -0.3386 | -0.2503 | -0.4478 |
| CRP | -0.2747 | -0.3537 | -0.2626 | -0.4853 | -0.4622 | -0.4696 | -0.3457 | -0.2770 | -0.3323 | -0.3377 | -0.2740 | -0.4535 |
| NMM | -0.2475 | -0.3187 | -0.2483 | -0.4450 | -0.4425 | -0.4500 | -0.3210 | -0.2546 | -0.3109 | -0.3199 | -0.2475 | -0.4399 |
| I_S | -0.2460 | -0.3177 | -0.2460 | -0.4433 | -0.4401 | -0.4434 | -0.3182 | -0.2534 | -0.3095 | -0.3199 | -0.2460 | -0.4394 |
| NFM | -0.2460 | -0.3238 | -0.2460 | -0.4433 | -0.4414 | -0.4441 | -0.3184 | -0.2534 | -0.3091 | -0.3182 | -0.2460 | -0.4386 |
| FMP | -0.2549 | -0.3210 | -0.2492 | -0.4531 | -0.4459 | -0.4470 | -0.3215 | -0.2596 | -0.3111 | -0.3207 | -0.2548 | -0.4404 |
| TRN | -0.2042 | -0.3166 | -0.2373 | -0.4677 | -0.4606 | -0.4500 | -0.3080 | -0.2188 | -0.2800 | -0.3143 | -0.2039 | -0.4250 |
| OME | -0.2637 | -0.4195 | -0.2274 | -0.4535 | -0.4648 | -0.4519 | -0.3142 | -0.2486 | -0.2848 | -0.3110 | -0.2584 | -0.4236 |
| OMF | -0.2023 | -0.3982 | -0.2073 | -0.4382 | -0.4486 | -0.4456 | -0.2982 | -0.2129 | -0.2739 | -0.2981 | -0.2022 | -0.4113 |
| EGW | -0.2528 | -0.3233 | -0.2711 | -0.4688 | -0.4519 | -0.4471 | -0.3318 | -0.2620 | -0.3242 | -0.3414 | -0.2528 | -0.4560 |
| CNS | -0.2460 | -0.3176 | -0.2460 | -0.4434 | -0.4400 | -0.4434 | -0.3192 | -0.2535 | -0.3101 | -0.3204 | -0.2460 | -0.4386 |
| T_T | -0.3221 | -0.4295 | -0.4694 | -0.5433 | -0.5975 | -0.7025 | -0.5427 | -0.3971 | -0.5375 | -0.5311 | -0.3264 | -0.6145 |
| OSP | -0.2880 | -0.3424 | -0.3243 | -0.6615 | -0.5756 | -0.5533 | -0.4351 | -0.3063 | -0.4301 | -0.5641 | -0.2883 | -0.5985 |
| OSG | -0.2856 | -0.3185 | -0.3053 | -0.4439 | -0.4408 | -0.4743 | -0.3454 | -0.2798 | -0.3580 | -0.3781 | -0.2863 | -0.4840 |
| DWE | -0.2793 | -0.3330 | -0.3609 | -0.4437 | -0.5050 | -0.4436 | -0.3550 | -0.2830 | -0.3499 | -0.3627 | -0.2790 | -0.4562 |

not supported by the empirical evidence presented by Rimmer and Powell (1992), who have found that marginal budget shares vary with income. In particular, when those authors examined demand patterns over different levels of economic development, they found that the marginal budget shares of certain goods (e.g., food, beverages and tobacco, and clothing) decline with per capita income, while for other goods (e.g., household furnishings, rent, and fuel), the marginal budget shares increase with per capita income. Under these circumstances, use of the LES of demand would limit an AGE model's ability to depict accurately household behavior in simulations that result in significant household expenditure changes.

For GTAP, we choose the CDE functional form for the expenditure function. The CDE expenditure function was introduced by Hanoch (1978), who discussed models that were more general than the CES but less general than a flexible functional form, for example, the translog.[3] The CDE is based on the assumption of implicit additivity, which, in the case of $N$ commodities, constrains the symmetric $N{\times}N$ matrix of elasticities of substitution to depend on only $N$ parameters. The CDE also allows for a richer representation of income effects in the demand system. In particular, marginal budget shares may vary with expenditure levels. Calibration of the CDE expenditure function requires data on average budget shares and on income and own-price elasticities of demand for all commodities, as noted above. Calibration procedures are straightforward; however, it is possible that the prespecified information may be inconsistent or may not fit the CDE expenditure function model. In such cases some compromise must be reached. This will be discussed in the section on calibration, below.

### Theoretical development of the CDE

In general, an expenditure function can be represented in the following manner:

$$E = G(p,u) = \{\min p'x{:}f(x){\geq}u\}, \tag{4.3}$$

where $p$ and $x$ are $N$-dimensional vectors of prices and demands, $u$ is utility, and $E$ is minimum expenditure. The function $f(\cdot)$ represents utility, and $G(\cdot)$ is the minimum expenditure function. Function $G(\cdot)$ is homogeneous of degree 1 in prices, allowing the following normalization of prices and expenditure by minimum expenditure:

$$G(E^{-1}p,u) = G(z,u) \equiv 1, \tag{4.4}$$

where the $z$'s are the normalized prices. To obtain the CDE expenditure function, Hanoch (1975) restricts the number of substitution effects to $N$ by imposing additivity in the normalized prices. The implicit function proposed takes the form:

$$G(z,u) = \sum_{i=1}^{N} B_i u^{e_i b_i} z_i^{b_i} \equiv 1, \qquad (4.5)$$

where the $b_i$'s are the $N$ parameters, which determine substitution possibilities among commodities in consumption; the $e_i$'s are $N$ expansion parameters, which appear owing to nonhomotheticity in consumption; and the $B_i$'s are scale parameters necessary to specify the function. It is required that $B_i > 0$ and $e_i > 0$, and $b_i < 1$, with either $0 < b_i < 1$ or $b_i < 0$ for all $i$ (Hertel et al. 1991).

If the substitution parameters are rewritten as $\alpha_i = 1 - b_i$, the Allen partial elasticities of substitution can be expressed as:

$$\sigma_{ij} = \alpha_i + \alpha_j - \sum_k s_k \alpha_k - \frac{\delta_{ij}\alpha_i}{s_i}, \qquad (4.6)$$

where $\delta_{ii} = 1$, and $\delta_{ij} = 0$ for $i \neq j$, and the $s_i$'s are expenditure shares. The name *constant difference in elasticities* arises due to the fact that the difference between the elasticities of substitution $\sigma_{ij}$ and $\sigma_{ih}$ is invariant to index $i$ (Hertel et al. 1994):

$$(\sigma_{ij} - \sigma_{ih}) = (\alpha_j - \alpha_h). \qquad (4.7)$$

The expressions for income elasticities of demand are:

$$\eta_i = \left( \sum_k s_k e_k \right)^{-1} \left[ e_i(1-\alpha_i) + \sum_k s_k e_k \alpha_k \right] + \left( \alpha_i - \sum_k s_k \alpha_k \right), \qquad (4.8)$$

and the expressions for compensated own-price elasticities of demand are:

$$-v_{ij} = -s_i \left[ 2\alpha_i - \sum_k \alpha_k s_k - \alpha_i / s_i \right]. \qquad (4.9)$$

### Calibration of the CDE

The income and uncompensated own-price elasticities of private household demand used in GTAP derive from a variety of sources, *none* of which involve econometric estimation using the CDE form. This is a common difficulty when choosing elasticities for AGE models. That is, the functional forms used in the econometric studies from which estimates are drawn do not correspond to the functional forms specified in the model. Furthermore, the sample period used in estimation may not include the benchmark equilibrium year. Finally, econometric studies are based on consumer goods prices, whereas AGE models typically evaluate consumption at producer prices. These divergences cause difficulty, as not all sets of income and own-price elasticities will be representable via the CDE functional form, evaluated at 1992 producer prices.

The problem can be seen clearly for the consumption budget shares and own-price elasticities shown at the top of Table 4.4. These are derived from

Table 4.4. *A 3X3 Example of the CDE*

| | USA | EU | ROW |
|---|---|---|---|
| | Consumption Shares | | |
| Foods | 0.082048 | 0.151911 | 0.212457 |
| Manufactures | 0.173766 | 0.200349 | 0.198768 |
| Services | 0.744186 | 0.64774 | 0.588775 |
| | Own-Price Elasticities | | |
| Foods | -0.172441 | -0.177254 | -0.149364 |
| Manufactures | -0.547482 | -0.501926 | -0.31344 |
| Services | -0.428958 | -0.418842 | -0.282822 |
| | $\alpha_i$ Parameters Derived by Solving Equation (4.9) | | |
| Foods | -0.40 | -0.23 | -0.10 |
| Manufactures | -0.80 | 0.09 | 0.20 |
| Services | 8.51 | 3.46 | 1.60 |

a three-region, three-commodity aggregation of GTAP (see Chapter 5 for details on aggregation). The $\alpha_i$ parameters derived by solving equation (4.9) for each region are also given in Table 4.4. Plainly, none of these sets of values satisfies the requirement that $0 < \alpha_i < 1$ for all $i$. Therefore, a procedure must be formulated that, for any set of *target* income and own-price elasticities, determines values of the CDE parameters that yield *model* income and own-price elasticities sufficiently close to the target income and own-price elasticities. This section describes such a calibration procedure for determining CDE parameters.

It is evident from the outset that certain aspects of this calibration procedure, such as the choice of a measure of "closeness," will be, to some extent, arbitrary. Another element of choice is the weight to be given to deviations of own-price elasticities from target values as compared with income elasticities. In the case of the CDE functional form, a "natural" choice in this regard is suggested by equations (4.8) and (4.9), relating elasticities to CDE parameters. The own-price elasticities are determined by the $\alpha_i$ parameters, while the income elasticities depend on both $\alpha_i$ and $e_i$ parameters. Thus the procedure adopted was to determine $\alpha_i$'s to ensure closeness of the own-price elasticities implied by equation (4.9) with target elasticities, and to use these $\alpha_i$'s in equation (4.8) when determining an appropriate set of $e_i$ parameters.

The calibration procedure for CDE parameters entails solving two constrained minimization problems. The first determines the CDE $\alpha_i$ parameters by seeking a good fit to the target own-price elasticities. The second, taking the $\alpha_i$ values from the first as given, determines the $e_i$ parameters by seeking a good fit to the target income elasticities. The constraints imposed are of two types. First are those on CDE parameters required for the regularity of the CDE form. Second is the requirement that income elasticities are greater than (less than) or equal to 1 if the corresponding targets are greater than (less than) 1. This latter constraint ensures that goods that were superior (inferior) as represented by the target elasticities remain so after calibration.

The constrained minimization problem for determining the CDE $\alpha_i$ parameters can be represented formally as: given $v_{ii}^{\text{target}}$, choose $v_{ii}$, and $\alpha_i$ to minimize:

$$\sum_i v_{ii}[\log_e(v_{ii}/v_{ii}^{\text{target}}) - 1] \qquad (4.10)$$

subject to $0.01 \leq \alpha_i \leq 0.99$, and equation (4.9), where $v_{ii}^{\text{target}}$ = target-compensated own-price elasticities; $v_{ii}$ = compensated own-price elasticities arising from calibration; $\alpha_i$ = CDE substitution parameters arising from calibration.

The regularity requirement that $0 < \alpha_i < 1$ has been replaced by the inequality constraint shown. Otherwise the problem may not have a solution if the objective function attained its minimum on the boundary of the region $\{\alpha_i: 0 < \alpha_i < 1$ for all $i\}$. The objective function is strictly convex, and the feasible region convex, so a unique minimum exists.

The constrained minimization for determining the CDE $e_i$ parameters can be represented formally as: given $\eta_i^{\text{target}}$, choose $\eta_i$, and $e_i$ to minimize:

$$\sum_i s_i(\eta_i - \eta_i^{\text{target}})^2 \qquad (4.11)$$

subject to equation (4.8),

$$0.01 \leq e_i, \sum_i s_i\eta_i = 1, \text{ and } (\eta_i - 1) * (\eta_i^{\text{target}} - 1) \geq 0,$$

where $\eta_i^{\text{target}}$ = target income elasticities; $\eta_i$ = income elasticities resulting from calibration; and $e_i$ = CDE expansion parameters resulting from calibration.

The regularity requirement that $e_i > 0$ has been replaced by the inequality constraint shown, for the same reason that the regularity condition on the $\alpha_i$ was altered in the first minimization. It should be noted that the second constraint ensures that the income elasticities derived as the solution to this minimization will satisfy the Engel condition. The third constraint ensures that the calibrated income elasticities lie on the same side of one as the target elasticities.

Although many software packages exist in which these constrained minimizations could be formulated and solved with ease, they have been implemented in GEMPACK. This has been done to ensure that GTAP users do not require access to any other software in order to perform the entire range of operations, from data aggregation to printing of simulation results.

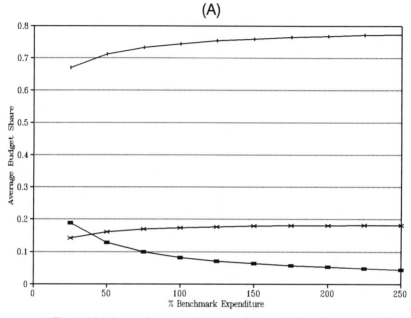

**Figure 4.1** (*above and opposite*). Behavior of average budget shares as expenditure increases in *USA*: (A) average; (B) marginal.

## Performance of the CDE implicit expenditure function

We now examine the behavior of the average and marginal budget shares, and income elasticities of demand, as the level of expenditure in each region varies from the benchmarklevels. Using the calibrated parameters for the 3x3 model (including the scale parameters ($B_i$'s)) and equation (4.5), utility levels are computed using a range of 25–250% of the benchmark level of expenditure for each region. Once per capita utility has been calculated, demands for each good in each region are computed using the following equation:

$$x_i = \frac{B_i b_i u^{b_i e_i} z_i^{b_i - 1}}{\displaystyle\sum_{k=1}^{N} B_k b_k u^{b_k e_k} z_k^{b_k}} \quad i = 1...N. \tag{4.12}$$

Average budget shares are computed by using the following formula:

$$s_i = \frac{p_i x_i}{\displaystyle\sum_{k=1}^{3} p_k x_k}. \tag{4.13}$$

The income elasticities are computed using equation (4.8). Finally, the marginal budget shares are computed using:

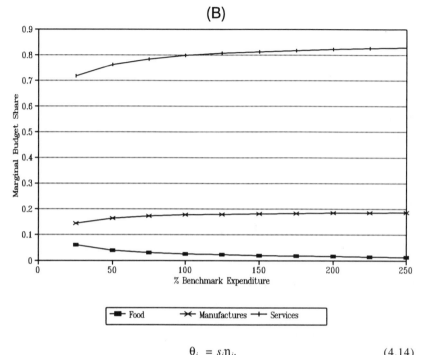

$$\theta_i = s_i \eta_i. \tag{4.14}$$

Figure 4.1 shows plots of the average (panel *a*) and marginal (panel *b*) budget shares for the US; Figures 4.2*a* and *b* and 4.3*a* and *b* display average and marginal budget shares for the EU and the rest of the world (ROW), respectively. As total expenditure increases, the average budget shares for services and manufactured goods increase in all three regions. As the economies grow, the demand for these goods grows. The average budget shares for food decline as the level of expenditure increases in all regions. This decline is greatest for food in the US.

Notice that as expenditure increases, the marginal budget shares for services and manufactures grow in all regions, but both are quite flat for the US. In the EU and ROW the marginal shares for services also change relatively little as incomes grow. The marginal budget shares for food decline gradually for all three regions. This behavior agrees with the results of Rimmer and Powell (1992) for food in Australia. As the economy grows, households spend a smaller proportion of marginal increases in income on food.

Figure 4.4*a–c* shows the behavior of the income elasticities as expenditure increases in each region. These elasticities decline in all regions for all three goods as income increases. This result coincides with prior beliefs about the income responsiveness of demand as wealth increases. In sum, the CDE

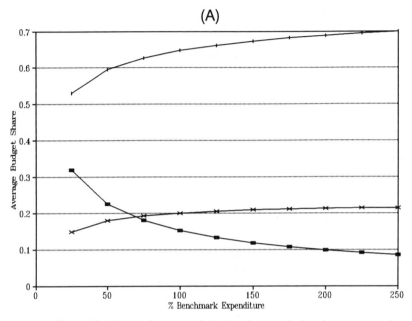

**Figure 4.2** (*above and opposite*). Behavior of average budget shares as expenditure increases in *EU*: (A) average; (B) marginal.

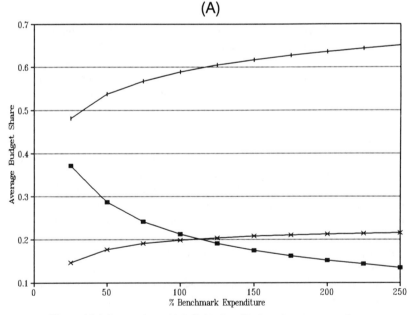

**Figure 4.3** (*above and opposite*). Behavior of budget shares as expenditure increases in *ROW*: (A) average; (B) marginal.

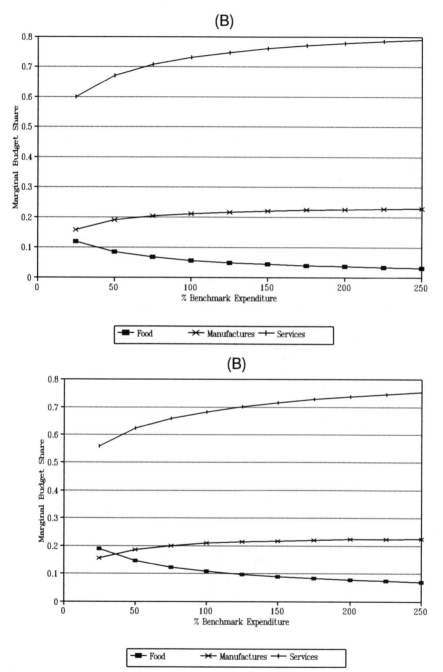

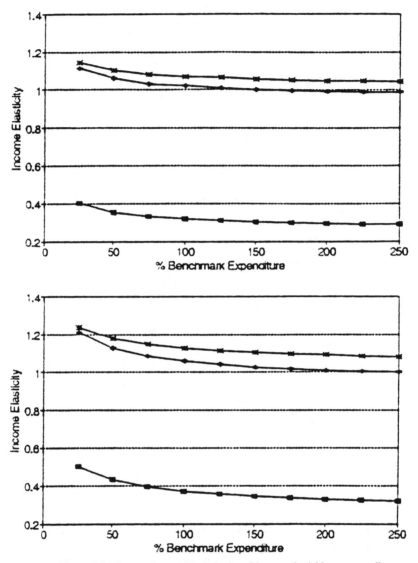

**Figure 4.4** (*above and opposite*). Behavior of income elasticities as expenditure increases: (top) *USA*; (bottom) *EU*; (opposite) *ROW*.

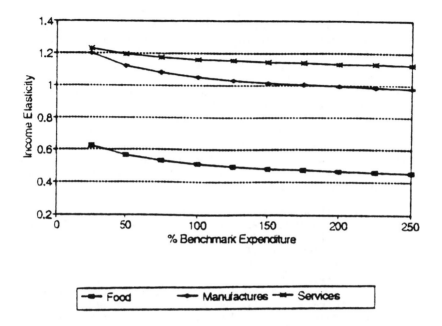

expenditure function appears to behave satisfactorily under a growth scenario. As such, it appears to be a good choice for modeling household preferences.

## NOTES

1. By *average household budget shares*, we mean $p_i x_i / E$, where $p_i$ and $x_i$ are the price and quantity demanded, respectively, for commodity $i$, and $E$ is total expenditure.
2. By *marginal budget shares*, we mean $p_i \partial x_i / \partial E$.
3. The term *flexible functional form* is usually used for those forms that provide a second-order approximation at a point to the true function (Fuss, McFadden, and Mundlak 1978).

## REFERENCES

Codsi, G., and K. R. Pearson (1988) "GEMPACK: General-Purpose Software for Applied General Equilibrium and Other Economic Modelers," *Computer Science in Economics and Management* 1:189–207.

Dixon, P. B., B. R. Parmenter, J. Sutton, and D. P. Vincent (1982) *ORANI: A Multisectoral Model of the Australian Economy.* Amsterdam: North-Holland.

Food and Agriculture Organization (1993) "World Food Model," Supplement to the *FAO Agricultural Projections to 2000,* Rome.

Frisch, R. (1959) "A Complete Scheme for Computing All Direct and Cross Elasticities in a Model with Many Sectors," *Econometrica* 27:177–196.

Fuss, M., D. McFadden, and Y. Mundlak (1978) "A Survey of Functional Forms in the Economic Analysis of Production." In M. Fuss and D. McFadden (eds.), *Production Economics: A Dual Approach to Theory and Applications*. Amsterdam: North-Holland.

Hanoch, G. (1971) "CRESH Production Functions," *Econometrica* 39(September):695–712.

Hanoch, G. (1975) "Production and Demand Models with Direct or Indirect Implicit Additivity," *Econometrica* 43:395–419.

Hanoch, G. (1978) "Polar Functions with Constant Two Factors–One Price Elasticities." In M. Fuss and D. McFadden (eds.), *Production Economics: A Dual Approach to Theory and Applications*. Amsterdam: North-Holland.

Hertel, T. W., J. M. Horridge, and K. R. Pearson (1991) "Mending the Family Tree: A Reconciliation of the Linearization and Levels Schools of CGE Modelling," Impact Project Preliminary Working Paper No. IP-54, Australian Industry Commission and Monash University, June.

Hertel, T. W., J. M. Horridge, and K. R. Pearson (1992) "Mending the Family Tree: A Reconciliation of the Linearization and Levels Schools of AGE Modelling," *Economic Modeling* 9:385–407.

Hertel, T. W., E. B. Peterson, P. V. Preckel, Y. Surry, and M. E. Tsigas (1991) "Implicit Additivity as a Strategy for Restricting the Parameter Space in CGE Models," *Economic and Financial Computing* 1(1):265–289.

Jomini, P., J. F. Zeitsch, R. McDougall, A. Welsh, S. Brown, J. Hambley, and J. Kelly (1991) SALTER: *A General Equilibrium Model of the World Economy, Vol. 1. Model Structure, Database and Parameters*. Canberra, Australia: Industry Commission.

Keller, W. J. (1980) *Tax Incidence: A General Equilibrium Approach*. Amsterdam: North-Holland.

Klein, L. R., and H. Rubin (1948–49) "A Constant Utility Index of the Cost of Living," *Review of Economic Studies* 15:84–87.

Lluch, C., A. A. Powell, and R. A. Williams (1977) *Patterns in Household Demand and Savings*. New York: Oxford University Press.

Putnam, J. J., and J. E. Allshouse (1993) *Food Consumption, Prices, and Expenditures, 1970–92*, Statistical Bulletin No. 867, Commodity Economics Division, Economic Research Service, USDA, Washington, DC, September.

Rimmer, M. T., and A. A. Powell (1992) "Demand Patterns Across the Development Spectrum: Estimates of the AIDADS System," Impact Project Preliminary Working Paper No. OP-75, Australian Industry Commission and Monash University.

Stone, R. (1954) "Linear Expenditure System and Demand Analysis: An Application to the British Pattern of Demand," *Economic Journal* 64(255):511–532.

Theil, H., C. F. Chung, and J. L. Seale, Jr. (1989) "International Evidence on Consumption Patterns," Supplement 1 to *Advances in Econometrics*. Greenwich, CT: JAI Press.

Zeitsch, J., R. McDougall, P. Jomini, A. Welsh, J. Hambley, S. Brown, and J. Kelly (1991) "SALTER: A General Equilibrium Model of the World Economy," SALTER Working Paper No. 4. Canberra, Australia: Industries Assistance Commission, January.

CHAPTER 5

# Aggregation and computation
# of equilibrium elasticities

*Thomas W. Hertel, D. Kent Lanclos, Kenneth R. Pearson, and Padma V. Swaminathan*

## I    Introduction and overview

The Global Trade Analysis Project (GTAP) benchmark data and parameters are specified for 37 commodities and 24 regions. Due to the size of this data set, an aggregated version of the data base and parameters will be desired for most GTAP simulations. The precise dimensions of each aggregation will depend on the problem at hand. Experienced users tend to favor strategic aggregations that allow them to focus on key sectors and regions of interest. This makes the job of sorting through the simulation results less daunting. For teaching purposes, we usually begin with the three-region, three-commodity (3x3) aggregation referred to in Chapters 2 and 4. Section II introduces you to the GTAP aggregation facility that created this 3x3 data set. We will also examine some of the key value flows, as well as the full parameter file. In section III, local behavior of the 3x3 model will be examined through the use of general equilibrium demand elasticities. This offers a valuable summary of the interaction between theory, data, and parameters in the model.

## II    Aggregation of the GTAP data

The user specifies the desired aggregation of the GTAP data base by filling in a *template* file.[1] This involves defining names for the aggregated commodities and associating them with disaggregate GTAP commodity categories, then doing the same for regions. Figure 5.1 presents the aggregation template file for the 3x3 aggregation used in this chapter. In part 1 of this file, we define the three aggregated tradeable commodities, which are denoted as *food* (food and agriculture), *mnfcs* (resources and manufacturing), and *svces* (services). In Part 2, these are linked with the 37 individual commodities in the GTAP data base. Parts 3 and 4 of the template file accomplish the same thing for regions. In this case, *USA* and European Union (*EU*) are left

149

```
! 1. AGGREGATED COMMODITIES
!    In this section, the user fills in:
!        a) short names
!        b) (optional) explanatory text
!   NAME        |   Explanatory Text
!               |   (Rest of line)
= = = = = = = = = = = = = = = = = = = = = =
food                & food and agriculture
mnfcs               & resources and manufactures
svces               & all services
= = = = = = = = = = = = = = = = = = = = = = = = =
! 2. COMMODITY AGGREGATION MAPPING
!    In this section the user fills in the short name of
!    the appropriate aggregated commodity (from the previous
!    list) for each GTAP commodity.
!
!     GTAP COMMODITY    |   Aggregated Commodity
= = = = = = = = = = = = = = = = = = = = = = = = = = = = =
pdr, paddy rice                     & food
wht, wheat                          & food
gro, grains                         & food
ngc, nongrain crops                 & food
wol, wool                           & food
olp, other livestock                & food
for, forestry                       & mnfcs
fsh, fisheries                      & mnfcs
col, coal                           & mnfcs
oil, oil                            & mnfcs
gas, gas                            & mnfcs
omn, other minerals                 & mnfcs
pcr, processed rice                 & food
met, meat products                  & food
mil, milk products                  & food
ofp, other food products            & food
b_t, beverages and tobacco          & food
tex, textiles                       & mnfcs
wap, wearing apparel                & mnfcs
lea, leather etc.                   & mnfcs
lum, lumber                         & mnfcs
ppp, pulp, paper, etc.              & mnfcs
p_c, petroleum and coal             & mnfcs
crp, chemicals, rubbers, and plastics   & mnfcs
nmm, nonmetallic minerals           & mnfcs
i_s, primary ferrous metals         & mnfcs
nfm, nonferrous metals              & mnfcs
fmp, fabricated metal products      & mnfcs
trn, transport industries           & mnfcs
ome, machinery and equipment        & mnfcs
omf, other manufacturing            & mnfcs
egw, electricity, water, and gas    & svces
cns, construction                   & svces
t_t, trade and transport            & svces
osp, other services (private)       & svces
osg, other services (govt)          & svces
dwe, ownership of dwellings         & svces
= = = = = = = = = = = = = = = = = = = = = = = = =
```

**Figure 5.1.** Template file for the 3x3 aggregation.

```
!
! 3. AGGREGATED REGIONS
!   In this section, the user fills in:
!
!       a) NAMES
!       b) (optional) explanatory text
!
!               |   Explanatory Text
! NAME          |   (Rest of line)
= = = = = = = = = = = = = = = = = = = = = = =
  USA           &   United States of America
  EU            &   European Union
  ROW  &  Rest of the World
= = = = = = = = = = = = = = = = = = = = = = = =
!
! 4. REGIONAL AGGREGATION MAPPING
!
!   In this section, the user fills in the short
!   name for the aggregated region to which each
!   of the GTAP regions belongs.
!
!   GTAP REGION   |   Aggregated Region
= = = = = = = = = = = = = = = = = = = = = = = = = = = = =
  AUS   Australia                       &  ROW
  NZL   New Zealand                     &  ROW
  CAN   Canada                          &  ROW
  USA   United States of America        &  USA
  JPN   Japan                           &  ROW
  KOR   Republic of Korea               &  ROW
  EU    European Union                  &  EU
  IDN   Indonesia                       &  ROW
  MYS   Malaysia                        &  ROW
  PHL   Philippines                     &  ROW
  SGP   Singapore                       &  ROW
  THA   Thailand                        &  ROW
  CHN   China                           &  ROW
  HKG   Hong Kong                       &  ROW
  TWN   Taiwan                          &  ROW
  ARG   Argentina                       &  ROW
  BRA   Brazil                          &  ROW
  MEX   Mexico                          &  ROW
  LAM   Rest of Latin America           &  ROW
  SSA   Sub Saharan Africa              &  ROW
  MNA   Middle East and North Africa    &  ROW
  EIT   Economies In Transition         &  ROW
  SAS   South Asia                      &  ROW
  ROW   Rest of World                   &  ROW
```

**Figure 5.1.** (*Continued*) Template file for the 3x3 aggregation.

disaggregated, while all other regions are lumped together in the rest of the world (*ROW*). Since this file is the definitive statement of what is in each composite category, it is always provided with any aggregation of the data base.

### Aggregation of value flows

Aggregation of value flows in the benchmark data involves the simple summation of appropriate component elements. For example, disaggregate consumer expenditures for agricultural and processed food products are summed to obtain total consumer expenditures for the aggregate category, food. Similarly, when aggregating regions, consumer expenditures for each commodity are summed across disaggregate regions. For variables that are source-specific (e.g., trade flows), the regional aggregation also aggregates across these sources.

Even the 3x3 aggregation results in a sizeable data set. Tables 5.2 and 5.3 present *portions* of this data base. In Table 5.1, the disposition of domestic output in the US is presented. At the top of the table the value of output at domestic market prices is presented for each of the aggregate traded commodities. The next three lines break out domestic and export sales, as well as sales to the global transport sector. Since the latter entry (VST) comprises only trade and transport services, it is equal to zero for food and manufactures. Part II of this table reports the breakdown of exports across destinations. Note that there is no intraregional trade for an individual country such as *USA*.

Part III of Table 5.1 decomposes domestic sales into those destined for private and government households and intermediate inputs. The bulk of manufactured goods are sold to other firms, while sales to households constitute a majority of the food and services output in the US. Intermediate sales are broken out at the bottom of Table 5.4. At this level of aggregation, own-use of inputs is very important. Indeed, the bulk of farm and food intermediate sales takes place within the food sector, as defined by the aggregation template in Figure 5.1. This is followed by sales to the services sector. The manufacturing and services sectors are important purchasers of one another's outputs. These sectors also supply virtually all the inputs to the capital goods (investment) sector.

Table 5.2 shows the sources and uses of imports, at domestic market prices, in the *USA* region. At the top of this table, imports sourced from the three regions of origin are reported. Again, the absence of intraregional trade at the national level is noted. The bulk of US imports is shown to be sourced from the composite, ROW region. The sum of imports from all sources, VIM, is reported in the next line of Table 5.2. Note that manufacturing imports exceed imports of food or services by an order of magnitude. This line is followed by the disposition of imports across households and intermediates uses within the *USA* region. The majority of trade is shown to take place in intermediate goods. Finally, the breakdown of imports for intermediate use by individual sector is shown in part II of Table 5.2.

*Aggregation of parameters*

Aggregation of behavioral parameters of the model is more involved than aggregation of value flows. The relevant behavioral parameters are the uncompensated own-price and income elasticities of demand, the elasticities of

**Table 5.1.** *Disposition of Domestic Output in the US: 3x3 Aggregation*

|  | i = food | i = mnfcs | i = svces |
|---|---|---|---|
| **I. Domestic Output** | | | |
| $VOM(i,USA)$[a] | **663,932**[b] | **2,856,656** | **6,548,007** |
| = $VDM(i,USA)$ | 615,418 | 2,480,245 | 6,395,376 |
| + $\sum_{s \in REG} VXMD(i,USA,s)$ | 48,514 | 376,411 | 135,049 |
| + $VST(i,USA)$ | 0 | 0 | 17,582 |
| **II. Exports** | | | |
| $\sum_{s \in REG} VXMD(i,USA,s)$ | **48,514** | **376,411** | **135,049** |
| = $VXMD(i,USA,USA)$ | 0 | 0 | 0 |
| + $VXMD(i,USA,EU)$ | 8,564 | 92,695 | 51,672 |
| + $VXMD(i,USA,ROW)$ | 39,950 | 283,716 | 83,377 |
| **III. Domestic purchases** | | | |
| $VDM(i,USA)$ | **615,418** | **2,480,245** | **6,395,376** |
| = $VDPM(i,USA)$ | 318,045 | 525,012 | 2,998,010 |
| + $VDGM(i,USA)$ | 10,993 | 191,368 | 870,490 |
| + $\sum_{j \in PROD\_COMM} VDFM(i,j,USA)$ | 286,380 | 1,763,865 | 2,536,876 |
| **IV. Intermediate, domestic purchases** | | | |
| $\sum_{j \in PROD\_COMM} VDFM(i,j,USA)$ | **286,380** | **1,763,865** | **2,536,876** |
| = $VDFM(i,food,USA)$ | 205,558 | 84,772 | 146,429 |
| + $VDFM(i,mnfcs,USA)$ | 6,410 | 817,396 | 570,221 |
| + $VDFM(i,svces,USA)$ | 74,399 | 624,365 | 1,362,530 |
| + $VDFM(i,cgds,USA)$ | 13 | 237,332 | 457,696 |

*a* Aggregate values in boldface.
*b* All units in 1992 $US million.

substitution in value-added, and the elasticities of substitution among foreign goods and between domestic and foreign goods. The own-price and income elasticities of demand vary by commodity and region, whereas the substitution elasticities vary only by commodity. Rather than simply computing arithmetic means of the disaggregate parameters, we compute their expenditure share-weighted means.

In the case of consumer demand elasticities, we proceed as follows:

1. We ensure that the Engel aggregation condition holds for the disaggregate data and parameters by proportionally adjusting all income elasticities as required.

**Table 5.2.** *Sources and Uses of Imports in the US: 3x3 Aggregation*

|  | i = food | i = mnfcs | i = svces |
|---|---|---|---|
| **I. Sources and Uses of Imports** | | | |
| $VIMS(i, USA, USA)$ | 0 | 0 | 0 |
| + $VIMS(i, E\_U, USA)$ | 6,859 | 97,204 | 15,146 |
| + $VIMS(i, ROW, USA)$ | 26,046 | 472,786 | 54,940 |
| **$VIM(i, USA)$** | **32,905** | **569,990** | **70,086** |
| = $VIPM(i, USA)$ | 14,563 | 179,406 | 28,790 |
| + $VIGM(i, USA)$ | 429 | 31,457 | 3,530 |
| + $\sum_{j \in PROD\_COMM} VIFM(i, j, USA)$ | 17,912 | 359,127 | 37,766 |
| **II. Uses of Intermediate Imports** | | | |
| $\sum_{j \in PROD\_COMM} VIFM(i, j, USA)$ | **17,912** | **359,127** | **37,766** |
| = $VIFM(i, food, USA)$ | 13,631 | 8,208 | 1,002 |
| + $VIFM(i, mnfcs, USA)$ | 373 | 207,796 | 12,859 |
| + $VIFM(i, svces, USA)$ | 3,906 | 63,590 | 18,537 |
| + $VIFM(i, cgds, USA)$ | 1 | 79,531 | 5,366 |

*a* Aggregate values in boldface.
*b* All units in 1992 $US million.

2. We apply the Slutsky condition to derive *compensated* own-price elasticities based on the GTAP data for *uncompensated* own-price elasticities and the income elasticities from the previous step.
3. We obtain expenditure share-weighted means of the disaggregate income and *compensated* own-price elasticities for the aggregation in question.
4. We again make sure that the Engel aggregation condition holds for the aggregated data and income elasticities by proportionally adjusting all income elasticities. The underlying parameters of the CDE expenditure function are calibrated to the income and compensated own-price elasticities from items 3 and 4.

Since the elasticities of substitution are not region-specific, only aggregation across commodities is necessary. Hence, the share weights used in commodity aggregation are global values. For the elasticities of substitution in value-added, sectoral payments to land, labor, and capital are summed to obtain total value-added by sector, which is the weight used in the aggregation. For the elasticities of substitution among foreign goods and between domestic and foreign goods, total expenditures for imports and total expenditures for

**Table 5.3.** *Equilibrium Price Elasticities of Demand: 3X3 Aggregation*

| qo\pm | usa_f | usa_m | usa_s | eu_f | eu_m | eu_s | row_f | row_m | row_s |
|---|---|---|---|---|---|---|---|---|---|
| | | | | A. Full GE Closure | | | | | |
| *usa_f* | -0.663 | 1.074 | 0.225 | 0.112 | -0.196 | -0.041 | 0.369 | -0.600 | -0.162 |
| *usa_m* | 0.071 | -1.990 | 0.662 | -0.017 | 0.209 | -0.086 | -0.060 | 0.434 | -0.277 |
| *usa_s* | 0.014 | 0.526 | -0.205 | -0.001 | -0.051 | 0.027 | -0.002 | -0.095 | 0.090 |
| *eu_f* | 0.098 | -0.209 | -0.015 | -0.625 | 0.727 | 0.420 | 0.317 | -0.503 | -0.151 |
| *eu_m* | -0.019 | 0.224 | -0.065 | 0.080 | -1.405 | 0.624 | -0.071 | 0.477 | -0.294 |
| *eu_s* | -0.005 | -0.052 | 0.024 | 0.045 | 0.393 | -0.261 | -0.013 | -0.104 | 0.117 |
| *row_f* | 0.126 | -0.271 | -0.018 | 0.110 | -0.211 | -0.031 | -0.415 | 0.290 | 0.528 |
| *row_m* | -0.030 | 0.295 | -0.080 | -0.038 | 0.304 | -0.109 | 0.057 | -0.689 | 0.512 |
| *row_s* | -0.009 | -0.081 | 0.037 | -0.002 | -0.095 | 0.052 | 0.046 | 0.246 | -0.309 |
| to(i,r) | -0.760 | -2.593 | -1.467 | -0.734 | -1.848 | -1.571 | -0.748 | -1.371 | -2.004 |
| | | | *B. PE Closure with Endowment Prices and Regional Incomes Fixed* | | | | | | |
| *usa_f* | -0.701 | -0.255 | -0.462 | 0.107 | 0.027 | 0.018 | 0.391 | 0.031 | 0.053 |
| *usa_m* | -0.085 | -1.809 | -0.834 | 0.007 | 0.339 | 0.065 | 0.029 | 0.915 | 0.220 |
| *usa_s* | -0.080 | -0.340 | -0.959 | 0.002 | 0.031 | 0.026 | 0.009 | 0.078 | 0.069 |
| *eu-f* | 0.097 | 0.035 | 0.039 | -0.696 | -0.272 | -0.306 | 0.341 | 0.048 | 0.052 |
| *eu_m* | 0.007 | 0.284 | 0.073 | -0.140 | -1.690 | -0.665 | 0.017 | 0.886 | 0.172 |
| *eu_s* | 0.001 | 0.020 | 0.024 | -0.103 | -0.299 | -0.901 | -0.001 | 0.031 | 0.040 |
| *row_f* | 0.139 | 0.044 | 0.051 | 0.119 | 0.026 | 0.015 | -0.527 | -0.334 | -0.334 |
| *row_m* | -0.002 | 0.406 | 0.097 | -0.000 | 0.471 | 0.051 | -0.176 | -1.325 | -0.734 |
| *row_s* | -0.000 | 0.045 | 0.042 | -0.001 | 0.038 | 0.026 | -0.140 | -0.427 | -0.861 |
| to(i,r) | -0.688 | -0.676 | -0.745 | -0.663 | -0.620 | -0.812 | -0.653 | -0.572 | -0.729 |

imported and domestic commodities are calculated. As above, share weights are then calculated for the disaggregate members of each aggregate commodity and used to weight the disaggregate substitution elasticities prior to summation.

Figure 5.2 reports the parameter file used in the 3x3 aggregation. It begins with the calibrated CDE parameters, SUBPAR and INCPAR, which are

```
! The matrix SUBPAR(%1,%2) with %1 in IND, %2 in REG.
!%2= USA        EU          ROW
   0.866678     0.897081    0.967472        !%1=food
   0.239291     0.317116    0.669294        !%1=mnfcs
   9.999990E-03        9.999990E-03    9.999990E-03    !%1=svces

! The matrix INCPAR(%1,%2) with %1 in IND, %2 in REG.
!%2= USA        EU          ROW
   0.133962     0.160812    0.331707        !%1=food
   0.793119     0.789978    0.838876        !%1=mnfcs
   1.14379      1.26177     1.29555         !%1=svces

! Values of ESUBD(IND) - an array of size 3
!--------------------
!  food          mnfcs              svces
   2.39901       2.79556            1.94365

! Values of ESUBM(IND) - an array of size 3
!--------------------
!
!  food          mnfcs              svces
   4.63905       6.08810            3.91673
!
! Values of ESUBVA(IND) - an array of size 4
!--------------------
!
!  food          mnfcs              svces
   0.789314      1.21992            1.38946
!  CGDS
   0.000000
!
! Values of ETRAE  (a single number)
!---------------
!
   -1.00000
!
! Values of RORFLEX(REG) - an array of size 3
!--------------------
!
!  USA          EU           ROW
   10.0000      10.0000      10.0000
!
! Values of RORDELTA  (a single number)
!------------------
!
   0.000000
```

**Figure 5.2.** Parameters for the 3x3 aggregation.

commodity- and region-specific. These are followed by the region-generic elasticities of substitution between domestic goods and imports (ESUBD), between imports from different sources (ESUBM), and among the components of value-added (ESUBVA). The next entry, ETRAE, specifies the elasticity of transformation between alternative uses of the sluggish endowment commodities – in this case, farmland. The final sets of parameters are relevant to the interregional allocation of investment. RORFLEX, the flexibility of investment allocation, is permitted to vary by region. It is operational only when RORDELTA is equal to 1. In this parameter file *RORDELTA* = 0, so that the global banking sector's regional investment portfolio is fixed.

## III  Equilibrium elasticities

Price and income elasticities are the driving mechanisms behind agents' demand (and supply) responses to changes in market prices. The new postshock equilibrium reached by the model critically depends on these elasticities. Elasticities are, by definition, partial equilibrium phenomena. Therefore, the meaning of elasticities in a general equilibrium (GE) framework requires further discussion. For example, it will be seen that the choice of closure influences not only the magnitude but also the sign of the elasticities. In this section we examine two closures: (1) the standard GE closure and (2) a partial equilibrium closure in which we abstract from income effects and supply-side interactions.

The matrix of price elasticities of demand, $[\varepsilon_{(i,r),(j,s)}]$, is generated for all traded commodities in all regions, $(i,j \in TRAD\_COMM, r,s \in REG)$, by shocking $to(i,r)$ by enough to raise the market price, $pm(i,r)$, by 1%, one commodity and one region at a time. We then record the effect on output $qo(i,r)$. The own-price elasticity of demand is simply the ratio $qo(i,r)/pm(i,r)$. The own- and cross-price elasticities form a square matrix whose dimension is the product of *#TRAD\_COMM* and *#REG*. The matrix of price elasticities for two important closures will be discussed below. The task of computing these elasticities for a disaggregated model, say, with five regions and six traded commodities, can become very cumbersome and time-consuming even for a single choice of closure. However, the reader will be relieved to know that this has been automated via a series of GEMPACK programs that can produce these matrices in one stroke.[2]

### Standard closure

In the standard (GE) closure of the GTAP model, prices, quantities of all nonendowment commodities, and regional incomes are endogenous variables. Conversely, policy variables, technical change variables, and population are exogenous to the model. By virtue of Walras' Law, we omit the equation forcing global savings to equal investment. Their equality may be checked after the fact by examining the value of *walraslack*. If this is zero, then the solution is consistent in a general equilibrium sense. The price elasticities that result from this GE closure are true *general equilibrium* demand elasticities, reflecting adjustment in all markets. These elasticities for the 3x3 aggregation are presented in part A of Table 5.3.[3] Each column may be generated by shocking the associated power of the output tax by the amount indicated in the last row of this table. For example, $to("usa", "food") = -.760$ will cause the market price of food produced in the US region to rise by 1%, and the demand (and hence supply) to fall by 0.663%, as noted by the first diagonal entry.

The diagonal elements in part A of Table 5.3 represent the GE, own-price elasticities of demand, $\varepsilon_{(i,r),(i,r)}$, and are negative. They are largest for the heavily traded manufacturing products, and smallest for the dominant, lightly traded service sector. The blocks of submatrices along the diagonal contain the intraregional cross-price elasticities of demand, $\varepsilon_{(i,r),(j,r)}, i \neq j$. These entries are positive, indicating GE substitutability. The off-diagonal blocks of submatrices show interregional cross-price elasticities of demand, $\varepsilon_{(i,r),(j,s)}, r \neq s$, and are of mixed sign. Furthermore, the matrix is qualitatively symmetric.

The importance of the elasticities reported in Table 5.3 cannot be overemphasized. For example, the GE own-price elasticity of demand for a given product is critical for determining the distribution of benefits from technical change in an industry (see Chapter 13). These own-price elasticities depend on a number of factors including: the mix of final demands, private households' own-price elasticity of demand, and exposure to trade.

Cross-price elasticities determine the nature of the relationship between a pair of commodities. In this 3x3 aggregation, with the standard GE closure, we observe block substitutability along the diagonal such that $\varepsilon_{(i,r),(j,r)} > 0$ for $i \neq j$. This is due to the interplay of both demand and supply considerations. In particular, an increase in $pm(i,r)$ causes a contraction in the demand for commodity $i$ in region $r$ as agents substitute away from the higher-priced commodity. At this point, GE supply-side forces come into play, since the resources released from sector $i$ in $r$ must be absorbed by other sectors. Therefore, outputs of all sectors $j \neq i$ in region $r$ increase. This increase in other sectors' outputs underscores the key role of intersectoral competition for mobile resources in determining the sectoral responses to any shock to the economy.

The blocks of off-diagonal submatrices measure the responses across regions for both own- and cross-commodities. Many, although not all, of the strongest cross-region linkages exist for similar commodities, $\varepsilon_{(i,r)(i,s)}, r \neq s$. These elasticities are positive, indicating substitutability. This is to be expected, given the strong substitutability between imports and domestic goods ($\sigma_D$ = ESUBD) shown in Figure 5.2. Meanwhile, the interregional cross-price elasticity between dissimilar products, $\varepsilon_{(i,r)(j,s)}, i \neq j, r \neq s$, exhibits complementarity, although the magnitude of this response is generally smaller. This derives from the supply-side interactions again. With $qo(i,s) > 0$ in response to $pm(i,r) > 0$, resources are drawn away from other sectors in region $s$. Therefore, $qo(j,s) < 0$ for $j \neq i$ in $s \neq r$.

To summarize, let us consider what happens when the price of manufactures supplied by the *USA* region increases by 1% owing to an output tax on that sector. This may be ascertained by looking down the second column in part A of Table 5.3. The first point to note is that the demand for *USA* manufacturing output falls by almost 2%. This releases resources to the other two sectors, which *expand* as a result. This expansion is especially strong in the food sector, where output increases by 1.07%. This strong response is a result of the sector's relatively small claim on economywide resources, and its significant export opportunities. (Note the large share of *USA* food exports in output in Table 5.1.) The proportionate response of services is only half as large, for precisely the opposite reasons (large sector with little trade).

The impact of the *USA* manufactures price hike on the other two regions is also significant, with the *EU* and *ROW* regions' manufacturing output increasing by .22% and .29%, respectively. This serves to draw resources *away from* the food and services sectors in these other regions. When these supply-side forces are combined with reduced prices for the competing *USA* food and services outputs, due to an expansion in those sectors, there is a significant reduction in food and services outputs outside the *USA*. This multiregion, GE linkage is particularly striking in the case of *ROW* food production, where the 1% increase in *USA manufacturing* price has resulted in a .27% *reduction* in *ROW food* production.

All the results discussed above are dependent on the GE closure that we have used. These are properly viewed as *unconditional* elasticities, since all endogenous variables are permitted to adjust to their new equilibrium values, following the price shock. However, it is also useful to examine various *conditional* elasticities to obtain insight into individual components of the full model. In the next closure we abstract from supply-side effects by fixing endowment prices. Also, regional income (and hence expenditure) is fixed. This permits us to focus on the substitution relationships deriving from the demand side of the model.

### Partial equilibrium (PE) closure with endowment prices and regional incomes fixed

By exogenizing regional incomes, we can focus on the uncompensated price elasticities of final demand. It also allows us to generate income elasticities of demand. This is accomplished by endogenizing *incomeslack(r)* and exogenizing $y(r)$. Endowment prices are fixed by swapping *pm(i,r)* $i \in$ *ENDW_COMM*, with *endwslack(i,r)*. This allows us to isolate pure expansionary (contractionary) effects in the supply of TRAD_COMM. Producers have no incentive to substitute among primary factors in their value-added nests because primary factor prices do not change. The fixed-coefficients nature of the model at the topmost level in the utility/production trees means the expansionary (contractionary) effect in the value-added nest is matched in sign and magnitude by all the intermediate input nests. The only firm side substitution will occur in the Armington nests (ESUBD and ESUBM). Finally, note that since we have destroyed the GE consistency of the model, we can no longer expect Walras' Law to hold. Therefore, *walraslack* is exogenized and *psave* (formerly the numeraire) is endogenized.

The conditional PE price elasticities are shown in part B of Table 5.3. In contrast to the earlier matrix, this one is not fully symmetric in a qualitative sense. Also, now the blocks of submatrices along the diagonal show net complementarity, $\varepsilon_{(i,r),(j,r)} < 0$, $i{\neq}j$. This is the relationship opposite from that identified among commodities within a region under the GE closure. The difference is entirely due to the absence of supply-side competition for resources. [With *endwslack(i,r)* endogenous, the factor market clearing conditions are no longer applicable.] Therefore, the only remaining linkage is through the demand side. Here, one might expect the increase in the manufactures price, for example, to stimulate the demand for food and services, thereby *increasing* their outputs (i.e., intraregional substitution). However, this effect is dominated by the role of manufactures as an intermediate input in the other sectors. Higher prices for this input raise the price of food and manufacturing products, thereby reducing demand. This is the dominant effect for all intraregional commodity relationships. Regarding *interregional* commodity relationships in the model, we see that substitution is the dominant response.

Income elasticities of demand are obtained, using this same PE closure, by perturbing regional incomes by 1%, one region at a time. These are reported in Table 5.4. They measure the percentage change in demand for output of commodity $i$ in region $r$, $qo(i,r)$, when income in region $s$, $j(s)$, rises by 1%. Unlike the private household income elasticities of demand presented in Chapter 4, the elasticities do not satisfy Engel aggregation on a regional basis. To see this, one simply has to note that *all* income elasticities of demand in this table are less than 1. This is due to the presence of *leakages*. For example, some of the income in the EU region is spent on goods produced in the *USA* and *ROW* regions.

The presence of these interregional leakages, coupled with intermediate demands and the presence of large government sectors (with homothetic demands), tends to blunt the differences in private household income elasticities of demand reported in Chapter 4. The demand for services is the most elastic, followed by manufacturing and then food. There is considerable variation in the own-income elasticities of demand for food across regions, with that in ROW being most responsive to income. This follows from the fact that per capita income in ROW is considerably lower. Cross-region effects

**Table 5.4.** *Equilibrium Income Elasticities of Demand: 3X3 Aggregation*

| qo | PE Closure with Endowment Prices and Regional Incomes Fixed | | | |
|---|---|---|---|---|
| | y(usa) | y(eu) | y(row) | y(world) |
| *usa_f* | 0.397 | 0.015 | 0.060 | 0.472 |
| *usa_m* | 0.647 | 0.051 | 0.136 | 0.834 |
| *usa_s* | 0.869 | 0.019 | 0.045 | 0.933 |
| *er_f* | 0.008 | 0.415 | 0.055 | 0.479 |
| *eu_m* | 0.039 | 0.600 | 0.189 | 0.828 |
| *eu_s* | 0.012 | 0.841 | 0.085 | 0.938 |
| *row_f* | 0.013 | 0.024 | 0.541 | 0.578 |
| *row_m* | 0.077 | 0.100 | 0.665 | 0.845 |
| *row_s* | 0.024 | 0.053 | 0.864 | 0.940 |

are strongest for manufactures, which have substantial trade linkages among regions.

The final column in Table 5.4 shows that impact on regional outputs when *global* incomes increase by 1%. This further blunts the differences across regions. Services outputs increase by .93–.94%, followed by manufactures, .83–.84%, and food, .47–.57%.

### Decomposition of aggregate demand elasticities

The aggregate demand elasticities reported in Table 5.3 may also be *decomposed* into their component parts. In this section we develop the analytical formula for this decompositionof the aggregate demand elasticity, denoted: $\varepsilon_{(i,r)(j,s)} = qo(i,r)/pm(j,s)$, and then provide a numerical illustration.

The physical quantity balance for tradeable $i$ in region $r$ is given by:

$$QO(i,r) = QPD(i,r) + QGD(i,r) + QST(i,r)$$
$$+ \sum_{k \in PROD\_COMM} QFD(i,k,r,) + \sum_{t \in REG} QXS(i,r,t). \qquad (5.1)$$

This tracks total output to all its potential uses by various agents. Proportionately differentiating (5.1) and multiplying through by the common market price $PM(i,r)$ gives an equation relating the value-weighted change in proportional output to the sum of the weighted proportional changes in demands. Dividing this through by $VOM(i,r) * pm(j,s)$ gives equation (5.2):

**Table 5.5.** *Decomposition of the Aggregate Demand Elasticity: 3X3 Aggregation*

| Agent's Elasticity | | Agents' Share of Demand | | Contribution to Aggregate Elasticity |
|---|---|---|---|---|
| $qpd(i,r)/pm(j,s)$ | = -0.291 | $VDPM(i,r)/VOM(i,r)$ | = 0.479 | -0.139 |
| $qgd(i,r)/pm(j,s)$ | = -1.032 | $VDGM(i,r)/VOM(i,r)$ | = 0.017 | -0.017 |
| $qfd(i,food,r)/pm(j,s)$ | = -0.807 | $VDFM(i,food,r)/VOM(i,r)$ | = 0.310 | -0.250 |
| $qfd(i,mnfcs,r)/pm(j,s)$ | = -0.057 | $VDFM(i,mnfcs,r)/VOM(i,r)$ | = 0.010 | -0.001 |
| $qfd(i,svces,r)/pm(j,s)$ | = -0.101 | $VDFM(i,svces,r)/VOM(i,r)$ | = 0.112 | -0.011 |
| $qfd(i,cgds,r)/pm(i,s)$ | = -0.224 | $VDFM(i,cgds,r)/VOM(i,r)$ | = 0.000 | 0.000 |
| $qxs(i,r,usa)/pm(j,s)$ | = -2.649 | $VXMD(i,r,usa)/VOM(i,r)$ | = 0.000 | 0.000 |
| $qxs(i,r,eu)/pm(j,s)$ | = -3.614 | $VXMD(i,r,eu)/VOM(i,r)$ | = 0.013 | -0.047 |
| $qxs(i,r,row)/pm(j,s)$ | = -3.293 | $VXMD(i,r,row)/VOM(i,r)$ | = 0.060 | -0.198 |
| $qst(i,r)/pm(j,s)$ | = 0.000 | $VXS(i,r)/VOM(i,r)$ | = 0 | 0.000 |
| $qo(i,r)/pm(j,s)$ | = -0.663 | $VOM(i,r)/VOM(i,r)$ | = 1.000 | -0.663 |

Note: $\epsilon_{(i,r)(j,s)} = -0.633$; $i = j = food$; $r = usa$.

$$\frac{qo(i,r)}{pm(j,s)} = \frac{VDPM(i,r)}{VOM(i,r)} * \frac{qpd(i,r)}{pm(j,s)} + \frac{VDGM(i,r)}{VOM(i,r)} * \frac{qgd(i,r)}{pm(j,s)}$$

$$+ \sum_{k \in PROD\_COMM} \frac{VDFM(i,k,r)}{VOM(i,r)} * \frac{qfd(i,k,r)}{pm(j,s)}$$

$$+ \sum_{t \in REG} \frac{VXMD(i,r,t)}{VOM(i,r)} * \frac{qxs(i,r,t)}{pm(j,s)} + \frac{VST(i,r)}{VOM(i,r)} * \frac{qst(i,r)}{pm(j,s)}. \quad (5.2)$$

The aggregate demand elasticity, $\varepsilon_{(i,r),(j,s)} = qo(i,r)/pm(j,s)$, on the left-hand side gives the interregional cross-price elasticity. The right-hand side shows the contribution to the aggregate response by different agents that consume the sector's output. The value flows making up these weights may be found in Table 5.1, for $r = usa$. These operate as weights on the individual agents' price elasticities. Relatively elastic agents that consume a higher proportion of the output contribute more to the aggregate demand response.

Table 5.5 presents a numerical illustration of equation (5.2) whereby $i = j = food$ and $r = s = usa$, under the standard GE closure. From Table 5.3 we see that the aggregate, GE, own-price elasticity of demand for US food is equal to $-0.663$. The last column in Table 5.5 breaks this elasticity into its component parts. The largest contributor is the food sector itself ($-0.250$ of the total). This is due to the relatively large share of farm and food output used as intermediate inputs in this sector (.31 from column 2 of Table 5.5), and the relatively price-responsive demand in this sector ($-0.807$ from column 1).

In contrast to the intermediate demands by the food industry, final demands by private households (see the first row in Table 5.5) account for almost half of all sales (agent's share = 0.479) but embody relatively little price responsiveness (agent's elasticity = −0.291), therefore, they contribute only half as much to the GE demand elasticity for food (−0.139 vs. −0.250). Finally, note that the contribution of domestic final demands for US food are eclipsed in column 3 by export demands, which account for −0.245 (= −.047 + −0.198) of the total.

## IV    Summary

This chapter has demonstrated how the theory, data, and parameters of the standard GTAP framework interact for a particular aggregation, under alternative closure assumptions. The resulting *equilibrium elasticities* are quite informative. For example, when only demand-side forces are considered, the predominant, equilibrium, cross-price relationships in the model are those of intraregional complementarity and interregional substitutability. However, when factor market equilibrium conditions are brought into play, goods become *intraregional substitutes*. Interregional relationships are mixed; like commodities in different regions are substitutes, and other interregional cross-price relationships exhibit complementarity. Finally, each of these equilibrium elasticities may be broken into its component parts. In sum, the computation and scrutiny of equilibrium elasticities is a very useful exercise. Chapter 6 will discuss how to access the software necessary to do this – and many other types of computing with GTAP.

NOTES

1. This template file may be found in the File Transfer Protocol (FTP) site, also accessible via the GTAP Web site, along with existing GTAP aggregations. Readers interested in ordering additional aggregations may contact GTAP staff by sending a message to GTAP@FTP.PURDUE.EDU.
2. A detailed explanation of this procedure used to generate the matrices automatically is given in the Hands-On document (examples 32–39) described in Chapter 6, and available on the Web site.
3. The row and column labels in Table 5.3 need a little explanation. The "*f*" stands for commodity food, "*m*" for *mnfcs*, and "*s*" for *svces*. For example, *usa.f* is an abbreviation for (*food, usa*), and *eu-s* is an abbreviation for (*svces, eu*).

CHAPTER 6

# Implementing GTAP
# using the GEMPACK Software

*Kenneth R. Pearson*

## I    Introduction and overview

The purpose of this chapter is to introduce you to the publicly available
software accompanying this book, and to tell you how you can use this software
to carry out, on a PC, the applications presented in Part III (Chapters 7–13)
of this book. These programs are based on the GEMPACK suite of software
(Harrison and Pearson 1994), which is designed specifically for the nonlinear
solution of partial and general equilibrium models. The files with which you
will work have been specially tailored to the needs of the Global Trade
Analysis Project (GTAP), and they offer users a great deal of flexibility, within
this standard framework. The software accompanying this book is referred to
as the *GTAP Book Version of GEMPACK*.

GEMPACK separates the theory of GTAP (Chapter 2) from the basic data
base (Chapter 3) and the behavioral parameters (Chapter 4). All the applications
in Part III draw on the same theoretical structure, which we refer to as the
"standard GTAP model." Indeed, the software accompanying this book does
not permit the user to modify the basic theory.[1] Within this broad structure,
however, there is ample flexibility for addressing a wide variety of issues,
including: the impact of economic growth on trade and factor markets, regional
integration, multilateral trade policy reform, distributional consequences of
technological change, implications of environmental policies, and more. Furthermore, as demonstrated in Chapter 5, users can specify alternative model
closures that can be useful, both for decomposing the effects of a simulation
as well as for capturing different market environments.

As noted in Chapter 5, we never work with the fully disaggregated GTAP
data base. It is simply too large. Rather, we strategically aggregate the data
base to meet the needs of a particular application. Thus each of the seven
applications which follow is based on a different aggregation of the same data
base. For this reason, the first thing the reader will want to do is become

164

familiar with the particular aggregation used in an application. This involves examining key shares and summary variables, as well as computing equilibrium elasticities such as those presented in the previous chapter. The procedures for conducting this type of preliminary analysis are described below in section VI. In addition to the standard GTAP data synopsis, users are given the capacity to create their own summary measures. However, it should be noted that users are discouraged from modifying the value flows in the data base, since doing so is very likely to destroy the consistency of the benchmark equilibrium.

In contrast to the value data, the behavioral parameters associated with a GTAP application may be readily modified, adhering to the theoretical restrictions outlined in the model chapter (Chapter 2). Thus, after replicating the results in Part III (see section V below), the reader may examine the sensitivity of model solutions to changes in key parameters. For example, the trade elasticities may be systematically reduced, or increased, as may the elasticities of substitution in production. The user may also alter the degree of intersectoral factor mobility and the sensitivity of international investment to regional rates of return.

You may also construct your own experiments. We recommend that you begin by marginally altering existing applications, thereupon branching out to new applications. However, there is nothing to prevent you from embarking on an entirely different path of enquiry, and we expect that many readers will eventually turn in this direction. At some point, users may feel constrained by the limitations of the standard GTAP model, in which case they may purchase the requisite software for modifying the theory.[2] Finally, readers may also order their own aggregations of the GTAP data base; they may even purchase the full data base, complete with aggregation software (see section II in Chapter 5).[3]

In summary, using the *GTAP Book Version of GEMPACK*, you can

- Examine the data in any of the aggregations used in the applications in Part III.
- Uncover many useful pieces of summary information about these aggregations.
- Replicate the results of the applications in Part III.
- Modify these applications (including changing the closure, shocks, and parameters).
- See how sensitive the results are to the values of various parameters.
- Carry out completely new applications using the standard GTAP model and selected aggregations from Part III of the book.

The purpose of this chapter is to tell you how to do these things.

Instructions for obtaining the software and data accompanying this book are given in section II of this chapter. Detailed instructions for using the software to carry out these tasks are given in sections III to VI of this chapter. These spell out the steps in running the software and give suggestions for hands-on computing you can carry out to familiarize yourself with the software and with GTAP. Further information about the computer version of the standard GTAP model can be found in section VII, and more information about GEMPACK is given in section VIII.

The programs, data, and files accompanying this book are available only for use on a DOS 80386/80486/Pentium PC with a hard disk, at least 8 Mb of RAM (memory), a numeric coprocessor, and version 3.3 or later of DOS.

The theory of the GTAP model (that is, the formulas and equations in Chapter 2) is written down in the TABLO Input file GTAP94.TAB, which is supplied with the *GTAP Book Version of GEMPACK*. Note that, although the equations are written in a linearized form, the software is still able to produce accurate solutions of the nonlinear levels equations of the model [see Hertel, Horridge, and Pearson (1992) and section 4 of Harrison and Pearson (1994)].

## II      Installing programs, data, and applications files on your PC

To obtain the files you will need a PC that is connected to the World Wide Web and has a Web browser or File Transfer Protocol (FTP) software available. Before attempting to obtain the files, you should first make a new directory (we suggest that you call it \GTAPBOOK) on your PC for the files, and then put all the files in this directory. To do this, use the commands

**md \gtapbook**
**cd \gtapbook**

If you have World Wide Web access, you should download all files from

*http://www.agecon.purdue.edu/gtap/software/gtapbook.htm*

If not, you can use FTP to obtain the files. To do this, first connect to the relevant machine by entering the command

**ftp ftp.purdue.edu**

When you receive the prompt to indicate that you are connected, you should log in as user "anonymous" and give your Internet address for the password. The sequence of commands for doing this will be similar (but possibly not identical) to the two below shown in boldface. [In this chapter, we use the convention that the text you type in is shown in **boldface sans serif** type. Any text starting with an exclamation mark ! begins a *comment* (which is in *sans serif italics*); you should not type in the exclamation mark or the text that follows it.] You will, of course, need to type in your Internet address instead of the response "<Internet address>" shown below.

**login anonymous**
**<Internet address>**    *! E.g. Ken.Pearson@BusEco.monash.edu.au*

(Note that all commands below, while connected to this machine *ftp.purdue.edu,* are case-sensitive. So, for example, "login anonymous" is required, and use of a different case such as "LOGIN ANONYMOUS" may fail. Below, all commands are in lowercase.) All the files relating to this book are in a subdirectory called *pub/gtap/book.* To change to this directory, type in the commands

**cd pub**
**cd gtap**
**cd book**

Most of the files are stored in PKZIP archives (which compress the files). To decompress them on your PC, you will need the program PKUNZIP.EXE. To get this to your PC, issue the commands (use lowercase)

**binary**
**get pkunzip.exe**    *! (This will download PKUNZIP.EXE to your PC)*

Most of the files you need are .ZIP files. To get them all, issue the commands (again in lowercase)

**binary**
**prompt off**    *! (This may not be necessary.)*
**mget *.zip**    *! (This should download several .zip files.)*

Some of the files are text files (each has the suffix .txt). To get these to your PC, issue the commands

**ascii**
**mget *.txt**    *! (This should download one or more .txt files)*

Now issue the command

**quit**

to exit from FTP. The command

**dir**

on your PC should show you the file PKUNZIP.EXE, several .ZIP files, and one or more .TXT files.

To extract all the files from a .ZIP archive, issue the command

**.\pkunzip <archive-name>**    *! E.g. ".\pkunzip gempie" to extract files in GEMPIE.ZIP*

At this point, simply extract the files in the archives GEMSIM.ZIP, GEMPIE. ZIP, TABLO.ZIP, SEEHAR.ZIP, SLTOHT.ZIP, TMEM.ZIP, TP1010.ZIP, CMF2-01.ZIP, and AGG2-01.ZIP; the others can wait until later. Also, you should read the text file README.TXT, which contains any changes or corrections made since this book was printed.

### *Memory required for the programs*

When you start running a program that has been compiled and linked with the Lahey Fortran compiler (as the executable images supplied here have been), the program displays a box that tells you how much memory is available. All the programs you have obtained for solving GTAP will run when this box shows that at least 6850K (that is, 6850 kilobytes, or about 6.85 megabytes) of memory is available.

You can test how much memory is available to Lahey programs by running the test program TMEM.EXE. Type in

**cd \gtapbook**
**tmem**

If the box shows less than 6850K available, you may not be able to run all the programs. You may be able to increase the amount of memory available by removing device drivers and/or caches (such as SMARTDRV.EXE). (You will probably need to edit your AUTOEXEC.BAT and/or CONFIG.SYS files to do this. You will need to reboot, by holding down the **Ctrl, Alt,** and **Del** keys simultaneously, for such changes to take effect.) As long as you have 8Mb or more of memory on your computer, you should be able to arrange things so that the Lahey box shows 6850K or more available.

### *Editing text files*

When installing and using the GEMPACK software, you will need to be able to edit text files. This is often best done using a text editor (that is, an editor designed for handling text files exclusively). A text editor, **EDIT**, is supplied with version 5 or later of DOS. There are many other text editors available on DOS machines. Alternatively, you can use a word processor (such as

Microsoft Word or WordPerfect) to edit text files; if so, you must be careful to save the resulting file as a text file.

*Changes to the DOS settings*

Check the file CONFIG.SYS in your default directory \. Look for the lines

**FILES = xx**
**BUFFERS = yy**

If necessary, change these (use your text editor) so that the number xx is at least 40 and yy is at least 10. If either of these lines is not present, add new lines

**FILES = 40**
**BUFFERS = 10**

as appropriate. (If you do not have a CONFIG.SYS file, create a new one containing the two lines above.)

If you change CONFIG.SYS, you need to reboot your system (press **Ctrl**, **Alt**, and **Del** simultaneously) before using the software.

*Running GEMPACK programs*

Under DOS, this is done simply by typing in the name of the program, as in, for example,

**gempie**

(You will need to be in directory \GTAPBOOK before typing in these commands.[4])

To exit from the program once it has started running, simply type **Control-C** (that is, hold down the **Ctrl** key, which is usually on the left of your keyboard, and, while holding it down, touch the **C** key). This will interrupt the program and return you to the DOS prompt. (You may have to type **Control-C** twice to achieve this.)

## III     Using the software: An introduction

You can use the software provided

- To carry out simulations with GTAP
- To look at the data in a GTAP data set
- To find out other useful information about the data in a GTAP data set

This section contains an introduction to these different uses of the software. Detailed instructions for running the programs are given. You are encouraged to run the programs, giving the responses indicated below. In doing so, you will learn about the software and about the GTAP model.

The first part of this section contains an introduction to carrying out simulations with GTAP. It is followed by a subsection on how to look at the data and important consequences of it. Here, you will use the 3x3 GTAP data set discussed in Chapter 5. However, the techniques you will learn will apply equally to the larger GTAP data sets used in the applications in Part III of this book.

### Carrying out simulations with GTAP

Simulations with GTAP can be carried out in two steps (see Figure 6.1).[5] The first step in a simulation is to run the program TP1010. You should think of this as the computer version of the theory of GTAP (the human-readable version is the TABLO Input file GTAP94.TAB). TP1010.EXE is produced from GTAP94.TAB by running the GEMPACK program TABLO; see section VII below for more information. When running TP1010, you also specify the base data (that is, the GTAP aggregation you are working with), the closure, and the shocks. The output from TP1010 is a so-called Solution file, a binary file containing the results of the simulation, that is, the percentage changes in the endogenous variables as a result of the shocks to the exogenous variables.

Because this Solution file is a binary file, it must be converted to a text file (that is, to human-readable form). This is done by running the GEMPACK program GEMPIE in the second of the two steps. The output from GEMPIE is a so-called GEMPIE Print file that contains the simulation results (that is, percentage changes in the endogenous variables). This file can be printed or viewed in an editor.

**An example.** We illustrate this by considering a numeraire simulation with the 3x3 aggregation of the GTAP data. In this simulation, the price of savings is increased by 10%. That is, we supply a shock of 10 to the variable *psave*. To carry out this simulation, proceed as follows.

**Step 1    Run the program TP1010** by entering the commands

**cd \gtapbook**
**tp1010**

(The first changes directory into directory \GTAPBOOK. The second starts TP1010.EXE running.) When prompted by the program, give the two responses

**cmf**
**num2-01.cmf**

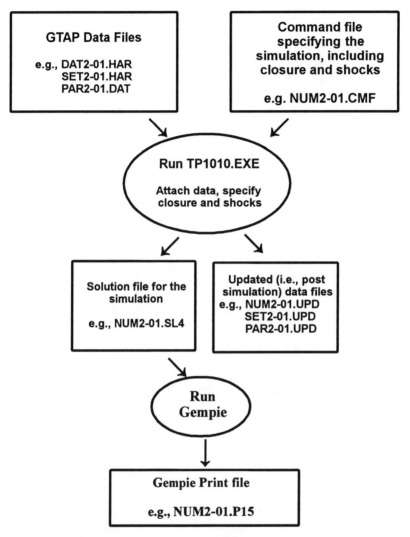

**Figure 6.1.** Carrying out a simulation with GTAP.

The program will take several minutes to run. It is taking all its input from the GEMPACK Command file NUM2-01.CMF. This file tells which base data to read (that is, which aggregation of the GTAP data to use), which variables are exogenous and which endogenous, and what shocks to give. (We explain the contents of this file below in section IV.) Once the program finishes running, check that the Solution file NUM2-01.SL4 has been created, via the command

**dir num*.sl4**

**Step 2.    Run the GEMPACK program GEMPIE** by entering

**gempie**

When prompted by GEMPIE, give the responses below. (The first and fourth are carriage returns. After each response, we have given, in italics, a comment, which starts with an exclamation mark; when running the program, you should not type in the exclamation mark or the comment following it.)

### User Input to GEMPIE

| | |
|---|---|
| `<carriage-return>` | *! Take default options and finish option selection* |
| `num2-01` | *! Name of Solution file (from Step 1 above)* |
| `a` | *! Print all endogenous variables* |
| `<carriage-return>` | *! Accept default name NUM2-01.PI5 for Print file* |
| `Numeraire shock with 3x3 data` | *! Heading for each page of Print file* |
| `5` | *! Number of decimal places in the results* |

### End of User Input to GEMPIE

This should create the GEMPIE Print file NUM2-01.PI5. You can check this via the command

**dir *.pi5**

This file contains the percentage changes in the endogenous variables of the model resulting from the shocks.

You can look at the results of this simulation by printing NUM2-01.PI5 (if you have a printer attached) or by viewing it in an editor. For example, if you have version 5 or later of DOS, you can view the results by issuing the command

**edit num2-01.pi5**

(The specific instructions below about keys for moving, searching, and exiting all apply to this DOS editor; if you are using another editor, use the appropriate keys in that editor.) You can move around the file using the **PgDn** and **PgUp** keys. Notice the sections at the start of the file reminding you which variables are exogenous and which are endogenous, and what the shock is.

In this simulation, because the numeraire *psave* has been increased by 10%, you should expect that prices and dollar values will increase by 10% and that quantities will stay unchanged. Is this what you observe? For example, look at the results for variables **qo** (a quantity) and **ps** (a price). [In **edit**, to search for the **qo** results, first go to the top of the file via **Ctrl+Home** (that is, hold down the **Ctrl** key and touch the **Home** key). Then, to search, touch the **Alt** key, then the **s** (search) key, then the **f** (find) key, then type in "**qo** (" as the 4-letter string to search for,[6] and enter a carriage return. This should bring you to the start of the **qo** results.]

To exit from **edit**, touch the **Alt** key, then the **f** (file) key, and then the **x** (exit) key.

### *Looking at the data in a GTAP data set*

You will need to be able to look at the data in a GTAP data set in order to understand simulation results. This involves looking at the data directly and being able to derive important consequences of the data (for example, the share of imports in total household consumption). We have prepared suggestions for hands-on computing to enable you to look at the data in these ways, and to do other GTAP-related computing. These suggestions are contained in a document "Hands-On Computing to Introduce GEMPACK and GTAP" (Pearson 1994); below we refer to this as the *Hands-On document.*

This Hands-On document is one of the files you have installed on your PC. There are two versions of it: first a text version and second a Microsoft Word for Windows version. If you have Microsoft Word for Windows on your computer,[7] you should access the Word version, since it contains boldface and other formatting to make it easier to follow. Otherwise, access the text version (which contains exactly the same information without the formating).

Both of these versions are in the file DOC.ZIP in your \GTAPBOOK directory. To extract the appropriate one, first change directory into \GTAPBOOK via

**cd \gtapbook**

Then, to access the Word-for-Windows version HANDSON.DOC, first extract it via the command

**.\pkunzip doc handson.doc**

and then open this file HANDSON.DOC in Microsoft Word for Windows (or another word processor that can read Word for Windows files). Alternatively, to access the text version HANDSON.TXT, first extract it via the command

**.\pkunzip doc handson.txt**

and then open this file HANDSON.TXT in your favorite editor. (For example, if you have version 5 or later of DOS, issue the command "edit handson.txt.") In either case, you may like to print the Hands-On document. Examples 1–4 in the Hands-On document show you how to look at the data and various shares, etc., directly. We encourage you to work through at least examples 1–8 in the Hands-On document before you attempt to replicate any of the applications in this book (see section V, below).

### GEMPACK documentation

GEMPACK is fully documented for users in GEMPACK documents numbered GPD-1, GPD-2, and GPD-3 (see the References section at the end of this chapter). We have tried to make this chapter and the Hands-On document (see above) self-contained. If, however, you feel that you need to look at the GEMPACK documents, there are text versions (which do not include the diagrams or figures) of these on your computer in the files GPD1.ZIP, GPD2.ZIP, and GPD3.ZIP, respectively. To extract these text versions, issue the commands

**cd \gtapbook**
**.\pkunzip gpd1 gpd1.txt**

for GPD-1, and similarly for the other two. Alternatively, you can purchase printed copies of these GEMPACK documents (including diagrams and figures) from the Impact Project (the address is provided in section VIII).[8]

### IV      Specifying a simulation: An introduction to Command files

Each of the applications in this book was carried out by running the program TP1010, and using a GEMPACK Command file to specify the data, closure, and shocks. The Command file contains all input required by the program TP1010 and also provides a record of the simulation. Below we describe the syntax of these Command files by looking in detail at the file NUM2-01.CMF used in the simulation executed in step 1 in section III, above. The file NUM2-01.CMF is shown in Figure 6.2.

*(a) Syntax and Comments in GEMPACK Command files.* Any part of a line starting with a single exclamation mark ! is treated as a comment. (We suggest using comments liberally to make Command files self-documenting.) A semi-colon ";" ends each statement in a Command file. Any statement can extend over several lines (as in the list of exogenous variables in Figure 6.2). The order of the statements does not matter. Keywords can be abbreviated as long as they remain unambiguous. (For example, "Aux file" can be used as an abbreviation for "Auxiliary files.") Finally, like most GEMPACK files,

```
!_____num2-01.cmf_____
! This GEMPACK command file simulates a numeraire shock in gtap94.tab,
! using the 3x3 data files referred to as aggregation 2-01.
!_____
!
! Which model
Auxiliary files = tp1010 ;
!
! Original (i.e. pre-simulation) data files
File GTAPSETS = set2-01.har;
File GTAPPARM = par2-01.dat;
File GTAPDATA = dat2-01.har;
!
! Equations file information
Equations File  = TP2-01 ;
         Model = TP1010 ;
         Version = 1 ;
         Identifier = GTAP94.TAB with standard condensation and 3x3 data ;
!
! Closure
Exogenous pop
          psave
          profitslack incomeslack endwslack
          cgdslack saveslack govslack tradslack
          ao af afe ava atr
          to txs tms tx tm
          qo(ENDW_COMM,REG)  ;
!
Rest Endogenous ;
!
! Shock
Shock psave = 10 ;
!
! Solution method
Method = Johansen ;
!
Verbal Description =
      +++++++++++++++++++++++++++++++++++++++++++++++++++++++++++
      +                    Model TP1010                         +
      +         Experiment NUM2-01: numeraire shock             +
      +              Solution Method: Johansen                  +
      +++++++++++++++++++++++++++++++++++++++++++++++++++++++++++;
! Output File Specification (they are experiment dependent)
 Save Environment File   tp2-01 ;
Solution         File = num2-01 ;
Log              File = num2-01.LOG ;
!
! Updated (i.e. post-simulation) data files
Updated file GTAPSETS = set2-01.upd;
Updated file GTAPPARM = par2-01.upd;
Updated file GTAPDATA = num2-01.upd;
!
Display file = tp2-01.dis ;
!
! Options
Extrapolation accuracy file = YES ;
CPU = yes ;
! Next needed if reusing pivots is to succeed in multistep sim
Iz1 = no ;
!_____End of file_____
```

**Figure 6.2.** The GEMPACK Command file NUM2-01.CMF.

Command files are not case-sensitive. You can put "Johansen" or "johansen." (Command files are case-sensitive only for file names on systems such as Unix, on which file names are case-sensitive.)

*(b) Which model.* The statement

```
Auxiliary files = tp1010 ;
```

tells the program TP1010 to use the Auxiliary files TP1010.AXS and TP1010.AXT. These are computer representations of the theory in GTAP94.

TAB as implemented with the standard GTAP condensation. (That is, with the omissions and backsolves indicated in section VII, below.)

*(c) Base data.* The statements

```
File GTAPSETS = set2-01.har ;
File GTAPDATA = dat2-01.har ;
File GTAPPARM = par2-01.dat ;
```

specify the names of the three data files used in this simulation. These contain, respectively, the set information, the global data base, and the parameters for the 3x3 GTAP data set (aggregation number 1). (Other aggregations of the GTAP data are used in the applications in this book; see section V below for details.)

*(d) Closure.* This is specified by the statements

```
Exogenous pop
         psave
         profitslack incomeslack endwslack
         cgdslack saveslack govslack tradslack
         ao af afe ava atr
         to txs tms tx tm
         qo(ENDW_COMM,REG) ;
Rest Endogenous ;
```

which list the exogenous variables and state that all other variables are endogenous. (Alternatively, you could list the endogenous variables and state that the remainder are exogenous, or even list all exogenous and all endogenous variables.)

*(e) Shock.* This is specified by the statement

```
Shock psave = 10 ;
```

which indicates that variable *psave* (the price of capital goods supplied to savers, which is the numeraire of GTAP) is to be increased by 10%.

*(f) Solution file and verbal description.* The Solution file name is specified via the statement

```
Solution File = num2-01 ;
```

TP1010 automatically adds the suffix ".SL4" so that the full name is NUM2-01.SL4.

The verbal description is specified by the statement

```
Verbal Description =
  ++++++++++++++++++++++++++++++++++++++++++++++++++
  +                     Model TP1010                  +
  +         Experiment NUM2-01: numeraire shock       +
  +             Solution Method: Johansen             +
  ++++++++++++++++++++++++++++++++++++++++++++++++++;
```

This verbal description (five lines of text) is put on the Solution file and is echoed when the Solution file is accessed, so that it appears on the GEMPIE Print file.

*(g) Updated (i.e., postsimulation) data.* The names of the updated files are specified by the statements

```
Updated file GTAPSETS = set2-01.upd;
Updated file GTAPPARM = par2-01.upd;
Updated file GTAPDATA = num2-01.upd;
```

Of these, the only interesting one is the updated global data file NUM2-01.UPD, which contains the global data as it would be once the numeraire has been increased by 10%. The updated set information and parameters files are redundant (since they will be identical to the original ones), but the software requires that names be given for them.

*(h) Solution method.* This is specified by the statement

```
Method = Johansen ;
```

which tells TP1010 to use Johansen's method. While Johansen's method is satisfactory for this numeraire simulation (which is essentially a linear perturbation of the economy), if you want accurate solutions of the underlying nonlinear equations of the model, it is usually necessary to use Gragg's method (the default in GEMPACK) or Euler's method. For example, to use Gragg's method and to extrapolate from 2,4,6-step calculations, replace the above statement by[9]

```
Method = Gragg ;
Steps = 2 4 6 ;
```

*(i) Other information.* The statements

```
Equations File = TP2-01 ;
      Model = TP1010 ;
      Version = 1 ;
      Identifier = GTAP94.TAB with standard conden-
      sation and 3x3 data ;
```

specify the name of the so-called Equations file and associated information. This is required information whenever you carry out a simulation (unless you start from an existing Equations file). The statement

```
Save Environment File tp2-01 ;
```

tells TP1010 to save the closure on a so-called Environment file. Then, to specify this closure in another Command file, you could use the statement

```
Use Environment file tp2-01 ;
```

which would save having to list the exogenous variables there. The statement

```
Log File = num2-01.LOG ;
```

tells TP1010 to record all screen output in the LOG file NUM2-01.LOG. After the run, you can look at this LOG file to check that things went as expected. The statement

```
Display file = tp2-01.dis ;
```

names the display file produced. The statements

```
Extrapolation accuracy file = YES ;
CPU = yes ;
```

tell TP1010 to produce a so-called Extrapolation Accuracy file and to report CPU (that is, processing) times. If you employ a multistep (i.e., nonlinear) solution procedure, the Extrapolation Accuracy file contains information about the accuracy of the results. The statement

```
Iz1 = no ;
```

is added because we know that it speeds up multistep calculations with GTAP. This is a rather technical point that you shouldn't worry about until you are very experienced with GEMPACK and its solution process.

Other Command files you might like to look at are TMSEU.CMF and TMSEUN.CMF (see examples 20–24 in the Hands-On document).

*Specifying components of a variable*

Individual components of a variable can often be specified using the element name(s), as in, for example, **qo("food","usa")**. Groups of components can often be expressed in a similar way, as in, for, example, **qo("food",REG)**.

Sometimes you will need to specify component numbers or to understand output from a program given in terms of component numbers. If so, the order of the components is specified by the rule that *the first index varies fastest, followed by the second index, and so on.*

Consider the 3x3 aggregation in which **TRAD_COMM = (food, mnfcs, svces)**, and **REG = (USA, EU, ROW)**. Consider variable *qxs*(**i,r,s**), **i** in TRAD_COMM, and **r,s** in REG [exports from r to s]. In this case, **i** varies fastest, **r** next fastest, **s** most slowly. There are 3*3*3=27 components. This gives rise to the following ordering for *qxs*:

| component number | component |
|:---:|:---:|
| 1 | *qxs*("food","USA","USA") |
| 2 | *qxs*("mnfcs","USA","USA") |
| 3 | *qxs*("svces","USA","USA") |
| 4 | *qxs*("food","EU","USA") (etc) |
| 9 | *qxs*("svces","ROW","USA") |
| 10 | *qxs*("food","USA","EU") |
| 11 | *qxs*("mnfcs","USA","EU") (etc) |
| 27 | *qxs*("svces","ROW","ROW") |

**V     Carrying out the applications simulations**

Below you will find a list of the seven applications in Part III (Chapters 7–13) of this book. Next to each application is the number identifying the aggregation of the GTAP data base used in the application. (Aggregation number 1 is the 3x3 data used above. Aggregation number 2 is employed in Chapter 14 of this book.)

| Identifying number of aggregation | Topic |
|:---:|:---|
| 3 | Growth and Wages (Chapter 7) |
| 4 | Agricultural Liberalization (Chapter 8) |
| 5 | APEC Liberalization (Chapter 9) |
| 6 | MFA Liberalization (Chapter 10) |
| 7 | Climate Change (Chapter 11) |
| 8 | Environmental Policy (Chapter 12) |
| 9 | Technical Change (Chapter 13) |

Associated with each application are two .ZIP files, called **AGG2-0X.ZIP** and **CMF2-0X.ZIP** (where **X** is replaced by the identifying number of the aggregation used in the topic). For example, associated with the application "Growth and Wages" in Chapter 7 are the two files AGG2-03.ZIP and CMF2-03.ZIP. (The files AGG2-0X.ZIP and CMF2-0X.ZIP should be in directory \GTAPBOOK.) The file **AGG2-0X.ZIP** contains compressed versions of the four files

> DAT2-0X.HAR  Global data file
> SET2-0X.HAR  Set information
> PAR2-0X.DAT  Parameters
> AGG2-0X.TXT  Mapping file describing the aggregation

The file **CMF2-0X.ZIP** contains the Command files and any associated shocks files used in reproducing the results in the application.

If you wish to run the simulations for any of these applications, you will first need to uncompress the files. First change directory into \GTAPBOOK and then run PKUNZIP to uncompress the files. Use the following commands (in which you should replace **X** by the relevant number 3, . . . , 9).

**cd \gtapbook**
**.\pkunzip agg2-0x**     *! example: .\pkunzip agg2-03*
**.\pkunzip cmf2-0x**     *! example: .\pkunzip cmf2-03*

Each of the CMF2-0X.ZIP files contains a README file called **READ2-0X.ME**. This file contains instructions and advice about carrying out the simulations for the particular application. You should always read this file before starting to replicate the results in an application.

### *Example*

Below we show you how to replicate the results of one of the simulations in the Technical Change application in Chapter 13. This simulation, which looks at the effects of a 2% rate of total factor productivity growth in Australasian crops, uses the data in GTAP aggregation number 9. To extract the data files for this aggregation, enter the commands

**cd \gtapbook**
**.\pkunzip agg2-09**

First check the size of this aggregation by examining the set information file SET2-09.HAR following the method in example 1 of the Hands-On document. You will see that this aggregation recognizes five tradeable commodities (crops, livestock, fish & food, manufactures, and services) and six regions (North America, EU, Australasia, East Asia, Southeast Asia, and ROW).

To carry out the simulation, follow the steps in Figure 6.1. The Command file to use is C2-09E1.CMF, which can be extracted from CMF2-09.ZIP via the command

**.\pkunzip cmf2-09**

You might like to look at this file C2-09E1.CMF to see the shock, which is an increase of 2% to **ao("crops","AustrNZ")**.
First run TP1010 by typing

**tp1010**

and then give the two responses

**cmf**
**c2-09e1.cmf**

When TP1010 finishes running, check that the Solution file C2-09E1.SL4 has been created via the command

**dir c2-09*.sl4**

Then run GEMPIE by typing

**gempie**

Respond as in step 2 in section III above, but replace "num2-01" with "c2-09e1" as the Solution file name, and enter a suitable heading for each page of the Print file.

The first two entries in the first column of Table 13.3 in Chapter 13 give the effects of this shock on Australasian crops and livestock output. To check these values, look in the Print file C2-09E1.PI5, find the output results (the variable is **qo**), and verify that: (1) output of crops in Australasia increases by 2.32%, and (2) output of livestock in Australasia decreases by 0.04%. You can follow a similar procedure to replicate other results in this chapter (or other chapters) in Part III of the book.

*Modifying the applications*

It is one thing to reproduce the results of the applications in this book, but it may be more interesting and instructive to carry out other simulations of your own choosing. With the software you have obtained from the FTP site, you can vary the shocks, closure, and/or solution method used. We say something about each of these options below. Note that complete documentation of the syntax allowed in Command files is given in Appendix A.1 of GEMPACK document GPD-1; however, the examples given above in section IV will probably cover most (ideally, all) of the cases of relevance to you. If you edit a Command file in a word processor (as opposed to a text editor), remember to save the new file as a text file.

**Varying the shocks, closure, and/or solution method.** To do any of these, all you need to do is to make the obvious changes to the Command file used to run TP1010. For example, to change the shocks, just change the shock statements in the Command file; to change the closure, change the exogenous statements. You might like to see how changing from Gragg's method to the midpoint or Euler's method changes the accuracy of the extrapolated results for the shock given in TMSEUN.CMF (see examples 23–24 in the Hands-On document). (The statements "Method = midpoint;" or "Method = Euler;" instead of "Method = Gragg;" will change the solution method to the midpoint or Euler's method, respectively.)

**Varying the data.** You can modify the parameters by editing the appropriate PAR2-0X.DAT file. (It is a text file.) For example, if you wish to examine the sensitivity of any of the application results in Part III to the parameter values used, you can systematically vary the parameters of interest and recompute the simulation results.

However, we do not recommend modifying the global data in any of the GTAP aggregations, since this is likely to destroy the consistency of the benchmark equilibrium.

**Varying the theory and condensation of the model.** The theory of the GTAP is contained in the TABLO Input file GTAP94.TAB. (You might like to look at this file to see how the GTAP equations in Chapter 2 have been written in the algebraic syntax used in TABLO Input files.) The standard condensation used to generate the program TP1010 and the Auxiliary files TP1010.AXS and TP1010.AXT files is that given by running TABLO taking all inputs (in particular, omissions and backsolves) from the Stored-input file TP1010TG. STI . (See section VII below for more details.) With the software provided in the *GTAP Book Version of GEMPACK*, you cannot change the theory or condensation. (To do so, you would need a Source-code version of GEMPACK or a larger Executable-Image version.)

*Errors you may encounter while running*
*GEMPACK programs*

Most error messages from the programs should be self-explanatory. For example, if you choose an invalid closure when you carry out a simulation, this is likely to show up when the relevant matrix (called the left-hand-side matrix) is reported as being structurally or numerically singular. However, due to the rounding that inevitably occurs whenever a large arithmetic calculation is carried out on a computer, the software is not always able to distinguish between a singular matrix and one that is nearly singular. Accordingly, invalidity of a closure may not always be identified by the program. It should, however, be evident in the simulation results (which will probably contain implausibly large movements).

If you receive warnings about the accuracy of the results, you should check carefully to ensure that you are using a valid closure. (Note that warnings about a "possibly ill-conditioned matrix" can usually be ignored with GTAP.)

**Dimension limits may be exceeded.** Each of the programs in the *GTAP Book Version of GEMPACK* (e.g., SEEHAR.EXE and GEMSIM.EXE) can handle only limited model sizes. They have been dimensioned so as to be able to carry out most (ideally, all) tasks associated with aggregations up to 10 regions and 10 tradeable commodities that you may wish to use them for. It is, however, possible that you may ask them to carry out a calculation that exceeds these limits. If so, you will see a message similar to the following.

```
You have exceeded the size limits of
the GTAP Book version of GEMPACK.
(To complete your current task, you
would need a source-code version of GEMPACK.)
```

With the GTAP book version of the software, your best alternative is to find another way of carrying out the same task. (The only other alternative is to obtain a source-code version of GEMPACK; this allows you to reconfigure programs to take advantage of all memory on your computer.)

**If a multistep simulation does not converge.** Gragg's method or the midpoint method converges much more quickly than Euler's method for many simulations. (That is, they produce much more accurate results for the same number of steps.) However, it is known that Gragg's method and the midpoint method are not suitable for some simulations; see part E of the Hands-On document for details.

## VI    Data reporting and equilibrium elasticities

### *Data reporting*

The three TABLO Input files GTAPCHK.TAB, SHOCKS.TAB, and GTAPVOL.TAB are important adjuncts to the GTAP model. GTAPCHK.TAB is used to report many useful pieces of information from a GTAP data set. SHOCKS.TAB is used to calculate the distortions (such as import tariffs and output subsidies) in a GTAP data set, and to write the shocks required to eliminate these distortions. GTAPVOL.TAB is used to report volume changes (rather than percentage changes) implied by a GTAP simulation.

**Information about a GTAP data set via GTAPCHK.TAB.** See examples 5–8 of the Hands-On document for details about GTAPCHK. It is easy to modify GTAPCHK to add extra calculations and reports. Examples 9–11 in the Hands-On document show how to do this.

**Preparing shocks using SHOCKS.TAB.** For the use of SHOCKS.TAB, see examples 12 and 13 in the Hands-On document.

**Reporting volume changes via GTAPVOL.** When you carry out a simulation using GTAP, the Solution file (or GEMPIE Print file) give information about percentage changes in quantity indices. (For example, the **qo** results give information about changes in the outputs of different commodities in the different regions.) The TABLO Input file GTAPVOL.TAB has been designed to report the corresponding **changes** (rather than percentage changes) in some of these volumes. See examples 28–31 in the Hands-On document for details about the use of GTAPVOL.

*Computing equilibrium elasticities (see Chapter 5)*

You can compute the equilibrium elasticities for the 3x3 data set described in Chapter 5. To do so, simply follow the steps in examples 32–39 in the Hands-On document. Before you try these examples, you will first need to extract SAGEM.EXE from its archive via the commands

```
cd \gtapbook
.\pkunzip sagem
```

**VII    Producing TP1010.EXE from the TABLO Input file GTAP94.TAB**

*Condensation and omission of variables*

The theory of the GTAP model (as described and used in this book) is contained in the TABLO Input file GTAP94.TAB. This allows different aggregations with up to 10 regions and up to 10 tradeable commodities.[10] In order to solve the model on an 8Mb PC, a particular implementation, referred to as **TP1010**, is supplied. In this implementation[11]

(a) certain policy variables have been **omitted**. This means that these variables are effectively exogenous but cannot be shocked. (When you work with this implementation, it is as if these variables had never been present in the model.) The variables omitted are:

**tf tpm tpd tgm tgd tfm tfd**

(b) certain variables have been selected for **backsolving**. This means that these variables are hard-wired as endogenous. When you run a simulation, you can obtain results for these variables. However, they cannot be set exogenous in this implementation. The variables that are backsolved for are:

**pfd ppm pfm pms pfob pcif pf ppd pgm pgd qfm qfd pva qfe qva qf pgov qg pg qgm qgd qp qpd qpm**

You can look in GTAP94.TAB to find out more about these variables.

The computer version of TP1010 consists of the file TP1010.EXE and the two **Auxiliary files** TP1010.AXS and TP1010.AXT. These files, which should be in directory \GTAPBOOK on your computer, were produced by running the GEMPACK program TABLO taking inputs from the Stored-input file TP1010TG.STI.[12] The file TP1010TG.STI, which should also be in directory \GTAPBOOK on your computer, includes instructions to omit and to back-solve, as indicated above.

The full GTAP94.TAB has approximately 14,400 equations and 22,600 variables for a 10x10 aggregation of the model. The condensation in TP1010TG .STI omits approximately 2,900 of these variables and leaves a condensed system of about 3,150 equations in about 8,460 variables. Thus, with a 10x10 aggregation, TP1010 solves a system of about 3,150 linear equations in the middle of each step of a multistep calculation. During each step, about 260 variables are backsolved for. See section 3.9 of GPD-1 for more about condensation and section 4.2 of GPD-1 for information about how a multistep calculation is done.

*Levels and linearized equations*

The TABLO Input file GTAP94.TAB has all its EQUATIONs expressed in linearized form. GEMPACK also allows *levels* EQUATIONs in TABLO Input files, and a mixture of levels and linearized equations can be given in such files. For example, see the TABLO Input file SJ.TAB for the Stylized Johansen model, which is discussed and given in full in sections 3.1 to 3.3 of GPD-1. Detailed advice about linearizing equations can be found in Appendix A of GPD-2.

## VIII     GEMPACK

GEMPACK is a suite of general purpose software especially designed for implementing and solving general and partial equilibrium models. The software can handle a wide range of economic behavior, including forward-looking behavior in intertemporal models. GEMPACK is used to solve many different models besides GTAP [see, for example, the models listed in section 2.6 of Harrison and Pearson (1994)]. Part F of the Hands-On document gives information about some available models other than the GTAP.

An introduction to the current release of GEMPACK, Release 5.1, and to the different versions of GEMPACK can be found in Harrison and Pearson (1994) and also in sections 1.1-1.3 of GPD-1. Information about GEMPACK can be obtained from

> The GEMPACK Manager
> Centre of Policy Studies and Impact Project
> Monash University
> Clayton 3168, Australia
> Telephone: +613-9905-5484
> Fax: +613-9905-5486
> email: impact@vaxc.cc.monash.edu.au

*Programs provided in the GTAP Book Version*
*of GEMPACK*

**GEMPIE.** Use this to convert a Solution file to human-readable form. (See Figure 6.1.)

**TP1010.** Use this to carry out simulations with the GTAP. (See section VII above for the procedure for producing TP1010.EXE.)

**TABLO.** Use this to process TABLO Input files, both those for models (such as GTAP94.TAB–see section VII above) and those for carrying out data manipulation tasks (such as GTAPCHK.TAB–see section VI above). [See step 1 in figure 3.3 in Harrison and Pearson (1994) or in figure 2.1 in GPD-1.]

**SEEHAR.** Use this to look at the data in GEMPACK Header Array files including the set information and global data files in a GTAP data set. See examples 1, 2, and 4 in the Hands-On document for the use of SEEHAR.

**GEMSIM.** Use this to carry out the calculations in data manipulation TABLO Input files (such as GTAPCHK.TAB–see section VI above). It can also be used to solve (small) models (see section 2.1 of GPD-1).

**SLTOHT.** Use this to convert Solution files to other forms, notably to Header Array files. To see how SLOTHT is used, see the GTAPVOL part of section VI above.

**SAGEM.** Use this to calculate several Johansen solutions in one run, as in, for example, its use in computing several equilibrium elasticities (see section VI above). In producing several solutions in one run, SAGEM takes only about as long as TP1010 takes to do one step of a multistep calculation. Of course, Johansen results are not accurate solutions of the underlying nonlinear equations of the model, so they must be used with care. But they can be helpful in forming preliminary ideas about a new scenario.

### The Harwell subroutines

The speed with which GEMPACK programs such as TP1010, GEMSIM, and SAGEM solve the system of linear equations on each step of a multistep simulation is due to the efficiency of the Harwell sparse linear equations routines MA28 [see Duff (1977)] developed by AEA Technology at Harwell, UK.[13]

NOTES

1. Readers with access to a source-code version of GEMPACK [see section 11 of Harrison and Pearson (1994)] can modify the standard model, if they wish.
2. The theory can be modified using a source-code version of GEMPACK. Enquiries about purchasing such a version should be addressed to the Impact Project, whose address is given in section VIII.
3. Inquiries regarding purchase of the GTAP data base should be directed to GTAP@FTP.PURDUE.EDU. Additional information is available on the GTAP Web site.
4. (a) If you want to be able to run the programs from other directories, you will need to add directory \GTAPBOOK to your DOS PATH. To do this, edit the file AUTOEXEC.BAT, which is usually in your default directory \ . You should add \GTAPBOOK to the PATH statement in that file. For example, if you find a line
**PATH = C:\;C:\DOS;**
add "C:\GTAPBOOK;" at the end (be careful to separate directory names by semicolons ";") to make it
**PATH = C:\;C:\DOS;C:\GTAPBOOK;**
(You will need to reboot your PC to put such a change into effect.)
(b) If your PC runs under Windows, you will need to run the software in a DOS box.
5. These two steps are those called steps 2 and 3 in figure 3.3 in Harrison and Pearson (1994). Step 1 in that figure has already been carried out for you: see section VII.
6. The four letters are **q**, then **o**, then a **space**, and finally an opening parenthesis (. The space and parenthesis ( are added to bypass several occurrences of **qo** earlier in the file.
7. You will need version 2.0 or later of Word for Windows or another word processor that can read Word for Windows 2.0 files (such as version 5.1 or later of Word-Perfect).
8. At the time of publication of this book, the cost is $A70 in Australia, New Zealand, or Papua New Guinea or $US70 elsewhere. (This cost includes postage by airmail.)
9. Since Gragg is the default method in GEMPACK, the statement "Method = Gragg ;" could be omitted.

10. To work with more than 10 regions or more than 10 tradeable commodities, you would need a source-code version of GEMPACK and an aggregation of the GTAP data base not provided with this book.
11. Of course, other implementations could be made using a source-code version of GEMPACK. However, you cannot make other implementations using the software accompanying this book.
12. See step 1 in figure 3.3 of Harrison and Pearson (1994) or in figure 2.6.1 in GPD-1.
13. MA28 is just one of the large number of general purpose routines in the Harwell Subroutine Library that can be used to carry out a wide range of numerical calculations (including matrix calculations, solving differential equations, statistical calculations, numerical integration, root finding, and so on). For more information about the software in this library, contact Harwell Subroutine Library, AEA Technology, 329 Harwell, Didcot, Oxfordshire OX11 0RA, UK.

REFERENCES

Duff, I. S. (1977) *MA28 A Set of FORTRAN Subroutines for Sparse Unsymmetric Linear Equations*, Harwell Report R.8730 (HMSO, London), p. 104.

Harrison, W. Jill, and K. R. Pearson (1994) *Computing Solutions for Large General Equilibrium Models Using GEMPACK*, Centre of Policy Studies and Impact Project Preliminary Working Paper No. IP-64, Monash University, June. [Revised version to be published in *Computational Economics* in 1996.]

Hertel, T. W., J. M. Horridge, and K. R. Pearson (1992) "Mending the Family Tree: A Reconciliation of the Linearization and Levels Schools of Applied General Equilibrium Modeling," *Economic Modelling* 9:385–407.

GEMPACK documents

GPD-1, *An Introduction to GEMPACK*, 2nd edition, April 1994, pp. 252ff.

GPD-2, *User's Guide to TABLO, GEMSIM and TABLO-generated Programs*, 2nd edition, April 1994, pp. 138ff.

GPD-3, *How to Create and Modify GEMPACK Header Array Files Using the Program MODHAR*, 3rd edition, April 1993, pp. 27ff.

Hands-On document

Pearson, K. R. (1994) "Hands-On Computing to Introduce GEMPACK and GTAP." [This is the document in the files HANDSON.TXT and HANDSON.DOC available via FTP–see section III in the text of this chapter. This is referred to as the "Hands-On document" in the text.]

PART III

APPLICATIONS OF GTAP

CHAPTER 7

# Developing country expansion and
# relative wages in industrial countries

*Robert McDougall and Rod Tyers*

## I    Introduction and overview

Changes in the labor markets of the developed countries since the 1970s have
been the subject of extensive empirical analysis (Murphy and Welch 1989;
Freeman 1993; Gregory and Vella 1993; Katz, Loveman, and Blanchflower
1993; Freeman and Katz, 1994). The principal stylized facts to emerge from
this analysis are that (1) real wage inequality has increased in most Organization for Economic Cooperation and Development (OECD) member countries
(the few exceptions including Japan), (2) this trend has been strongest in the
US in the 1980s and weaker in those countries where wage determination is
more centralized, and (3) the rate of unemployment has risen more where the
trend toward wage dispersion has been weakest. Numerous explanations have
been advanced for the trend in the US. Those that emphasize labor supply
include that growth in the supply of skilled workers slowed in the 1980s
(Katz, Loveman, and Blanchflower 1993) and that immigration of unskilled
workers has accelerated (Borjas, Freeman, and Katz 1991). Those emphasizing
labor demand argue that technological change has been unskilled labor–saving
(Mincer 1991; Bound and Johnson 1992) and that an expansion in imports
that are intensive in unskilled labor has shifted the product composition of
domestic output in ways that foster growth in the demand for skilled rather than
unskilled labor (Murphy and Welch 1991; Wood 1991a,b 1994; Leamer 1993).

It is the last of these explanations that we explore further. We find the
labor demand approach more attractive than the labor supply explanations
because the latter are country-specific and the trend toward more wage dispersion seems general. Although we accept that labor saving technical change
has played a role, it is possible that fine shifts in the mix of products in a
given industry, which are induced by competition with imports, may show
up in empirical analysis as changes of technology. Bound and Johnson (1992),
for example, use only 17 industry groups, of which the manufacturing sector

191

is a part of only two. The remainder are mainly nontraded service industry categories. Clearly, it has been the manufacturing sector in the developed countries that has endured enhanced competition from labor-intensive imports while at the same time expanding its exports of skill-intensive products. The documented decline in employment in that sector, combined with an apparent increase in its average wage in the US, is consistent with the possibility that both the level of employment and the average wage of unskilled workers in manufacturing there has fallen substantially.

Recent analysis at the two-digit International Standard Industrial Classification (ISIC) level by Lawrence and Slaughter (1993) [also drawn upon extensively by Krugman and Lawrence (1993)] finds that employment has become more skill-intensive in all sectors, despite a decline in the relative cost of unskilled labor. To them, this suggests that domestic technology changes dominate trade effects in causing increased wage dispersion. While this may indeed be true, their paper concedes that changes in trade composition may also have contributed, and no empirical apportionment is attempted. Moreover, the studies to date have emphasized the analysis of the domestic product and labor markets and not the international setting in which the pattern of trade flows is determined. Yet, the latter is required if one is to understand the factors that have induced the rise in labor-intensive imports and, presumably, the corresponding rise in exports by developed countries of products intensive in other factors.

Since the 1970s, a growing number of developing countries have changed their trade policy regimes in favor of "outward orientation" (Whalley 1989). This "opening up" has been associated with substantial growth in exports by developing countries and with a shift in the composition of those exports away from products intensive in natural resources toward labor intensive manufactures (IMF 1993, chap. VI). There is, of course, little doubt that these developments have fostered growth in the global economy and that factors other than unskilled labor have been beneficiaries in the developed countries. Indeed, the improvements in productivity and factor use associated with developing country growth are very likely Pareto-improving *across* countries (Kemp, Ng, and Shimomura 1993). Our concern is to explore the effect of these developments on inequality *within* the developed countries.

In part, this concern has its origins in two basic theorems of the traditional two-factor, two-sector Heckscher–Ohlin–Samuelson (HOS) trade model: the factor price equalization (FPE) and Stolper–Samuelson (SS) theorems. The FPE theorem provides conditions under which free trade, which is assumed to equalize product prices across countries, also equalizes factor rewards. The SS theorem relates changes in product prices to factor rewards. An increase in the price of the relatively labor intensive product increases the real return to labor and reduces the real return to capital. This implies that if developed countries have used trade interventions to protect relatively labor-intensive import competing sectors and developing countries have similarly protected their relatively capital-intensive import competing sectors, then protection would be at least partly responsible for real wages being higher in the developed countries. As trade restrictions are scaled down by both groups of trading partners, this would suggest a convergence of factor rewards in both and a decline in the real return to pure labor in developed countries. Hereafter, we refer to this as the HOS result.

There are, however, a number of reasons why the HOS result might not be observed. To start with, some results from the HOS model either disappear or need reinterpretation once its more restrictive assumptions are relaxed. In particular, extensions to more than two products, factors, or countries; unequal numbers of products and factors; and the allowance of some specialization in production all reduce the sharpness with which the conclusion may be drawn that trade reform leads to factor price convergence (Ethier 1984; Deardorf 1986; Falvey 1991). But the potential for extensions does not end there. A more accurate model would allow for the following:

1. The existence of nontraded goods and services, many of which are intensive in unskilled labor
2. The differentiation of products at the level of the firm or the country of origin
3. The comparative international mobility of some forms of capital
4. Consumption behavior driven by nonhomothetic preferences, such that rich households whose income is derived principally from capital have higher propensities to consume labor-intensive goods and services.

These extensions of the basic model enhance the role of income effects of trade reforms in ways that run counter to substitution effects in demand. As trade reforms raise incomes in both the developing and developed countries, the shifting of demand in the developed countries from home products to imports is less complete. Indeed, nontraded and some traded labor-intensive home product and service industries would actually face rising demand. The international mobility of capital ensures that remaining distortions and product differentiation do not retard the growth of capital income in the developed countries. And nonhomothetic preferences allow the wealthier households to spend this new income more than proportionately on labor-intensive home products and services. Moreover, the poorer households in the developed countries would then have consumption bundles that are more intensive in the imported products of the developing countries. Other things equal, trade reform should raise the purchasing power of those households.

In this chapter we explore the consequences of some of these extensions to the basic model of trading economies. For this we use the global data base assembled originally for the SALTER Project (Jomini et al. 1991) and updated and modified for the Global Trade Analysis Project (GTAP) (see Chapter 3) The analysis to be presented also uses the GTAP modeling framework as laid out in Chapter 2 of this book.[1] For consistency with other work presented in this volume, we do not go so far as to examine nonhomotheticity of preferences by disaggregating among rich and poor households.[2] Moreover, our analysis is constrained by the model's consolidation of both skilled and unskilled labor into a single factor. It is therefore impossible to separate derived demands for pure labor and human capital. Both this, and the model's differentiation of products by country of origin, render the pure HOS result unlikely. Nonetheless, labor as a broad group in the older industrial economies (OIEs) emerges as losing, relative to capital and land, from reforms and subsequent rapid growth in the rapidly developing Asian economies (RDEs). However, it gains relative to final product prices.

## II     Aggregation strategy

The GTAP data base divides the world into 24 countries and has 37 commodities and 3 primary factors (labor, capital, and agricultural land). For our purpose it is aggregated to 6 regions and 10 commodity groups, as indicated in Table 7.1. This regional aggregation best highlights the contrasts between the OIEs and the RDEs whose impacts on the former we wish to estimate. The commodity aggregation is based on an analysis of the factor proportions adopted in each industry in the OIEs. The 10 commodity groups are chosen so as to maximize *between*-group differences and minimize *within*-group differences in the split of factor payments between labor and the other factors. This is done for the average of the three OIEs: North America, the European Union (EU), and Australasia.

In any examination of factor market impacts of economic reform, the results depend crucially on the extent of the between-group differences in factor intensities. Shares of direct and total (direct and indirect) expenditure on the three primary factors, as derived from the 1992 data base, are listed in Table 7.2. (Aggregated trade elasticities are reported in Table 7.3.[3]) The two groups of capital-intensive manufactures have only slightly different total factor requirements, when indirect factor demands are added. The "highly capital-intensive" group is consistently more capital-intensive so long as capital is defined broadly to include land. Petroleum and coal products are also relatively capital-intensive.

The labor-intensive manufacturing groups have compositions that are non-traditional. The light manufactures mainly exported by developing countries

Table 7.1. *Regional and Commodity Aggregation*

| Regional Aggregation | Commodity Aggregation |
|---|---|
| **1. Australasia**<br>Australia<br>New Zealand | **1. Crops**<br>Paddy rice<br>Wheat<br>Grains<br>Nongrain crops |
| **2. North America**<br>Canada<br>US | **2. Other agriculture, forestry, and fishing**<br>Wool<br>Other livestock |
| **3. EU**<br>The former European Community of 12 | Forestry<br>Fisheries |
| **4. Rapidly developing**<br>China<br>Indonesia<br>Hong Kong<br>Malaysia<br>Singapore<br>Republic of Korea<br>Taiwan<br>Thailand | **3. Mining**<br>Coal<br>Petroleum<br>Gas<br>Other minerals<br><br>**4. Highly capital-intensive manufacturing**<br>Processed rice<br>Meat products<br>Milk products<br>Other food products |
| **5. Japan** | |
| **6. Slowly developing**<br>Argentina<br>Brazil<br>Mexico<br>Rest of Latin America<br>sub-Saharan Africa<br>Middle East<br>North Africa | **5. Moderately capital-intensive manufacturing**<br>Beverages and tobacco<br>Chemicals, rubbers, and plastics<br>Other manufacturing<br><br>**6. Moderately labor-intensive manufacturing**<br>Textiles<br>Leather goods<br>Lumber and wood products<br>Pulp and paper<br>Nonmetallic minerals<br>Fabricated metal products |
| | **7. Highly labor-intensive manufacturing**<br>Wearing apparel<br>Primary ferrous metals<br>Transport industries<br>Machinery and equipment |
| | **8. Petroleum and coal products** |
| | **9. Labor-intensive services**<br>Electricity, water, and gas<br>Construction<br>Trade and transport<br>Other private services<br>Other government services |
| | **10. Capital-intensive services**<br>Ownership of dwellings |

are not concentrated in the "highly labor-intensive" group but are distributed across the four manufacturing groups. This stems in part from the consolidation of skilled with unskilled labor in the data base, since the skill level and the average wage of most workers in light manufacturing might be expected to be lower than in heavy manufacturing.[4] It also stems from the use of factor proportions in the OIEs in designing the industry aggregation. According to Wood (1994), light manufactures imported from developing countries have more labor content than the home goods with which they now compete in the

**Table 7.2.** *Factor Proportions by Industry in the OIEs*

| | North America | | | European Union | | | Australia | | |
|---|---|---|---|---|---|---|---|---|---|
| | Labor | Capital | Land | Labor | Capital | Land | Labor | Capital | Land |
| Crops | (38)[a] 49 | (42) 40 | (20) 11 | (68) 67 | (21) 26 | (11) 7 | (55) 56 | (16) 19 | (29) 25 |
| Other agriculture, forestry and fishing | (44) 52 | (46) 41 | (10) 7 | (61) 63 | (30) 31 | (9) 6 | (48) 52 | (25) 28 | (27) 20 |
| Mining | (25) 36 | (75) 64 | (0) 0 | (69) 67 | (31) 33 | (0) 0 | (26) 37 | (74) 63 | (0) 0 |
| Highly capital-intensive manufacturing | (52) 54 | (48) 42 | (0) 3 | (57) 62 | (43) 34 | (0) 3 | (61) 59 | (39) 32 | (0) 9 |
| Moderately capital-intensive manufacturing | (54) 56 | (46) 44 | (0) 0 | (69) 67 | (31) 32 | (0) 0 | (54) 59 | (46) 40 | (0) 1 |
| Moderately labor-intensive manufacturing | (70) 67 | (30) 33 | (0) 0 | (73) 71 | (27) 29 | (0) 0 | (63) 62 | (37) 36 | (0) 1 |
| Highly labor-intensive manufacturing | (79) 73 | (21) 27 | (0) 0 | (80) 76 | (20) 24 | (0) 0 | (75) 69 | (25) 30 | (0) 0 |
| Petroleum and coal products | (62) 56 | (38) 44 | (0) 0 | (11) 22 | (89) 78 | (0) 0 | (40) 54 | (60) 45 | (0) 0 |
| Labor-intensive services | (65) 65 | (35) 35 | (0) 0 | (73) 72 | (27) 28 | (0) 0 | (69) 68 | (31) 32 | (0) 0 |

Share of (Direct[a]) and Total[b] Industry Expenditure on Domestic Factors

[a] Shares of factors employed directly in each industry to total value-added are reported in parentheses. Note that the excluded final category, ownership of dwellings, employed only capital.
[b] Includes indirect factor requirements, i.e., factor content of intermediate inputs into the industry. Total requirements coefficients were normalized to exclude indirect taxes and imports.
**Source:** GTAP model data base version 2. (See Chapter 3.)

Table 7.3. *Aggregate Elasticities of Substitution in Demand*[a]

|  | Between Home Goods and Generic Imports | Between Imports According to Source |
|---|---|---|
| Crops | 2.2 | 4.4 |
| Other agriculture, forestry, and fishing | 2.8 | 5.5 |
| Mining | 2.8 | 5.6 |
| Highly capital-intensive manufacturing | 2.2 | 4.4 |
| Moderately capital-intensive manufacturing | 2.2 | 4.4 |
| Moderately labor-intensive manufacturing | 2.5 | 5.4 |
| Highly labor-intensive manufacturing | 3.5 | 7.0 |
| Petroleum and coal products | 1.9 | 3.8 |
| Labor-intensive services | 1.9 | 3.9 |

[a] Note that the final category, ownership of dwellings, is not traded and therefore is excluded from above.

Table 7.4. *The Regional Share of World Population and GDP in 1970(%)*[a]

|  | Population | GDP |
|---|---|---|
| Australasia | .5 | 1.7 |
| North America | 6.9 | 41.5 |
| EU | 9.7 | 26.2 |
| Rapidly developing | 31.3 | 5.1 |
| Japan | 3.2 | 7.7 |
| Slowly developing | 48.4 | 17.8 |
| Total | 100.0 | 100.0 |

[a] Shares of global nominal gross domestic product (GDP), calculated by adding nominal regional GDP values, converted to $US using current exchange rates.
Source: World Bank, *World Tables* data base.

OIEs. This militates further against the model exhibiting strong HOS effects from developing country trade reform. Although a simulated surge of developing country imports might accurately predict the resulting change in home industry outputs, it is likely to yield an underestimate of the resulting change in the home sector's labor intensity.

## III    Growth and economic openness: The stylized facts

The contrast between the performance of economies that were poor in 1970 but have performed well since and those that were then already industrialized is best drawn between the OIEs of North America, Western Europe and Australasia, and the RDEs, which include Mainland China, Taiwan and Hong Kong, the Association of South East Asian Nations (ASEAN), and the Republic of Korea. It is evident from Table 7.4 that the rapidly developing group had about a third of the world's population in 1970 and about a twentieth of its recorded output.[5]

**Table 7.5.** *Economic Openness: Interregional Exports as Shares of GDP, (%)*

|  | 1970 | 1990 | Change, % GDP |
|---|---|---|---|
| Australasia | 12.6 | 13.1 | 0.6 |
| North America | 3.7 | 5.7 | 1.9 |
| EU | 7.9 | 9.0 | 1.0 |
| Rapidly developing | 6.8 | 25.8 | 19.0 |
| Japan | 9.5 | 9.8 | 0.3 |
| Slowly developing | 14.7 | 17.8 | 3.1 |

* Exports exclude intraregional trade.
Source: GDP estimates are from the World Bank, *World Tables* data base. Exports are from the United Nations International Trade Statistics, as supplied by the Australian National University's International Economic Databank.

**Table 7.6.** Measures of Growth, 1970—1990, (%)*

|  | Labor Use | Capital Stock | Total Factor Productivity | Real GDP |
|---|---|---|---|---|
| Australasia | 33 | 114 | 19 | 77 |
| North America | 22 | 82 | 30 | 76 |
| EU | 7 | 101 | 42 | 69 |
| Rapidly developing | 41 | 554 | 75 | 334 |
| Japan | 18 | 320 | 61 | 134 |

* Because their sources are disparate, there is no necessary consistency between the four columns of this table and any particular GDP function. Complete statistics on all columns are unavailable for the slow-growing developing group of economies.
Source: Labor use growth is based on population statistics from the World Bank, *World Tables* data base. The use of population here implies the assumption that age distributions and participation rates remained constant. Capital use and total factor productivity growth estimates are from Nehru and Dhareshwar (1993). Real GDP changes are from a revised version of the *Penn World Tables*, described originally by Summers and Heston (1991).

The RDEs were typical of many developing countries until the early 1970s in that their international commerce was retarded by a combination of high infrastructure costs, poor communications, and, most important, substantial tariff and nontariff barriers to trade. Beginning at various times after 1970 they, and numerous other developing countries, began to pursue export-led growth (World Bank 1993). Barriers to trade were reduced and international commerce actively fostered. A consequence of this, as indicated in Table 7.5, was a surge in exports and a considerable increase in economic openness during the subsequent two decades. By 1990, the RDEs were by far the most open of the regions identified.[6]

Associated with this increase in economic openness in many developing countries was comparatively strong growth performance. This is evident from Table 7.6, in which the contributions to overall growth of increased primary factor use and total factor productivity are separated out. From the last column it is clear that, of the regions identified in the model, the RDEs are aptly named. Their growth was facilitated primarily by a substantial increase in the capital stock, although rapid population growth also contributed. There is also evidence that comparatively large gains were made in these countries in total factor productivity (Nehru and Dhareshwar 1993). The sectoral impact of their

Table 7.7. *Trade Between the RDEs and the OIEs[a] (1992 $US billion)*

|  | From Rapidly Developing to Industrial | From Industrial to Rapidly Developing |
|---|---|---|
| Crops | 5 | 7 |
| Other agriculture, forestry, and fishing | 3 | 4 |
| Mining | 4 | 6 |
| Highly capital-intensive manufacturing | 5 | 5 |
| Moderately capital-intensive manufacturing | 35 | 27 |
| Moderately labor-intensive manufacturing | 41 | 19 |
| Highly labor-intensive manufacturing | 114 | 81 |
| Petroleum and coal products | 1 | 2 |
| Labor-intensive services | 31 | 23 |
| Ownership of dwellings | 0 | 0 |
| Total | 238 | 174 |

[a] The OIEs include Australasia, North America, and the EU.
Source: The GTAP data base version 2. (See also Chapter 3.)

expansion, combined with increased openness, is indicated by the composition of their trade with the OIEs in 1990, shown in Table 7.7. Half the value of their exports is in the highly labor-intensive group of products. However, the industry aggregation chosen tends to mask the contrast between the composition of their exports to the OIEs and their imports from them. Their imports include a smaller proportion of "moderately labor-intensive" products than their exports, but the substantial share in their imports due to labor-intensive products clearly includes heavy manufactures, which are intensive in human capital rather than raw labor.[7]

## IV    Experimental design

The effects on the OIEs of the trade, and other reforms that brought about the increased openness in the RDEs, are readily examined using the GTAP model. Since it is comparative static, however, the GTAP model cannot represent all the mechanisms that link those reforms to growth. The analysis therefore focuses, first, on the pure comparative static effects of the trade reforms necessary to achieve the observed increase in openness and, second, on the associated growth, introduced as exogenous changes in regional primary factor use. For this, the three scenarios delineated in Table 7.8 are sufficient.

In the first scenario, we ask how the world would have looked in the early 1990s, had the RDEs not shown extraordinary openness and growth performance over the two decades since 1970. They are assumed to have

**Table 7.8.** *Scenarios for the RDEs, 1970—1990*[a]

| | Growth, 1970—1990, % | | | 1990 Openness[a] |
|---|---|---|---|---|
| | | | | $\dfrac{X}{(GDP-X+M)}$ |
| | Labor Use | Capital Use | Total Factor Productivity | Percent |
| Scenarios for 1990: | | | | |
| Scenario 1: Reference Remain closed and grow like OIEs[b] | 14 | 92 | 0 | 7 |
| Scenario 2: Open Open but still grow like OIEs | 14 | 92 | 0 | 26 |
| Scenario 3: Open with growth Open and grow rapidly | 41 | 554 | 0 | 26 |

[a] The ratio of exports to absorption. This is used because these are the two components of total supply (C + I + G + X) and their ratio is comparable across regions. In scenario 1 this is assumed to expand between 1970 and 1990 in the same proportion as (and hence not faster than) the older industrial countries.
[b] The OIEs are Australasia, North America and the EU.
Source: Derived from observations presented in Tables 7.5 and 7.6.

opened more gradually and grown more slowly (at the precise average rate of the OIEs). This provides a reference against which it is possible to compare the remaining two scenarios. Scenario 2 introduces the economic reforms necessary to bring the levels of openness of these economies up to their observed values in the current GTAP data base.[8] Factor use in this scenario is as for the first. It is important to note that the closure chosen for all scenarios fixes factor use and renders unit factor rewards endogenous. Unlike the first two scenarios, the third requires no model simulation. It is that in which the policy reforms are undertaken and the comparatively rapid growth ensues in the RDEs, leading ultimately to the world characterized in the current data base.

Note that the scenarios are not different as to total factor productivity (TFP). The results on TFP to which we have access [such as those from Nehru and Dhareshwar (1993)] are at the economywide level only. Substantial single-country evidence suggests that productivity gains have been unevenly distributed across industries and that, in developing countries, they have been associated with exports (World Bank 1993, chap. 6). In the absence of an industry-specific data base on TFP we chose to construct scenarios 1 and 2 based on factor use and openness alone. The scenario 1 gain in GDP in the RDEs turned out to be precisely that anticipated from the final column of Table 7.6.[9] Pending further information on the industry distribution of changes in technology, no complementary technology shocks have been applied.[10]

## V     Simulated effects of openness and growth

Comparing scenarios 2 and 3 with 1, the effects of openness and growth on the quantities produced in the OIEs are given in Table 7.9. There are two consistent effects. First, agriculture expands in the OIEs. This is a clear HOS

**Table 7.9. Changes in Sectoral Output in the OIEs***

| | North America | | European Union | | Australasia | |
|---|---|---|---|---|---|---|
| | Open | Open With Growth | Open | Open With Growth | Open | Open With Growth |
| Crops | .9 | 4.9 | -.7 | 1.8 | .8 | 6.8 |
| Other agriculture, forestry, and fishing | .3 | 1.3 | -.1 | .4 | .9 | 3.4 |
| Mining | .5 | -.3 | -.3 | -.6 | 3.6 | -3.3 |
| Highly capital-intensive manufacturing | .1 | .4 | -.1 | .2 | -.4 | 1.1 |
| Moderately capital-intensive manufacturing | -.6 | -.7 | -.7 | -.7 | -2.7 | -3.6 |
| Moderately labor-intensive manufacturing | -1.2 | -1.9 | -.7 | -1.1 | -1.9 | -2.2 |
| Highly labor-intensive manufacturing | -.8 | -1.3 | -1.2 | -1.4 | -4.2 | -5.6 |
| Petroleum and coal products | .1 | .2 | .0 | .0 | .7 | .6 |
| Labor-intensive services | .2 | .2 | .3 | .3 | .1 | .2 |
| Ownership of dwellings | .2 | .3 | .2 | .2 | .7 | 1.3 |

*Spanning header:* Percent Change in the Volume of Output

* Listed are proportional departures of scenarios 2 and 3 from the reference scenario (Table 9.8).
Source: Simulations of the GTAP model, as discussed in the text.

result, since the RDEs comprise predominantly land-scarce, densely populated countries. Their expansion raises the excess demand for the land-intensive agricultural exports of the OIEs. Second, all but the most capital-intensive of the manufacturing industry groups decline. This is another HOS result, since the OIEs have a comparative disadvantage in labor-intensive manufacturing relative to the RDEs. Both emerge as purely comparative static effects of the policy reform (openness only) and are enhanced by the associated growth reflected in scenario 3.

The particularly large amplification of the expansion of OIE agriculture when RDE growth is added is a further HOS effect, consistent with the Rybczynski Theorem. The principal source of RDE growth is an increase in the region's capital stock. Terms-of-trade changes are not large, since the RDEs still supply only 6% of global GDP.[11] The tradeable goods sector most intensive in capital – namely, manufacturing – expands while other tradeable goods sectors, including agriculture, contract. There is another reason for this enhancement that helps to explain why the crops sector of the EU contracts under the pure comparative statics of the trade reform (openness only). It is not due to any HOS effect but, instead, to the differentiation of home products from imports. The EU contraction results from a decrease in domestic absorption of agricultural products. This occurs because of a contraction in capital-intensive manufacturing (particularly food processing), which is a major user of agricultural products. The combination of openness with growth, however, raises export demand in the EU sufficiently to compensate for the decline in domestic absorption.

A final point to emerge from Table 7.9 is that the OIE structural change that stems from RDE openness and growth is most extensive in Australasia. This is because the intensity of Australasia's trade with the populous Asian economies is greater than that for either North America or the EU.

The corresponding aggregate effects on welfare, GDP, and exports are given in Table 7.10. OIE welfare, measured as an index of the volume of aggregate consumption, tends to rise with the combination of RDE openness and growth. Across regions, at least, this combination of changes appears Pareto-improving. The same is true of the volume measure of GDP, though the increases recorded in North America and the EU are imperceptible. And, not surprisingly, the combined shock raises the volume of exports everywhere. Among the OIEs, Australasia derives the most net benefit from RDE expansion, by virtue of its high trading intensity with RDE countries and its more substantial increase in agricultural production. Of course, it also undergoes considerably more structural change than do the other OIEs. North America and the EU experience only modest structural change, deriving little or no net benefit.

Finally, the factor market effects in the OIEs are summarized in Table 7.11. In general, their wage–rental ratios decline – more so against land, the

**Table 7.10.** *Percent Changes in Regional Welfare, GDP, and Exports[a]*

| | Welfare (per capita)[b] | | GDP | | Exports | |
|---|---|---|---|---|---|---|
| | Open | Open with growth | Open | Open with growth | Open | Open with growth |
| Australasia | 1.6 | 2.4 | 0.2 | 0.3 | 1.9 | 4.2 |
| North America | 0.4 | 0.5 | 0.0 | 0.0 | 1.8 | 4.3 |
| European Union | 0.7 | 0.7 | 0.1 | 0.0 | 0.7 | 4.3 |
| Rapidly developing | 8.7 | 40.4 | 10.9 | 59.7 | 45.3 | 84.4 |
| Japan | 1.9 | 2.4 | 0.1 | 0.1 | 1.2 | 9.7 |
| Slowly developing | 0.6 | 0.7 | 0.0 | 0.0 | 1.3 | 1.4 |

[a] Listed are proportional departures of scenarios 2 and 3 from the reference scenario (Table 7.8).
[b] A quantity index of per capita regional aggregate household consumption. See Chapter 2. No adjustment has been made for the changes of population implied in the growth shocks for the rapidly developing economies.
Source: Simulations of the GTAP model, as discussed in the text.

**Table 7.11. Changes in Relative Unit Factor Rewards in the OIEs[a]**

| Percent Change in Unit Reward | North America | | European Union | | Australasia | |
|---|---|---|---|---|---|---|
| | Open | Open With Growth | Open | Open With Growth | Open | Open With Growth |
| **1. Relative to the rate of return on capital** | | | | | | |
| Labor | -.7 | -.10 | -.06 | -.06 | -.38 | .0 |
| Land | 1.16 | 8.28 | -.95 | 2.02 | .77 | 10.45 |
| **2. Relative to the CPI[b]** | | | | | | |
| Labor | .17 | .29 | .18 | .24 | .69 | 1.35 |
| Land | 1.39 | 8.67 | -.70 | 2.32 | 1.85 | 11.81 |
| Capital | .24 | .38 | .24 | .30 | 1.08 | 1.36 |

[a] Listed are proportional departures of scenarios 2 and 3 from the reference scenario (Table 7.8), expressed as percentages of 1990 values.
[b] The CPI is a region-specific index of final consumption prices.
Source: Simulations of the GTAP model, as discussed in the text.

owners of which appear to be the principal OIE beneficiaries of RDE expansion. This is consistent with HOS model predictions. The further HOS prediction that labor would also lose relative to final product prices is not borne out, however. Comparisons with region-specific indices of final consumption prices show labor gaining in both scenarios 2 and 3, throughout the OIEs.[12] This confirms our expectation that the HOS effects would be diluted by the assumption that home products are differentiated from imports and by the aggregation bias effects associated with consolidating raw labor and human capital.

Again, because of its high trade intensity with the RDEs, Australasia stands out as showing substantially larger gains in real factor rewards. The advent of openness with growth in the RDEs makes capital considerably cheaper there, raising their output of minerals and processed raw materials. These sectors are unrestrained in the GTAP model by specific factors (such as mineral or energy deposits); therefore, they expand in competition with the capital-intensive minerals sector of Australasia. Thus, Australasia's expanding labor-intensive agriculture and contracting capital-intensive natural resource–based goods sector raises demand for labor relative to capital. It is therefore the only OIE group not experiencing an apparent fall in the wage–rental ratio due to RDE expansion. These effects are less significant for North America and the EU, since their natural resource–based goods sectors are much less important.

## VI    Inferring changes in the distribution of employment by occupation in the OIES

The consolidation of labor into a single factor in the GTAP model notwithstanding, it is possible to estimate shifts in labor demand across occupation by drawing upon separate data on the human capital content of the labor force in each industry. We have collected sufficient data to make it possible to split payments to labor by industry for the OIEs alone, though we have not used direct measures of human capital (such as years of education). Instead, we have used the International Labor Organization (ILO) standard occupational classification, which forms the basis of survey data on the skill composition of labor forces in all the OIEs, to divide payments to labor in each industry between a high-skill "more highly paid" category and a low-skill "less highly paid" category.[13] The results, which are summarized in Table 7.12, make it clear that manufacturing in the OIEs generally is intensive not only in labor but, more particularly, in low-skill labor.[14]

Applying this occupational distribution to the changes in generic labor use in each sector that emerge from the model simulations, we are able to estimate changes in employment, by occupation, which occur as a consequence of

Table 7.12. *Occupational Shares (%) in Direct Payments to Labor in the OIEs*[a]

| | North America | | European Union | | Australia | |
|---|---|---|---|---|---|---|
| | More Highly Paid | Less Highly Paid | More Highly Paid | Less Highly Paid | More Highly Paid | Less Highly Paid |
| Crops | 58 | 42 | 60 | 40 | 61 | 39 |
| Other agriculture, forestry, and fishing | 57 | 43 | 63 | 37 | 62 | 38 |
| Mining | 33 | 67 | 32 | 68 | 21 | 79 |
| Highly capital-intensive manufacturing | 23 | 77 | 25 | 75 | 17 | 83 |
| Moderately capital-intensive manufacturing | 41 | 59 | 33 | 67 | 27 | 73 |
| Moderately labor-intensive manufacturing | 29 | 71 | 25 | 75 | 20 | 80 |
| Highly labor-intensive manufacturing | 42 | 58 | 33 | 67 | 22 | 78 |
| Petroleum and coal products | 36 | 64 | 55 | 45 | 30 | 70 |
| Labor-intensive services | 41 | 59 | 42 | 58 | 41 | 59 |

[a] Based on the ILO Classification of Occupations, the more highly paid include managers and administrators, professionals, and paraprofessionals. The less highly paid include plant and machine operators and drivers, tradespersons, clerks, laborers and related workers, salespersons, and personal services workers.
Source: For the US: Bureau of the Census (1993); for the EU: Eurostat (1991a,b) and Ryan(1993); for Australia: Kenderes and Strzelecki (1993). The industrial classification in each case was concorded to the SALTER level (Hambley (1993)) prior to aggregation to the 10 sectors shown.

**Table 7.13.** *Percent Changes in Employment by Occupation, "Open High Growth" Over Reference Scenario*

|  | Agricultural | More Highly Paid[a] | Less Highly Paid[b] |
|---|---|---|---|
| North America | 3.94 | .00 | -.07 |
| EU | 1.08 | .05 | -.07 |
| Australasia | 6.74 | .52 | -.27 |

[a] Managers and administrators, professionals, and paraprofessionals, as in Table 7.12, including more highly paid agricultural workers.
[b] Plant and machine operators and drivers, tradespersons, clerks, laborers and related workers, salespersons, and personal services workers, as in Table 7.12, including less highly paid agricultural workers.
Source: Estimates obtained by imposing the distribution of employment among occupations in the older industrial economies (Table 7.12) on the changes in generic labor use by industry emerging from the simulation.

openness and growth in the RDEs. If anything, this approximation underestimates the change in the distribution of employment across skill groups, since it assumes that employment composition within industries remains the same.[15] Given the broad industry groups adopted here, this is very unlikely. The results for the OIEs are given in Table 7.13. They show a tendency toward declining demand for low-skill workers and rising demand for high-skill workers. This contrast is strongest for Australasia, possibly because the industries that expand (agriculture and services) tend to use skilled labor, while the sectors that decline (natural resource–based products and manufacturing) are intensive in unskilled labor.

## VII Conclusion

The opening and rapid expansion of Asian developing countries is examined for its effects on the OIEs. Although the process is found to cause substantial changes in the structure of the OIE economies, none appears to suffer reduced economic welfare or GDP as a consequence. The resulting surge of labor-intensive exports from the RDEs does have unequal effects on workers and the owners of capital and land, however. The wage–rental ratio declines throughout the OIEs, and more so relative to land rents.

This inequality notwithstanding, all unit factor rewards rise relative to final consumption prices in all the OIE regions. Their economies enjoy a favorable shift in their terms of trade and increased consumer demand, which tends to mitigate the effects on demand due to cheaper imports. And, in any case, the labor (including human capital) share of value-added in their export industries tends to be just as high as in those that compete with Asian imports. Nevertheless, we present evidence that the results imply a shift in the composition of labor demand in the industrial economies against low-skill workers and hence; had we been able to disaggregate the labor force by skill level,[16] low-skill workers might have appeared as losers from Asian economic reform and growth.

This analysis is constrained somewhat by the structure of the existing GTAP data base and model. While its strength lies in its representation of the reciprocal nature of international trade, so that the RDEs are both competitors and customers of the OIEs, the weakness of the current version is that its data base does not capture the dispersion of skill and capital intensities across industries. (See Chapter 14 for an early attempt at remedying this deficiency.) In the OIEs, the apportionment of value-added between generic labor and other factors seems similar in light and heavy manufacturing. Yet separate evidence indicates that their skill mixes differ substantially. Disaggregation by skill level would therefore greatly improve the model's representation of factor markets. Further, the disaggregation of households in each region between those supplying unskilled labor, on the one hand, and those supplying human or physical capital, on the other, would provide scope to capture the effects of different preferences between winners and losers on derived labor demand.[17]

NOTES

1. The interested reader is referred to Chapter 2 for more detail on the specification of the model.
2. Of course, some nonhomotheticity is already built into the GTAP constant difference of elasticities (CDE) demand system, which is described in Part II.
3. As is common with such models (Brown and Stern 1989), results tend to be critically sensitive to the estimates of elasticities of substitution in demand that are used. Indeed, when these elasticities are in the range commonly estimated (1–5), large-country effects are prominent and income changes dominate relative price shifts in determining the mix of consumption among home goods and imports. In this framework, trade reform can move border distortions away from their optimal levels for some countries and have little effect in switching domestic demand toward imports. Some recent studies have suggested, however, that the common range of estimates of elasticities of substitution in demand is too low (Horridge 1987; Tyers et al. 1996).
4. This pattern is exhibited by US data presented in Leamer (1993). The difference in the occupational pattern between the four types of manufacturing is substantial, however, as indicated later, in Table 7.12.
5. In this analysis, we ignore errors in the use of market exchange rates as weights in international comparisons. The use of weights based on purchasing power parity (PPP) makes an especially large difference in the case of China. When these are used, China's share of world GDP by 1990 is raised from 2% to over 6% (IMF 1993, Annex IV). By contrast, that of Japan is reduced from 17% to only 8%.
6. The regional aggregation chosen tends to hide similar transformations in some other developing countries during this period. The large change in China's openness would be moderated somewhat were its GDP measured assuming PPP.
7. The trade contrast is better drawn in an earlier version of this chapter [McDougall and Tyers (1993), table 7], which showed that "heavy manufactures" dominate RDEs imports.
8. Scenario 1 is derived by forcing on the RDEs a level of openness equivalent to what they would have achieved had they opened at the rate of the OIEs over

1970–1990. This required the imposition of a generic 170% increase in the power of their 1990 tariffs (the resulting ratio of domestic to border prices, controlling for marketing margins). Barriers thus enlarged are removed in scenarios 2 and 3.

9. To see this, note that the average real growth in GDP achieved in the OIEs between 1970 and 1990 was approximately 74%. The growth achieved by the RDEs was 333%. Had the RDEs grown as slowly as the OIEs in that period, their 1990 GDP would have been smaller by 100 (433 − 174)/433 = 60%. This is the precise gain that scenario 1 yields.

10. It is likely that the observed difference in growth rates has been due to a combination of trade barrier reductions and technical change, where the technical change is distributed unevenly across both sectors and factors. New information is required before realistic shocks of this type can be constructed.

11. As stated in note 5, above, this is probably an underestimate.

12. In North America particularly, the net gains in all factor prices relative to final product prices contrast with the negligible gains in GDP and welfare indicated in Table 7.10. This suggests that the structural change there supports subsidized industries (e.g., agriculture), reducing allocative efficiency. Factor income gains are offset by net reductions in the revenue from indirect taxes.

13. We avoided human capital measures because of their lack of homogeneity. Their use tends to inflate the skill content of the labor force relative to the use of occupational criteria. The occupational data also have their biases, however. In particular, the predominance of the self-employed in agriculture tends to lead to the classification of a disproportionate share of the rural population as "managers." This is evident from the first two rows of Table 7.12, which show agriculture to be intensive in "more highly paid" workers.

14. The largely nontraded labor-intensive services sector, however, appears to use mostly high-skill workers. This is very likely a property of the skill mix in OIEs that does not extend to the developing countries.

15. That changes in factor proportions have occurred within industry is confirmed for the US by Berman et al. 1994.

16. This result is reported in McDougall and Tyers (1994).

17. It should be noted that the analysis of Australasian factor markets in the face of Asian growth is impaired by the lack of any specific factor (mineral, energy, or other fixed resource) to constrain the response of the mining and petroleum and coal industries' responses to changes in the cost of capital. This tends to enhance the expansion of this sector with growth in Asia to an unrealistic extent, weakening the analysis of trade with Australasia, where that sector tends to dominate exports.

## REFERENCES

Berman, E., J. Bound, and Z. Griliches (1994) "Changes in the Demand for Skilled Labor within U.S. Manufacturing: Evidence from the Annual Survey of Manufacturers." *Quarterly Journal of Economics* 109(May):367–397.

Borjas, G. J., R. B. Freeman, and L. F. Katz (1991) "On the Labor Market Effects of Immigration and Trade," NBER Working Paper No. 3761. Cambridge, MA.

Bound, J., and G. Johnson (1992) "Changes in the Structure of Wages in the 1980s: An Evaluation of Alternative Explanations." *American Economic Review* 82(June):371–392.

Brown, D. K., and R. M. Stern (1989) "US–Canada Bilateral Tariff Elimination: The Role of Product Differentiation and Market Structure," chapter 7. In R. C. Feenstra (ed.) *Trade Policies for International Competitiveness*. Chicago: University of Chicago Press.

Bureau of the Census, Government of the United States (1993) *Current Population Survey of March 1992*. Washington, DC: USGPO.

Deardorf, A. (1986) "FIRless and FIRwoes: How Preferences Can Interfere with the Theorems of International Trade," *Journal of International Economics* 20:131–142.

Ethier, W. (1984) "Higher Dimensional Issues in Trade Theory," *Handbook of International Economics,* Vol. 1. In R. W. Jones and P. B. Kenen (eds). Amsterdam: North-Holland.

Eurostat (1991a) *Earnings: Industry and Services*. Luxembourg.

Eurostat (1991b) *Labor Costs: Survey 1988*. Luxembourg.

Flavey, R. (1995) "Trade Liberalization and Factor Price Convergence," Project Paper No. 1, Trade and Wage Dispersion Project, Department of Economics, The Faculties, Australian National University.

Freeman, R. B. (1993) "Working Under Different Rules," Cambridge, MA: *NBER Reporter*.

Freeman, R. B., and L. F. Katz, eds. (1994) *Differences and Changes in Wage Structures*. Chicago: University of Chicago Press.

Gregory, R. G., and F. Vella (1993) "Real Wages, Employment and Wage Dispersion in US and Australian Labor Markets," Department of Economics, Research School of Social Sciences, Australian National University.

Hambley, J. (1993) "Early Stage Processing of International Trade and Input–Output Data for SALTER, SALTER Working Paper No. 15. Canberra, Australia: Australian Industry Commission.

Heckscher, E. (1949) "The Effect of Foreign Trade on the Distribution of Income." In H. S. Ellis and L. A. Metzler (eds.), *Readings in the Theory of International Trade*. Homewood, IL: Irwin.

Horridge, M. (1987) "The Long Term Costs of Protection: Experimental Analysis with Different Closures of an Australian Computable General Equilibrium Model." Ph.D. dissertation, Department of Economics, University of Melbourne.

IMF (1993) *World Economic Outlook*. Washington, DC: International Monetary Fund.

Jomini, P., J. F. Zeitsch, R. McDougall, A. Welsh, S. Brown, J. Hambley, and J. Kelly (1991) *SALTER: A General Equilibrium Model of the World Economy*, Vol. 1, "Model Structure, Database and Parameters." Canberra, Australia: Australian Industry Commission.

Katz, L. F., G. W. Loveman, and D. G. Blanchflower (1993) "A Comparison of Changes in the Structure of Wages in Four OECD Countries." In R. B. Freeman and L. F. Katz (eds.), *Differences and Changes in Wage Structures*. Chicago: University of Chicago Press.

Kemp, M. C., Y. K. Ng, and K. Shimomura (1993) "The International Diffusion of the Fruits of Technical Progress," *International Economic Review* 34(2):381–385.

Kenderes, M., and A. Strzelecki (1993) "Listing of the 1986–87 ORANI Database," Industry Commission Research Memorandum No. 0A-569, Canberra, Australia.

Krueger, A. (1968) "Factor Endowments and Per Capita Income Differences Among Countries," *Economic Journal* 77:641–659.

Krugman, P., and R. Lawrence (1993) "Trade, Jobs and Wages," NBER Working Paper No. 4478. Cambridge, MA.

Lawrence, R. Z., and M. J. Slaughter (1993) "Trade and US Wages: Great Sucking Sound or Small Hiccup?" *Brookings Papers on Economic Activity: Microeconomics.* Washington, DC.

Leamer, E. E. (1993) "The Wage Effects of a US–Mexican Free Trade Agreement," NBER Working Paper No. 3991, Cambridge, MA.

McDougall, R., and R. Tyers (1993) "Asian Expansion and Labor Saving Technical Change: Factor Market Effects and Policy Reactions," Principal paper presented at the session on Trade Patterns in the Pacific Rim: Outlook for the Next Decade, 1994 Summer Meetings of the American Agricultural Economics Association. San Diego, CA.

McDougall, R., and R. Tyers (1994) "Developing Country Expansion and Factor Markets in Industrial Countries," *American Journal of Agricultural Economics,* 76(December):1111–1118.

Mincer, J. (1991) "Human Capital, Technology and the Wage Structure: What Do the Time Series Show?" NBER Working Paper No. 3581, Cambridge, MA.

Murphy, K. M., and F. Welch (1989) "Wage Premiums for College Graduates: Recent Growth and Possible Explanations," *Educational Researcher* 18:17–26.

Murphy, K. M., and F. Welch (1991) "The Role of International Trade in Wage Differentials." In M. Kosters (ed.), *Workers and Their Wages.* Washington, DC: American Enterprise Institute.

Nehru, V., and A. Dhareshwar (1993) "New Estimates of Total Factor Productivity Growth for Eighty Three Industrial and Developing Countries," World Bank Policy Working Paper No. 1128. World Bank, Washington, DC.

Ohlin, B. (1993) *Interregional and International Trade.* Cambridge, MA: Harvard University Press.

Ryan, C. (1993) "The SALTER Model: Construction of the European Database," SALTER Working Paper No. 10. Canberra, Australia: Australian Industry Commission.

Samuelson, P. A. (1948) "International Trade and Equalization of Factor Prices," *Economic Journal* 58:163–184.

Summers, R., and A. Heston (1991) "The Penn World Table (Mark 5): An Expanded Set of International Comparisons, 1950–1988," *Quarterly Journal of Economics* 106(2).

Tyers, R., P. Gibbard, J. Golley, M. Austria, and C. S. Suh (1996) "Imperfect Competition and Returns to Scale in General Equilibrium: Results for Four Archetype Western Pacific Economies," expansion of an earlier report to the Australian Research Council, *Pacific Economic Papers.* Australian National University.

Whalley, J. (1989) "Recent Trade Liberalization in the Developing World: What Is Behind It and Where Is It Headed?" NBER Working Paper No. 3057, Cambridge, MA.

Wood, A. (1991a) "How Much Does Trade with the South Affect Workers in the North?" *World Bank Research Observer* 6(1):19–36.

Wood, A. (1991b) A New-Old Theoretical View of North-South Trade, Employment and Wages," Discussion Paper No. 292, Institute of Development Studies, University of Sussex.

Wood, A. (1994) *North-South Trade, Employment and Inequality.* Oxford: Clarendon Press.

World Bank (1993) *The East Asian Miracle: Economic Growth and Public Policy.* New York: Oxford University Press.

CHAPTER 8

# An evaluation of the Cairns Group strategies for agriculture in the Uruguay Round

*Donald MacLaren*

## I    Introduction and overview

The scope of the agenda for the agricultural trade negotiations in the Uruguay Round of the General Agreement on Tariffs and Trade (GATT) was influenced to a considerable degree by the coalition known as the Cairns Group, an agenda-moving group that succeeded in subjecting its domestic agricultural policies to international negotiation.[1,2] This initial outcome of the coalition's activities was a significant achievement and a departure from the agricultural agenda in previous negotiating rounds, an agenda that had been deficient because the contracting parties had avoided the issue of domestic agricultural policies.[3] The main leadership of the group has been, and continues to be, provided by Australia. In the four years following that country's petulant behavior at the GATT Ministerial Meeting in 1982, a more positive attitude was adopted toward international diplomacy in the area of agricultural trade policy, for example, by producing the so-called Red and Gold books, thereby bringing into the public domain an evaluation of the self-inflicted economic harm done by agricultural policies.[4] Hence, at Punta del Este in 1986, the Cairns Group was able to help establish, through skillful diplomacy with the US and the European Union (EU), the agenda for the agricultural negotiations.[5]

During the negotiations, the coalition maintained substantial and unified pressure on these major players. This, in itself, was an achievement because, since the group's inception, there had been internal tensions within it: between "North" and "South" over the issue of services, and between Canada and Australia over agricultural policy matters. Canada, although being party to the Cairns Group submission to the GATT in 1987, insisted on submitting its own national views because these were not wholly consistent with those of its partners, and in particular Australia's. These obvious tensions arose between the two countries partly because of traditional differences in the style of diplomacy pursued and partly because of differences in their definition of the

212

basic underlying goal of agricultural policy reform (Higgott and Cooper 1990; Cooper 1992).

Throughout the round, it was apparent that Canada was more accommodating toward domestic agricultural policies and the associated income objectives for the farm sector, and it continued to subsidize its agriculture and to insist on maintaining the supply management regimes for dairy and poultry products. On the other hand, after 1983, the commonwealth government in Australia sought to deflect the political costs of deregulating the agricultural sector, to the extent permitted by constitutional constraints, by promulgating the view in the rural sector that multilateral trade reform would more than compensate for a reduction in commonwealth government assistance (Higgott and Cooper 1990). The Canadian government did not follow this lead and has been more sensitive politically to the issue of farm incomes (Cooper 1992).

As the round dragged on, the Cairns Group, as reflected in the utterances of the Australian government, became more strident in its criticism of the stances taken by both the US and the EU on the reform of their agricultural policies. This increased stridency reflected, no doubt, the increasing frustration felt by the group that, once again, any final deal on agriculture was in danger of being negotiated bilaterally between the US and the EU, the very outcome that the Cairns Group had been established to prevent. That frustration was justified because at the important Blair House Accord between the US and the EU in November 1992, the Cairns Group was not a participant. On balance, the EU was the main target of Australian criticisms, the belief being that the Common Agricultural Policy is more destructive of the well-being of the Australian farm sector, of the national economy, and of international agricultural trade in general than are the agricultural policies of the US.[6]

The purpose of this chapter is twofold. The first objective is to investigate quantitatively the individual gains to Australia and to Canada of unilateral agricultural trade liberalization by the US and the EU. By measuring the gains to each of Australia and Canada, it will be possible to determine whether the Cairns Group was correct in supporting the Australian position of attacking the Common Agricultural Policy more than the agricultural policy of the US. The second objective is to measure the distributional effects of agricultural policy liberalization within Australia and Canada. By quantifying the effects of their unilateral liberalization, it will be possible to determine whether political sensitivity to farm incomes had a sound economic foundation in political economy.

## II    Aggregation

For purposes of this chapter, the Global Trade Analysis Project (GTAP) data base was aggregated to six regions: Australia, Canada, the US, Japan, the EU, and the rest of the world (ROW). Because version 2 of the data base does not identify all the Cairns Group countries individually, and because agriculture appears to be of greater concern to Australia and Canada than to the South American and Association of South East Asian Nations (ASEAN) members of the group, the Cairns Group countries, minus Australia and Canada, could not be aggregated into a separate region. An alternative to the aggregation chosen would have been to consider the effects of the Cairns Group strategy on the major subgroups within the group and to evaluate the North–South tensions over services together with those for agriculture. However, the policy simulations are restricted to those involving the agenda for agriculture; therefore, only the two countries of interest within the group – namely, Australia and Canada – are identified separately. This is also why the commodity aggregation is heavily agriculture-focused, breaking out: wheat, other grains, wool, rice, meat products, milk products, other agricultural and food products, manufacturing and services.[7]

Agriculture and food are important sectors in all the regions identified. This is particularly true for Australia, where food's contribution to export earnings is one of the highest in the industrialized world. For that reason the model was run with a general equilibrium closure. The basic production data from the aggregation of countries and commodities are shown in Table 8.1. There are considerable differences among the regions with respect to the relative importance of the separate commodity aggregates. For example, wool is very important to Australia, but less so to the other regions. Rice stands out in Japan, as do grains in the US and Canada.

The patterns of gross exports in tradeable products are shown in Tables 8.2 and 8.3. (The emphasis on exports rather than on imports should not be interpreted as mercantilist; rather, it reflects the concern of the Cairns Group for improved market access, and for less distorted international markets for agricultural products.) For Australia (Table 8.2), the EU (at 15%) is a more

**Table 8.1.** *Value of Sectoral Output (1992 $US million)*

|  | Australia | Canada | USA | Japan | EU | ROW |
|---|---|---|---|---|---|---|
| Wheat | 2,037 | 5,564 | 22,652 | 4,583 | 38,572 | 32,807 |
| Other grains | 707 | 3,295 | 44,697 | 7,041 | 32,210 | 103,436 |
| Wool | 3,393 | 2 | 236 | 7 | 1,004 | 3,932 |
| Rice | 350 | 85 | 5,547 | 76,010 | 6,991 | 249,910 |
| Meat products | 7,558 | 12,858 | 79,822 | 32,953 | 179,362 | 152,969 |
| Milk products | 4,002 | 8,256 | 47,855 | 19,803 | 112,971 | 46,409 |
| O. Ag. and food | 30,601 | 57,712 | 469,736 | 408,465 | 881,982 | 1,090,260 |
| Mnfc and Svces | 455,710 | 1,005,880 | 8,951,790 | 6,184,810 | 9,987,410 | 9,171,640 |

Source: GTAP data base.

Table 8.2. *Pattern of Australia's and Canada's Agricultural Exports (fob basis)*

|  | Australia | Canada | US | Japan | EU | ROW | Total |
|---|---|---|---|---|---|---|---|
|  |  |  | Share of Total, % |  |  |  | $US m |
| *Wheat* |  |  |  |  |  |  |  |
| Australia | 0 | 0 | 0 | 15 | 0 | 85 | 1,200 |
| Canada | 0 | 0 | 5 | 8 | 3 | 84 | 3,986 |
| *Other grains* |  |  |  |  |  |  |  |
| Australia | 0 | 0 | 0 | 29 | 2 | 69 | 354 |
| Canada | 0 | 0 | 21 | 24 | 4 | 51 | 643 |
| *Wool* |  |  |  |  |  |  |  |
| Australia | 0 | 0 | 4 | 17 | 38 | 40 | 2,834 |
| Canada | 0 | 0 | 100 | 0 | 0 | 0 | 1 |
| *Rice* |  |  |  |  |  |  |  |
| Australia | 0 | 0 | 0 | 0 | 15 | 85 | 93 |
| Canada | 0 | 0 | 0 | 0 | 0 | 100 | 1 |
| *Meat products* |  |  |  |  |  |  |  |
| Australia | 0 | 4 | 33 | 35 | 5 | 23 | 2,625 |
| Canada | 1 | 0 | 67 | 18 | 6 | 8 | 931 |
| *Milk products* |  |  |  |  |  |  |  |
| Australia | 0 | 0 | 2 | 20 | 2 | 76 | 676 |
| Canada | 1 | 0 | 10 | 9 | 15 | 65 | 157 |
| *O. Ag. and food prod.* |  |  |  |  |  |  |  |
| Australia | 0 | 3 | 5 | 24 | 12 | 56 | 3,499 |
| Canada | 1 | 0 | 60 | 14 | 12 | 13 | 6,211 |
| *Total* |  |  |  |  |  |  |  |
| Australia | 0 | 2 | 10 | 23 | 15 | 49 | 11,281 |
| Canada | 1 | 0 | 39 | 13 | 8 | 39 | 11,930 |

Source: GTAP data base.

important destination for exports than is the US (10%), even with trade-distorting agricultural policies in place. However, ROW (49%) and Japan (23%) are even more important. For Canada (Table 8.2), the US (39%) and ROW (39%) are equally important and easily dominate the EU (8%) and Japan (13%) as export destinations. This base period information provides insight into the differences between the Australian and Canadian positions and into their respective sensitivity to the US and the EU. These data are also important in understanding the outcomes of the unilateral trade liberalization experiments for the US and the EU as demonstrated in section IV below. For

**Table 8.3.** *Pattern of US's and EU's Agricultural Exports (fob basis)*

|  | Australia | Canada | USA | Japan | EU | ROW | Total |
|---|---|---|---|---|---|---|---|
|  | Share of Total, % | | | | | | $US m |
| *Wheat* | | | | | | | |
| US | 0 | 0 | 0 | 14 | 2 | 83 | 4,219 |
| EU | 0 | 0 | 0 | 0 | 0 | 100 | 1,269 |
| *Other grains* | | | | | | | |
| US | 0 | 1 | 0 | 30 | 6 | 63 | 6,465 |
| EU | 0 | 0 | 0 | 3 | 0 | 97 | 783 |
| *Wool* | | | | | | | |
| US | 0 | 0 | 0 | 8 | 54 | 38 | 13 |
| EU | 5 | 1 | 5 | 35 | 0 | 53 | 110 |
| *Rice* | | | | | | | |
| US | 0 | 6 | 0 | 0 | 21 | 73 | 923 |
| EU | 0 | 0 | 2 | 0 | 0 | 97 | 243 |
| *Meat products* | | | | | | | |
| US | 0 | 12 | 0 | 49 | 5 | 34 | 4,431 |
| EU | 0 | 0 | 7 | 19 | 0 | 73 | 3,865 |
| *Milk products* | | | | | | | |
| US | 1 | 6 | 0 | 6 | 2 | 85 | 410 |
| EU | 1 | 1 | 6 | 4 | 0 | 88 | 4,701 |
| *O. Ag. and food prod.* | | | | | | | |
| US | 1 | 11 | 0 | 18 | 25 | 45 | 30,821 |
| EU | 1 | 3 | 17 | 8 | 0 | 71 | 30,671 |
| *Total Exported to* | | | | | | | |
| US | 1 | 9 | 0 | 22 | 18 | 51 | 47,282 |
| EU | 1 | 2 | 14 | 8 | 0 | 75 | 41,642 |

Source: GTAP data base.

the US (Table 8.3), ROW (51%) is the most important destination, with Japan (22%) and the EU (18%) almost equally important. The pattern of EU exports is more concentrated, with 75% of exports going to ROW (Table 8.3) and only 14% destined for the US; Australia and Canada are insignificant export destinations.

## III    Experimental design

The experiments in this chapter were designed to help evaluate two strands in the Cairns Group strategy for negotiating reforms in agriculture as part of the Uruguay Round in the GATT. The first strand reflects the group's concentration on the damage done to international agricultural trade and, hence their economies, by the EU's Common Agricultural Policy (CAP). The second strand reflects the different treatment of agriculture by the governments of Australia and Canada: the former trying to convince those in the agricultural sector that the short-run pain created by deregulation of the sector would be more than offset by the longer-term gains from multilateral agricultural trade liberalization; the latter country remaining much more susceptible to lobbying by those in its agricultural sector.

The policy experiments run are as follows.

- Experiment 1 (E1) considers the unilateral removal of domestic agricultural policy instruments and agricultural trade policy instruments by the US without adjustment for the existence of set-aside. It is assumed that such set-aside land is prevented from reentering production by means of an expanded conservation reserve program. Also, the EU is assumed to insulate its agricultural sector. This is achieved on the import side by swapping $pr(i,e\_u)$, the price ratio of imports to domestic goods, with $tm(i,e\_u)$, thereby mimicking the variable levy. On the export side, $tx(i,e\_u)$ is permitted to vary, and output $qo(i,e\_u)$ is fixed. This mimics the workings of the variable export subsidies. [See Hertel, Gehlhar, and McDougall (1994) for more details on this closure.]
- Experiment 2 (E2) simulates unilateral agricultural domestic and trade liberalization by the EU through removal of the CAP and without its replacement by national agricultural policies.
- Experiment 3 (E3) examines unilateral removal of domestic agricultural policies and agricultural trade policies by Australia. The EU insulates its agricultural sector.
- Experiment 4 (E4) simulates unilateral removal of domestic agricultural policies and agricultural trade policies by Canada. The EU insulates its agricultural sector.

The first objective is evaluated through a comparison of results of experiments 1 and 2; an evaluation of the second objective requires a comparison of the results of experiments 3 and 4, followed by a comparison with some of the results of experiments 1 and 2.

These four experiments, although none of them are novel, have not been conducted before in the context of assessing the political economy of the Cairns Group negotiating strategy. The outcomes are studied from the Australian and Canadian perspectives within the context of the Cairns Group coalition of self-styled "fair trading" agricultural exporting countries. Since the mid-1980s, a substantial literature has developed in which the results of simulation experiments involving the liberalization of agricultural policies have been published. In previous studies the focus has been largely on the effects of industrialized country liberalization or world liberalization on regional and world welfare [see, e.g., Anderson and Tyers (1991); Blandford (1990); Goldin, and Knudsen (1990); Meilke (1987); Nguyen, Perroni, and Wigle (1993); OECD (1990); and Tyers and Anderson (1992)]. In addition, many studies have paid attention to the US and EU economies and the effects of agricultural trade policy liberalization on each other [see, e.g., Commission of the European Communities (1988)]. In some of these latter studies, a Nash outcome to the negotiating game has been formally derived [see, e.g., Johnson, Mahé, and Roe (1993)]. A number of studies have focused on liberalization by a single country [see, e.g., Stoeckel and Breckling (1989) for the EU; Vincent (1989) for Japan; Hertel, Thompson, and Tsigas (1989) for the US; and Higgs (1989) for Australia] and on the political economy of agriculture in the GATT [see, e.g., Avery (1993)]. By contrast, in the experiments described in this chapter, the motivation is provided by political economy and, in particular, an evaluation of the strategy adopted by the Cairns Group as reflected in the positions of Australia and Canada.

## IV     Results

A subset of the policy liberalization shocks administered in E1–E4 are reported in Tables 8.4 and 8.9. These involve removal of policies relating to taxes on agricultural output (*to*), agricultural export taxes (*txs*), and agricultural import tariff and nontariff equivalents (*tms*) in the unilaterally liberalizing region. (In order to conserve space, bilateral export and import shocks are reported only for ROW; these are indicative of the shocks to rates for other regions.) Entries in the vector of shocks *to* that are negative indicate that a subsidy is to be removed so that the domestic producer price will fall. Conversely, a positive entry denotes elimination of a net producer tax. Negative (positive) entries in the vector of shocks *tms* indicate that a border import tax (subsidy) is to be removed. This lowers (raises) domestic market prices. In the case of the vector *txs*, negative (positive) entries indicate the removal of an export subsidy (tax), which depresses (raises) domestic prices relative to world prices.

### Experiment 1: Liberalization by the US

The shocks required for US agricultural trade liberalization, as outlined above, are shown in Table 8.4. It is noticeable that the pattern of support between domestic and trade instruments varies considerably across the eight commodities and underlines the comment made above that for certain commodities, earlier negotiations on agriculture in the GATT had missed the main source of trade distortions. The most heavily distorted products in terms of domestic

**Table 8.4.** *Percentage Shocks[a] for Complete US and EU Agricultural Policy Liberalization*

|                      | Domestic Output (to) | Exports to ROW (txs) | Imports from ROW (tms) |
|----------------------|:---:|:---:|:---:|
| *Wheat*              |       |       |       |
| US                   | -24.5 | -16.7 | -9.2  |
| EU                   | -5.9  | -67.6 | -33.9 |
| *Other grains*       |       |       |       |
| US                   | -23.4 | -1.3  | -3.4  |
| EU                   | -2.4  | -70.7 | -40.3 |
| *Wool*               |       |       |       |
| US                   | -38.7 | 0.0   | -4.9  |
| EU                   | -0.4  | -0.0  | -0.7  |
| *Rice*               |       |       |       |
| US                   | -24.4 | -1.6  | -4.2  |
| EU                   | -2.2  | -25.4 | -56.3 |
| *Meat products*      |       |       |       |
| US                   | 0.3   | -1.5  | -15.4 |
| EU                   | -0.2  | -44.8 | -35.9 |
| *Milk products*      |       |       |       |
| US                   | -4.1  | -34.1 | -49.9 |
| EU                   | 0.4   | -47.8 | -57.1 |
| *O. Ag. and food prod.* |    |       |       |
| US                   | 2.7   | -0.0  | -8.7  |
| EU                   | -9.3  | 1.6   | -28.2 |

[a] Shocks for import and export policies are restricted to the region ROW only for considerations of space. but they are indicative of the shocks for the other regions.
Source: GTAP data base.

subsidy instruments are wheat, other grains, wool, and rice (large negative entries in *to*), while meat products are taxed rather than subsidized under existing policies. Products most supported through export subsidies are wheat and milk products (negative entries in *txs*), while those most protected from imports are meat products and milk products (negative entries in *tms*).

Only a few of the important features of the outcome of this simulation will be analyzed and presented here. The results for the variable *qo*, the percentage change in the quantity of sectoral output, are shown in Table 8.5, together with the corresponding changes in the volume of output.[8] There are important falls in the volume of US production of wheat (24%, $US 4,129m) and of other grains (11%, $US 3,623m). There are also substantial percentage falls in the outputs of the less important products (see Table 8.1), namely, wool (49%) and rice (21%). For meat products, milk products, and other agricultural and food products the percentage reductions are small: they amount to $US

**Table 8.5.** *Liberalization of US (E1) and EU* (E2) Agricultural Policies: Changes in Volume Output (1992 $US million; percentage change in volume in parentheses)*

|  | Australia | Canada | US | Japan | EU | ROW |
|---|---|---|---|---|---|---|
| *Wheat* | | | | | | |
| E1 | 363 (19) | 1,358 (29) | -4,129(-24) | 864 (22) | 0   (0) | 2,832 (9) |
| E2 | 120 (6) | 677 (14) | 1,229  (7) | 65  (2) | -7,830 (-22) | 1,713 (5) |
| *Other grains* | | | | | | |
| E1 | 110 (16) | 428 (14) | -3,623(-11) | 1,197 (20) | 0   (0) | 4,694 (4) |
| E2 | 29 (4) | 139 (5) | 1,753  (5) | 87  (2) | -7,409 (-24) | 3,549 (3) |
| *Wool* | | | | | | |
| E1 | 19 (1) | 0 (18) | -71(-49) | 0  (1) | 0   (0) | 62 (2) |
| E2 | -12 (-0) | 0 (3) | 4  (3) | 0  (5) | 38   (4) | 36 (1) |
| *Rice* | | | | | | |
| E1 | 18 (5) | 16 (19) | -890(-21) | -222 (-0) | 0   (0) | 1,131 (0) |
| E2 | 46 (13) | 2 (2) | 643 (15) | 15  (0) | -2,465 (-36) | 3,815 (1) |
| *Meat products* | | | | | | |
| E1 | 215 (3) | 155 (1) | -694 (-1) | -195 (-0) | 0   (0) | 128 (0) |
| E2 | 597 (8) | 241 (2) | 1,432  (2) | 324  (1) | -16,494  (-9) | 8,039 (5) |
| *Milk products* | | | | | | |
| E1 | 166 (4) | 162 (2) | -2,131 (-5) | 0  (0) | 0   (0) | 1,472 (3) |
| E2 | 812 (19) | 569 (7) | 837  (2) | 292  (2) | -16,796(-15) | 8,864(20) |
| *O. Ag. and food prod.* | | | | | | |
| E1 | 91 (0) | 1,348 (2) | -4,646 (-1) | -2,982 (-1) | 0   (0) | 1,096 (0) |
| E2 | 1,386 (5) | 1,175 (2) | 10,747  (2) | 635  (0) | -115,612 (-14) | 58,057 (5) |
| *Manuf. and services* | | | | | | |
| E1 | -1,036 (-0.2) | -3,589 (-0.3) | 11,533  (0) | -1,723 (-0) | 0 (0) | -13,984(-0) |
| E2 | -2,127 (-0) | -2,446 (-0) | -10,479 (-0) | -834 (-0) | 128 399 (1) | -77,513(-1) |

Source: GTAP simulation
* The EU is assumed to insulate its agricultural sector in this simulation.

694m, $US 2,131m, and $US 4,646m, respectively. The contractions in the output of the US agricultural sector are mirrored by an increase in manufacturing and service sector output of $US 11,533m. These changes in the output mix of the US economy, in general, affect world prices, trade flows, and output in other regions.[9] The magnitude of these changes in average world prices, by commodity, is shown in Table 8.6. The international price effects are greatest for cereals (wheat 14.3%, other grains 15.2%, and rice 6.3%) and for milk products (4.8%). The directions of these effects are consistent with expectations, and their magnitudes are consistent with the relative sizes of the liberalization shocks.

**Table 8.6.** *Liberalization of Agricultural Policies: Changes in World Prices Indices* [*pxwcom(i)*]

|                      | E1    | E2   | E3   | E4   |
|----------------------|-------|------|------|------|
| Wheat                | 14.3  | 5.6  | 0.1  | 5.4  |
| Other grains         | 15.2  | 3.9  | 0.0  | 1.0  |
| Wool                 | 1.3   | 2.2  | 0.9  | 0.3  |
| Rice                 | 6.3   | 3.1  | 0.0  | 0.1  |
| Meat products        | 0.5   | 7.0  | -0.2 | 1.0  |
| Milk products        | 4.8   | 21.6 | 1.2  | 2.1  |
| O. Ag. and food prod.| 0.3   | 2.0  | 0.0  | 0.2  |
| Manuf. and services  | -0.0  | 0.2  | 0.0  | -0.0 |

Source: GTAP simulation.

As shown in Table 8.5, for Australia the largest percentage changes occur in the outputs of wheat (19%) and other grains (16%), which amount to $US 363m and $US 110m, respectively. Small increases are shown for rice (5%), meat products (3%), and milk products (4%), amounting to $US 18m, $US 215m, and $US 166m, respectively. The increases in agricultural output are accompanied by a reduction in the value of output of the manufacturing and services sector (−0.2%, or $US 1,036m). A similar pattern emerges for Canada, with wheat outputs increasing by 29% ($US 1,358m) and other grains by 14% ($US 428m), and the manufacturing and services sector contracting in value by −0.3%, or $US 3,589m.

It should be noted that there are no changes in agricultural output in the EU because the insulating effect of the threshold price/variable levy system of the CAP prevents changes in international prices from affecting domestic agricultural markets. However, there are budgetary consequences for the EU as world prices rise for its imports from major suppliers (these are not shown here but are found in the matrix *pcif(i,r,e_u)*). This same qualitative picture emerges from noting the changes in the global price indices by commodity, *pxwcom(i)*, reported in Table 8.6. Here we see price increases ranging from 0.5% for meat products to 15.2% for other grains. This increase in world prices also causes EU expenditures on export subsidies to fall. These decreases range from 0.3% for other agricultural and food products to 6.3% on milk products and 8.8% on wheat, and may be found in the vector *tx(i,e_u)* (not reported here).

The focus of the Cairns Group was on the removal of policies that distort agricultural trade. Therefore, it is important to consider the changes in export volume stimulated by the removal of US policies and to *calculate the resulting benefits to Australia and Canada*. The percentage changes in bilateral trade are obtained from the variable *qxs(i,r,s)*. This information, together with base period flows at market prices, *VXWD(i,r,s)*, enable us to calculate the changes in volume of exports by region r to all other regions, at base period market prices. Results are shown in Table 8.7. The greatest differences between the two countries in exports of agricultural and food products are in exports of

**Table 8.7.** *Impact of Liberalization of US and EU Agricultural Policies on Exports Volumes from Australia and Canada*

|  | Australia | | Canada | |
|---|---|---|---|---|
|  | % | $US m | % | $US m |
| **Wheat** | | | | |
| E1 | 30.3 | 356 | 31.3 | 1344 |
| E2 | 7.2 | 85 | 15.6 | 670 |
| *Other grains* | | | | |
| E1 | 30.1 | 105 | 41.6 | 315 |
| E2 | 4.5 | 16 | 11.7 | 88 |
| *Wool* | | | | |
| E1 | 0.7 | 21 | 18.1 | 0 |
| E2 | -0.3 | -9 | 3.3 | 0 |
| *Rice* | | | | |
| E1 | 14.4 | 13 | 41.2 | 1 |
| E2 | 35.4 | 33 | 36.2 | 1 |
| *Meat products* | | | | |
| E1 | 7.7 | 202 | 16.0 | 149 |
| E2 | 20.8 | 544 | 21.4 | 200 |
| *Milk products* | | | | |
| E1 | 16.3 | 132 | 35.3 | 99 |
| E2 | 80.4 | 653 | 139.7 | 392 |
| *O. Ag. and food prod.* | | | | |
| E1 | -1.3 | -44 | 18.1 | 1139 |
| E2 | 17.9 | 624 | 8.2 | 514 |
| *Manuf. and services* | | | | |
| E1 | -1.7 | -634 | -1.7 | -2264 |
| E2 | -3.6 | -1371 | -1.1 | -1499 |

Source:  GTAP simulation.

wheat and other agricultural and food products, from which Canada gains over $US 1 billion in each case, whereas Australian exports increase for wheat but decline by $US 44m for other agricultural and food products. Part of the explanation is that 60% of Canada's exports of other agricultural and food products goes to the US as compared with only 5% for Australia (Table 8.2) and the output of other agricultural and food products in the US has fallen by $US 4646m (Table 8.5).

Finally, the increase in the real price of the sector-specific asset, agricultural land, in Australia and Canada can be used as a proxy for the change in producer surplus. This information is useful in the second set of experiments, in which the political economy of unilateral removal of protectionism by these countries is investigated. Using the base period value of land (*EVOA*), the percentage change in the agents' price of land (*ps*), and the percentage change in the price index of private household expenditure (*ppriv*) as the deflator, the real increase in producer surplus in Australia is $US 265m and in Canada is $US 604m (Table 8.8). Overall, national welfare, as measured by equivalent variation, increases in Australia and Canada by $US 389m and $US 458m, respectively.

### Experiment 2: Liberalization by the EU

The shocks required to remove the domestic and trade policy instruments associated with the EU's CAP are presented in Table 8.4. The size of the shocks to remove the domestic instruments are relatively small (*to*); it should be remembered that income support for the farm sector in the EU, unlike the position in the US, comes largely from transfers from consumers rather than from taxpayers [see Blandford (1990), p. 406]. Therefore, the shocks required to remove the insulating trade policies, that is, the export subsidies (*txs*) and the import levies (*tms*), are substantial. Output of the milk products sector is taxed (the entry in *to* is positive) rather than subsidized, and exports of other agricultural and food products are also taxed (the entry in *txs* is positive) and not subsidized. For all other products, the signs of the shocks indicate a removal of output subsidies, export subsidies, and import taxes. In comparing the shocks for the EU with those for the US (Table 8.4), it would appear that, in general, much more support for US agriculture comes from domestic instruments, except for livestock products, whereas in the EU, the support is through the use of import barriers and aids to exports. However, the size of the shocks on their own does not lead to an inference about the disruptive effects of the CAP on international trade; changes in trade volumes and world prices are also required.

Selected results of this policy experiment are as follows. The outputs of the agricultural sector of the EU contract, as anticipated (Table 8.5). The largest percentage reductions occur in grains: wheat −22%, other grains −24%,

**Table 8.8.** *Summary Measures of Agricultural Policy Liberalization*

| | Equivalent Variation ($US m) [EV(r)] | | | |
|---|---|---|---|---|
| | E1 | E2 | E3 | E4 |
| Australia | 389 | 811 | -0.7 | 133 |
| Canada | 458 | 254 | -1.3 | 814 |
| US | 3,193 | 1,210 | -20.0 | 175 |
| Japan | -3,456 | 1,662 | -73.0 | -588 |
| EU | 414 | 7,120 | 83.1 | 240 |
| ROW | -2,626 | 15,106 | -77.2 | -752 |
| World | -1,628 | 26,162 | -89.1 | 20 |
| | *Producer Surplus ($US m)[a]* | | | |
| Australia | 265 | 322 | -86 | 72 |
| Canada | 604 | 306 | 3 | -927 |
| US | -1525 | 1009 | 6 | 325 |
| Japan | 837 | 110 | 5 | 109 |
| EU | 0 | -5863 | 0 | 0 |
| ROW | 2516 | 11213 | 53 | 452 |
| | *Terms of Trade (%) [psw(r) - pdw(r)]* | | | |
| Australia | 0.5 | 1.1 | 0.0 | 0.2 |
| Canada | 0.5 | 0.4 | 0.0 | -0.3 |
| US | 0.0 | 0.4 | 0.0 | 0.1 |
| Japan | -0.1 | 0.2 | 0.0 | 0.0 |
| EU | 0.0 | -1.6 | 0.0 | 0.0 |
| ROW | 0.0 | 0.7 | 0.0 | 0.0 |

[a] The change in producer surplus is approximated as the change in the value of the sector-specific asset, land deflated by the price index [ppriv(r)].
Source: GTAP simulation.

and rice −36%. However, in volume terms the greatest effects of liberalization occur in the livestock sector, with the volume of production of meat products falling by $US 16,494m and milk products by $US 16,796m. There is also a substantial decline in other agricultural and food products of $US 115,612m. As EU agriculture contracts, resources become available to enable the nonagricultural sectors to expand; manufacturing and services do so by $US 128,399m. The international price effects of the liberalization of the CAP are not as dramatic as those that might have been anticipated and, with the important exception of milk products, are generally smaller than those generated by liberalization of US agricultural policy (Table 8.6). This finding must be qualified by noting that E1 does not account for the price dampening effect of possible reentry of set-aside land in the US. Also, it is the result of the *price insulating* effects of the CAP, as implemented in E1. Because the EU does not participate in the adjustment to higher world prices, a greater movement in price is required to attain a new equilibrium.

Column two of Table 8.5 shows that Australian agriculture benefits from EU agriculture liberalization, particularly in other agricultural and food products ($US 1,386m), milk products ($US 812m), and meat products ($US 597m). The wheat sector makes a small gain of 6%, or $US 120m, and the wool sector contracts by $US 12m. Mirroring the expansion in agriculture is the contraction in manufacturing and services of $US 2,127m. In Canada, the wheat sector benefits most in percentage terms (14%), but in volume terms the greatest gain is in other agricultural and food products ($US 1,175m). The output of the livestock sector expands with meat products growing by ($US 241m) and milk products by $US 569m. The Canadian manufacturing and services sector contracts by $US 2,446m.

With the trade distorting instruments of the CAP removed, Australian and Canadian exports of agricultural products expand. The changes in the volume of exports are obtained as before and are presented in Table 8.7. For Australia, exports of all agricultural products increase, with the exception of wool – the increases being greater than those reported for E1 for livestock products but less than those for wheat and other grains. At the same time, there is a loss of exports in manufacturing and services of $US 1,371m. On the other hand, Canadian exports of manufacturing and services fall less in this experiment than in the previous one. The offsetting gains in wheat and in other agricultural and food products are about one half as large as those obtained in E1, while those for livestock products are substantially greater.

The gains in the Australian and Canadian agricultural sectors, as measured by the increase in the real value of sector-specific assets, are shown in Table 8.8. For Australia, producer surplus increases by $US 322m, while Canada shows an increase of $US 306m. However, in terms of national welfare, Australia gains by $US 811m, and Canada gains by $US 254m.

**Evaluation of the first objective.** The first objective of this chapter was to determine whether the political rhetoric of the Cairns Group with respect to the relative distortions created by the agricultural policies of the US and the EU has a basis in economics. These policies, once liberalized unilaterally, generate a different set of international prices, thereby altering output levels as well as the pattern of trade flows. Unilateral liberalization by the US has a greater effect on world prices for grains than for livestock products: the effects of removing the CAP are the reverse (Table 8.6).

The overall changes in welfare in each of the six regions are provided by the equivalent variation (Table 8.8). There are a number of interesting features in this table. First, there are gains to Australia, Canada, and the US, as expected, and a small gain to the EU following unilateral liberalization of US agricultural policies. Second, there are large losses to Japan, which, as a net importing region of agricultural and food products, loses from higher world prices for these products, and loses further from the fall in the world price of manufactures and services. Hence, Japan's terms of trade decline by 0.1%. Third, there is a loss to world welfare from US liberalization. This is a *second-best* result that follows from the fact that the rise in world prices causes other regions (e.g., Japan) to exacerbate their misallocation of resources. It also depends critically on the assumptions of no change in US set-aside land and EU insulation. Fourth, the changes in regional welfare generated by removal of the CAP are quite different. The welfare gains to Australia are positive ($US 811m) and greater than they were in E1, whereas the gain to Canada ($US 254) is less than in the first experiment. As expected, there are large gains in the EU. ROW gains due to its dominant role as an exporter of agricultural products into the EU and as an importer of manufactures and services from the EU. [See also Hertel, Gehlhar, and McDougall (1994) on this point.] Finally, there is a net gain of $US 26 billion across all regions. This contrasts with the loss of $US 1.6 billion in E1.

From the changes in real income, as measured by equivalent variation, it is clear that for Australia the CAP depresses regional income more than the agricultural policy of the US, that is, by $US 811m as compared with $US 389m, respectively. For Canada, the reverse is true, with US policy depressing real incomes by $US 458m, as compared to $US 254m owing to the existence of the CAP. Moreover, the improvement in Australia's terms of trade under E2 (1.1%) exceeds that achieved under E1 (0.5%), while for Canada, the improvement under E1 (0.5%) exceeds that under E2 (0.4%) (Table 8.8).

The political stance of the Cairns Group in supporting Australia's concentrated attack on the CAP is partially vindicated by the results of these two simulations. Moreover, by focusing on liberalizing the CAP, the Cairns Group was assisting in raising world real income. But the greater caution Canada demonstrated with respect to the agricultural policies of the US and the EU is also shown to be justified and helps to explain, in part, the tension between Australia and Canada within the Cairns Group that arose over agricultural policy.

*Experiment 3: Liberalization by Australia*

The second objective in this chapter was to explore the distributional effects of unilateral liberalization of agricultural policies within Australia and Canada, and to compare these outcomes with the income effects created by unilateral liberalization by the US and the EU. It is then possible to assess the political judgments made by the governments of Australia and Canada with respect to deregulation of their respective agricultural sectors. The Australian government has chosen to ignore the farm lobby, while the Canadian government has continued to pursue its objective of supporting farm incomes. This set of experiments focuses on changes in producer surplus and national welfare.

Australia's removal of domestic agricultural policies and trade policies requires the shocks shown in the upper entries of Table 8.9. These are of a

Table 8.9. *Percentage Shocks[a] for Complete Australian and Canadian Agricultural Policy Liberalization*

| | Domestic Output (to) | Exports to ROW (txs) | Imports from ROW (tms) |
|---|---|---|---|
| Wheat | | | |
| Australia | -3.9 | 2.1 | -0.2 |
| Canada | -14.4 | -7.1 | -22.4 |
| *Other grains* | | | |
| Australia | -3.5 | 2.2 | -1.8 |
| Canada | -7.1 | -15.1 | -12.7 |
| *Wool* | | | |
| Australia | -3.2 | 1.3 | -2.0 |
| Canada | -3.3 | 0.0 | -2.2 |
| *Rice* | | | |
| Australia | -0.8 | 0.2 | -4.2 |
| Canada | 0.3 | 0.0 | -1.0 |
| *Meat products* | | | |
| Australia | 0.7 | 0.5 | -5.6 |
| Canada | -18.0 | 0.0 | -18.0 |
| *Milk products* | | | |
| Australia | 6.0 | -16.7 | -25.9 |
| Canada | -4.3 | -44.1 | -57.5 |
| *O. Ag. and food prod.* | | | |
| Australia | -0.3 | 0.5 | -4.7 |
| Canada | -2.3 | -1.4 | -6.6 |

[a] Shocks for import and export policies are restricted to the region ROW only for considerations of space but they are indicative of the shocks for the other regions.
Source: GTAP simulation.

much smaller order of magnitude than the shocks presented above for the US and the EU (Table 8.4). Domestic assistance (indicated by negative entries shocks *to*) is provided for all products except for meat products and milk products, which are taxed. Exports are taxed (the entries in *txs* are positive) with the exception of milk products which are subsidized. Imports are all taxed, with milk products receiving the greatest protection (the entries in *tms* are negative).

Removal of the policies implicit in the shocks shown in Table 8.9 result in adjustments in Australian output, exports, and imports (Table 8.10). It is interesting to note that while the output of most agricultural sectors declines, it expands for meat products by $US 132m. Output in the manufacturing and services sector also increases ($US 483m). As expected, the greatest contraction in output occurs in milk products (or 9.3%, $US 394m), the most heavily supported sector. Changes in the volume of exports parallel those in domestic output, with the exception of exports of other agricultural and food products, which increase by $US 102m. As domestic production and exports contract, imports rise, but by small amounts. The largest percentage change in imports occurs in milk products (56.4%), and the largest volume change occurs in other agricultural and food products ($US 266m). Imports of manufactures and services fall by $US 136m, reflecting the expansion in domestic output. The removal of assistance on output and on exports, together with the removal of protection from imports, result in a decline in real producer surplus of $US 86m, an overall loss of $US 0.7m (Table 8.8).

**Evaluation of second objective for Australia.** In the context of the second objective of the study, the loss in producer surplus of $US 86m should be compared with the corresponding figures from the first two experiments. In these experiments it was concluded that under unilateral liberalization by the US, producer surplus in Australia would rise by $US 265m, and through removal of the CAP the corresponding gain would be $US 322m. Clearly, the gain from US and EU agricultural liberalization dominates the loss from unilateral liberalization by Australia. Hence, the Australian government's argument to the farm lobby that their income losses caused by the removal of assistance would be more than offset by the gains from trade liberalization appears to be correct.

*Experiment 4: Liberalization by Canada*

The shocks required to remove Canada's domestic agricultural policies and associated trade policies are given in the lower entries of Table 8.9. The

**Table 8.10.** *Impact of Liberalizing Australian and Canadian Agricultural Policies ($US million; percentages in parentheses)*

|  | Output [qo] | Exports [qxw] | Imports [qim] |
|---|---|---|---|
| Wheat |  |  |  |
| Australia (E3) | -51 (-2.6) | -45 (-3.8) | 0 (6.7) |
| Canada (E4) | -1763 (-37.0) | -1711 (-39.9) | 3 (83.7) |
| *Other grains* |  |  |  |
| Australia (E3) | -12 (-1.8) | -9 (-2.7) | 0 (10.2) |
| Canada (E4) | -654 (-21.4) | -374 (-49.5) | 27 (23.7) |
| *Wool* |  |  |  |
| Australia (E3) | -47 (-1.4) | -45 (-1.6) | 3 (9.0) |
| Canada (E4) | -0 (-4.5) | -0 (-4.5) | -0 (-3.1) |
| *Rice* |  |  |  |
| Australia (E3) | -4 (-1.3) | -1 (-1.4) | 2 (10.1) |
| Canada (E4) | -1 (-1.3) | 0 (8.9) | -4 (-4.5) |
| *Meat products* |  |  |  |
| Australia (E3) | 132 (1.7) | 122 (4.7) | 7 (19.6) |
| Canada (E4) | -1914 (-18.1) | -520 (-55.8) | 1144 (109.6) |
| *Milk products* |  |  |  |
| Australia (E3) | -394 (-9.3) | -277 (34.1) | 81 (56.4) |
| Canada (E4) | -1277 (-16.2) | -258 (-92.0) | 1437 (466.3) |
| *O. Ag. and food prod.* |  |  |  |
| Australia (E3) | -233 (-0.8) | 102 (2.9) | 266 (13.6) |
| Canada (E4) | -5748 (-10.3) | -357 (-5.7) | 2338 (30.7) |
| *Manuf. and services* |  |  |  |
| Australia (E3) | 483 (0.1) | 270 (0.8) | -136 (-0.2) |
| Canada (E4) | 9297 (0.9) | 5156 (4.0) | -1766 (-1.3) |

Source: GTAP simulation.

negative signs in the vector of liberalization shocks, *to*, indicate that outputs are subsidized. This domestic support varies across commodities, with wheat (14.4%) and meat products (18%) receiving the greatest degrees of support. Export support (the negative sign in *txs* indicating a subsidy) is largest for other grains (15.1%) and for milk products (44.1%), while the import shock (the negative sign in *tms*) on milk products (57.5%) is again substantially higher than for the other agricultural products. Wheat (22.4%) and other grains (12.7%), as well as meat products (18.0%) also receive protection from imports of not inconsequential amounts.

The results of unilateral Canadian liberalization, for a selection of variables, are presented in Table 8.10. The outputs of all agricultural sectors decline, with the largest percentage falls occurring in wheat (37%) and other grains (21.4%). There are also falls in the outputs of meat products (18.1%) and milk products (16.2%). In volume terms, the largest declines occur in other agricultural and food products ($US 5,748m), meat products ($US 1,914m), and wheat ($US 1,763m). The contraction in the agricultural sectors is accompanied by an expansion of $US 9,297m in the manufacturing and services sector. The falls in domestic output are matched (except for rice) by falls in exports, the most important of which occur in wheat ($US 1,711m) and meat products ($US 520m). There are attendant increases in imports of meat products ($US 1,144m), milk products ($US 1,437m), and other agricultural and food products ($US 2,338m). The effects of these adjustments in output are reflected in international markets through the price changes shown in Table 8.6. However, with the exception of the price of wheat (5.4%), the remaining price increases for agricultural products are inconsequential in comparison with those generated under E1 and E2.

The removal of Canadian for agricultural policies leads to a decline in producer surplus of $US 927m (Table 8.8). However, there is an overall national welfare gain of $US 814m from unilateral reform of Canadian farm and food policies.

**Evaluation of the second objective for Canada.** A part of the second objective in this chapter was to assess whether the Canadian government's political sensitivity to farm incomes was justified in the context of the trade negotiations and the stance of the Cairns Group under Australian leadership. In E1 and E2 the gains in producer surplus in the Canadian farm sector were $US 604m and $US 306m, respectively, whereas under unilateral Canadian liberalization, the loss is $US 927m. Hence, the government's sensitivity to welfare in the Canadian agricultural sector in the context of trade negotiations appears to have a sound foundation in political economy.

**V    Conclusions**

This chapter had two principal objectives. The first was to determine whether the support the Cairns Group gave to the US in its sustained attack on the CAP was supported by economic analysis as reflected in the payoff to both

Australia and Canada. The results of the first two simulation experiments indicate that Australia would gain more from unilateral removal of the CAP than it would from unilateral removal of agricultural policies of the US; for Canada, more would be gained from a unilateral removal of US policies than from removal of the CAP. It must be stressed, however, that in the case of US liberalization, it has been assumed that existing land that is currently set aside is not brought back into production when price support policies are removed but that the land remains idle, for example, becoming part of a conservation reserve. In addition, it should be remembered that *except in the CAP liberalization experiment*, the EU's domestic markets for agricultural products have been totally insulated from international price changes in these experiments. With these caveats, it has been substantiated that the CAP is more of an impediment than is US agricultural policy to international agricultural trade and national welfare as perceived by Australia. This finding may explain both Australia's aggressive stance in relation to the CAP and also the Canadian government's more balanced approach as Canada gains more from US liberalization than from removal of the CAP.

The second objective was to investigate the stances adopted by the Australian and Canadian governments with respect to domestic political economy in their own farm sectors. For Australia, it was shown that losses to the farm sector from unilateral deregulation were smaller than the gains from successful unilateral international agricultural trade liberalization by the US and by the EU. In the case of Canada, the loss to the agricultural sector from the removal of government assistance exceeds the gains from unilateral agricultural trade liberalization by the US and the EU. Therefore, the respective positions adopted by each of these Cairns Group countries appear to have some justification in the political economy of domestic agricultural policy.

Historically, Australia has exhibited a sense of grievance at the conditions under which agricultural trade takes place and has perceived itself as being particularly vulnerable to the international political economy of agricultural policy. Until recently, these features have combined to produce a less than sensitive diplomatic touch in the area of international trade negotiations. Canada, on the other hand, has been constrained by its different agricultural structure with respect to provincial / federal relationships and by the importance of the US as a trading partner. This constraint has produced a more subtle style of diplomacy in trade negotiations as a balance has had to be struck between international obligations and domestic agricultural interests. Given such differences in the political forces operating on national governments in these two countries, it is remarkable that the Cairns Group remained an effective third force acting between the interests of the US and the EU in the Uruguay Round for as long as it did. Perhaps equally striking is the fact that the needs of the respective domestic political agendas are largely coincident with the economic conclusions derived from these simulations.

## NOTES

1. The Cairns Group comprises the following countries: Argentina, Australia, Brazil, Canada, Chile, Colombia, Fiji, Hungary, Indonesia, Malaysia, New Zealand, Philippines, Thailand, and Uruguay. For a detailed description of the origins of the group, see Higgott (1988), and for an assessment of its role in the Uruguay Round until 1990, see Higgot and Cooper (1990).
2. An agenda moving coalition is one in which the principal aim is to ensure that the issues of particular interest to the member countries are properly dealt with in the negotiations (Hamilton and Whalley 1989).
3. "GATT has been ineffective in agriculture because it has tried to separate the international trade aspects of agriculture from the internal policies which lead to restrictions on international trade in agricultural products" [see reference to Dam, cited by Warley (1976), p. 339].
4. The "Red" book is the volume put out by the Bureau of Agricultural Economics (1985), and the "Gold" book is by Miller (1986).
5. Throughout this chapter, reference will be made to the EU, even although the change of name from European Community did not occur until November 1993.
6. After all, the US government claimed that it introduced the Export Enhancement Program (EEP) provisions only to counter subsidized exports of agricultural products by the EU and not to seek "unfair" advantage in international markets.
7. One specific commodity would have been of interest to Australia, particularly in its trade relations with the US and the EU, namely, sugar, but it is not present as a distinct commodity in the data base.
8. Volumes are obtained by running the program GTAPVOL, described in Chapter 6. This computes the following item: $0.01*qo(i, r)*VOM(i, r)$.
9. In the case of Japan, the effect is to transfer marginal resources from the manufacturing and services sector to certain of the agricultural sectors, for example, wheat and other grains (Table 8.5). If it is accepted that Japan has a comparative disadvantage in agriculture, then this inefficient use of resources is consistent with the loss of welfare of $US 3456m (Table 8.8).

## REFERENCES

Anderson, K., and R. Tyers (1991) *Global Effects of Liberalizing Trade in Farm Products*. Hemel Hempstead: Harvester Wheatsheaf, for the Trade Policy Research Centre, London.

Avery, W. P., ed. (1993) *World Agriculture and the GATT*. Boulder, CO: Lynne Rienner Publishers.

Blandford, D. (1990) "The Costs of Agricultural Protection and the Difference Free Trade Would Make." In F. H. Sanderson (ed.), *Agricultural Protectionism in the Industrialized World*. Washington, DC: Resources for the Future.

Bureau of Agricultural Economics (1985) *Agricultural Policies in the European Community: Their Origins, Nature and Effects on Production and Trade*. Policy Monograph No. 2, Canberra: Australian Government Publishing Service.

Commission of the European Communities (1988) *Disharmonies in EC and US Agricultural Policies: A Summary of Results and Major Conclusions.* Brussels: EU Commission.

Cooper, A. F. (1992) "Like-minded Nations and Contrasting Diplomatic Styles: Australian and Canadian Approaches to Agricultural Trade," *Canadian Journal of Political Science* 25:349–379.

Cooper, A. F., and R. A. Higgott (1993) "Australian and Canadian Approaches to the Cairns Group: Two-Level Games and the Political Economy of Adjustment." In W. P. Avery (ed.), *World Agriculture and the GATT.* Boulder, CO: Lynne Rienner Publishers.

Goldin, I., and O. Knudsen (1990) *Agricultural Trade Liberalization: Implications for Developing Countries.* Paris: OECD.

Hamilton, C., and J. Whalley (1989) "Coalitions in the Uruguay Round," *Weltwirtschaftliches Archiv* 125:547–561.

Hertel, T. W., M. Gehlhar, and R. A. McDougall (1994) "Reforming the European Community's Common Agricultural Policy: Who Stands to Gain?" In A.V. Deardorff and R. M. Sterns (eds.), *Analytical and Negotiating Issues in the Global Trading System.* Ann Arbor: University of Michigan Press.

Hertel, T. W., R. L. Thompson, and M. Tsigas (1989) "Economywide Effects of Unilateral Trade and Policy Liberalization in US Agriculture." In A. B. Stoeckel, D. Vincent, and S. Cuthbertson (eds.), *Macroeconomic Consequences of Farm Support Policies.* Durham, NC: Duke University Press.

Higgott, R. A. (1988) "Trans-regional Coalitions and International Regimes: The Cairns Group, Agricultural Trade and the Uruguay MTN Round," *Australian Quarterly* (Summer), 415–434.

Higgott, R. A., and A. F. Cooper (1990) "Middle Power Leadership and Coalition Building: Australia, the Cairns Group, and the Uruguay Round of Trade Negotiations," *International Organization* 44:589–632.

Higgs, P. J. (1989) "The Taxation of Australian Agriculture through Assistance to Australian Manufacturing." In A. B. Stoeckel, D. Vincent, and S. Cuthbertson (eds.), *Macroeconomic Consequences of Farm Support Policies.* Durham, NC: Duke University Press.

Johnson, M., L. Mahé, and T. Roe (1993) "Trade Compromises Between the European Community and the United States: An Interest Group Game Theoretical Approach," *Journal of Policy Modeling* 15:199–222.

Meilke, K. D. (1987) *A Comparison of the Simulation Results from Six International Trade Models.* Working Paper WP87/3, Department of Agricultural Economics and Business, University of Guelph, February.

Miller, G. (1986) *The Political Economy of International Agricultural Policy Reform.* Canberra: Australian Government Publishing Service.

Nguyen, T., C. Perroni, and R. Wigle (1993) "An Evaluation of the Draft Final Act of the Uruguay Round," *Economic Journal* 103:1540–1549.

OECD (1990) *OECD Economic Studies.* No. 13 (Winter), 1989–1990.

Stoeckel, A. B., and J. Breckling (1989) "Some Economywide Effects of Agricultural Policies in the European Community: A General Equilibrium Study." In A. B. Stoeckel, D. Vincent, and S. Cuthbertson (eds.), *Macroeconomic Consequences of Farm Support Policies.* Durham, NC: Duke University Press.

Tyers, R., and K. Anderson (1992) *Disarray in World Food Market: A Quantitative Assessment.* Cambridge: Cambridge University Press.

Vincent, D. (1989) "Effects of Agricultural Protection in Japan: An Economywide Analysis." In A. B. Stoeckel, D. Vincent, and S. Cuthbertson (eds.), *Macroeconomic Consequences of Farm Support Policies*. Durham, NC: Duke University Press.

Warley, T. K. (1976) "Western Trade in Agricultural Products." In A. Shonfield (ed.), *International Economic Relations of the Western World 1959–1971*. Vol. 1. The Royal Institute for International Affairs. London: Oxford University Press.

CHAPTER 9

# Free trade in the Pacific Rim:
# On what basis?

*Linda M. Young and Karen M. Huff*

## I    Introduction and overview

The Pacific Rim contains many dynamic, export-oriented economies that have
grown rapidly in recent years, shifting the world's economic center of gravity
toward the east. The Asia Pacific Economic Cooperation (APEC) group was
established in 1989, with 12 founding members. Its goal is to promote multilateral trade reform and to facilitate regional trade. Since its inception, APEC
has expanded to its present membership of 18, including: the Association of
South East Asian Nations (ASEAN) of Malaysia, Thailand, Indonesia, the
Philippines, Singapore, and Brunei; the "three Chinas" – China, Hong Kong,
and Taiwan; South Korea; Australia; New Zealand: Papua New Guinea; the
US; Canada; Mexico; and Japan. Papua New Guinea and Mexico were admitted
during the APEC summit in November of 1993 and Chile was admitted in
1994. Its member economies now account for almost 50% of the world's
production and 40% of world trade (*Far Eastern Economic Review* 1993). In
November 1994 the APEC members signed the Bogor Accord, which states
that they will "adopt the long-term goal of free and open trade and investment"
in the region. This will be accomplished by 2010 for industrialized countries
and by 2020 for developing countries (*Wall Street Journal* 1994). The purpose
of this chapter is to analyze the implications of such an agreement for trade
and welfare in the region.

  An initial reason given for the creation of a free trade zone in the Pacific
is disillusionment over the effectiveness of the General Agreement on Tariffs
and Trade (GATT) to sustain multilateral trade liberalization. It is unclear
whether the long awaited conclusion of the Uruguay Round has done much
to alleviate these concerns, in light of the limited measure of trade liberalization
that it achieved. However, the increase in regionalism throughout the world,
in particular, the trade diverting consequences of the European Union (EU)
and North American Free Trade Agreement (NAFTA), has given impetus to

the idea that the Pacific Rim should undertake action to create its own free trade area. In addition, the rise of trade friction between the US and countries in East Asia, particularly Japan, has resulted in suggestions of more effort to manage trade between countries bilaterally.

The idea of a Pacific Rim free trade area was first proposed by the Japanese economist Kyoshi Kojima in 1964, and has been discussed in various venues since then. One reason the area has not developed regional institutions earlier on is that when the Asian countries were ready for an economic takeoff, GATT had already succeeded in creating a relatively open trading regime (Eminent Persons Group 1993). Another reason is the diverse nature of the economies, cultures, and political systems, combined with the lack of a history of unifying institutions. For example, the countries in APEC have per capita incomes ranging from US $30,000 in Japan to less than US $1,000 in the People's Republic of China and Indonesia. These economies are quite likely to be affected in different ways by a free trade agreement. Moreover, the region contains not only two of the world's largest national economies but also some of the smallest. There is a perception that the smaller Pacific Rim countries would lose if such arrangements impinged on the growth of open trade.

Beyond the question of regional integration, there is the question of what form of economic integration to pursue. Some have argued that European-style integration is inappropriate for the Pacific region. For example, Drysdale (1988) argues that regional negotiations should not focus on discriminatory trade liberalization, but should be based on most favored nation (MFN) principles. He believes that the formation of a discriminatory free trade zone would damage the capacity for fluid changes in market share that has been crucial to the growth of these rapidly changing economies. Drysdale and Garnaut (1993) further argue that the countries in the Western Pacific have unilaterally liberalized trade, leading to an increase in trade throughout the region. They contrast this to GATT negotiations in which countries assume that liberalization is a concession, and in which they characterize trade expansion in the Western Pacific as a "prisoner's delight."

The feeling that multilateral trade liberalization is best for the region was also articulated by the prime minister of Australia, R. J. Hawke, who said at the first ministerial meeting of APEC in 1989, "A move towards some kind of a Pacific trading block ... would be a foolish one, in that it would run counter to the region's absolutely compelling interest in the maintenance of a strong and open multilateral trading system. It is on such a system that the region's economic prosperity has been built, and continues to rely" (Hughes 1991). These arguments are similar in nature to those used in the debate over regionalism versus multilateralism in the global trading system.

This chapter focuses on the issue of multilateral versus preferential free trade in the Pacific Rim. We proceed as follows. First a brief discussion of the regional and commodity aggregation employed for the simulations is given. This is followed by an outline of the APEC trade liberalization scenarios to be examined. Next the results of the preferential trade liberalization scenario are discussed in detail and then the MFN scenarios are compared to it. The last section contains our conclusions.

## II    Aggregation strategy

The data base accompanying the GTAP model is well suited to examine the consequences of a free trade area in the Pacific Rim, since, with the exception of Brunei and Papua New Guinea, all the countries concerned are detailed in the data. The following 10-region aggregation was employed:

1. US, Canada, and Mexico (NAM)
2. Japan (JPN)
3. Australia and New Zealand (ANZ)
4. China and Hong Kong (CHN _ HKG)
5. South Korea (SKOR)
6. Taiwan (TWN)
7. Malaysia and Singapore (MYS _ SGP)
8. Thailand and the Philippines (THA _ PHL)
9. Indonesia (IDN)
10. Rest of the World (ROW)

Individual countries were separated as much as possible in order to distinguish the welfare and trade effects of policy changes by country. However, in order to keep the analysis of a manageable size, in five cases two or more economies were combined. Owing to NAFTA an economic grouping of the US, Canada, and Mexico seems natural; in fact, the analyses in this chapter are conducted using a "post-NAFTA" data set. Combining China and Hong Kong is also sensible, since the trade data for the two regions are so intertwined. The other groupings are based on geographic considerations and / or the composition of trade. The ROW region is dominated by the EU. With the exception of Brunei, Chile, and Papua New Guinea, this ROW region faithfully aggregates those countries currently excluded from APEC.

The commodities are divided into three groups: food and agriculture, resources and manufacturing, and services. While this three-commodity grouping is admittedly aggregate, it begins to capture some of the differences in trade patterns in the APEC region under the various scenarios studied. Clearly, future analyses will need to investigate the consequences for specific subsectors within the food, resources and manufacturing, and services industries.

Table 9.1 reports the value of bilateral trade flows (imports) among the APEC members and with ROW. Seventy-two percent of APEC imports were from member countries in 1992, and that trade was valued at US $1,494 billion. Around 70% of trade by APEC members is in resources and manufacturing, with about 20% in services and 10% in food.

## III    Experimental design

All experiments were conducted with a multicountry, general equilibrium closure. The general equilibrium closure is appropriate for capturing the substitution in production and consumption that occurs between goods and the resulting changes in trade flows and values. Output levels, prices, and income are endogenous for all regions. Finally, the global bank's allocation of investment is fixed ($RORDELTA = 0$). Provided there is little change in the global composition of savings, this effectively fixes the trade balance for each country/region (see also Chapter 2).[1]

The experiments involve the complete removal of *ad valorem* import tariffs and tariff equivalents of bilateral nontariff barriers (NTBs) among the APEC regions. Export subsidies and taxes are not altered. This choice was made because the major export interventions present in the GTAP data base are those relating to the Multifibre Arrangement (MFA) and agricultural export subsidies. Since both of these areas have been addressed under the Uruguay Round agreement, they logically do not fall under the domain of an APEC free trade zone. It also seems unlikely that the US would participate in an agreement involving the liberalization of agricultural export subsidies without the involvement of the EU. For these reasons, the APEC liberalization scenarios analyzed involve import protection instruments only.

As mentioned in the previous section, the APEC trade liberalization experiments conducted in this chapter are based on a post-NAFTA data set. These data constitute an update of the standard GTAP data set that results from the removal of import tariffs and NTBs on the composite resources and manufacturing commodity within the North American region.[2] The results of this experiment are not discussed here and simply provide the starting point for each of the trade liberalization scenarios studied in this chapter. For example, the flows in Table 9.1 are estimated *post-NAFTA* imports at *post-NAFTA* market prices.

Table 9.2 shows the bilateral tariff (and tariff equivalent) rates for food (upper entry), and for resources and manufacturing (lower entry), for the 10 regions. (GTAP does not have protection data for the services sector.) Each row in this table refers to a particular source (exporter), while the columns

Table 9.1. *Total Value of Post-NAFTA Imports at Importer's Market Prices (1992 U.S. $ million)*

| SOURCE | Destination | | | | | | | | | |
|---|---|---|---|---|---|---|---|---|---|---|
| | NAM | JPN | ANZ | CH/HK | TWN | SKOR | MA/SG | TH/PH | IDN | ROW |
| NAM | 363,197 | 111,187 | 17,821 | 27,435 | 21,593 | 31,311 | 19,687 | 11,218 | 5,712 | 316,844 |
| JPN | 140,422 | 0 | 11,793 | 44,165 | 26,429 | 26,773 | 26,701 | 20,988 | 8,002 | 159,846 |
| ANZ | 7,729 | 23,536 | 5,765 | 4,428 | 2,644 | 5,216 | 3,231 | 1,927 | 2,018 | 21,133 |
| CH/HK | 46,830 | 26,276 | 4,484 | 82,803 | 2,370 | 10,021 | 7,604 | 4,235 | 1,672 | 63,106 |
| TWN | 32,054 | 14,410 | 2,493 | 20,851 | 0 | 2,581 | 6,235 | 4,414 | 1,832 | 29,427 |
| SKOR | 24,627 | 17,792 | 2,101 | 10,409 | 2,620 | 0 | 5,799 | 3,717 | 2,631 | 39,085 |
| MA/SG | 26,823 | 16,929 | 4,035 | 11,069 | 6,278 | 5,637 | 21,432 | 9,295 | 3,000 | 39,420 |
| TH/PH | 15,480 | 13,228 | 967 | 3,956 | 958 | 2,339 | 4,777 | 517 | 590 | 18,891 |
| IDN | 6,056 | 15,138 | 1,257 | 3,356 | 1,524 | 3,008 | 3,964 | 825 | 0 | 9,857 |
| ROW | 263,993 | 128,009 | 20,800 | 47,349 | 14,106 | 34167 | 29,477 | 22,406 | 11,505 | 1,052,901 |
| TOTAL IMPORTS | 927,211 | 366,506 | 71,517 | 255,821 | 78,522 | 121,052 | 128,907 | 79,543 | 36,962 | 1,750,508 |

**Table 9.2. Bilateral Tariff Rates for Food, and Resources and Manufacturing by Source and Destination (%)**

| SOURCE | | NAM | JPN | ANZ | CH/HK | TWN | SKOR | MA/SG | TH/PH | IDN | ROW |
|---|---|---|---|---|---|---|---|---|---|---|---|
| | | | | | | Destination | | | | | |
| NAM | fd | 12.40 | 128.75 | 5.52 | 7.54 | 144.67 | 156.33 | 0.84 | 35.19 | 41.55 | 21.22 |
| | r&m | 0.00 | 2.94 | 17.58 | 9.10 | 7.54 | 16.02 | 2.20 | 27.52 | 10.73 | 8.52 |
| JPN | fd | 5.38 | n.a. | 4.39 | 4.10 | 21.09 | 106.75 | 3.69 | 40.11 | 26.92 | 15.12 |
| | r&m | 21.17 | n.a. | 21.17 | 13.58 | 5.84 | 18.19 | 3.72 | 33.83 | 14.34 | 16.08 |
| ANZ | fd | 16.24 | 92.62 | 8.81 | 8.54 | 37.66 | 74.61 | 1.07 | 23.96 | 32.40 | 23.14 |
| | r&m | 4.24 | 1.06 | 15.18 | 17.91 | 1.68 | 8.78 | 2.71 | 20.49 | 5.36 | 5.15 |
| CH/HK | fd | 5.07 | 76.13 | 5.75 | 5.30 | 36.05 | 276.81 | 0.57 | 33.44 | 47.71 | 24.28 |
| | r&m | 10.88 | 7.15 | 21.90 | 13.63 | 5.53 | 14.67 | 2.16 | 29.48 | 13.74 | 10.25 |
| TWN | fd | 4.55 | 34.87 | 4.70 | 5.81 | n.a. | 86.49 | 0.68 | 56.30 | 40.98 | 44.68 |
| | r&m | 10.74 | 5.95 | 17.17 | 13.55 | n.a. | 19.21 | 5.60 | 37.84 | 19.06 | 9.91 |
| SKOR | fd | 5.24 | 28.37 | 4.66 | 1.91 | 47.16 | n.a. | 1.47 | 53.73 | 26.76 | 11.46 |
| | r&m | 8.81 | 7.00 | 18.57 | 9.69 | 6.37 | n.a. | 3.37 | 30.27 | 17.96 | 11.79 |
| MA/SG | fd | 6.80 | 22.77 | 6.62 | 14.86 | 30.49 | 170.12 | 0.63 | 37.11 | 21.71 | 16.12 |
| | r&m | 6.11 | 2.55 | 19.82 | 6.58 | 5.68 | 14.03 | 4.35 | 28.93 | 11.28 | 9.27 |
| TH/PH | fd | 5.57 | 39.26 | 5.02 | 10.77 | 54.44 | 187.92 | 8.27 | 26.44 | 12.94 | 29.33 |
| | r&m | 8.56 | 4.67 | 13.69 | 4.73 | 4.07 | 16.22 | 2.21 | 37.18 | 15.18 | 9.32 |
| IDN | fd | 6.41 | 23.01 | 6.34 | 12.22 | 40.66 | 180.48 | 0.80 | 52.28 | n/a | 23.05 |
| | r&m | 9.60 | 3.16 | 10.08 | 15.03 | 3.19 | 9.09 | 1.79 | 25.80 | n/a | 9.92 |
| ROW | fd | 10.0 | 51.54 | 8.51 | 9.89 | 45.77 | 110.55 | 1.71 | 47.20 | 32.04 | 23.42 |
| | r&m | 8.07 | 3.08 | 16.23 | 14.51 | 6.15 | 11.84 | 2.55 | 26.82 | 12.89 | 8.75 |

refer to destinations (importers). Several points stand out. First of all, looking at the diagonal elements of the table, notice that some regions have internal levels of import protection and for others this is not applicable (n.a.). The regions with internal trade barriers are always aggregate groupings of individual countries, such as North America and China and Hong Kong. The bilateral import protection represents an aggregated level of protection based on the levels of protection between the individual, disaggregate regions in the GTAP data base. The regions without entries on the diagonal are individual countries without internal trade barriers. Finally, the diagonal entry for North America for resources and manufactures is 0. This is because Table 9.2 corresponds to the *post-NAFTA* data base, which represents the starting point for experiments in this chapter.

The top entry in each row of Table 9.2 represents the import tariff equivalents for food and agriculture. Notice that the tariff equivalents on food imports into most of the East Asian markets are very high. For example, the average tariff equivalent on North American food exports to Japan (column headed "JPN," row labeled "NAM-fd") is almost 130%. The comparable figures for Taiwan and South Korea are 144% and 156%, respectively. Unfortunately, nontariff barriers facing agricultural imports were not available at the time of this study for Malaysia, Singapore, the Philippines, and Hong Kong (see Chapter 3). Consequently, the food protection estimates for these regions are understated.

Turning to the resources and manufacturing protection data, reported in the italicized entries in alternating rows of Table 9.2, we note that the average level of protection is lower than for food. These entries account for applied tariff rates, as well as antidumping duties in the case of the US, Canada, and the EU. The effect of these duties shows up in the bilateral rate of protection on imports from Japan to North America. The average applied tariff rates on merchandise imports into the US and Canada from Japan are only 7.6% and 5.2%, respectively. However, the antidumping duties are much higher – 31.4% in the case of US imports of machinery and equipment from Japan (see Chapter 3). Consequently, the combined bilateral protection rate on NAM imports from Japan is fairly high (21.17%).

The experimental design in this chapter *abstracts from* the changes proposed under the Uruguay Round of the GATT negotiations. At the time of this analysis, the outcome of that agreement was still unclear and it had not yet been adopted by all member countries. The associated trade reforms, when known, *could be* incorporated in the analysis, thereby permitting an assessment of the impact of additional (post-GATT) liberalization by the APEC countries. This would involve implementing a Uruguay Round trade liberalization scenario first, thereafter implementing the APEC trade reforms, using the updated data from the GATT scenario as the starting point. This is *not* done here.

Three experiments were performed:

- *Experiment 1: APEC Preferential Free Trade Area.* Import protection (both tariffs and NTBs) within the nine APEC regions were removed but maintained between the rest of the world and APEC. Although it is unlikely that an agreement would result in the complete removal of all import barriers, this experiment provides an upper bound for the benefits of APEC that can be captured by the model. (Export interventions are *not* altered.)
- *Experiment 2: APEC Trade Reform on a Most Favored Nation Basis (MFN); ROW does not reciprocate.* In this experiment the nine APEC regions remove import barriers for all regions including ROW; however, ROW does not reciprocate. As many leaders in APEC have argued against reforms on a preferential basis, this experiment provides an estimate of the consequences of extending these reforms on an MFN basis, without reciprocity from ROW.
- *Experiment 3: APEC Trade Reform on an MFN Basis; ROW reciprocates.* Now, import barriers are also removed on APEC–ROW trade. (However, they remain in place on ROW–ROW trade.) The purpose of this scenario is to provide an alternative benchmark for a multilateral trade liberalization experiment on an MFN basis. It seems unlikely that APEC members would agree to extend MFN status to ROW without some degree of reciprocity. Again export taxes and subsidies are not altered.

## IV    Results

The consequences of the preferential elimination of import barriers within APEC are examined first. These results are then compared to reform on an MFN basis, both with and without the reciprocity of ROW.

When a country participates in a free trade area, it may experience gains due to trade creation and either a gain or a loss due to trade diversion. The former has a positive effect on welfare, since the removal of tariffs within the region allows the country to allocate its resources more efficiently in production. The country is now able to import the goods that it formerly produced inefficiently behind its tariff wall from member regions that are more efficient producers (Caves and Jones 1981). Trade diversion in the context of a preferential APEC trading region might arise as follows. Prior to the removal of tariffs within APEC, Indonesia sourced more of its imports from the ROW region. This can be seen by looking at Table 9.1 across the row for ROW under the IDN column. Following a preferential APEC agreement, we find that the volume of merchandise Indonesia imported from ROW falls by

$2.4 billion. Other APEC member countries are now able to undercut ROW even if they were not as efficient as ROW in production. For example, South Korean exports to Indonesia rise by about $2.2 billion. Trade has been diverted from ROW to South Korea in this instance. If South Korea is, in fact, a less efficient producer, a welfare loss arises due to Indonesia switching the source of its imports away from the more efficient source. However, this loss may or may not be offset by the gain in welfare that results from tariff removal (Caves and Jones 1981). Both of these effects enter into the results of the preferential trade liberalization experiment and help to explain differences between this experiment and the MFN experiments.

Table 9.3 presents the effects of APEC trade liberalization on the volume of total trade including services.[3] The top figure in each row represents the change in the volume of total exports (valued at the exporter's market prices, in the initial equilibrium, measured in $US million), relative to the base data, under the preferential trade agreement. The lower figure in parentheses represents the *difference* between the volume changes under the preferential basis and the MFN basis. If the figure in parentheses is subtracted from the top figure, then the change in volume for the MFN experiment is obtained (see also footnote *b*, Table 9.3). This table shows that all APEC members gain export volume under both experiments (positive row totals) at the expense of ROW, which experiences a $37,563 million reduction in export volume. When the basis of trade liberalization changes from preferential treatment to MFN treatment, ROW does not lose nearly as much volume [37,563 − (−32,358) = $5,205 million], since under the latter scenario APEC countries also eliminate protection on ROW imports.

Recall from Table 9.2 that some of the APEC member countries had very high initial tariff equivalents, particularly on food. This indicates that the trade liberalization experiment should have the greatest impact in these regions. An examination of the volume of exports into South Korea (SKOR) shows that all other APEC members experience an increase in volume of exports to South Korea except for Australia and New Zealand (ANZ). Thus, it is not surprising that the *initial* bilateral tariff on ANZ imports was *relatively* low. For example, from Table 9.2, South Korea has import tariff equivalents of 74.61% and 8.78% on imports of food and of resource and manufactures, respectively, from ANZ versus tariff equivalents of 156.33% and 16.02% on North American imports of food and of resources and manufactures, respectively.

The ROW region loses export volume, relative to the base, in all APEC member regions except Japan and Malaysia and Singapore under the preferential trade liberalization scenario (across the row headed ROW). These two regions had the smallest tariffs on imports of ROW resources and manufactures (3.08 and 2.55, respectively); therefore, after formation of the APEC block, ROW is still competitive in those markets. When the experiment is conducted

Table 9.3. *Effect of Trade Reform on Volume* of Total Exports (1992 US million, evaluated at exporter market prices)*

| From/To | NAM | JPN | ANZ | CH/HK | TWN | SKOR | MA/SG | TH/PH | IDN | ROW | TOTAL |
|---|---|---|---|---|---|---|---|---|---|---|---|
| NAM | -41658 | 77,008 | 6,179 | 6,083 | 15,268 | 13,295 | 1,880 | 4465 | 1971 | -2196 | 82294 |
|  | (11,144)ᵃ | (3,417) | (1,901) | (2,083) | (859) | (2,394) | (-82) | (2021) | (670) | (-45173) | (-20767) |
| JPN | 97,124 | 0 | 3,203 | 6,179 | 76 | 7,847 | -2,165 | 7979 | 1058 | -30816 | 90486 |
|  | (8,004) | (0) | (1,305) | (3,442) | (480) | (2,100) | (-110) | (3452) | (741) | (-17144) | (2268) |
| ANZ | 1,956 | 6,051 | 1,427 | 2,544 | -252 | -309 | 256 | 185 | 317 | -927 | 11247 |
|  | (267) | (-84) | (366) | (342) | (5) | (136) | (-94) | (263) | (163) | (-2906) | (-1541) |
| CH/HK | 10,303 | 6,197 | 1,482 | 23,714 | 22 | 8,563 | -556 | 1179 | 597 | -8158 | 43341 |
|  | (103) | (-816) | (291) | (-4,600) | (-32) | (-484) | (-271) | (529) | (134) | (-9183) | (-4161) |
| TWN | 6,719 | 809 | 450 | 5,315 | 0 | 755 | 826 | 4172 | 1017 | -2985 | 17078 |
|  | (950) | (-108) | (223) | (-1,632) | (0) | (121) | (-101) | (1131) | (227) | (-3932) | (141) |
| SKOR | 10,169 | 7,425 | 1,154 | 3,745 | 1,113 | 0 | 1,484 | 3362 | 2180 | 1405 | 32036 |
|  | (1,003) | (-106) | (277) | (966) | (65) | (0) | (-75) | (966) | (408) | (-6082) | (-2577) |
| MA/SG | 593 | -142 | 1,294 | 178 | 549 | 1,368 | 1,633 | 2914 | 392 | -4104 | 4675 |
|  | (1,089) | (101) | (481) | (816) | (190) | (421) | (137) | (1548) | (305) | (-4506) | (581) |
| TH/PH | 8,175 | 3,050 | 428 | 1,145 | 308 | 1,584 | 2,100 | 730 | 230 | 2950 | 20700 |
|  | (326) | (-227) | (89) | (-206) | (2) | (122) | (-211) | (138) | (61) | (-3469) | (-2963) |
| IDN | 1,520 | 1,893 | 24 | 1,699 | 111 | 423 | 119 | 414 | 0 | -316 | 5887 |
|  | (150) | (-315) | (91) | (274) | (6) | (150) | (-114) | (159) | (0) | (-1414) | (-1013) |
| ROW | -27,021 | 2,371 | -5,016 | -7,151 | -519 | -7,667 | 206 | -9802 | -2441 | 19478 | -37563 |
|  | (-33,622) | (2,124) | (-5,747) | (-15,941) | (-1,077) | (-7,562) | (1,883) | (-11799) | (-3300) | (42682) | (-32358) |

ᵃ The volume of exports corresponds to *one component* of the *(PM)* value flow [*VXMD*(*i*,*r*,*s*) = *PM*(*i*,*r*) * *QXS*(*i*,*r*,*s*)]. The change in the value of exports is driven by both the change in market price (*PM*) and the change in quantity component (*QXS*). The volume change refers to the change in the quantity component, which is valued at the *initial* exporter market prices. This provides the common, source-generic, metric.

ᵇ The terms in parentheses represent the difference between the preferential experiment and the MFN experiment without ROW reciprocity. Therefore, the preferential change in volume minus the difference equals the MFN change in volume (DIFF = PREF - MFN, therefore, MFN = PREF - DIFF) for measuring volume.

on an MFN basis, ROW is once again able to compete in most markets and increases export volume in all APEC regions with the exception of Japan, South Korea, and Malaysia and Singapore.

For the most part, trade among the APEC member regions is enhanced by a preferential agreement. For example, all the APEC members gain export volume into North America (down the column headed NAM) at the expense of NAFTA members and ROW, which both lose volume. Similar results hold for changes in export volume among the other APEC regions. When trade liberalization is conducted on an MFN basis, the members gain volume in the APEC region, but often to a lesser extent due to the increased involvement of ROW. For example, under the preferential agreement, North American exports to ANZ increase in volume by over $6 billion, while under the MFN reforms they increase by just over $4 billion. Adding up the export volumes from ROW to APEC regions (adding across the row headed ROW, but not including ROW, yields a *reduction* of over $57 billion in trade volume under the preferential reforms versus an *increase* of roughly $18 billion under the MFN reforms).

Under preferential trade reform, the volume of APEC exports into the ROW region falls, except from South Korea and Thailand and Philippines. ROW intraregional trade is enhanced. When MFN principles are used for trade reform, these results are mostly reversed. All APEC members except Japan gain export volume into ROW, and the volume of ROW intraregional trade declines. Specifically, in the first experiment there is an increase in intra-ROW trade volume of $19,478 million, whereas in the second experiment there is a decline of $19,478–$42,682 = $23,204 million.

Tables 9.4 and 9.5 detail changes in the terms of trade, real gross domestic output (GDP), and household utility for each region. Table 9.3 showed that the formation of the free trade area increased the volume of exports in all the member regions; however, this increase in exports is not necessarily accompanied by an increase in real GDP or utility. North America, Australia and New Zealand, Thailand and Philippines, and Indonesia all experience a decline in utility. As noted in Chapter 2, this change in terms of trade is often sensitive to the treatment of investment. As noted in an earlier footnote, Australia and New Zealand's terms-of-trade change is reversed when the investment is flexible. This can be explained by the deterioration these countries experience in their terms of trade. Notice that South Korea also experiences a deterioration in its terms of trade, but this effect is offset by the significant improvement in efficiency of domestic resource use, as reflected in the increased real GDP.

The terms of trade are defined as the ratio of the price received for tradeables (export price index) to the price paid for tradeables (import price index).[4] McDougall (1993) explains that in a model like GTAP, which differentiates

**Table 9.4.** *Effect of Preferential Trade Reform on Terms of Trade, Real GDP and Utility (% change)*

| Region | Terms of Trade | GDP Quantity Index[a] | Household Utility |
|---|---|---|---|
| North America | -1.03 | .07 | -.11 |
| Japan | 4.08 | .78 | 2.29 |
| Australia and New Zealand | -.84 | .18 | -.07 |
| China and Hong Kong | .96 | .53 | 1.28 |
| Taiwan | .81 | 1.78 | 2.40 |
| South Korea | -2.01 | 4.32 | 3.16 |
| Malaysia and Singapore | 1.17 | .38 | 2.42 |
| Thailand and Philippines | -6.29 | 1.30 | -3.05 |
| Indonesia | -1.05 | .46 | -.17 |
| ROW | -1.17 | -.04 | -.34 |

[a] The percentage change in the GDP quantity index equals the quantity change component of the percentage change in the value of GDP ($vgdp = pgdp + qgdp$). The change in the value of GDP is composed of a price change component ($pgdp$) and a quantity change component ($qgdp$). This quantity change component can be thought of as the change in real GDP.

products by country of origin, changes in the terms of trade can arise from changes in the relative prices of different source-specific varieties of the same commodity. A region's terms of trade will tend to improve if its exports of a commodity rise in price relative to the exports of other regions. A region's terms of trade will tend to worsen if it imports source-specific varieties that rise in price relative to other sources of the good. He proceeds to demonstrate how changes in the terms-of-trade index can be decomposed into three components: a component representing the contribution of changes in world prices, a component representing the contribution of changes in regional export prices, and a component representing the contribution of changes in regional import prices. An illustration of this type of decomposition for the changes in South Korea's terms of trade are presented and discussed in the appendix and the end of this chapter.

For the trade reform experiments conducted in this chapter, the negative changes in the terms of trade arise mainly due to the deterioration of regional export prices for resources and manufactures, particularly in North America, Australia and New Zealand, South Korea, Thailand and Philippines, Indonesia,

**Table 9.5.** *Effect of MFN Trade Reform on Terms of Trade, Real GDP, and Utility (% change)*

| Region | Terms of Trade | GDP Quantity Index | Household Utility |
|---|---|---|---|
| North America | -2.15 | -.10 | -.27 |
|  | (1.12)[a] | (-.03) | (.16) |
| Japan | 2.60 | .82 | 1.83 |
|  | (1.48) | (-0.04) | (.46) |
| Australia and New Zealand | -2.38 | .33 | -.38 |
|  | (1.54) | (-0.15) | (.31) |
| China and Hong Kong | -.43 | .80 | .60 |
|  | (1.39) | (-0.27) | (.68) |
| Taiwan | -.42 | 1.78 | 1.59 |
|  | (1.23) | 0 | (.81) |
| South Korea | -3.19 | 4.56 | 2.58 |
|  | (1.18) | (-.24) | (.58) |
| Malaysia and Singapore | .39 | .29 | 1.02 |
|  | (.78) | (.09) | (1.40) |
| Thailand and Philippines | -7.79 | 2.46 | -2.97 |
|  | (1.50) | (-1.16) | (-.08) |
| Indonesia | -2.84 | .78 | -.99 |
|  | (1.79) | (-.32) | (.82) |
| ROW | .65 | 0.02 | .19 |
|  | (-1.82) | (-0.06) | (-.53) |

[a] The terms in parentheses represent the difference between the preferential experiment and the MFN experiment without ROW reciprocity. Therefore, MFN percentage change plus the difference equals preferential percentage change as displayed in Table 9.4 (MFN + DIFF = PREF).

and ROW. World prices and composite regional import prices contribute relatively little to the terms-of-trade changes under the scenarios examined. Resources and manufactures make up the bulk of merchandise trade and, since the price received for exports declines relative to the price received for imports in these regions, a deterioration in terms of trade is experienced.

Although these results capture only a comparative static analysis of preferential trade reform, they suggest that this type of free trade area would promote growth in many member regions, but this could be at the expense of households in some cases. The North American region has experienced most of its gains through NAFTA, which is assumed to have been implemented already, prior to the APEC experiment. These results suggest that membership in the APEC region may not be beneficial for North America. Of course, this ignores the long-run effects of such an arrangement and the important political benefits of maintaining close ties within the Pacific Rim area. Although North America winds up losing under all three of the APEC simulations (see Table 9.6), it is important to keep in mind that these trade reform scenarios involve import protection liberalization only. Studies examining the impact of eliminating *export restraints*, like the one mentioned in Chapter 10 on reform of the Multifibre Arrangement (MFA), show significant gains accruing to the North American region.

When the APEC liberalization experiment is conducted on an MFN basis without the ROW region reciprocating, the welfare results obtained are qualitatively similar to those from the preferential experiment, except for ROW. Changes in terms-of-trade, real GDP, and utility under the MFN experiment are presented in Table 9.5. The figures in parentheses represent the differences between the results using a preferential basis and the MFN basis. Adding the difference to the percentage change for the MFN experiment yields the percentage change in the variable for the preferential experiment (Table 9.4). Notice now that the ROW region benefits from the APEC region liberalizing tariffs on its exports to the region. The benefits ROW experiences come at the expense of APEC member regions. North America, Australia and New Zealand, Thailand and Philippines, and Indonesia experience a decline in household utility that is larger in magnitude than under the preferential trade reforms. Although the other member regions still experience a gain from the liberalization, it is not as great as under the preferential scenario. This is supported by the fact that now more of the member regions experience a deterioration in their terms of trade, namely, North America, Australia and New Zealand, China and Hong Kong, Taiwan, South Korea, Thailand and Philippines, and Indonesia. Therefore, these comparative static simulations indicate that a trade reform package that extends MFN status to ROW, but does not require it to reciprocate, is not desirable for the APEC member countries.

Table 9.6 presents the welfare effects of the two previously discussed trade liberalization scenarios, as well as the third experiment, in which the ROW region reciprocates. It is interesting to note how well Japan fares under each of the scenarios. Under preferential trade reform Japan experiences a welfare gain of over $71 billion, which represents about 77% of the $93 billion in gross welfare gains. Japan's share of gross welfare gains drops to about 65% under MFN reform, without ROW reciprocating, but this increase bounces back to 76% when ROW does reciprocate in the reforms. The fact that Japan dominates the welfare gains in this analysis may be explained by its large initial share of APEC exports, which amounts to 20%. As well, Japan experiences a

Table 9.6. *Effect of Trade Liberalization on Welfare ($US million)*

| Region | Preferential Reform 1 | MFN Reform 2 | Difference 1 — 2 | MFN with ROW Reciprocating 3 |
|---|---|---|---|---|
| North America | -6,625 | -16,745 | (10,120) | -2,260 |
| Japan | 71,564 | 57,339 | (14,225) | 93,955 |
| Australia and New Zealand | -205 | -1,134 | (929) | 738 |
| China and Hong Kong | 5,891 | 2,778 | (3,113) | 7,360 |
| Taiwan | 5,041 | 3,348 | (1,693) | 6,430 |
| South Korea | 8,424 | 6,894 | (1,530) | 10,967 |
| Malaysia and Singapore | 2,120 | 896 | (1,224) | 2,802 |
| Thailand and Philippines | -4,577 | -4,449 | (-128) | -1,533 |
| Indonesia | -202 | -1,186 | (984) | 569 |
| ROW | -31,668 | 17,592 | (-49,260) | -47,195 |
| **TOTAL** | 49,763 | 65,333 | (-15,570) | 71,833 |

large increase in export volume under the reforms (see Table 9.3) and a noticeable improvement in terms of trade (Tables 9.4 and 9.5).

Some general observations on the effects of the different trade liberalization scenarios on welfare follow. When reform is conducted on a preferential basis, North America, Australia and New Zealand, Thailand and Philippines, Indonesia, and ROW all experience a reduction in welfare; the other APEC member regions gain. When the reforms are conducted using MFN principles, the results depend upon whether or not the ROW reciprocates in the reforms. When it does not reciprocate, ROW's welfare increases by over $17 billion; it falls by $47 billion when it does reciprocate. This loss in welfare is larger than the loss incurred under preferential reforms, but it is considerably reduced when the ROW region also liberalizes *intra*regional trade. When ROW does not reciprocate under the MFN reforms, all APEC members, with the exception of Thailand & Philippines, are worse off than under the preferential reforms. When ROW participates in the MFN reform experiment by cutting its import tariffs as well, the APEC members are better off than they are without its reciprocity. In fact, all the APEC members are even better off under the MFN reforms with ROW reciprocity than they are under the preferential liberalization scenario. These results seem to suggest that pursuing multilateral trade reforms is a wise strategy for the APEC member nations.

## V    Conclusions and qualifications

The results of the chapter highlight the importance of experimental design and the usefulness of GTAP in conducting an analysis of regional integration. Three different scenarios for APEC regional trade liberalization are examined and compared. The results show that the formation of an APEC trading block could result in both winners and losers in the group, as well as in ROW. The distribution of the gains and losses are affected by the assumptions that are made about the basis under which trade reform is conducted.

Conducting the APEC trade reform experiment on an MFN basis without the reciprocity of ROW delivers lower benefits for APEC members, and seems to support the arguments of Prime Minister Hawke in favor of *multilateral* trade liberalization involving ROW in trade negotiations. It has been argued, however, that regional reforms can lead to reform on a wider basis by providing impetus toward global trade reform. In that case, the analysis of this chapter suggests that APEC members would be better off to withhold tariff reductions on ROW imports until such time as they agree to reciprocity.

This chapter has demonstrated the suitability of the GTAP modeling framework for examining the impact of different types of trade agreements for the Pacific Rim, especially given its excellent coverage of the countries involved. However, some significant limitations must be noted. First, version 2 of the data base does not have complete coverage of agricultural protection for the countries involved in APEC. The protection data base also does not cover all the nontariff barriers that exist, although substantial progress has been made with the inclusion of the MFA and antidumping duties. This is a part of the data base that is constantly being improved as further information becomes available. Future analyses of alternative APEC agreements will benefit from these improvements.

Finally, note that the benefits of a preferential trading agreement cannot be fully captured by a perfectly competitive, static model. The benefits of increased competition, potential economies of scale, and the incentives for investment brought about by a preferential agreement will be fully realized only in the long run. These forces will likely increase incomes and with them, imports from ROW (McCalla 1992). While the GTAP model cannot capture all these dynamic effects from trade liberalization, it is a useful tool for generating comparative static results for a variety of trade reform scenarios, the comparison of which can provide direction in the path toward further trade reform.

## Appendix: Decomposition of changes in terms of trade for South Korea

McDougall (1993) demonstrates that the change in the terms of trade can be decomposed into the contribution of world price indexes of all goods ($c1\_r$), the contribution of regional export prices ($c2\_r$), and the contribution of regional import prices ($c3\_r$).

$$c1\_r + c2\_r - c3\_r = tot.$$

Substituting in the values of the components for South Korea yields:

$$(.04) + (-1.81) - (.26) = -2.01.$$

As discussed in the chapter, this change in the terms of trade is dominated by the changes in the export prices for the region. This term ($c2\_r$) can in turn be decomposed:

$$c2\_r = sum(i \ \varepsilon \ TRAD\_COM, \ c2\_ir).$$

The term ($c2\_ir$) represents the contribution of the change in regional export price for good $i$ to the change in terms-of-trade. Substituting in the values of the components for this equation yields:

$$(-.44) + (-1.51) + (.4) + (-.26) = -1.81.$$

The first term refers to changes in the price of Food exports for the region, the second term to changes in the export price of resources and manufactures for the region, the third term to the change in the export price of services for the region, and the last term to changes in the price of capital goods exports for the region. The change in the export price of resources and manufactures clearly dominates this calculation. This is reinforced by the fact that capital goods are constructed as a composite of the first three produced goods; thus, a portion of its price change reflects the change in the price of resources and manufactures.

## NOTES

1. In a separate exercise, these experiments were all conducted using the flexible investment portfolio specification ($RORDELTA = 1$ and $RORFLEX = 10$). This dampens the terms-of-trade effects and actually reverses their sign for the ANZ region, which subsequently gains from preferential liberalization. Further analysis of the impact of APEC on investment patterns in the region is clearly warranted. The interested reader can pursue this issue by accessing the files associated with this chapter, following the instructions in Chapter 6.

2. Both the Canada–US Free Trade Agreement and NAFTA avoided full liberalization of food and agricultural trade. Rather, exceptions were granted, as well as more gradual implementation of agreed-upon cuts.

3. The volume of exports corresponds to *one component* of the (*PM*) value flow [*VXDM*(*i,r,s*) = *PM* (*i,r*) * *QXS*(*i,r,s*)]. The change in the value of exports is driven by both the change in market price (*PM*) and the change in quantity component (*QXS*). The volume change refers to the change in the quantity component, which is valued at the *initial* exporter market prices. This provides the common, source-generic, metric for measuring volume.

4. McDougall (1993) provides a methodology for decomposing changes in the terms of trade.

## REFERENCES

Caves, R., and R. Jones (1981) *World Trade and Payments*. Boston: Little, Brown.

Drysdale, P., (1988) *International Economic Pluralism: Economic Policy in East Asia and the Pacific*. New York: Columbia University Press.

Drysdale, P. and R. Garnaut (1993) "The Pacific: An Application of a General Theory of Economic Integration." In C. F. Bergsten and M. Noland (eds.), *Pacific Dynamism and the International Economic System*. Washington, DC: Institute for International Economics.

Eminent Persons Group (1993) "A Vision for APEC: Towards an Asian Pacific Economic Community," Report of the Eminent Persons Group to the Ministers of APEC, Singapore, October.

*Far Eastern Economic Review* (1993) "Loose Knit Family," Dec. 2, pp. 12–13.

Hughes, H. (1991) "Does APEC Make Sense?" *ASEAN Economic Bulletin* 8:125–136.

McCalla, A. (1992) "GATT, Preferential/Regional Trading Blocs and Agricultural Trade," *Review of International Economics* 1:73–89.

McDougall, R. (1993) "Two Small Extensions to SALTER," SALTER Working Paper No. 12.

*Wall Street Journal* (1994) "APEC Nations Agree to Remove Trade Barriers in the Pacific Rim," November 16, p. A30.

CHAPTER 10

# Evaluating the benefits
# of abolishing the MFA
# in the Uruguay Round package

*Yongzheng Yang, Will Martin, and Koji Yanagishima*


## I    Introduction and overview

The use of quantitative restrictions on textile imports from developing countries
dates back to the 1930s (Keesing and Wolf 1980). At that time, the restrictions
were mainly directed against the increasingly competitive Japanese cotton
textile industry. After the Second World War, Japan's textile exports to the
industrial countries spearheaded its export-led industrialization. However, the
pressure for protection in industrial countries came not only from competition
overseas, but perhaps more important, from the stagnant or even declining
output and employment as a result of sluggish domestic demand (Keesing
and Wolf 1980). Despite Japan's "voluntary" export restraints, a Short-Term
Arrangement (STA) in cotton textile trade was reached in 1961 at the initiative
of the US and under the auspices of the General Agreement on Tariffs and
Trade (GATT). The conclusion of a Long-Term Arrangement (LTA) in 1962
established a system of quantitative protection against textile exports from
developing countries (GATT 1984).

Despite the LTA, developing countries were able to expand their exports
of textiles to industrial countries in the 1960s. Technological change strengthened the competitiveness of developing countries in textiles throughout this
period. The emergence of synthetic fibers also enabled developing countries
to find holes in industrial country restrictions, thereby increasing their market
penetration. In addition, restrictions on Japanese products led to rapid growth
of exports from other Asian countries, namely, Hong Kong, Taiwan, and
Korea (Keesing and Wolf 1980). Under renewed pressure of competition from
overseas, the US initiated the negotiations on the Multifibre Arrangement
(MFA) in 1973. The MFA went into effect on January 1, 1974. It has been
renewed several times since then.

The prominent feature of the MFA is its stipulation of the use of quantitative
restrictions on textile exports from developing countries. Under the umbrella

of the MFA, industrial and developing countries negotiate bilateral agreements on export quotas regulating textile trade. Thus, the MFA is discriminatory by country of origin. This is primarily achieved via voluntary export restraints (VERs). As a result, exporting countries capture the quota rents. The MFA stipulates 6% annual growth of exports from developing countries, but in practice the growth rates of bilateral quotas are frequently below the stipulated rate, and in some cases, even negative growth rates have been applied. Developing countries' exports are allowed to transfer a portion of an unfilled quota from one category to another ("swing"), use the unused quotas from the previous year ("carry-over") and borrow quotas from the following year ("carry-forward"). But limits are set on the ensuing flexibility.

The MFA restriction has become increasingly complex as the number of countries and commodities has been enlarged. Today, the MFA includes most major industrial and developing countries and covers products made of cotton, synthetic fibers, wool, silk and ramie, or their blends. In addition, the growth rates of quota volumes seem to be declining (Yang 1992). Global restrictions have also been applied by industrial countries in recent years. Under this arrangement, *all exports* are subject to quota when total exports from an exporting country reach a certain share of total imports in the country of destination.

In addition to the bilateral quotas, nondiscriminatory tariffs are frequently applied on imports of textiles and clothing, even when these products are subject to the MFA. The interaction between the tariffs and the MFA quotas introduces some complexities into the evaluation of the phase-out of the MFA proposed under the Uruguay Round agreement. The effects of quota removal depend upon second-best considerations, and theory alone is not sufficient to guide the selection of policies to improve the allocation of resources.

A path breaking feature of the Uruguay Round was an agreement to bring MFA-restricted goods under GATT disciplines. This liberalization process is being undertaken very gradually over a 10-year period, with MFA-restricted goods being returned to the normal GATT system (i.e., freed from export quotas) progressively over a 10-year period. Under the agreement, import tariffs are also being reduced, on both textiles and clothing and on a wide range of other goods. However, the rates of tariff reduction vary considerably between commodities, with considerably lower rates of tariff reduction on textiles than on most other goods.

The objective of this paper is to assess the effects of the removal of the MFA in the context of more general liberalization under the Uruguay Round agreement. To do this, we consider four separate experiments that shed some light on the nature of the welfare effects of liberalizing the MFA in the context of the Uruguay Round agreement:

1. Elimination of MFA quotas with non-MFA distortions in place
2. Reduction in tariffs on MFA goods alone
3. Non-MFA reforms
4. Implementation of the comprehensive Uruguay Round package.

To introduce the basic economic mechanisms at work, we first formulate the problem in simple partial equilibrium terms. Second, we briefly consider the nature of the liberalization undertaken under the Uruguay Round. Then, we consider the formulation of the problem in the Global Trade Analysis Project (GTAP) model. Finally, we discuss the nature of the experiments conducted. We report the results, then conclude our experiments.

## II    Consequences of liberalizing tariffs and MFA quotas

Normal tariffs are levied by the importing country, with the tariff revenue accruing to the importing country. Because of the precarious standing of the MFA in the international trading system, however, the developed country importers seeking to restrict exports from developing countries felt it necessary to "purchase" compliance by giving the exporters the right to control exports. Because export rights are scarce, they become valuable assets in those supplying countries that are internationally competitive suppliers. These assets are typically distributed free to exporting firms by governments on the basis of some criterion such as past export performance (Hamilton 1990).

If these export quota rights are freely traded, their value to exporters is equalized at the margin: exporters for whom their value is less than their market price sell them in the market; exporters for whom their value is initially more than the market price typically buy them. Even where quota transfers are illegal or restricted, typically there are arrangements for quota rental or for quota fulfillment through subcontracting so that it is realistic as a first approximation to assign a single quota premium across exporting firms in a single country. In this situation, the overall national quota can be thought of as imposing a tax on exporters equal to the purchase price of a unit of quota. For an exporter who has received a quota allocation, the cost of exporting is increased by the price for which the quota could have been sold, or the opportunity cost of holding the quota. For an exporter who does not initially have a unit of quota, the cost of exporting includes the purchase price of a unit of quota.

The assumptions we have made above treat the MFA more favorably as a policy instrument than it may deserve. There is evidence that the procedures used to allocate export quotas in developing countries may sometimes lead to substantial efficiency losses. There is also evidence that the developing country exporters do not receive the full benefits of the MFA quota rents. At least a part of the quota rents may be shared with the importing countries because of the market power of importing firms at the individual product level (Krishna, Erzan, and Tan 1994). In this analysis, we deal with the standard case in which the quotas restrict exports efficiently and the rents are transferred to the exporters.

When both a quota and a tariff are levied on the import of a good, and the import quota is binding, the quota level determines the volume of imports of the good. The domestic price of the good is, in turn, determined solely by domestic demand and the volume of the import quota. At a given world price, the difference between the domestic price in the restricted market and the world price consists of the tariff and the quota rent. The tariff rate is an exogenous policy variable; the tariff equivalent of the quota is endogenously determined by the level of the quota and the strength of domestic demand. Algebraically:

$$p_d = p_w(1+t)(1+q), \tag{10.1}$$

where $p_d$ is the domestic price of the good; $p_w$ is the world price of the good; $t$ is the *ad valorem* tariff rate; and $q$ is the tariff rate that would be equivalent in its restrictive effect to the export quota.

To aid understanding, we first consider the case in which a single exporting region faces two sources of demand: the restricting market, and the rest of the world (ROW). To illustrate this, we draw an extended version of a diagram presented in Martin and Suphachalasai (1990, figure 3.3). The major extension in this diagram is the incorporation of the effects of a tariff on imports into the quota-restricted market. In Figure 10.1, total import demand consists of two components: $Z_p^1(t)$ is the net demand for imports by the developed regions in the presence of an initial tariff, $t$, on imports into this market; and $Z_p^2$ is the net demand for imports by ROW. The resulting total import demand is given as $ED(t)$. The supply of exports from the developing countries is given as $-Z_p^0$.

Without the MFA quota, the market clears at world price, $p_e(t)$ in Figure 10.1. With imposition of an MFA export quota, the total import demand becomes the kinked curve $abc$. In the presence of both the tariff and the quota, the world market clears at a lower world price, $p_w$, which is the price received by developing country exporters for their exports to the non-MFA market. The price received by developing country exporters for their exports to the MFA-restricted market is p $(=p_w(1+q))$; the price paid by consumers within the restricted market is $p_c$ $(=p_w(1+t)(1+q))$. The quota regime results in rents of $(p-p_w)Q^*$ being transferred from the restricting importer to the exporting region where $Q^*$ equals the quantity of exports into the MFA-restricted market.

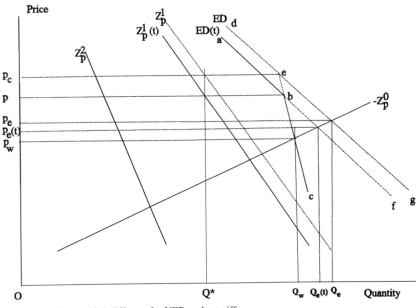

**Figure 10.1.** Effects of a VER and a tariff.

Starting from the distorted equilibrium depicted in Figure 10.1, the effects of removing the tariff and the quota can be considered in turn. Removal of the tariff shifts the import demand curve for the restricted market up to $Z_p^1$ and is associated with a rise in the price received by MFA exporters for these exports to $p_c$. The total import demand curve, $ED(t)$, shifts upward only to the left of the kink point $b$, that is, in situations when the quota was not previously binding. The new total import demand curve is thus the kinked curve, *dec*. Assuming a binding quota, the world price, $p_w$, is unaffected by this change, as are the volume of imports and exports in all markets. This illustrates the fact that *the tariff in this case is purely a rent shifting tariff*: its sole effect is to determine the allocation of the difference between the world price and the price in the restricted market between quota rents to exporters, and tariff revenues to importers.

The effects of abolishing the MFA quota are considerably more complex than those of removing the tariff on the quota-constrained goods. With the tariff in place, the total import demand curve becomes *abf*, and without the tariff it is the curve *deg*. The quantity of exports to both importing markets rises from $Q_w$ to $Q_e(t)$ while the world market price rises to $p_e(t)$ in the presence of the tariff. In the absence of the tariff, total imports increase to $Q_e$ and the world market price is $p_e$. As a consequence, the exporters are able to expand their output, reaping an efficiency gain in the process, as emphasized by de Melo and Winters (1993). With a tariff, the price received for products sold in the restricted market, however, declines from $p$ to $p_e(t)$, implying a loss of quota rents on the goods sold to the restricted market. The overall welfare effects of the change depend upon whether the loss of rents on products sold in the restricted market is outweighed by the increase in prices received from unrestricted markets and the efficiency gains associated with increasing output.

Whether an exporter will gain or lose from quota liberalization clearly depends upon the magnitude of the price changes in the restricted and unrestricted markets, and upon the relative importance of each market for that exporter. The magnitude of the price effects, in turn, depends upon the price responsiveness of the restricted and the unrestricted markets. In the appendix to this chapter, we use a simple theoretical model, consistent with the diagram, to show that the welfare effects of liberalization depend in a relatively straightforward way upon the share of its exports sold to quota-restricted markets, and on the relative magnitude of the price decline in the restricted market and the price increase in the unrestricted market.

Where tariffs apply to goods other than the restricted good, government revenue changes in markets other than the restricted one must also be considered. Liberalization of textile and clothing quotas will lower the domestic prices of textiles and clothing and therefore can be expected to reduce demand for imports of goods that are close domestic substitutes. The resulting changes in tariff revenue must be considered when evaluating the welfare effects of liberalization (Anderson and Martin 1993). Thus, the larger the reductions in tariffs on imports of goods that are substitutes for textiles and clothing, the more likely it is that removal of MFA quotas will be welfare-improving.

In addition to the distortions facing developing country exporters, other important influences on whether they will gain or lose from removal of the MFA quotas are the shares of their products sold in the MFA markets, and the elasticities of demand they face in each market. If a supplier has a low elasticity of demand in the restricted market (and hence achieves large price gains per unit of sales forgone), then it is more likely to lose from the MFA removal. An exporter that has a large quota relative to its supply potential, and hence sells a higher proportion of its exports in the restricted markets, is also more likely to lose from the abolition. Given the structure of the GTAP model, export demand elasticities across markets are quite similar. Thus, the share of exports to the restricted market is most relevant in making these assessments. Table 10.1 identifies the commodities/regions used in our aggregation, and Table 10.2 reports the restricted export shares. For textiles, the newly industrializd economies (NIEs), Association of South East Asian Nations (ASEAN), and China all send only a small share of their exports to the restricted markets. South Asia and Latin America have a higher orientation to these markets, while the ROW region has the highest degree of orientation

Table 10.1. *Regional and Commodity Aggregation*

| Regional Aggregation | Commodity Aggregation |
|---|---|
| **1. Australia**<br>Australia<br>New Zealand | **1. Agriculture**<br>Paddy rice<br>Wheat<br>Nongrain crops<br>Wool |
| **2. North America**<br>US<br>Canada | Other livestock<br>Forestry<br>Fisheries |
| **3. EU** | Processed rice |
| **4. Japan** | **2. Mining**<br>Coal |
| **5. NIEs**<br>Hong Kong<br>Republic of Korea<br>Taiwan | Oil<br>Gas<br>Other minerals<br>Nonmetallic minerals |
| **6. ASEAN**<br>Indonesia<br>Malaysia<br>Philippines<br>Singapore<br>Thailand | **3. Processed food**<br>Meat products<br>Milk products<br>Other food products<br>Beverages & tobacco<br><br>**4. Textiles** |
| **7. China** | **5. Clothing**<br>Wearing apparel |
| **8. South Asia** | |
| **9. Latin America**<br>Argentina<br>Brazil<br>Mexico<br>Rest of Latin America | **6. Iron and steel**<br>Primary ferrous metals<br><br>**7. Machinery and equipment**<br><br>**8. Transport equipment**<br>Transport industries |
| **10. ROW**<br>Sub-Saharan Africa<br>Middle East & North Africa<br>Economies of Transition<br>ROW | **9. Other manufactures**<br>Leather, etc.<br>Lumber<br>Pulp paper, etc.<br>Petroleum and coal<br>Chemicals<br>Rubbers and plastics<br>Nonmetallic minerals<br>Nonferrous metals<br>Fabricated metal products<br>Other manufacturing |
| | **10. Nontradeable services**<br>Construction<br>Trade and transport<br>Electricity, water, and gas<br>Other serives (private)<br>Other services (government)<br>Ownership of dwellings |

to the MFA-restricted markets. However, ROW includes some developed countries whose access is not restricted by the MFA, so this region effectively faces limited restrictions. (This is reflected in its relatively low average export tax equivalent.)

Table 10.2. *Export Shares and Tax Equivalents of MFA Quotas (% of fob prices)*

| | Textiles | | | | Clothing | | | |
|---|---|---|---|---|---|---|---|---|
| | Share Restricted | Tax Equivalents | | Share Restricted | Tax Equivalents | | | |
| Exporter | | North America | EU | | North America | EU | | |
| NIEs | 0.11 | 8.8 | 10.3 | 0.71 | 18.9 | 16.3 | | |
| ASEAN | 0.23 | 12.0 | 16.0 | 0.55 | 36.5 | 38.2 | | |
| China | 0.16 | 18.9 | 27.4 | 0.26 | 40.4 | 36.1 | | |
| South Asia | 0.39 | 19.0 | 27.4 | 0.78 | 40.4 | 36.1 | | |
| Latin America | 0.48 | 9.6 | 14.2 | 0.87 | 20.2 | 17.6 | | |
| ROW | 0.66 | 4.6 | 6.2 | 0.86 | 8.6 | 8.7 | | |

*Source:* GTAP data base.

Table 10.3. *Tariff Reductions in Industrial Countries Agreed Under the Uruguay Round* (%)

| Rate of tariff reductions imported from: | All | Developing | Developed |
|---|---|---|---|
| Agricultural products | 36.0 | | |
| Mining products | 34.4 | 35.0 | 33.7 |
| Processed food | 21.3 | 22.4 | 19.5 |
| Textiles and clothing | 20.0 | 21.2 | 18.9 |
| Iron and steel | 62.2 | 66.7 | 60.6 |
| Machinery and equipment | 48.8 | 48.6 | 48.8 |
| Transport equipment | 21.6 | 18.4 | 21.8 |
| Other manufactures | 41.9 | 39.7 | 42.5 |

Source: Computed from table 11, GATT (1993).

In the clothing market, the developing country exporters tend to rely much more heavily on the MFA importing markets than is the case in textiles. There are very large differences in the extent of this reliance, however, with China exporting a much smaller share to MFA markets than the other suppliers. ASEAN is also relatively more diversified, with only 55% of its exports going to MFA importing markets. Latin America is the most dependent upon the MFA importing markets, with 87% of its exports going to these two markets.

## III    Liberalization under the Uruguay Round

In this analysis, we focus on the gains in market access provided for under the Uruguay Round agreement, rather than the systemic reforms to the trading system, which may well be of even greater importance. Specific estimates of the gains in market access under the round were not available at the time of writing. The broad estimates presented in Table 10.3 are generally similar to those used in earlier studies (e.g., Goldin, Knudsen, and van der Mensbrugghe 1993) and provide a broad estimate of the intended nature of the liberalization. We draw upon more recent GATT (1994) estimates of tariff reductions of 10% and 15% for textiles and clothing and transport equipment, respectively, in North America. For developing countries, we follow Brandão and Martin (1993) in assuming that agricultural trade distortions will be reduced by two-thirds of the developed country reductions. In addition, we assume here, for want of better information, that developing countries reduce their industrial sector protection by two-thirds of the reduction achieved by industrialized countries.

Although the phase-out of the MFA will occur gradually, our framework is really suitable for analyzing only comparative static effects. Because we are primarily concerned with understanding the consequences of liberalization in the presence of multiple distortions using a comprehensive general equilibrium model, rather than determining the actual impact of the Uruguay Round, we first evaluate the effects of an immediate phase-out of the arrangement. Given the rapid changes occurring in comparative advantage in this industry, and the likely tendency for the arrangement to become more restrictive over time (Yang 1994b), the effects of MFA liberalization seem more likely to be favorable for developing countries at the end of the phase-out period.

The effects of liberalization depend heavily upon the magnitude of the initial distortions. We draw on the GTAP data base for estimates of the magnitude of these distortions (see Chapter 3). All industrialized regions (except Australasia) and the NIEs have sizeable production subsidies for agriculture, with the European Union (EU) having the highest level of support. Only North America and the EU maintain sizeable export subsidies for agricultural exports. Tariffs or their equivalents on agricultural commodities are very high in the EU, Japan, and the NIEs. They are also quite high in ASEAN and China. Among manufactured goods, only processed food and textiles and clothing are subject to relatively high tariffs in industrial countries. The NIEs have the lowest tariffs on manufactured goods among developing countries, and China seems to have the highest.

The export tax equivalents of the MFA on textiles are reported in the first group of columns in Table 10.2. They are higher in the EU than in North America; for clothing (second group of columns) North America is generally more restrictive. ASEAN, China, and South Asia are the most severely restricted textile and clothing exporters. These regions were not major exporters of textiles and clothing when the MFA was established, and their exports of goods under the MFA are lower, relative to their total exports, than is the case in the NIEs.

For simplicity, we assume that all textile and clothing categories are restricted by the MFA, although we know that not all textile and clothing categories are covered by binding MFA import quotas [for estimates of these coverage ratios see Hamilton (1990)]. Ideally, we would divide total imports of textiles and clothing into two groups: those restricted by the MFA, and those unrestricted. However, this would involve introducing additional commodities, and hence introducing a fundamental distinction between commodities and industries that is not present in the current data base. Further, the distinction is probably less important than it might appear, since many of the products not explicitly restricted by the MFA are essentially under its shadow, and would come under its restrictions if their export levels increased.

## IV    Experimental design

### Experiment 1 (E1)

Our first experiment consists of the elimination of MFA quotas in the presence of the pre–Uruguay Round tariffs. Because the quotas are being fully liberalized, it is appropriate to impose the shock by specifying the quotas as though they were implemented by using export taxes of equivalent restrictiveness (see Table 10.4 for a summary of the four experiments). The MFA phase-out is simply implemented by imposing shocks that will reduce the export tax equivalents (*txs*) of the MFA quotas to zero. Exogenous variables in this closure include population, the numeraire price of savings, all technological change shifters, all slack variables except the Walrasian slack variable, all policy variables, and all endowments.

## *Experiment 2 (E2)*

In our second experiment the reduction of tariffs on textiles and clothing alone is imposed directly by reducing these tariffs (*tms*) by the amount (an average of 21% for industrial countries and 14% for developing countries) estimated to have been agreed under the Uruguay Round. At the same time, the export tax equivalents of the MFA for textiles and clothing (*txs*) are endogenized, and the corresponding exports (*qxs*) from developing countries are fixed. The results of this experiment provide something of a check on the model. We know that the welfare gains to developing countries of this experiment should be almost equal to the change in their export tax revenues, plus any welfare impact of their own tariff reductions in textiles and clothing. This is because there are no quantity adjustments occurring, and hence no price changes. The only effect of the tariff reduction is to increase the quota rents accruing on exports of these goods.

## *Experiment 3 (E3)*

Similarly, in experiment 3, the export tax equivalents for MFA quotas on textiles and clothing are endogenized and the corresponding exports from developing countries are modeled as being determined by exogenous quotas. The shocks now, however, cover all non-MFA reforms. Thus, policy variables subject to shocks include import tariffs for all commodities (see Table 10.3) and agricultural output subsidies (20% cut) and export subsidies (36% cut). The effect of liberalizing all non-MFA distortions depends upon the usual considerations such as efficiency gains, terms-of-trade gains, and induced changes in tariff and other tax revenues (second-best effects). Since trade liberalization is a positive sum game, the overall gains will be positive, although there is no guarantee that some regions will not lose.

One second-best consideration likely to be important in experiment 3 is the possibility of changes in the export tax equivalent on textiles and clothing when other goods are liberalized. Assuming other goods are substitutes for textiles and clothing, reductions in other tariffs will reduce the import demand for textiles and apparel, and hence reduce the quota rents accruing to exporters.

**Table 10.4.** *Experimental Design*

| Experiment | Exogenous variable[a] | Variables shocked[b] |
|---|---|---|
| E1 | *txs* | *txs* (textiles and clothing only) |
| E2 | *qxs* (textile and clothing exports from developing to industrial regions only) | *tms* (textiles and clothing only) |
| E3 | *qxs* (textile and clothing exports from developing to industrial regions only) | *to* (agriculture only), *tms*, *txs* (agriculture only) |
| E4 | *txs* | *to* (agriculture only), *tms*, *txs* (agriculture, textiles and clothing only) |

[a] All four experiments have a standard general equilibrium closure that includes the following exogenous variables: *pop, ao, psave, tm. tx, to, tms, and the usual slack variables*. The additional exogenous variables listed above are experiment-specific.
[b] For depth of tariff reductions, see Table 10.3. For reductions in bilateral export tax equivalents, see Table 10.2.

This possible loss must be set against the certain gain in quota rents resulting from reductions in the tariff on textiles and clothing. Whether the gain or the loss is larger depends upon the closeness of substitution between textiles/clothing and other goods and on the relative magnitude of both initial tariffs and the rates of tariff reduction. High initial tariff rates on nontextiles, and large proportional rates of reduction, especially if combined with high substitutability, may reduce the quota rents.

### Experiment 4 (E4)

Experiment 4 considers a complete Uruguay Round reform. This allows us to evaluate the importance of the MFA reform in the entire Uruguay Round package by subtracting the results of the non-MFA reforms from this experiment. Whether the gains are greater or smaller than previously (or even positive or negative) depends upon how MFA and non-MFA distortions interact in the process of liberalization. An alternative approach to the evaluation of the role of the MFA reform is to eliminate the export tax equivalents from the data base resulting from the third experiment. This effect can, however, be calculated by subtracting results of E3 from those of E4.

## IV    Simulation results

### Eliminating the MFA in the pre–Uruguay Round environment

As discussed earlier, our first experiment is typical of the previous studies of the MFA. The MFA is abolished alone, leaving all other pre–Uruguay Round distortions intact. Table 10.5 reports the impact of this policy change on the production and exports of textiles and clothing. As a result of MFA abolition, textile and clothing output increases in developing countries but falls in industrialized countries. The relocation of world production and export sources appears to be substantial. It occurs not only between industrialized and developing countries, but also among developing countries themselves. For example, while clothing production and exports in ASEAN, China, and South Asia increase substantially, they declined considerably in the NIEs, Latin America, and ROW. This result is hardly surprising given the protection pattern of the MFA across developing countries (see Table 10.2). The more restricted developing country exporters expand their exports at the expense of not only industrial countries but also less restricted developing countries.

The welfare effects of MFA removal as measured by equivalent variations are shown in Table 10.6, and the resulting changes in the terms of trade are reported in Table 10.7. The total welfare gain to the world economy is around

Table 10.5. *Impact of Pre-Uruguay Round MFA Removal (E1) and the full Uruguay Round (E4) on the Textile and Clothing Sector (%)*

| | Activity Level | | | | Exports | | | |
| | Textiles | | Clothing | | Textiles | | Clothing | |
| | E1 | E4 | E1 | E4 | E1 | E4 | E1 | E4 |
|---|---|---|---|---|---|---|---|---|
| Australasia | 0.5 | -3.1 | -0.3 | -3.6 | 4.7 | 1.1 | -25.5 | -10.6 |
| North America | -11.8 | -12.9 | -41.6 | -44.6 | -5.8 | -4.0 | 13.8 | -7.4 |
| EU | -4.2 | -3.9 | -33.0 | -34.1 | 3.2 | 7.6 | 6.6 | 15.2 |
| Japan | 1.1 | 2.1 | 0.3 | -0.8 | 6.2 | 15.5 | -27.2 | -23.4 |
| NIEs | 7.0 | 15.5 | -16.2 | -10.4 | 16.9 | 29.0 | -27.4 | 19.2 |
| ASEAN | 53.4 | 55.2 | 129.2 | 143.2 | 22.3 | 25.6 | 252.8 | 279.6 |
| China | 15.8 | 13.4 | 73.9 | 81.9 | 7.9 | 10.3 | 130.0 | 144.0 |
| South Asia | 17.3 | 16.8 | 91.7 | 91.1 | 24.9 | 26.0 | 253.7 | 252.5 |
| Latin America | -0.5 | -1.7 | -3.7 | -5.0 | 12.0 | 12.7 | -23.0 | -23.2 |
| ROW | -6.1 | -7.5 | -15.3 | -16.3 | -5.3 | -3.4 | -57.8 | -56.3 |
| World | 1.6 | 1.8 | -2.7 | -2.3 | 8.5 | 14. | 53.6 | 62.9 |

Table 10.6. *Welfare Effects of MFA Removal Vs. non-MFA Reforms (in both the Pre—Uruguay Round Setting and the context of the Uruguay Round (UR): (in 1992 $US million)*

| | E1 (pre-UR MFA REFORM) | E2 (UR tariff cuts on TXL & CLG) | E2 Δ rent premium | E3 (non-MFA UR) | E3 Δ rent premium | E4 (complete UR With MFA Reform) | Differences E4—E3 |
|---|---|---|---|---|---|---|---|
| Australia | 157 | 32 | | 646 | | 857 [0.3] | 211 |
| North America | 16,442 | -768 | | 1,306 | | 19,087 [0.3] | 17,781 |
| EU | 12,144 | -1,023 | | 10,620 | | 24,083 [0.4] | 13,463 |
| Japan | -1,615 | -95 | | 24,697 | | 23,012 [0.7] | -1,685 |
| NIEs | -4,52 | 1,048 | 478 | 4,488 | 559 | -108 [0.0] | -4,595 |
| ASEAN | 3,523 | 369 | 269 | 364 | 350 | 4,315 [1.2] | 3,951 |
| China | 5,184 | 790 | 299 | 649 | 283 | 6,204 [1.9] | 5,555 |
| South Asia | 2,128 | 270 | 203 | 12 | 146 | 2,020 [0.7] | 2,008 |
| Latin America | -1,602 | 183 | 150 | 1,566 | 86 | 308 [0.0] | -1,259 |
| ROW | -4,397 | 645 | 630 | 1,161 | 756 | -4,655 [0.2] | -5,816 |
| World | 27,437 | 1,404 | 2,029 | 46,523 | 2,180 | 75,124 | 28,600 |

Equivalent Variation (EV) in $US millions

Note: Numbers in brackets are percentages of 1992 income.

**Table 10.7.** *Terms-of-Trade Effects, by Experiment (% change)*

|  | Terms of Trade | | | |
|---|---|---|---|---|
|  | E1 | E2 | E3 | E4 |
| Australasia | 0.19 | -0.05 | -0.01 | 0.2 |
| North America | 1.16 | -0.10 | -0.05 | 1.2 |
| EU | 0.62 | -0.08 | 0.84 | 0.2 |
| Japan | -0.14 | -0.02 | 0.84 | 0.7 |
| NIEs | -1.05 | 0.23 | 0.08 | -1.1 |
| ASEAN | -0.94 | 0.08 | -0.17 | -1.2 |
| China | -1.41 | 0.08 | -0.49 | -2.0 |
| South Asia | -2.00 | 0.34 | 0.42 | -2.0 |
| Latin America | -0.54 | 0.03 | 0.22 | -0.3 |
| ROW | -0.4 | 0.06 | -0.17 | -0.6 |

$27 billion, similar to the $22 billion estimated by Trela and Whalley (1990) but much greater than the estimate of Yang (1994a), which is on the order of $6.5 billion (in 1986 prices). In terms of the benefits to developing countries, however, the results of the three studies are quite close. In fact, this study estimates that developing countries (excluding ROW) benefit less than shown in the Trela–Whalley and Yang studies.

Apart from the difference in price bases, the difference between this and Yang's estimate largely results from the overall higher MFA export tax equivalent applied in this model. It seems plausible that the estimate of this study captures the upper bound of the MFA effect and that of Yang the lower bound. As pointed out earlier, we have assumed that all textile and clothing exports from MFA-restricted developing countries are subject to constraint. If some textiles and clothing are not affected or affected only to a lesser degree by the MFA, our results will tend to overestimate the overall impact of the MFA. This is particularly true if there is a high a proportion of unrestricted products in a country's exports.

In both the Yang and Trela–Whalley studies, virtually every exporting country benefits from abolition of the MFA. In this study, however, although the more restricted and efficient exporters – namely, ASEAN, China, and South Asia – gain substantially, the exporters who face less stringent restrictions, either because of the size of their current quotas or because of their cost structures, lose from quota abolition. In the model simulation, this group includes the NIEs and Latin America (and ROW, to the extent that it includes some developing countries). This seems to result not only from the displacement of their exports by ASEAN, China, and South Asia, but also from the deterioration of their terms of trade and the loss of quota rents.

The terms of trade for the exporters with lower export shares in restricted markets also decline as a result of losing quota rents. However, the efficiency gains to these exporters are sufficient to outweigh these terms-of-trade losses, and lead to a welfare improvement for them. This confirms a well-established prediction that many developing countries will gain from the abolition of the MFA despite their loss of quota rents.

Our welfare estimates for North America and the EU lead us to two of the most robust conclusions from research on trade liberalization: (1) countries that impose trade restrictions tend to do more harm to themselves than to others, and (2) trade liberalization generally benefits those undertaking liberalization much more than those hoping to gain from the liberalization efforts of others. As a result of MFA removal, consumer prices in the two markets decline, as they no longer have to pay quota premia to exporting countries. This is reflected in the considerable improvement in the terms of trade for North America and the EU. Producers in MFA importing countries lose, but their losses are much smaller than the gains to consumers. One final factor contributing to the welfare gain of MFA importing countries is the increased tariff revenues. Despite the fact that tariff rates are not affected by the MFA removal, increases in import volume increase tariff collections.

Japan's loss from MFA abolition is also to be expected. The removal of the MFA raises world prices for textiles and clothing. As a net importer of these products, Japan's terms of trade deteriorate. The rises in world prices in non-MFA markets help domestic production, but Japan's clothing exports to North America and the EU are substantially reduced. As a result, both textile and clothing production increase only marginally. Overall, the terms-of-trade effect seems to have dominated other effects.

Regardless of who gains or loses from the demise of the MFA, the mechanism that determines the welfare impact of MFA removal on individual countries seems clear. Without simultaneous liberalization in other areas of the world economy, the abolition of the MFA will largely benefit the exporting countries that are subject to most severe restrictions and the MFA importing countries. Other countries are likely to lose as a result of deterioration in their terms of trade or loss of quota rents, or both.

*Implications of non-MFA reforms*

As pointed out earlier, second-best effects are an important factor in the context of the Uruguay Round reform. In particular, non-MFA reforms can also have important implications for the stringency of the MFA and quota rent transfers during the course of trade liberalization. Unlike tariffs, which provide constant rates of protection on domestic industries, MFA quotas provide variable protection because the associated quota rents are endogenous, while export volumes are exogenously fixed. In a general equilibrium context, when agricultural liberalization and tariff reductions occur before MFA quotas are completely abolished, the restrictiveness of the quotas changes and so do rent transfers. Given that the phase-out of MFA quotas is heavily loaded in the last few years of the 10-year transition period, and that non-MFA reforms are likely to be completed sooner, change in the restrictiveness of the MFA and hence quota rent transfers in the transition period is a relevant policy issue.

Two experiments were conducted to shed some light on these second-best considerations. In the first experiment, E2, tariffs on textiles and clothing are reduced by 21% in developed countries (15% in North America) and 14% in developing countries, leaving all other distortions (including the MFA) in place. The next experiment, E3, extends trade liberalization to include all non-MFA reforms, including tariff cuts on textiles and clothing. It should be noted that in both experiments, although textile and clothing exports from MFA exporting countries to MFA importing countries are fixed, the export tax equivalents on them are allowed to change, reflecting the endogenous nature of the MFA-imposed export taxes.

The welfare and terms-of-trade effects of the non-MFA reforms are shown in Tables 10.6 and 10.7, respectively. In Table 10.6 there are also entries referring to the changes in quota premiums as a result of the reforms. Tariff cuts on textiles and clothing in industrial countries lead to increases in import demand that raise the per unit quota rents accruing to exporting countries and increase the volume of exports on which rents are received. Because no import quantity adjustments occur, consumers in industrialized countries fail to benefit from the tariff reductions, as can be seen from the deterioration of their terms of trade due to their strengthened demand for imports. As a result, developing countries gain and industrialized countries lose.

It is worth noting that gains to developing countries from the tariff cuts account for a major or even dominant portion of their total gains and that the total gain to developing countries equals nearly 90% of the total welfare loss to North America and the EU. Had the same extent of protection on textiles and clothing been achieved by tariffs alone instead of a combination of the MFA and tariffs, MFA importing countries would have been likely to benefit from tariff reductions on textiles and clothing. This experiment thus highlights the point that the MFA is an inferior policy option to protect a domestic industry in comparison to tariffs. Politically, it has mitigated the resistance to the discriminatory restrictions by developing countries.

This experiment points to the vital role that the high tariffs on textiles and clothing play in the transfer of MFA quota rents from industrialized countries to developing countries. In the presence of the MFA, the tariffs serve as an instrument to extract quota rents that would otherwise have accrued to developing country exporters. In the extreme case, the entire rents generated by the MFA can be obtained by industrial countries if tariffs are set at such levels as to eliminate any quota premium generated by the MFA. It should be noted, however, that the tariffs that extract maximum quota rents are not necessarily optimal tariffs. Thus, industrialized countries might still lose from the MFA even if they were able to capture the full quota rents.

In contrast with the case of MFA removal, tariff reductions on textiles and clothing will benefit all MFA exporting countries, not only the more efficient ones, as is the case when the MFA is removed. If anything, the more established exporting countries, such as the NIEs, may benefit more from the tariff reductions as they tend to have larger market shares than their price competitiveness would dictate in MFA importing countries. The quota rents accruing to them can therefore be disproportionately large.

When trade liberalization extends to non-MFA commodities (ES), all countries benefit. Japan is the largest beneficiary from the extended trade liberalization. Despite a considerable deterioration of its terms of trade, the EU benefits nearly three times as much as North America, which enjoys an improvement in its terms of trade. In both North America and the EU, however, increases in quota rent transfers to developing countries are more than offset by the efficiency gains from tariff reductions.

The overall gains for developing countries from non-MFA reforms disguise the net contribution of the extended component of trade liberalization (i.e., E3-E2). While the NIEs, Latin America, and ROW benefit substantially from such an extension, China, and South Asia in fact lose from it. ASEAN barely gains. For these regions, increased rent transfers from industrial countries remain important to their total gains from non-MFA reforms. The losses to China and South Asia result from the adverse effect of the extended trade liberalization on the terms of trade for these regions and, to a lesser extent, from losses in MFA rent income (due to a decrease in export volume).

The deterioration in the terms of trade (Table 10.7) for the EU and China seem to be quite drastic, particularly in the case of China. Examination of the composite commodity price changes for exports leaving, and imports entering, each region (not shown here) reveals that for China the deterioration of terms of trade occurs most markedly in agricultural products, for which both ASEAN and China are substantial net importers. In addition, tariff reductions in the highly protected industrial sectors in China and, to a lesser extent, in ASEAN lead to an import surge in these sectors. Furthermore, tariff reductions substantially lower the costs for the exporting sector and boost manufactured exports. Under the regional product differentiation (Armington) assumptions in the model, this type of trade expansion translates into considerable declines in export prices. The declines are most pronounced for machinery and equipment, one of the largest export items for ASEAN and China.

Three factors may explain the deterioration in the terms of trade for the EU. In comparison to North America, the EU has higher tariffs on manufacturing imports, except for textiles and clothing. The EU's tariffs on manufactures are also considerably higher than those of Japan, except for clothing. In addition, agricultural reform shifts considerable resources from agriculture to manufacturing. Both of these factors boost manufactured exports in the EU more than in North America and Japan, and hence lead to greater suppression of its export prices. The third factor contributing to the larger decline in the EU's export prices derives from its export destinations. In both proportional and level terms, the EU exports less than North America and Japan to the liberalizing NIEs, ASEAN, and China, where tariff reductions have generated large demand for imports, particularly in contrast with ROW, for which a large portion of EU exports is destined. The relatively small tariff reductions in ROW result in a considerable improvement in terms of trade for the region at the expense of EU's export prices. Given these three factors, it is not surprising that export prices fall more than import prices for all industrial goods traded by the EU.

The increases in quota rent transfers from industrialized countries to developing countries are mirrored in the changes in the export tax equivalents of MFA quotas. Non-MFA reforms strengthen import demand for textiles and clothing in North America and the EU relative to supply of these exports by developing countries. This drives up the export quota rent premiums (Table 10.6). In the context of the Uruguay Round reform, this may mean that developing countries will face increasing restrictions on their textile and clothing exports during the period of transition. Much, of course, depends on how rapidly and effectively industrialized countries bring their textile and clothing sectors under the normal GATT rules. Whether tariff reductions on textiles and clothing will proceed before substantive tariffication of quota restrictions also makes a difference to the welfare of developing countries. As noted earlier, the tariff cuts alone will benefit developing countries significantly even if the MFA is left in place. Given that inefficient exporters are likely to lose from the abolition of the MFA, they are probably better off from speedy non-MFA reforms and a slow phase-out of the MFA. For efficient exporters, however, they must balance the increased quota rents arising from a slow MFA phase-out against the efficiency gains from a speedy phase-out. Given that the gain from the complete abolition of the MFA is at least several times larger than increased quota rents, these exporters are likely to benefit more from a rapid elimination of the MFA.

The increase in rent premiums has important implications for the political economy of MFA reform. Because MFA quotas on exports from the NIEs have come to account for a much higher share of their exports than of exports from ASEAN, China, and South Asia, there is relatively little incentive for the NIEs to see the MFA abolished. Indeed, if the competitive position of the NIEs were to stay unchanged, they might well have been better off if the MFA remained in place beyond the Uruguay Round. This contrasts sharply with the situation in the mid-1980s, when the abolition of the MFA would have benefited virtually all developing countries, according to Trela and Whalley (1990) and Yang (1994a). In the mid-1980s, when textile and clothing exports from developing countries were dominated by the strongly constrained East Asian economies, all major developing country exporters had an interest in reform.

### Effects of the complete Uruguay Round reform

Our final experiment, E4, simulates complete Uruguay Round trade liberalization. This not only allows us to assess the implications of the round for the world economy and its impact on the textile and clothing sector in particular, but also enables us to evaluate the contribution of MFA reform to the entire Uruguay Round package by deducting results from the previous experiment on the non-MFA reforms from those of the comprehensive reform (i.e., E4–E3, which is reported in the final column of Table 10.6).

The second set of entries in Table 10.5 summarizes the effect of the Uruguay Round on the output and exports of textiles and clothing. Comparing these entries with those from E1, we see that the predominant impact on production and exports of textiles and clothing came from MFA reforms, rather than from non-MFA reforms. In Australasia, however, non-MFA reforms had a greater impact on the textile and clothing sector because the initial tariffs on the sector were high and this region did not participate in the MFA. The clothing sector in the NIEs regains some ground from the substantial declines in production and exports following the abolition of the MFA. In addition, textile production and exports from the NIEs increased substantially from the pre–Uruguay Round MFA liberalization scenario, further reducing the adverse effect of MFA removal on their welfare. For countries other than Australasia and the NIEs, non-MFA reforms tend to amplify the effect of MFA reform. This is largely because tariffs on textiles and clothing are relatively high as compared with other manufactured goods, especially in industrial countries. Thus, for most countries, non-MFA reforms do not make adjustment in the textile and clothing sector any easier than if the MFA alone is liberalized.

The last two columns of Table 10.6 report the welfare effects of E4, the full Uruguay Round, and the difference, E4–E2. The latter represents the portion of E4 attributed to MFA reform. The global welfare gain from the comprehensive reform is around $75 billion, of which nearly $29 billion comes from the abolition of the MFA. For the world as a whole, the MFA reform accounts for 38% of total benefits of the Uruguay Round package. For the most affected countries, the share of the gain from MFA reform in the total gain is well above the world average. In fact, for these countries, the removal of the MFA is by far the most important reform. The MFA reform is of major importance to ASEAN, China, and South Asia, three of the most dynamic textile and clothing exporters in the last couple of decades. Even in North America and the EU, where agricultural reform is widely regarded as most important, MFA reform accounts for 84% and 55% of their total gains from the Uruguay Round, respectively. Non-MFA reforms are most important to Australasia, Japan, the NIEs, Latin America, and ROW. The reform of the MFA alone would in fact result in net welfare losses for some of these economies. This, nevertheless, highlights the vital influence of MFA reform in the overall welfare impact of the Uruguay Round trade liberalization on these countries.

It should be noted that the global welfare gain from MFA removal during the Uruguay Round is more than $1 billion larger than that arising from a pre–Uruguay Round reform (E1). The difference results from the fact that MFA quotas become more stringent following non-MFA reforms, as indicated by the increases in rent premiums shown under E3 in Table 10.6. Thus, abolition of the quotas after the other reforms have been implemented leads to a greater welfare improvement. Therefore, had the Uruguay Round failed to bring the MFA in the GATT framework, the annual cost of these bilateral quotas would have been even higher in a post–Uruguay Round world.

## V    Conclusions

The decision to abolish the MFA in the Uruguay Round trade negotiations has been hailed as a great victory for the GATT principles of nondiscrimination and the elimination of quantitative restrictions. With agriculture also brought under the normal GATT rules, the global multilateral trading system has been substantially strengthened.

Our simulation results show that the phase-out of the MFA is indeed important. Global welfare gains from MFA reform are well over one-third of the total gains from a complete Uruguay Round trade liberalization scenario. For the dynamic Asian textile and clothing exporters the MFA is by far the most important trade reform in the Uruguay Round. This is even true for North America and the EU, where the textile and clothing sector is small and far less important than in developing countries.

The significance of MFA reform in the Uruguay Round also lies in the fact that the cost of the MFA would have increased had it been allowed to stay beyond the round, while agriculture is being liberalized and industrial tariffs are being reduced. This is because non-MFA reforms, if implemented alone, would lead to increases in the trade restricting impact of MFA quotas.

Our results also point to the possibility that the developing country textile and clothing exporters, with larger quotas relative to their production potential, may lose from the elimination of the MFA because of the increased competition from their more efficient competitors and the deterioration in their terms of trade. One advantage of eliminating the MFA in the Uruguay Round is that developing country exporters with high shares of their exports going to restricted markets are substantially compensated for their possible losses by the gains from the non-MFA reforms. Given that the MFA is to be abolished, the best policy option for these inefficient exporters is to speed up tariff reductions and agricultural liberalization. A slow phase-out of the MFA may increase their quota rent revenue, at least in the transition period of MFA phase-out, but this gain is likely to be small compared with that from speedier non-MFA reforms. Speedy non-MFA reforms are also in the interest of more efficient exporters, although an effective, earlier phase-out of the MFA remains paramount to their interest.

In the pre–Uruguay Round context, second-best considerations suggest that it may be in the best interest of industrialized countries to maintain high tariffs on textiles and clothing. In the post–Uruguay Round, however, they are far better off to reduce all tariffs rapidly, as well as to phase out the MFA as quickly as possible. With the removal of the MFA, the high tariffs become more costly. Yet, any attempt to delay the effective phase-out of the MFA will also result in higher costs because of the increased quota rent transfer to developing countries.

Overall, second-best considerations do not warrant slow implementation of either MFA reforms or non-MFA reforms. The comprehensive coverage of the Uruguay Round means that while most countries will benefit from a fast and effective phase-out of the MFA, countries that may lose from MFA reform will be subject to a minimum adverse income effect because of the substantial gains from non-MFA reforms.

## Appendix: Determining whether a region will gain or lose from MFA liberalization

In this appendix, we consider the effects of a change in an export quota on the welfare of an exporting region. Since a region that exports subject to the MFA quota stands to gain from additional export demands and higher prices, but to lose from quota rent elimination, the net effect is unclear. In this appendix we attempt to determine the sign of this effect for particular supplying regions.

In the absence of distortions, the economy of each region can be characterized in terms of an expenditure function $e^i(p_w, U)$ which determines total expenditure in terms of the vector of consumer prices $(p_w)$ and the level of utility $(U)$, and a revenue function $r^i(p_w, V)$ which defines the value of output as a function of production prices and a vector of fixed endowments $(V)$.

For each region, $Z^i(p_w,U,V)$ gives the net expenditures on a commodity, where

$$Z^i(p_w,U,V) = e^i(p_w,U) - r^i(p_w,V). \qquad (A10.1)$$

Equation (A10.2) shows the trade market equilibrium condition for a commodity exported from region 0 to regions 1 and 2. $Z_p^i$ are the partial derivatives of the net revenue functions $(e^i - r^i)$ for regions $i(i=0,1,2)$ with respect to each region's trade price $(p_w)$. Noting that $e_p^i$ equals the Hicksian demand (which equals the Marshallian demand at equilibrium) and $r_p^i$ equals the supply of the commodity, then $Z_p^i$ represents net imports for region $i$, and

$$Z_p^0 + Z_p^1 + Z_p^2 = 0. \qquad (A10.2)$$

When exports from 0 to 1 are constrained by an export quota at the level of Q, the market equilibrium condition becomes:

$$Z_p^0 + Q + Z_p^2 = 0 \qquad (A10.3)$$

With the export quota, the exporter's welfare can be determined from equation (A10.4), where $(p-p_w)$ is a price wedge caused by the quota, $p_w$ is the world market equilibrium price, $p$ is the import price charged to the restricted market, and $U$ is the initial level of utility in the exporting region. The quota rent revenue is given as $(p-p_w)Q$ to country 0. As a result, the income expenditure condition for country 0 becomes,

$$e^0 - r^0 - (p - p_w)\, Q = 0. \qquad (A10.4)$$

Define the burden, $(B^j)$, as the additional financial inflow required to maintain a specified level of utility $U^j$ in the exporting country under the distorted market situation as follows:

$$B^j = e^0(p_w,\, U^{jrb}) - r^0 - (p - p_w)\, Q = Z^0\,(p_w,U^j) - (p - p_w)\, Q. \qquad (A10.5)$$

Here utility is fixed exogenously at level $j$. Therefore $B^j$ provides a money measure of welfare change.

By convention, a reduction in $B^j$ is a reduction in the cost of achieving a given level of utility and hence an increase in welfare. Holding utility constant at level $j$, and considering the impact of a change in quota, the change in the burden or cost of maintaining the level of utility of the exporting country $(dB)$ is given, up to a second-order approximation, as follows:

$$dB = Z_p^0 \frac{\partial p_w}{\partial Q}dQ - Q\left(\frac{\partial p_w}{\partial Q} - \frac{\partial p_w}{\partial Q}\right)dQ - (p - p_w)dQ$$
$$+ \frac{1}{2}\left[Z_{pp}^0\left(\frac{\partial p_w}{\partial Q}\right)^2 - 2\left(\frac{\partial p}{\partial Q} - \frac{\partial p_w}{\partial Q}\right)\right](dQ). \qquad (A10.6)$$

Dividing both sides of equation (A10.6) by the total value of exports $(X)$, which is the sum of the export value and quota rent revenue, and manipulating terms results in equation (A10.7).

$$\frac{dB}{X} = \frac{1}{X}\left[Z_p^0 p_w\left(\frac{\partial p}{\partial Q}\frac{Q}{p_w}\right) - Qp\left(\frac{\partial p}{\partial Q}\frac{Q}{p}\right) + Qp_w\left(\frac{\partial p_w}{\partial Q}\frac{Q}{p_w}\right)(p - p_w)Q\right]\frac{dQ}{Q}$$

$$+ \frac{1}{2X}\left[2\left(\frac{\partial p_w}{\partial Q}\frac{Q}{p_w}\right)Qp_w - 2\left(\frac{\partial p}{\partial Q}\frac{Q}{p}\right)Qp + Z_{pp}^0\left(p_w\frac{\partial p_w}{\partial Q}\frac{Q}{p_w}\right)^2\right]\left(\frac{dQ}{Q}\right)^2, \quad (A10.7)$$

where $X = -[Z_p^0 p_w - (p-p_w)Q]$ is the value of exports of the good in question.

Rearranging the right-hand side of equation (A10.7) yields:

$$\frac{dB}{X} = \left[\frac{(Z_p^0 p_w)}{X}\left(\frac{\partial p_w}{\partial Q}\frac{Q}{p_w}\right) - \frac{Qp}{X}\left(\frac{\partial p}{\partial Q}\frac{Q}{p}\right) - \frac{(p-p_w)Q}{X}\right]\frac{dQ}{Q}$$

$$+ \frac{1}{2X}\left[2\left(\frac{\partial p_w}{\partial Q}\frac{Q}{p_w}\right)Qp_w - 2\left(\frac{\partial p}{\partial Q}\frac{Q}{p}\right)Qp + Z_{pp}^0\left(p_w\frac{\partial p_w}{\partial Q}\frac{Q}{p_w}\right)^2\right]\left(\frac{dQ}{Q}\right)^2. \quad (A10.8)$$

Further modifying equation (A10.8), by using the relation that total export revenue equals the sum of the value of exports at the world price plus the export rent revenue yields:

$$\frac{dB}{X} = \left(\left[-1 + \frac{Qp}{X}\right]\left(\frac{\partial p_w}{\partial Q}\frac{Q}{p_w}\right) - \frac{Qp}{X}\left(\frac{\partial p}{\partial Q}\frac{Q}{p}\right) - \frac{(p-p_w)Q}{X}\right]\frac{dQ}{Q}$$

$$+ \frac{1}{2X}\left[2\left(\frac{\partial p_w}{\partial Q}\frac{Q}{p_w}\right)Qp_w - 2\left(\frac{\partial p}{\partial Q}\frac{Q}{p}\right)Qp + Z_{pp}^0\left(p_w\frac{\partial p_w}{\partial Q}\frac{Q}{p_w}\right)^2\right]\left(\frac{dQ}{Q}\right)^2. \quad (A10.9)$$

Rewriting equation (A10.9), by replacing the value ratio expressions with value shares, and flexibilities, gives:

$$\frac{dB}{X} = [(S_Q - 1)e_{wQ} - S_Q e_{1Q} - S_R]\frac{dQ}{Q}$$

$$+ \left[(S_Q - S_R)e_{wQ} - S_Q e_{1Q} + \frac{1}{2X}Z_{pp}^0(p_w e_{wQ})^2\right]\left(\frac{dQ}{Q}\right)^2, \quad (A10.10)$$

where $e_{wQ}$ is the flexibility of the world price with respect to the quota, $e_{1Q}$ is the flexibility of the restricted market price with respect to the quota, $S_R$ is the share of rents in total export value, and $S_Q$ is the share of export value to the restricted market in the total export value defined as follows:

$$e_{wQ} \equiv \frac{\partial p_w}{\partial Q}\frac{Q}{p_w}, \; e_{1Q} \equiv \frac{\partial p}{\partial Q}\frac{Q}{p}, \; S_R \equiv \frac{(p-p_w)Q}{X}, \text{ and } S_Q \equiv \frac{Qp}{X}.$$

Recalling that a fall in $B$ corresponds to an increase in welfare, from equation (A10.10), it is clear that the first-order effects of an increase in the export quota depend upon: (1) the share of exports going to the restricted market times the effect on the price in the quota market, (2) the share of exports going to nonquota markets multiplied by the change in the world market price and (3) the share of quota rent revenues in total export returns.

For complete quota removal, quota rents go to zero and the third first-order term $(-S_R)$ is eliminated as are the first two second-order terms. Under these circumstances, whether a region will gain or lose from liberalization depends upon the first two first-order terms and the final second order term in equation (A10.10). The first-order term, $(S_Q-1)e_{wQ}$, shows the impact of the rise in world prices on the welfare of the exporting country. The second term, $-S_Q e_{lQ}$, shows the impact of the decline in prices received in the restricted market on exporter's welfare. The quadratic second-order term, $(1/2X)Z^0_{pp}(p_w e_{wQ})^2$, shows the efficiency gains associated with output expansion following the rise in the world price.

## REFERENCES

Anderson, K. (1991) "Textiles and Clothing in Global Economic Development: East Asia's Dynamic Role," *World Competition* 14:97–117.

Anderson, J. E., and W. Martin (1993) "A Note on Four Measures for the Welfare Impact of Tariff Changes" paper presented at the Mid-West International Economics Meetings.

Brandão, A., and W. Martin (1993) "Implications of Agricultural Trade Liberalization for the Developing Countries," *Agricultural Economics* 8:313–343.

De Melo, J., and L. A. Winters (1993) "Do Exporters Gain from VER's?" *European Economic Review* 37:1331–1349.

GATT (1984) *Textiles and Clothing in the World Economy.* Geneva: GATT.

GATT (1993) *An Analysis of the Proposed Uruguay Round Agreement, with Particular Emphasis on Aspects of Interest to Developing Economies.* Geneva: GATT.

GATT (1994) *News of the Uruguay Round of Multilateral Trade Negotiations.* Geneva: GATT.

Gehlhar, M., T. H. Hertel, and W. Martin (1994) "Economic Growth and the Changing Structure of Trade in the Pacific Rim," *American Journal of Agricultural Economics* 76(5):1101–1110.

Goldin, I., O. Knudsen, and D. van der Mensbrugghe (1993) *Trade Liberalization: Global Economic Implications.* Paris and Washington, DC: OECD and the World Bank.

Hamilton, C. B. (ed.) (1990) *Textiles and Trade and the Developing Countries, Eliminating the Multi-Fibre Arrangement in the 1990s.* Washington, DC: The World Bank.

Hamilton, C. B. (1994) "ASEAN Systems for Allocation of Export Licenses Under VERs." In C. Findlay and R. Garnaut (eds.), *The Political Economy of Manufacturing Protection: Experiences of ASEAN and Australia.* Sidney: Allen and Unwin.

Keesing, B. K., and Wolf, M. (1980) "Textile Quotas Against Developing Countries," Thames Essay No. 23, Trade Policy Research Centre, London.

Krishna, K., R. Erzan, and L. Tan (1994) "Rent Sharing in the Multi-Fibre Arrangement: Theory and Evidence from US Apparel Imports from Hong Kong," *Review of International Economics* 2(1):62–73.

Martin, W., and S. Suphachalasai (1990) "Effects of the Multi-Fibre Arrangement on Developing Country Exporters: A Simple Theoretical Framework." In C. B. Hamilton (ed.), *Textiles and Trade and the Developing Countries, Eliminating the Multi-Fibre Arrangement in the 1990s.* Washington, DC: The World Bank.

Trela, I., and J. Whalley (1990) "Global Effects of Developed Country Trade Restrictions on Textiles and Apparel," *Economic Journal* 100:1190–1205.

Trela, I., and J. Whalley (1993) "Internal Quota Allocation Schemes and the Costs of the MFA," Centre for the Study of International Economic Relations, University of Western Ontario, London, Canada. (Mimeo.)

Yang, Y. (1992) "The Impact of the Multifibre Arrangement on World Clothing and Textile Markets with Special Reference to China," Ph.D. dissertation, Australian National University, Canberra.

Yang, Y. (1994a) "The Phasing Out of the Multifibre Arrangement," *Journal of Development Studies* 30(4):892–915.

Yang, Y. (1994b) "Pitfalls of Managed Trade: The Dynamics of MFA Restrictions," Australian National University, Canberra. (Mimeo.)

# CHAPTER 11

# Global climate change and agriculture

*Marinos E. Tsigas, George B. Frisvold, and Betsey Kuhn*

## I    Introduction and overview

Global population is projected to rise from today's 5.3 billion to more than 8.3 billion by 2025, with about 85% of that population living in developing countries (World Bank 1992). If that population is to be fed and if standards of nutrition are to improve, production of food will need to be increased several times from present levels. Cropland expansion and technological progress in farm production and in the processing sectors will help in meeting this goal. However, there are concerns that we may be running short on land suitable for cultivation and that further improvements in yields may be harder to achieve. Another factor that has recently attracted attention is the likelihood of change in climatic conditions. Climate change is an ongoing process, and global or local climates have changed in the past. Much of the present concern over climate change stems from the perceived negative consequences that might result from an enhanced greenhouse effect.

Some climatologists have long argued that the accumulation of carbon dioxide ($CO_2$) and other greenhouse gases would give rise to global warming and other climatic changes. However, they are not able to predict the exact timing and severity of this greenhouse effect. The best that can be done is to perform simulations with general circulation models (GCMs) that incorporate current knowledge of climatic phenomena and produce internally consistent climate scenarios. In particular, the level of atmospheric $CO_2$ is increased in a GCM, and the GCM is simulated through time until climatic variables reach a new equilibrium.

General circulation models do not agree in all aspects of their predictions of climate under a $CO_2$-rich atmosphere. The Intergovernmental Panel on Climate Change (IPCC) provides the following summary of results on climate change (IPCC 1990; Houghton, Jenkins, and Ephraums 1990; and Houghton, Callander, and Varney 1992): (1) the global mean temperature is likely to increase by 1°C above the present value by 2025 and by 3°C before the end of the next century; (2) regional climate changes will likely differ from the global mean, especially the distribution of precipitation; (3) high northern latitudes will warm more than the global mean in winter; (4) global average precipitation will increase 3–15%; and (5) soil moisture is likely to increase in high latitudes, but it is likely to decrease in northern midlatitude continents in summer due to evaporation.

Some of the most important impacts of this type of climate change might be those felt by agriculture because agricultural production is fine-tuned to temperature and moisture conditions in terms of cultivation practices and inputs. The US Environmental Protection Agency conducted research to evaluate the impact of climate change on crop yields, for several GCM scenarios. Agronomists in 18 countries used crop yield models developed by the US Agency for International Development for its International Benchmark Sites Network for Agrotechnology Transfer Project (1989). Crop models calculate yields based on factors such as weather (e.g., temperature, rainfall, and solar radiation), soil data, and cultivation practices (e.g., planting date, planting density and irrigation, and fertilizer practices). The GCM scenarios were developed by three institutions: the Goddard Institute of Space Studies (GISS) (Hansen et al. 1983), the Geophysical Fluid Dynamics Laboratory (Manabe and Wetherald 1987), and the United Kingdom Meteorological Office (Wilson and Mitchell 1987). These climates are assumed to occur in the year 2060. Crop response models for wheat, corn, rice, and soybeans were run for current and $2\times CO_2$-equivalent climatic conditions at 112 sites. Site-specific yield results were weighted by current production to generate national yield estimates. They also evaluated the direct effect of $CO_2$ on photosynthesis, evapotranspiration, and crop growth. The results from this research are reported in a volume edited by Rosenzweig and Iglesias (1994).

Several authors have looked into the economic implications of climate change with emphasis on agriculture [see Reilly and Thomas (1993) for a review of the literature]. Most of these studies focus on particular countries and agricultural commodities, and they provide partial equilibrium measures of welfare impacts.

The work of John Reilly and associates (Tobey, Reilly, and Kane 1992; Reilly and Hohmann 1993; Reilly and Thomas 1993) emphasizes the global nature of climate change and the importance of adjustments due to international trade. Kane, Reilly, and Tobey (1991) used the *Static World Policy Simul*ation (SWOPSIM) model to evaluate the economic effects of climate change. SWOPSIM is a partial equilibrium model of supply, demand, and international trade for 22 food and agricultural commodities and 36 countries/regions of the world (Roningen 1996). The SWOPSIM framework measures changes in producer and consumer surpluses. It assumes that income changes are small and that nonagricultural sectors are not affected by the shock examined. Kane, Reilly, and Tobey modeled climate change as shifts in commodity supply functions resulting from changes in crop productivity.

Reilly, Hohmann, and Kane (1991) also used SWOPSIM, and they specified shifts in commodity supplies based on Rosenzweig and Iglesias (1994). They concluded that climate change is unlikely to disrupt the world's food productive capacity and that the economic effects of climate change are likely to be small. They also concluded that this result depends to a large extent on the expected direct effect of $CO_2$ on crop growth.

All this work has been conducted under partial equilibrium assumptions, yet climate change is expected to have a large effect on some counties. This chapter intends to extend previous work to investigate whether partial equilibrium welfare measures can offer a reasonable approximation of the general equilibrium welfare impacts due to climate change. Kokoski and Smith (1987) evaluated partial equilibrium measures of the welfare impact resulting from climate change in a single economy. Their study was based on a synthetic data base designed to resemble the US economy. Six traded commodities were identified: agriculture, energy, chemicals, consumer durables, construction, and services. They found that partial equilibrium welfare estimates closely approximated general equilibrium measures for the model representing the US economy, but not for a model constructed to represent a developing country. Also, Kokoski and Smith (1987) did not evaluate this problem in a global context.

The purpose of the present study is to provide a comprehensive evaluation of the likely impact of climate change on global agriculture, *using both general and partial equilibrium closures*. This permits us to evaluate better the degree to which previous studies may have over-or understated the true effects.

## II    Aggregated data base and productivity shocks

Table 11.1 shows the regional and commodity aggregation for this chapter. We combine the 24 Global Trade Analysis Project (GTAP) regions into 8 aggregates: Canada, the US, Mexico, the European Union (EU), China, the Association of South East Asian Nations (ASEAN), Australia, and the rest of the world (ROW).[1] Likewise, we aggregate the 37 GTAP commodities into 8 aggregates: rice, wheat, other grains, other crops, livestock, processed agricultural commodities, and manufactures and services. The aggregate processed agricultural commodity includes processed foods, fisheries, as well as beverages and tobacco, textiles, and leather and leather products.

For our simulations we use available information on the aggregate effects of climate change by agricultural commodity. We examine the GISS climate change scenario and we implement climate change as Hicks-neutral technical

Table 11.1. *Regional and Commodity Aggregation*

| Regional Aggregation | Commodity Aggregation |
|---|---|
| 1. Canada | 1. Paddy rice |
| 2. US | 2. Wheat |
| 3. Mexico | 3. Other grains |
| 4. EU | 4. Nongrain crops |
| 5. China | 5. Livestock<br>Wool<br>Other livestock |
| 6. Association of Southeast Asian Nations<br>Indonesia<br>Malaysia<br>Philippines<br>Singapore<br>Thailand | **6. Processed agricultural commodities**<br>Fisheries<br>Processed rice<br>Meat products<br>Milk products |
| **7. Australia** | Other food products<br>Beverages and tobacco |
| **8. ROW**<br>New Zealand | Textiles<br>Leather, fur, and products |
| Japan<br>Republic of Korea | **7. Mining and manufactures**<br>Forestry |
| Hong Kong<br>Taiwan | Coal<br>Oil |
| Argentina<br>Brazil | Gas<br>Other minerals |
| Rest of Latin America<br>Sub-Saharan Africa | Wearing apparel<br>Lumber and wood products |
| Middle East & North Africa<br>Eastern Europe & former Soviet Union | Pulp, paper, and print products<br>Petroleum and coal products |
| South Asia<br>All other countries | Chemicals, rubber, and plastic<br>Nonmetallic mineral products<br>Primary iron and steel manuf.<br>Primary nonferrous metals<br>Fabricated metal products nec.<br>Transport industries<br>Other machinery & equipment<br>Other manufacturing |
| | **8. Services**<br>Electricity, gas, & water<br>Construction<br>Trade & transport<br>Other services (private)<br>Other services (gov't)<br>Ownership of dwellings |

change in the crop sectors of each region. For example, if output, $Q$, is a function of two inputs, $X_1$ and $X_2$, exogenous technical change is modeled as:

$$Q/A_0 = f(X_1 * A_1, X_2 * A_2).$$

Parameters $A_0$, $A_1$, and $A_2$ model technical change, and output and inputs are measured in *market* units (i.e., $Q$, $X_1$, and $X_2$) or *augmented* units (i.e., $Q/A_0$,

$X_1{*}A_1$, and $X_2{*}A_2$). Hicks-neutral technical progress is simulated by an increase in parameter $A_0$ (i.e., a positive shock would be applied to the GTAP variable $a_0$), and it implies that more output will be produced for the same quantities of both inputs. Parameters $A_1$ and $A_2$ represent Hicks-input augmenting technical change.

The assumed impacts on crop productivity are shown in Table 11.2. They are based on Rosenzweig and Iglesias (1994), as published in Reilly, Hohmann, and Kane (1993), for 33 regions and 9 crops: rice, wheat, corn, other coarse grains, soybeans, other oilseeds, cotton, sugar, and tobacco. We have aggregated across regions and commodities to compute shocks for our aggregation based on quantity and price data for 1989 (Sullivan et al. 1992). The top half of Table 11.2 (part A), shows productivity impacts that do not incorporate the direct effect of $CO_2$ on crop growth. Here, the impact of climate change on yields is clearly adverse across all regions, with worldwide productivity falling by 16–26%, depending on crop. Regional differences are quite dramatic, with average Mexican productivity dropping by 43%, followed by ASEAN with a decline of 34%. At the other extreme is Canada, where average regional productivity is hardly affected.

When one accounts for the direct effect of $CO_2$ on crop growth, the impact of climate change on agriculture is quite different. These estimates, are reported in the bottom half of Table 11.2 (part B). With the exception of Mexico and ASEAN, the adverse consequences of climate change are now offset, if not reversed! Canadian agricultural productivity now increases by 24%, on average. Most of the simulations in this chapter are based on the estimates in part B, because we feel that these estimates are more complete than those in part A. However, in the last section of the chapter, we also do a simulation with the shocks that do not incorporate the direct effect of $CO_2$ on crop growth to examine the sensitivity of results to this assumption.[2]

Three points should be made with respect to our modeling of climate change. First, we interpret the results in Rosenzweig and Iglesias (1994) as Hicks-neutral changes in crop productivity, that is, climate change will affect the productivity of all inputs in GTAP in the same way, and the magnitude of this effect does not depend on the levels of these inputs. This assumption fits well with the specification of production functions in GTAP (i.e., no substitution between value-added and intermediate inputs), and the degree of commodity aggregation in our data. To relax this assumption, we would implement a more flexible production system, obtain agronomic information to specify properly the effects of climate change under various input levels, and further disaggregate intermediate inputs.

Second, our approach does not capture any changes in technology that may be adopted by farmers in response to climate change. This appears to be an appropriate assumption given the medium-term time frame of our analysis.

**Table 11.2.** *Climate Change Impacts on Crop Productivity (%)*

| Commodity | | | | | Region | | | | |
|---|---|---|---|---|---|---|---|---|---|
| | CAN | US | MEX | EU | CHN | ASEAN | AUS | ROW | WORLD AVERAGE |
| *A. Impacts do not Account for Direct Effect of $CO_2$ on Crop Growth* | | | | | | | | | |
| Rice | 0 | -18 | -43 | 0 | -24 | -35 | -13 | -26 | -26 |
| Wheat | -12 | -21 | -53 | -12 | -5 | 0 | -18 | -22 | -16 |
| Other grains | -5 | -20 | -43 | -8 | -21 | -40 | -16 | -16 | -18 |
| Other crops | 1 | -15 | -43 | -10 | -15 | -35 | -16 | -23 | -19 |
| Regional average | -3 | -17 | -43 | -9 | -17 | -34 | -16 | -22 | |
| *B. Impacts Account for Direct Effect of $CO_2$ on Crop Growth* | | | | | | | | | |
| Rice | 0 | 1 | -24 | 0 | -3 | -8 | -12 | -8 | -7 |
| Wheat | 27 | -2 | -31 | 8 | 16 | 0 | 8 | 5 | 6 |
| Other grains | 15 | -16 | -35 | 1 | -14 | -33 | 5 | -3 | -9 |
| Other crops | 26 | 14 | -18 | 15 | 13 | -11 | 9 | 2 | 6 |
| Regional average | 24 | 2 | -24 | 11 | 3 | -11 | 8 | -1 | |

For most farmers in the world, implementation of changes in production technology would require a longer-run time frame.

Third, we do not consider the beneficial impact of potential expansion in arable land due to more favorable climatic conditions. However, to address this important issue satisfactorily, we would need to expand this study and say something about other limiting factors (e.g., soil conditions).

Table 11.3 reports a variety of summary information obtained from the aggregation of the GTAP data used in this study. This includes commodity-specific information on private household expenditure shares, regional quantity shares in world output, and demand and own-price elasticities of total demand. Throughout the paper we will draw on this information to aid in the interpretation of results. The production shares from part B of Table 11.3 have also been used to obtain the estimates of worldwide productivity effects reported in Table 11.2. For example, we can see that ROW and China account for 75% and 15%, respectively, of world rice production. Since both of these regions experience adverse productivity effects, even when the direct effect of $CO_2$ on crop growth is present, we see a worldwide decline in productivity for rice of 26% (part A) and 7% (part B), as reported in the last column of Table 11.2.

In contrast to rice, wheat production is more evenly distributed around the world, with ROW and the US producing 36% and 21%, respectively, of global production. Other important wheat producers are the EU and China. As a result, global productivity changes for wheat are dampened, relative to those for rice. In part A, there is a decline of 16% in part B, there is an average productivity increase of 6% worldwide. For other grains, ROW accounts for 43% of world production, and the US and China account for 21% each. As a result, global productivity for other grains is expected to decline by 18% in part A, whereas with the direct effect of $CO_2$ on crop growth, this decline is only 9%. For other crops, ROW accounts for 47% of world production. The US, EU, and China account for about 14% each. As a result, the world productivity for other crops is expected to decline by 19% in the absence of the direct effect of $CO_2$ on crop growth, but it increases by 6% when these are included.

In a climate change scenario where crop productivity is altered, the consequences for price will depend importantly on the nature of demands facing producers in each region. In order to obtain some insight regarding regional demands, it is useful to turn to the last block in Table 11.3, which reports partial equilibrium, own-price elasticities of total demand. In the GTAP model, each region produces a differentiated product, which faces a distinct set of demands due to the Armington assumption. Columns 1–8 in Table 11.3, part D, show own-price elasticities for each region's total demand. These elasticities incorporate: (1) substitution between domestic and foreign varieties; (2) changes in the regional composition of imports; and (3) changes in consumer demands due to price effects.

**Table 11.3. Household Budget Shares, Production and Use Shares, and Partial Equilibrium Demand Elasticities (%)**

| | | | | | Region | | | | |
|---|---|---|---|---|---|---|---|---|---|
| Commodity | CAN | US | MEX | EU | CHN | ASEAN | AUS | ROW | WORLD |
| *A. Private Household Budget Shares* | | | | | | | | | |
| Rice | 0.001 | 0.002 | 0.001 | 0.013 | 5.020 | 0.306 | 0.001 | 0.504 | |
| Wheat | 0.012 | 0.008 | 0.001 | 0.141 | 2.131 | 0.467 | 0.001 | 0.158 | |
| Other grains | 0.008 | 0.018 | 1.485 | 0.132 | 5.504 | 0.427 | 0.014 | 0.422 | |
| Other crops | 1.052 | 0.549 | 3.169 | 0.581 | 11.251 | 5.792 | 1.064 | 2.197 | |
| Livestock | 0.256 | 0.150 | 1.411 | 0.935 | 10.623 | 1.915 | 0.583 | 1.144 | |
| Proc. agr. | 1.277 | 8.571 | 23.887 | 17.299 | 26.982 | 28.086 | 14.839 | 18.647 | |
| Manufacture | 18.776 | 16.282 | 15.461 | 16.122 | 17.739 | 18.827 | 16.524 | 16.181 | |
| Services | 68.614 | 74.418 | 54.581 | 64.774 | 20.745 | 44.176 | 66.971 | 60.742 | |
| Column total | 100 | 100 | 100 | 100 | 100 | 100 | 100 | 100 | |
| *B. Production Shares* | | | | | | | | | |
| Rice | 0.01 | 1.17 | 0.16 | 0.26 | 15.22 | 8.38 | 0.06 | 74.75 | 100 |
| Wheat | 6.50 | 20.94 | 1.18 | 17.30 | 14.67 | 0.84 | 2.94 | 35.62 | 100 |
| Other grains | 1.66 | 21.60 | 4.81 | 5.89 | 21.18 | 1.34 | 0.45 | 43.07 | 100 |
| Other crops | 1.72 | 14.32 | 2.99 | 14.66 | 11.93 | 6.33 | 1.36 | 46.69 | 100 |
| Livestock | 2.32 | 15.02 | 2.56 | 33.90 | 7.80 | 1.94 | 1.70 | 34.76 | 100 |
| Proc. agr. | 1.83 | 15.22 | 2.11 | 28.09 | 4.76 | 3.24 | 1.06 | 43.68 | 100 |

Table 11.3. *Household Budget Shares; Production and Use Shares; and Partial Equilibrium Demand Elasticities* (Continued)

| | | | | | Region | | | | |
|---|---|---|---|---|---|---|---|---|---|
| Commodity | CAN | US | MEX | EU | CHN | ASEAN | AUS | ROW | WORLD |
| **C. Use Shares** | | | | | | | | | |
| Rice | 0.01 | 1.02 | 0.17 | 0.36 | 15.22 | 8.36 | 0.05 | 74.80 | 100 |
| Wheat | 0.65 | 15.02 | 1.42 | 15.78 | 17.29 | 2.28 | 1.17 | 46.38 | 100 |
| Other grains | 1.31 | 17.63 | 5.26 | 5.78 | 20.37 | 1.50 | 0.22 | 47.93 | 100 |
| Other crops | 1.91 | 13.52 | 2.91 | 17.79 | 11.51 | 5.75 | 1.18 | 45.44 | 100 |
| Livestock | 2.15 | 14.92 | 2.57 | 34.33 | 7.62 | 1.99 | 1.17 | 35.24 | 100 |
| Proc. agr. | 1.86 | 15.52 | 2.18 | 27.99 | 4.20 | 2.98 | 0.99 | 44.27 | 100 |
| **D. Demand Elasticities** | | | | | | | | | |
| Rice | -0.984 | -0.392 | -0.170 | -0.642 | -0.029 | -0.009 | -0.809 | -0.017 | -0.012 |
| Wheat | -2.789 | -0.881 | -0.418 | -0.453 | -0.381 | -1.128 | -2.207 | -0.898 | -0.029 |
| Other grains | -0.980 | -0.438 | -0.228 | -0.415 | -0.161 | -0.427 | -1.913 | -0.586 | -0.028 |
| Other crops | -1.01 | -0.763 | -0.552 | -0.806 | -0.248 | -0.905 | -0.736 | -0.467 | -0.039 |
| Livestock | -0.399 | -0.186 | -0.218 | -0.159 | -0.307 | -0.242 | -1.506 | -0.202 | -0.043 |
| Proc. agr. | -1.038 | -0.664 | -0.639 | -0.617 | -1.327 | -1.495 | -1.344 | -0.588 | -0.211 |

Let us consider, for example, the impact of a 1% increase in the price for US wheat. From the second entry in the second column of Table 11.3 we see that, in partial equilibrium, this induces a 0.881% reduction in total demand for US wheat. Similarly, a 1% increase in the price for Australian wheat induces a 2.207% reduction in total demand for Australian wheat. Why are these demand elasticities for the same commodity so different, by region? As the reader may recall from Chapter 2, all the relevant partial substitution elasticities have the same value across regions, for any given commodity.[3] Therefore, it is not the substitution elasticities that determine the relative size of the elasticities in Table 11.3. It is the domestic use shares and the import and export volume shares that determine the size of the own-price elasticities. For example, the own-price elasticities for Australian wheat and other grains are large because: (1) Australia is not a major supplier to other regions; and (2) Australia exports a large share of its production.

The last column in part D of Table 11.3 shows price elasticities for global demand. For example, a 1% increase in all regional prices of rice will cause global demand for rice to decline by 0.012%. The elasticities of global demand for wheat and other grains are −0.029 and −0.028, respectively. The elasticity of global demand for other crops is −0.039. These elasticities are very small, reflecting the inelastic demands by households and firms for these raw products. Therefore, we can see that a 7% reduction in global rice productivity will cause the equilibrium world price to increase substantially, but equilibrium world supply will decline by a very small percentage. Nevertheless, we expect to observe differences in regional commodity price changes due to differences in productivity shocks and in regional demand elasticities. For example, the US and China produce equivalent quantities of other grains (Table 11.3, part B) and experience equivalent shocks in other grains productivity (Table 11.2, part B). However, we expect the US price for other grains to increase by less than the price for China because the US faces a more elastic demand than China.

## III    Experimental design

In this paper we report the results from four different simulations of the model. We begin by examining the effects of climate change under two multiregion, partial equilibrium (PE) simulations, and then we obtain general equilibrium (GE) results. For the two PE simulations, we apply the productivity shocks that account for the direct effect of $CO_2$ on crop growth (Table 11.2, part B). These are compared to the GE results based on the same set of shocks. Finally we run the GE simulation with the productivity shocks in Table 11.2, part A. This permits us to assess the relative importance of the direct effect of $CO_2$ on crop growth in evaluating the impact of global climate change for agriculture and worldwide welfare.

In the first PE simulation (PE1), we concentrate on the effects of climate change on agricultural commodities alone. In particular: (1) output prices and quantities supplied by crops and livestock are endogenous; (2) output prices and quantities supplied by the other sectors of the economy are exogenous; (3) land rents are the only endogenous primary factor price; and (4) we do not consider the effect of household income changes on consumer demands. Thus, in this simulation, the crops and livestock sectors will face six new prices (i.e., rice, wheat, other grains, other crops, livestock, and land rents), and they will optimally adjust output supply and input demands. Other sectors will not change output supply and thus they will not change their demands for primary factors or *composite* intermediates (although they will alter their pattern of sourcing of a particular farm commodity in response to relative price changes). Household demands for all commodities will change due to relative price effects. All sectors and households will change their composition of demands with respect to domestic and imported varieties of crops and livestock, and region of origin.

As productivity in the crops sector declines, the price of its output will increase, and this will induce an increase in demand for primary factors and other inputs. Land rents will increase in proportion to the importance of land in the sector under question. Higher land rents and increased feed costs will increase the cost of producing livestock commodities. Changes in comparative advantage of producing farm commodities and trading patterns will determine the final equilibrium.

The second PE simulation (PE2) is slightly more general than the first. Here, we allow the agricultural processing sector to respond to new economic conditions (i.e., its output price and production level are endogenous). As a consequence, the increased farm prices will be reflected in higher costs for the agricultural processing sector. This in turn will affect the demand for processed commodities, and hence the derived demand for farm products. As in simulation PE1, the price of land is the only endogenous primary factor price, and household income does not affect consumer demands.

The GE closure follows the standard closure for GTAP. In this medium-term simulation, all sectors are assumed to adjust to new economic conditions, all markets clear, and changes in household income are fully reflected in consumer demands.

## IV     Results

### Partial equilibrium simulations

Table 11.4 shows results from the first PE simulation, in which the only endogenous prices are those relating to agricultural products. The first group

**Table 11.4.** *Results from Partial Equilibrium Simulation 1*

| | | | | | Region | | | | |
|---|---|---|---|---|---|---|---|---|---|
| | CAN | US | MEX | EU | CHN | ASEAN | AUS | ROW | WORLD |
| **Producer Prices, %** | | | | | | | | | |
| Rice | 1.74 | -0.78 | 50.04 | 0.00 | 3.73 | 13.42 | 15.42 | 11.99 | 10.73 |
| Wheat | -19.24 | 1.53 | 59.83 | -8.98 | -17.09 | -0.75 | -8.89 | -6.55 | -7.30 |
| Other grains | -10.85 | 19.92 | 79.94 | -1.07 | 21.63 | 65.81 | -1.23 | 4.80 | 14.91 |
| Other crops | -20.72 | -13.39 | 31.45 | -14.45 | -14.38 | 13.43 | -9.28 | -3.20 | -6.21 |
| Livestock | -3.87 | 3.83 | 17.59 | -0.63 | 0.75 | 1.39 | -0.15 | 0.59 | 1.00 |
| **Production, %** | | | | | | | | | |
| Rice | 0.75 | 5.01 | -6.99 | 4.55 | 0.22 | 0.27 | -4.57 | 0.30 | 0.33 |
| Wheat | 54.02 | -10.99 | -27.22 | -1.16 | 1.22 | -9.23 | -0.17 | -2.04 | -0.44 |
| Other grains | 38.86 | -3.44 | -11.28 | 7.44 | 1.11 | -13.88 | 34.42 | 5.80 | 2.08 |
| Other crops | 20.18 | 9.02 | -15.14 | 8.42 | 2.30 | -16.39 | 4.20 | -3.28 | -0.25 |
| Livestock | 3.49 | -0.37 | -3.49 | 0.22 | 0.12 | -0.42 | 1.23 | 0.01 | 0.03 |
| **Exports, %** | | | | | | | | | |
| Rice | 27.42 | 38.47 | -72.82 | 40.60 | 20.70 | -18.43 | -23.50 | -19.39 | 10.50 |
| Wheat | 59.27 | -34.51 | -90.77 | 0.57 | 54.04 | -26.58 | -0.28 | -8.01 | 4.55 |
| Other grains | 141.26 | -13.85 | -87.03 | 66.49 | -9.40 | -57.00 | 65.71 | 29.24 | 6.34 |
| Other crops | 79.00 | 31.50 | -73.25 | 37.98 | 42.90 | -50.65 | 20.98 | -15.18 | -3.41 |
| Livestock | 31.80 | -6.45 | -50.57 | 7.59 | -0.65 | -1.99 | 3.73 | -0.51 | 1.62 |
| **Imports, %** | | | | | | | | | |
| Rice | 3.82 | -16.99 | 126.77 | -6.70 | -13.63 | 13.22 | 21.21 | 17.28 | |
| Wheat | -37.63 | 50.75 | 158.19 | 7.81 | -10.26 | 4.08 | 22.83 | 1.72 | |
| Other grains | -42.61 | 54.92 | 91.73 | -21.30 | 68.86 | 50.11 | -9.51 | -8.98 | |
| Other crops | -16.07 | -23.61 | 86.88 | -15.63 | -21.67 | 33.64 | -7.04 | 6.05 | |
| Livestock | -8.01 | 9.81 | 43.95 | -3.16 | 1.58 | 1.17 | -1.70 | -0.46 | |

Table 11.4. *Results from Partial Equilibrium Simulation 1 (Continued)*

| | | | | | Region | | | | |
|---|---|---|---|---|---|---|---|---|---|
| | CAN | US | MEX | EU | CHN | ASEAN | AUS | ROW | WORLD |
| **Factor Prices, %** | | | | | | | | | |
| Land rent | 14.84 | -0.81 | 28.46 | -4.20 | -1.11 | 3.92 | -1.39 | 1.06 | |
| | | | | | | | | | |
| **Agricultural Employment, %** | | | | | | | | | |
| Labor | 7.88 | -0.56 | 14.64 | -2.40 | -0.81 | 2.04 | -0.85 | 0.35 | |
| Capital | 7.88 | -0.56 | 14.64 | -2.40 | -0.81 | 1.81 | -0.85 | 0.29 | |
| **CPI, %** | -0.18 | -0.06 | 2.30 | -0.08 | -0.50 | 0.93 | -0.10 | -0.00 | |
| **Cons. Surplus, %** | 0.13 | 0.05 | -1.90 | 0.06 | 0.29 | -0.56 | 0.07 | 0.00 | |
| **Cons. Surplus, $** | 700 | 2493 | -5620 | 3493 | 1309 | -2016 | 183 | -145 | 398 |
| **Income Change, $** | -15 | -1162 | 2953 | 252 | -474 | 972 | -45 | 4762 | 7243 |
| **Welfare Change, $** | 684 | 1331 | -2667 | 3745 | 835 | -1043 | 138 | 4618 | 7641 |

Note: Results are reported as changes from initial equilibrium. A dollar sign indicates that figures are in $US million. All other figures are in percentage changes. This simulation is based on the shocks in Table 10.2, part B.

of entries in this table refers to producer prices in each region. These changes vary considerably due to the product differentiation assumption. The last column in this block reports average world prices. As expected, the world prices for crop commodities change substantially, but the equilibrium world supplies (next block of results) do not change very much. The price of other grains increases the most (14.91%) because the global productivity shock for other grains is the largest. World productivity for wheat and other crops increases; therefore world prices for these products decline.

On a region-specific basis, Canada and the EU experience some of the largest *increases* in crop productivity, and as a result their producer prices decline the most. Mexico and ASEAN experience the largest *declines* in crop productivity and their producer prices increase the most. These productivity changes are magnified in the trade changes, where relatively small flows must change substantially in order to bring regional supply and demand into equilibrium. Canada and EU become larger net exporters of all crop commodities, except wheat in the EU. Mexico and ASEAN become larger net importers of all crop commodities. More generally, productivity losses for net exporters reduce the quantity traded in the world market. In contrast, productivity losses for net importers would increase the quantity traded. For the GISS scenario, the net effect is that world trade in rice, wheat, and other grains increases, with the biggest increase in rice and other grains (10.50% and 6.34%, respectively). World trade in other crops declines by 3.41%.

In this simulation, changes in livestock output are largely determined by changes in other grains and other crops prices. For example, in the US the other grains price increases substantially and livestock output falls, because feed grain costs in US livestock production are relatively large. On the other hand, livestock output in Canada increases significantly due to lower feed grain prices.

Land rents increase in Canada, Mexico, ASEAN, and ROW because demand for farmland increases. Land rents decline by similar percentages in China and Australia despite the fact that the average productivity gain for China is only 3% but for Australia it is 8% (Table 11.2, part A). This happens because Australia faces more elastic demands than China does. (The cost share of land in agriculture is similar in both countries.)

Changes in consumer prices are not exactly the same as producer price changes, because consumers, as all other users, demand imported commodities whose prices change at a different rate. The consumer price index (CPI) summarizes the impact on the overall price level facing consumers. The CPI changes for the US, EU, and Australia are small relative to other regions because (1) their consumer budget shares for farm commodities are small (Table 11.3, part A), and (2) consumer prices do not change as much as in other regions.

We take the sum of changes in consumer surplus, taxpayer surplus, and producer surplus as an indicator of welfare change in a PE simulation. The latter two surpluses are captured in the income change reported at the bottom of Table 11.4. In all regions, except ROW, the change in consumer surplus dominates the change in producer and taxpayer surplus. Welfare declines in Mexico and ASEAN, the regions that experience large crop productivity losses (Table 11.2, part B).

The results in Table 11.4 depend on the specification of elasticities in GTAP. A set of parameters that is most important in determining our results is the Armington elasticities for commodity demands of foreign varieties. The results for regional producer prices in Table 11.4 suggest that our Armington elasticities produce trade patterns that are relatively rigid. This makes it possible for wheat prices in Canada, the US, and Mexico to diverge to such a large degree. The US does import a small quantity of Canadian wheat, and this prevents the US price from rising even more. But the amount of imports from Canada is not enough to force the US wheat price to decline as in Canada. If the trading patterns were more flexible, we would expect wheat prices in Canada, the US, and Mexico to follow the world price and decline by about 7%. At the same time, however, Mexico would reduce its cropland substantially (because it faces such huge productivity losses for crops) and turn into a giant feedlot. Obviously, this is not something that can happen in the medium term. Thus, we feel that the Armington assumption is appropriate for GTAP.

Table 11.5 shows results from the second PE simulation, where we allow the agricultural processing sector to adjust to new economic conditions, following climate change. Producer prices for processed agricultural commodities increase by 6.34% and 3.031% in Mexico and ASEAN, respectively, because (1) farm product prices increase substantially in these regions and (2) farm products represent a significant part of total cost for their agricultural processing sector.

Global demand for processed agricultural commodities declines by 0.17%. As a result, farm commodity prices do not increase as much as in PE1, and in some regions, agriculture cannot attract enough labor and capital to offset productivity declines due to climate change. This is more pronounced in Mexico and ASEAN, where agricultural employment of capital and labor increases by less than in PE1.

Turning to the welfare results at the bottom of Table 11.5, we find that welfare now deteriorates further in Mexico and ASEAN because of the larger consumer surplus losses, owing to processed agricultural commodity price increases. Also, their gains in income are smaller in PE2 than in PE1. Welfare gains in the EU are now much more pronounced ($10.3 billion in PE2 vs. $3.7 billion in PE1), and ROW's welfare gain turns into a slight loss, owing to declining consumer surplus.

**Table 11.5. Results from Partial Equilibrium Simulation 2**

| | | | | | Region | | | | |
|---|---|---|---|---|---|---|---|---|---|
| | CAN | US | MEX | EU | CHN | ASEAN | AUS | ROW | WORLD |
| **Producer Prices, %** | | | | | | | | | |
| Rice | 2.09 | -0.82 | 45.32 | -0.08 | 3.93 | 10.34 | 15.77 | 11.63 | 10.22 |
| Wheat | -19.19 | 1.50 | 55.49 | -9.05 | -16.95 | -1.33 | -8.80 | -6.70 | -7.41 |
| Other grains | -10.67 | 19.87 | 75.20 | -1.14 | 21.82 | 62.15 | -1.12 | 4.63 | 14.57 |
| Other crops | -20.55 | -13.44 | 28.42 | -14.52 | -14.25 | 11.65 | -9.16 | -3.39 | -6.50 |
| Livestock | -3.83 | 3.82 | 15.29 | -0.70 | 0.89 | 1.03 | -0.07 | 0.69 | 0.95 |
| Proc. agr. | -1.70 | 0.03 | 6.34 | -1.14 | -0.25 | 3.03 | -0.75 | 0.94 | 0.28 |
| **Production, %** | | | | | | | | | |
| Rice | 1.76 | 4.73 | -12.12 | 5.18 | 0.67 | -4.53 | -3.67 | -0.33 | -0.49 |
| Wheat | 52.38 | -11.10 | -30.46 | -0.48 | 1.62 | -9.18 | -0.42 | -2.44 | -0.58 |
| Other grains | 39.43 | -3.74 | -13.49 | 8.11 | 1.38 | -15.56 | 34.01 | 5.35 | 1.79 |
| Other crops | 20.86 | 8.70 | -16.28 | 9.10 | 2.46 | -16.81 | 4.14 | -3.55 | -0.36 |
| Livestock | 5.61 | -0.25 | -8.10 | 1.16 | 0.47 | -3.44 | 2.04 | -0.52 | 0.08 |
| Proc. agr. | 2.86 | 0.22 | -6.41 | 1.20 | 1.36 | -5.49 | 1.93 | -0.77 | -0.17 |
| **Exports, %** | | | | | | | | | |
| Rice | 23.34 | 35.53 | -69.56 | 38.56 | 17.69 | -10.95 | -25.58 | -19.14 | 9.45 |
| Wheat | 57.27 | -35.20 | -89.68 | 0.07 | 50.09 | -26.91 | -1.86 | -8.46 | 3.44 |
| Other grains | 137.10 | -15.98 | -85.56 | 65.16 | -12.80 | -55.83 | 63.65 | 28.67 | 4.26 |
| Other crops | 75.55 | 29.39 | -70.99 | 36.39 | 39.28 | -48.51 | 17.05 | -15.28 | -3.90 |
| Livestock | 30.80 | -8.39 | -45.70 | 7.78 | -1.23 | -1.42 | 2.76 | -0.68 | 1.08 |
| Proc. agr. | 10.66 | 1.81 | -25.91 | 8.10 | 3.06 | -12.12 | 6.01 | -2.95 | -0.11 |
| **Imports, %** | | | | | | | | | |
| Rice | 6.68 | -16.34 | 99.84 | -5.74 | -12.33 | 4.55 | 25.89 | 16.28 | |
| Wheat | -36.27 | 50.71 | 132.12 | 8.53 | -9.63 | 0.91 | 24.89 | 0.83 | |
| Other grains | -41.07 | 54.78 | 75.05 | -20.61 | 70.07 | 40.77 | -8.14 | -9.81 | |
| Other crops | -14.88 | -23.02 | 71.96 | -14.69 | -20.60 | 26.72 | -6.36 | 5.42 | |
| Livestock | -7.51 | 10.27 | 28.46 | -2.90 | 2.00 | -0.62 | -0.70 | -0.83 | |
| Proc. agr. | -2.55 | -0.60 | 8.65 | -3.82 | -1.57 | 1.18 | -1.85 | 1.38 | |

Table 11.5. *Results from Partial Equilibrium Simulation 2 (Continued)*

| | | | | | Region | | | | |
|---|---|---|---|---|---|---|---|---|---|
| | CAN | US | MEX | EU | CHN | ASEAN | AUS | ROW | WORLD |
| **Factor Prices, %** | | | | | | | | | |
| Land Rent | 16.82 | -1.25 | 18.56 | -2.68 | -0.39 | -2.79 | -0.48 | -0.07 | |
| **Agricultural Employment, %** | | | | | | | | | |
| Labor | 8.94 | -0.81 | 9.58 | -1.53 | -0.41 | -1.55 | -0.34 | -0.26 | |
| Capital | 8.94 | -0.81 | 9.58 | -1.53 | -0.41 | -1.96 | -0.34 | -0.33 | |
| CPI, % | -0.35 | -0.05 | 3.55 | -0.26 | -0.49 | 1.57 | -0.19 | 0.16 | |
| *Cons. Surplus, %* | 0.24 | 0.04 | -2.89 | 0.19 | 0.29 | -0.95 | 0.13 | -0.11 | |
| *Cons. Surplus, $* | 1,274 | 2,313 | -8,613 | 10,910 | 1,288 | -3,397 | 348 | -8,063 | -3,940 |
| *Income Change, $* | -3 | -1,123 | 1,924 | -546 | -98 | -319 | -11 | 3,669 | 3,494 |
| *Welfare Change, $* | 1,271 | 1,189 | -6,689 | 10,364 | 1,190 | -3,716 | 337 | -4,394 | -447 |

Note: Results are reported as changes from initial equilibrium. A dollar sign indicates that figures are in $US million. All other figures are in percentage changes. This simulation is based on the shocks in Table 10.2, part B.

*General equilibrium simulations*

We now turn to the GE results in Table 11.6. The changes in output and trade are broadly similar to those in PE2; however, the same cannot be said of the welfare calculations, which are based on the regional equivalent variation (EV) associated with climate change. (Simple consumer, producer, and taxpayer calculations are no longer necessary.) Therefore, this section focuses on the welfare effects of climate change. First of all, note the two extreme cases represented by Canada and Mexico: Canada is a net exporter of agricultural commodities and it gains the most in crops productivity due to climate change; Mexico is a net importer of agricultural commodities and it loses the most in productivity. In Canada, agricultural production increases, and the nonfood part of the economy shrinks; the CPI increases because the prices of services and manufactures increase; but gains in producer surplus offset losses in consumer surplus, and welfare increases by about $US 2.6 billion. In Mexico, agricultural production declines, but the nonfood part of the economy shrinks too; the CPI increases because the farm and prices increase; both producers and consumers lose and welfare declines by about $US 8.2 billion.

A comparison of the welfare impacts from the PE simulations (Tables 11.4 and 11.5) with those from the GE simulation (Table 11.6) is provided at the bottom of Table 11.6. The first set of figures shows the degree to which the PE1 welfare results understate the GE results. In particular, they report $\{1 - EV(PE1)\}/EV(GE)$ multiplied by 100%. With the exception of the US, PE models that do not account for processed agricultural commodities (i.e., PE1) are likely to underestimate the welfare impact of climate change by more than 50%. For Canada, PE1 underestimates the welfare impact of climate change by 73.98%. With the exception of the US, inclusion of processed agricultural commodities is likely to improve measures of the welfare impact of climate change substantially: for Mexico, PE2 underestimates the welfare impact of climate change by only 19.15%.

Table 11.7 shows results from a GE simulation based on crop yield impacts that do not incorporate the direct effect of $CO_2$ on crop growth (Table 11.2, part A). World prices for all commodities increase; gains in producer surplus in some regions are not enough to offset losses in consumers surplus; and in all regions welfare declines. This leads us to the same conclusion as that of Reilly, Hohmann, and Kane (1993), namely, that the direct effect of $CO_2$ on crop growth will reduce substantially the adverse effects of climate change and it is important to account for it properly.

**V     Summary and conclusions**

This chapter has used an eight-region, eight-commodity aggregation of the GTAP model of global trade to estimate effects of climate change and to

**Table 11.6. Results from General Equilibrium Simulation**

| | | | | | Region | | | | |
|---|---|---|---|---|---|---|---|---|---|
| | CAN | US | MEX | EU | CHN | ASEAN | AUS | ROW | WORLD |
| **Producer Prices, %** | | | | | | | | | |
| Rice | 2.45 | -0.77 | 44.06 | 0.19 | 4.28 | 9.84 | 15.95 | 11.56 | 10.18 |
| Wheat | -18.90 | 1.56 | 54.28 | -8.80 | -16.66 | -2.06 | -8.63 | -6.75 | -7.31 |
| Other grains | -10.34 | 19.94 | 73.63 | -0.87 | 22.23 | 61.38 | -0.96 | 4.55 | 14.59 |
| Other crops | -20.25 | -13.40 | 27.21 | -14.29 | -13.95 | 11.05 | -8.99 | -3.46 | -6.50 |
| Livestock | -3.45 | 3.88 | 14.18 | -0.43 | 1.26 | 0.37 | 0.24 | 0.62 | 1.02 |
| Proc. agr. | -1.17 | 0.09 | 5.16 | -0.87 | 0.11 | 2.20 | -0.50 | 0.85 | 0.30 |
| Manufact. | 0.52 | 0.06 | -1.03 | 0.23 | 0.15 | -0.55 | 0.22 | -0.09 | 0.03 |
| Services | 0.57 | 0.07 | -1.39 | 0.28 | 0.30 | -0.98 | 0.27 | -0.11 | 0.05 |
| **Production, %** | | | | | | | | | |
| Rice | 1.04 | 4.66 | -11.41 | 4.89 | 0.53 | -3.39 | -4.01 | -0.24 | -0.35 |
| Wheat | 51.28 | -11.03 | -29.55 | -0.61 | 1.46 | -8.67 | -0.60 | -2.11 | -0.54 |
| Other grains | 38.34 | -3.78 | -13.03 | 7.90 | 1.19 | -14.85 | 33.70 | 5.57 | 1.85 |
| Other crops | 20.02 | 8.62 | -15.85 | 8.72 | 2.22 | -16.01 | 3.92 | -3.44 | -0.33 |
| Livestock | 4.95 | -0.28 | -7.55 | 1.03 | 0.32 | -2.71 | 1.71 | -0.41 | 0.07 |
| Proc. agr. | 2.25 | 0.19 | -5.90 | 1.05 | 0.89 | -4.27 | 1.62 | -0.66 | -0.15 |
| Manufact. | -1.35 | -0.04 | 1.84 | -0.29 | -0.09 | 2.01 | -0.41 | 0.18 | 0.01 |
| Services | 0.08 | 0.02 | -0.83 | 0.09 | 0.27 | -0.20 | 0.05 | -0.01 | 0.02 |
| **Exports, %** | | | | | | | | | |
| Rice | 21.53 | 35.18 | -68.47 | 37.02 | 16.06 | -9.29 | -26.04 | -18.85 | 9.40 |
| Wheat | 56.10 | -34.94 | -89.29 | -0.37 | 48.88 | -24.21 | -1.96 | -7.65 | 3.25 |
| Other grains | 134.65 | -16.05 | -84.96 | 63.99 | -13.59 | -54.70 | 63.31 | 29.54 | 4.06 |
| Other crops | 73.11 | 29.11 | -69.96 | 35.10 | 37.53 | -47.45 | 16.26 | -15.02 | -3.86 |
| Livestock | 28.92 | -8.88 | -42.75 | 6.52 | -2.73 | 0.83 | 2.27 | 0.10 | 0.83 |
| Proc. agr. | 7.88 | 1.48 | -21.39 | 6.65 | 1.28 | -8.50 | 4.67 | -2.46 | -0.12 |
| Manufact. | -2.79 | -0.31 | 6.27 | -1.36 | -0.86 | 3.13 | -1.21 | 0.59 | 0.09 |
| Services | -2.20 | -0.36 | 5.68 | -1.34 | -1.55 | 3.68 | -1.19 | 0.43 | 0.03 |

Table 11.6. *Results from General Equilibrium Simulation (Continued)*

| | | | | | Region | | | | |
|---|---|---|---|---|---|---|---|---|---|
| | CAN | US | MEX | EU | CHN | ASEAN | AUS | ROW | WORLD |
| **Factor Prices, %** | | | | | | | | | |
| Land rent | 15.76 | -1.29 | 18.64 | -2.75 | -0.33 | -1.55 | -0.80 | 0.08 | |
| Labor wage | 0.72 | 0.07 | -1.40 | 0.33 | 0.49 | -1.59 | 0.36 | -0.15 | |
| Capital rent | 0.69 | 0.07 | -1.67 | 0.36 | 0.67 | -1.50 | 0.37 | -0.15 | |
| **CPI, %** | 0.16 | 0.01 | 2.35 | -0.01 | -0.20 | 0.84 | 0.04 | 0.07 | |
| **Income Change, %** | 0.70 | 0.06 | -0.98 | 0.35 | 0.45 | -1.32 | 0.35 | -0.09 | |
| **Welfare Change, %** | 0.50 | 0.04 | -2.78 | 0.29 | 0.54 | -1.73 | 0.26 | -0.12 | |
| | 2,629 | 2,026 | -8,273 | 17,253 | 2,397 | -6,216 | 681 | -8,958 | 1,539 |
| **EV, Welfare Comparison, %** | | | | | | | | | |
| for PE1 | 73.98 | 34.30 | 67.76 | 78.29 | 65.16 | 83.22 | 79.74 | sign change | |
| for PE2 | 51.65 | 41.31 | 19.15 | 39.93 | 50.35 | 40.22 | 50.51 | 50.95 | |

Note: Results are reported as changes from initial equilibrium. A dollar sign indicates that figures are in $US million. All other figures are in percentage changes. This simulation is based on the shocks in Table 10.2, part B. The figures for the partial/general equilibrium comparison of welfare impacts are computed as: 100*[EV(GE) - EV(PE)]/EV(GE).

**Table 11.7. Results from General Equilibrium Simulation (without direct effect of CO₂ on crop growth)**

| | Region | | | | | | | | |
|---|---|---|---|---|---|---|---|---|---|
| | CAN | US | MEX | EU | CHN | ASEAN | AUS | ROW | WORLD |
| **Producer Prices, %** | | | | | | | | | |
| Rice | 11.51 | 28.64 | 128.50 | 4.23 | 50.02 | 80.53 | 30.31 | 59.61 | 59.31 |
| Wheat | 24.24 | 33.03 | 169.01 | 20.44 | 11.51 | 5.35 | 33.48 | 41.49 | 30.98 |
| Other grains | 15.37 | 31.54 | 123.50 | 14.24 | 42.52 | 97.29 | 32.32 | 31.04 | 36.99 |
| Other crops | 7.94 | 27.53 | 115.83 | 17.15 | 29.86 | 76.71 | 33.29 | 46.94 | 39.78 |
| Livestock | 8.48 | 12.03 | 33.20 | 3.49 | 12.78 | 10.78 | 7.66 | 10.66 | 8.98 |
| Proc. agr. | 3.68 | 5.60 | 14.88 | 3.80 | 11.53 | 19.33 | 5.74 | 10.95 | 8.26 |
| Manufact. | 1.07 | 0.50 | -1.61 | 0.68 | 0.57 | -1.13 | 1.13 | -0.25 | 0.20 |
| Services | 1.14 | 0.53 | -2.42 | 0.69 | -0.23 | -3.04 | 1.18 | -0.65 | 0.08 |
| **Production, %** | | | | | | | | | |
| Rice | 24.88 | 6.97 | -20.61 | 32.98 | -4.01 | -16.90 | 15.18 | -3.61 | -4.69 |
| Wheat | 16.83 | -2.17 | -42.29 | 8.65 | -3.75 | 11.37 | -7.35 | -13.15 | -4.37 |
| Other grains | 21.59 | 1.21 | -22.01 | 11.29 | -3.50 | -26.95 | 0.47 | -3.87 | -3.03 |
| Other crops | 36.35 | 9.24 | -24.28 | 21.78 | -1.91 | -25.25 | 6.06 | -7.84 | -2.02 |
| Livestock | 4.68 | 0.55 | -15.24 | 2.37 | -9.68 | -14.52 | 2.32 | -5.20 | -2.31 |
| Proc. agr. | 3.82 | 0.39 | -12.67 | 2.74 | -11.85 | -20.97 | 2.11 | -5.90 | -3.33 |
| Manufact. | -2.58 | -0.70 | 2.21 | -1.32 | -4.85 | 2.83 | -2.71 | -0.46 | -0.85 |
| Services | -0.35 | -0.33 | -2.22 | -0.78 | -4.73 | -2.28 | -0.57 | -1.10 | -0.84 |
| **Exports, %** | | | | | | | | | |
| Rice | 201.94 | 51.24 | -83.40 | 319.67 | -6.36 | -58.70 | 57.47 | -42.78 | 1.37 |
| Wheat | 18.38 | -6.80 | -95.59 | 38.45 | 76.12 | 98.78 | -14.20 | -30.24 | 1.84 |
| Other grains | 65.71 | 6.85 | -89.65 | 74.15 | -14.11 | -63.54 | -2.36 | -1.93 | 8.85 |
| Other crops | 175.83 | 45.05 | -81.78 | 103.72 | 40.34 | -58.27 | 34.36 | -19.18 | 1.79 |
| Livestock | 18.31 | -3.81 | -56.09 | 33.49 | -15.09 | -6.26 | 4.19 | -8.84 | -0.78 |
| Proc. agr. | 22.74 | 13.41 | -27.74 | 24.99 | -13.92 | -37.75 | 14.83 | -11.24 | -2.99 |
| Manufact. | -5.34 | -2.92 | 10.50 | -4.32 | -3.54 | 6.02 | -6.62 | 1.21 | -0.65 |
| Services | -4.98 | -3.89 | 9.32 | -5.13 | -2.08 | 10.13 | -6.69 | 0.94 | -1.12 |

**Table 11.7. Results from General Equilibrium Simulation (without direct effect of C), on crop growth) (Continued)**

| | | | | | Region | | | | |
|---|---|---|---|---|---|---|---|---|---|
| | CAN | US | MEX | EU | CHN | ASEAN | AUS | ROW | WORLD |
| **Factor Prices, %** | | | | | | | | | |
| Land rent | 63.97 | 60.99 | 64.76 | 39.30 | 33.64 | 48.23 | 37.42 | 50.70 | |
| Labor wage | 1.09 | 0.31 | -2.27 | 0.70 | 0.06 | -5.64 | 1.21 | -1.15 | |
| Capital rent | 1.13 | 0.54 | -3.18 | 0.48 | -5.52 | -6.21 | 0.68 | -1.55 | |
| CPI, % | 1.57 | 1.14 | 7.58 | 1.46 | 13.29 | 8.68 | 2.19 | 3.16 | |
| Income Change, % | 1.26 | 0.44 | -0.85 | 0.14 | 0.25 | -2.89 | 1.59 | -0.38 | |
| Welfare Change, % | -0.02 | -0.56 | -6.70 | -1.02 | -7.23 | -7.59 | -0.21 | -2.48 | |
| EV, $ | -93 | -29,499 | -20,356 | -60,323 | -33,596 | -28,149 | -533 | -180,957 | -353,505 |

Note: Results are reported as changes from initial equilibrium. A dollar sign indicates that figures are in $US million. All other figures are in percentage changes. This simulation is based on the shocks in Table 10.2, part A.

illustrate differences between partial and general equilibrium welfare impacts. Climate change is likely to affect human societies and natural ecosystems in several ways. Here, we have concentrated on the effects of climate change on agriculture. Furthermore, we examine the medium-term effects of climate change on world agriculture as it is today, and we have not accounted for possible future changes in government policies, technology, and population.

We applied direct impacts of climate change based on the Goddard Institute of Space Studies climate change scenario, and we implemented climate change as Hicks-neutral technical change in the crop sectors of each region. These climate change shocks are applied both with and without the direct effect of $CO_2$ on crop growth to examine the sensitivity of our results to this assumption. The base case accounts for the direct effect of $CO_2$ on crop growth, and these results suggest that the average consumer in most regions will have to pay higher prices, with Mexican and ASEAN consumers paying 2.3% and 0.8% more, respectively. Consumer prices in China are projected to decline by 0.2%.

Overall, welfare in Mexico and the ASEAN countries is estimated to decline by 2.7% and 1.7%, respectively. All other regions experience a relatively small increase in welfare, ranging from 0.06% for the US to 0.54% for China. Welfare in ROW will decline by 0.12%. Assuming that Mexico, ASEAN, and ROW are compensated by the regions that gain, the world as a whole would experience a very small increase in welfare.

Canada and, to a lesser degree, Australia are expected to increase their market shares in exports of agricultural commodities in general. The US is projected to increase its dominance of the rice trade. Despite significant loses in productivity for some crops, *world* demand (and production) for crops will change little, because final demand for farm commodities is quite inelastic. Thus, commodity prices for crops change substantially. However, the impact on consumers is blunted because they tend to consume processed agricultural commodities that require a variety of nonfarm inputs, the prices of which are not affected by climate change.

Our results also suggest that it is important to account properly for the direct effect of $CO_2$ on crop growth. If this is *ignored*, the impact of climate change is much more damaging. Welfare declines in all regions, with ASEAN, China, and Mexico losing about 7% of real income.

Finally, we show that partial equilibrium models that incorporate processed agricultural commodities are likely to produce satisfactory results for prices and quantities. However, these models will show welfare impacts that are substantially smaller than those from general equilibrium models because they likely do not capture the effects on labor and capital markets.

NOTES

1. We have modified the GTAP data for primary factor payments in Mexican agriculture because land rents appeared to be very low. In particular, we changed the

distribution of primary factor payments to reflect the GTAP data for Argentina and Brazil, where land rents and labor wages account for 37% and 26%, respectively, of primary factor payments. Capital rents account for 37% of primary factor payments.

2. Wolfe and Erickson (1993) note that full realization of $CO_2$ benefits requires optimal field conditions with respect to access and timing of irrigation and chemical inputs, and that such ideal conditions may not obtain in many developing countries.

3. The compensated price elasticities of demand for the private household differ by region, but they do not affect the relative size of the elasticities in Table 11.3, because private households consume a very small portion of domestic production of raw agricultural commodities.

## REFERENCES

Hansen, J., G. Russell, D. Rind, P. Stone, A. Lacis, S. Lebedeff, R. Ruedy, and L. Travis (1983) "Efficient Three-Dimensional Global Models for Climate Studies: Models I and II," *Monthly Weather Review* 111(4):609–662.

Houghton, J. T., B. A. Callander, and S. K. Varney (eds.) (1992) *Climate Change 1992: The Supplementary Report to the IPCC Scientific Assessment.* New York: Cambridge University Press.

Houghton, J. T., G. J. Jenkins, and J. J. Ephraums (eds.) (1990) *Climate Change: The IPCC Scientific Assessment.* New York: Cambridge University Press.

Intergovernmental Panel on Climate Change (1990) *Scientific Assessment of Climate Change: Policymakers Summary.* Geneva and Nairobi: World Meteorological Organization and the United Nations Environment Programme.

International Benchmark Sites Network for Agrotechnology Transfer (1989) *Decision Support System for Agrotechnology Transfer Version 2.1.* Department of Agronomy and Soil Science, College of Tropical Agriculture and Human Resources, University of Hawaii, Honolulu.

Kane, S., J. Reilly, and J. Tobey (1991) *Climate Change: Economic Implications for World Agriculture.* Agricultural Economics Report No. 647, Resources and Technology Division, Economic Research Service, USDA, Washington, DC.

Kokoski, M. F., and V. K. Smith (1987) "A General Equilibrium Analysis of Partial Equilibrium Welfare Measure," *The American Economic Review* 77(3):331–341.

Manabe, S., and R. T. Wetherald (1987) "Large-Scale Changes in Soil Wetness Induced by an Increase in $CO_2$," *Journal of Atmospheric Science* 44:1211–1235.

Reilly, J., and N. Hohmann (1993) "Climate Change and Agriculture: The Role of International Trade," *The American Economic Review* 83(2):306–312.

Reilly, J., N. Hohmann, and S. Kane (1993) "Climate Change and Agriculture: Global and Regional Effects Using an Economic Model of International Trade," Working Paper No. MIT-CEEPR 93-009, Center for Energy and Environmental Policy Research, Massachusetts Institute of Technology, August.

Reilly, J., and C. Thomas (1993) "Toward Economic Evaluation of Climate Change Impacts: A Review and Evaluation of Studies of the Impact of Climate Change," Working Paper No. MIT-CEEPR 93-012, Center for Energy and Environmental Policy Research, Massachusetts Institute of Technology, June.

Roningen, V. (1986) "A Static World Policy Simulation (SWOPSIM) Modeling Framework." Staff Report AGES 860625, Economic Research Service, USDA, Washington, DC.

Rosenzweig, C., and A. Iglesias (eds.) (1994) *Implications of Climate Change for International Agriculture: Crop Modeling Study.* US EPA, Washington, DC, June.

Sullivan, J., V. Roningen, S. Leetmaa, and D. Gray (1992) *A 1989 Global Database for the Static World Policy Simulation (SWOPSIM) Modeling Framework.* Staff Report No. AGES 9215, Agriculture and Trade Analysis Division, Economic Research Service, USDA, Washington, DC, May.

Tobey, J., J. Reilly, and S. Kane (1992) "Economic Implications of Global Climate Change for World Agriculture," *Journal of Agricultural and Resource Economics* 17(1):195–204.

World Bank (1992) *World Development Report, 1992.* New York: Oxford University Press.

Wilson, C. A., and J. F. B. Mitchell (1987) "A Doubled $CO_2$ Climate Sensitivity Experiment with a Global Climate Model Including a Simple Ocean," *Journal of Geophysical Research* 92(13):315–343.

Wolfe, D., and J. Erickson (1993) "Carbon Dioxide Effects on Plants: Uncertainties and Implications for Modeling Crop Response to Climate Change." In H. Kaiser and T. Drennen (eds.), *Agricultural Dimensions of Global Climate Change.* Delray Beach, FL: St. Lucie Press.

# CHAPTER 12

# Environmental policy modeling

*Carlo Perroni and Randall Wigle*

## I    Introduction and overview

One of the goals of the Global Trade Analysis Project (GTAP) is to make a versatile, well-documented "consensus" model broadly available. The advantage of such a tool is that it can help focus discussion on the economics of the analysis, rather than the mechanics of model formulation and solution. Although this model is reasonably versatile, no numerical model can be truly all-purpose, and GTAP is no exception. Of particular relevance to this chapter are environmental externalities and abatement costs, which GTAP does not currently incorporate. The goal of the exercises we present in this chapter is to illustrate how GTAP can be used to analyze issues that are not directly accommodated by the model. This work is meant to be illustrative rather than definitive; in other words, we are not arguing that the model we use is the best model; rather, we wish to illustrate how simple adaptations to an existing model structure can permit better insight into environmental policy issues.

This work is also motivated in part by studies cited in the popular press containing statements such as:

- Carbon taxes would cost the US economy 4% of gross national product (GNP).
- Environmental regulation would lead to reduced imports because they distort the economy.[1]

Often, the bases of such statements are simulation models, most of which have one or both of the following characteristics:

- There is no treatment of environmental feedbacks to the economy (particularly benefits of cleanup).
- There is no abatement technology.

As a practical matter, much analysis of environmental policy issues will be done in models without these features, and one objective of this chapter is to note the kinds of errors that cannot be avoided in such cases. However, we also show here how a computable general equilibrium (CGE) model without abatement or environmental benefits can be used to achieve better representation of the consequences of environmental policy. We concentrate on simple ways of representing an (absent) abatement technology for the analysis of emissions fees, and we also note how the welfare effects of the policy are changed by making allowance for benefits from abatement. Finally, we note the limitations of this approach.

## II    Purely "economic" models

In models like GTAP, the focus is normally on the interrelation between policy variables (taxes, subsidies, or quantity restrictions) on various economic magnitudes, such as employment, trade, or income. They may also abstract from several types of unmarketed goods, or nonmarket transactions. In the current context, the damages done to the environment by firms can be seen as important unmarketed inputs used by the firms. The firms damage the environment by their emissions but are not required to bear all (or perhaps any) of the costs of that damage. A similar argument could be made for positive externalities as unpriced outputs from firms.

The absence of environmental features in GTAP complicates the process of analyzing environmental policy for a number of reasons, to be discussed below, so why would one want to use an existing model like GTAP for such a purpose? Typically, analysts face a trade-off between a model with all the desirable model features (e.g., explicit treatment of abatement and emissions), and the level of industry detail or the quality of policy data and parameters in the model. In such circumstances, it may be advisable to use GTAP for some aspects of analysis or use a model like GTAP in tandem with a special purpose model that may lack some other important policy information that could interact with environmental policies.

## III    Benefits from abatement

Implicit in models without environmental benefits is the assumption that environmental feedbacks to the economy (particularly through preferences and utility) are separable from those market transactions forming the core of the model. This approach applies to many models addressing issues ranging from carbon taxes to environmental regulation schemes.[2] In some cases this omission makes sense, although at least four types of interactions may be missed by such models:

1. Changes in the relative valuation of the public good compared to private goods.
2. Changes in relative prices of goods occasioned by the shift of consumption shares and by the resulting shifts in intermediate use.
3. Changes in consumption patterns caused by changes in environmental quality. These changes can include not only reduced consumption of private goods to isolate individuals from poor environmental quality, but also changes in consumption patterns between substitutes and complements for environmental amenities.
4. Interactions between abatement activities taken by firms and private mitigating expenditures such as buying water purifiers or household air cleaners.

By way of an example of these last two interactions, suppose that instead of walking downtown you take your car to avoid the pollution. You shut the car windows and turn the air conditioner on. In doing so you contribute to pollution. In this case the social "cost" of abatement could be very small, since if everyone paid a small amount for abatement, they might not need their air conditioners. Without the air conditioners on, the pollution would be less, and abatement would be less costly. Truly evaluating the social cost of abatement in this case requires that the feedback through the benefit side be taken into account.

In a similar way, models that have no explicit abatement activities (but only model the effects of emissions fees or environmental regulations as output taxes) miss the interactions between abatement activities and other activities in the economy. Abatement activities typically have an input mix different from the polluting sector.

From a modeling perspective, we believe there are several specific limitations to which these problems may be traced:

1. Absence of benefits accruing from environmental cleanup
2. Improper specification of benefits evaluation
3. Absence of abatement technologies (implicit or explicit)
4. Improper specification of abatement technologies

In this chapter we look only at how one might remedy two of these problems, namely, the absence of an abatement technology, and some treatment of the benefits of abatement. As noted above, we feel that many models not designed for environmental policy could be used to generate some insights when used carefully, particularly when a more sparse special purpose model is available as a complementary tool.

The general approach to linking GTAP with a special purpose model for environmental policy is shown in Figure 12.1. We begin with a generalized

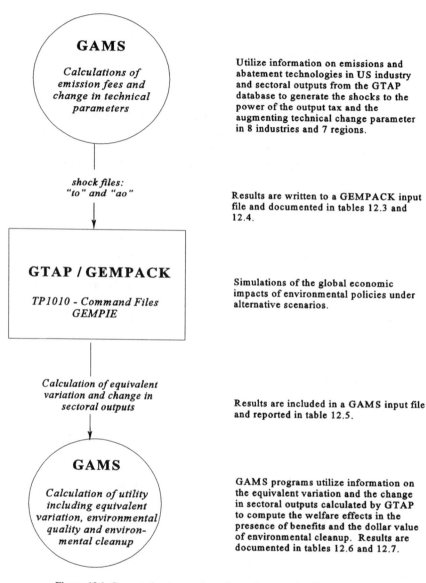

**GAMS**

*Calculations of
emission fees and
change in technical
parameters*

Utilize information on emissions and
abatement technologies in US industry
and sectoral outputs from the GTAP
database to generate the shocks to the
power of the output tax and the
augmenting technical change parameter
in 8 industries and 7 regions.

*shock files:
"to" and "ao"*

Results are written to a GEMPACK input
file and documented in tables 12.3 and
12.4.

**GTAP / GEMPACK**

*TP1010 - Command Files
GEMPIE*

Simulations of the global economic
impacts of environmental policies under
alternative scenarios.

*Calculation of equivalent
variation and change in
sectoral outputs*

Results are included in a GAMS input file
and reported in table 12.5.

**GAMS**

*Calculation of utility
including equivalent
variation, environmental
quality and environ-
mental cleanup*

GAMS programs utilize information on
the equivalent variation and the change
in sectoral outputs calculated by GTAP
to compute the welfare effects in the
presence of benefits and the dollar value
of environmental cleanup. Results are
documented in tables 12.6 and 12.7.

**Figure 12.1.** Computational procedures for environmental policy analysis using the
standard GTAP model.

Table 12.1. *Commodity and Regional Aggregation*

| Good | Description | Region | Description |
|------|-------------|--------|-------------|
| AGR | Agriculture | OHI | Other high income |
| FDM | Food manufacturing | NAM | Canada and US |
| RSC | Primary industry | JPN | Japan |
| CLO | Textiles and clothing | EU | EU |
| DRT | Dirty industry | MID | Middle income |
| FMN | Final manufacturing | CHN | China |
| SVC | Traded services | LOW | Low income (<$2000) |
| NTS | Nontraded services | | |

algebraic modeling system (GAMS) program that calculates the "shocks" to GTAP that are necessary in order to achieve a given combination of emission fees and abatement. These shocks are implemented in GTAP, and the resulting changes in sectoral output and equivalent variation associated with market goods are then used as inputs into a third step. This final exercise is also implemented in GAMS and permits the user to calculate welfare changes that take account of environmental quality and clean-up costs.

## IV Aggregation

In this application, we adopt the eight-good, seven-region aggregation described in Table 12.1. Commodities are grouped into agriculture, food manufacturing, primary industry, textiles and clothing, dirty industry, final manufacturing, and two service sectors that share a similar level of pollution. Since the willingness to pay for an improvement of environmental quality is correlated with income, the seven-region aggregation breaks out North America, Japan, the European Union (EU), and China, grouping other countries by income level.

## V Experiments

We look at the implementation of a set of emissions fees aimed at reducing the damage done by industrial pollution. The particular experiment we concentrate on involves setting environmental taxes at their economically appropriate level. The necessary taxes differ between sectors due to differences in emissions intensities. Table 12.2 presents estimated damages per dollar of output of the industries in the model, and abatement expenditures.

**Table 12.2.** *Damages and Abatement per Dollar Output[a,b,c]*

| Sector | Damages | Abatement Expenditures |
|--------|---------|------------------------|
| AGR | 0.011 | 0.005 |
| FDM | 0.001 | 0.003 |
| RSC | 0.010 | 0.011 |
| CLO | 0.009 | 0.003 |
| DRT | 0.021 | 0.009 |
| FMN | 0.004 | 0.003 |
| SVC | 0.015 | 0.001 |
| NTS | 0.015 | 0.001 |

Notes:

[a] The original source for the damage data is Lucas, Wheeler, and Hettige (1992; pp. 69—71). Damages represent the damage-weighted emissions (in equally toxic pounds per dollar of output) of US industries.

[b] Abatement costs are from Low (1992a). The data are again expenditures for dollar of output of US industries.

[c] All aggregated values are simple averages. Since the initial data did not include primary sectors or services, we assigned them values based on related sectors. In the case of AGR, this was based on averages across all sectors for damage data _and_ abatement costs. In the case of services, abatement costs are taken from printing and publishing and damage data from beverages.

We assumed that the benchmark (per unit of output) emissions of a given industry were the same in all countries, but that the damages caused by emissions were valued differently. The high-income regions (EU, NAM, JPN, OHI) share a common valuation of the damages. The same amount of emissions that causes $1 of damage in these regions causes 20 cents of damage in China and the low-income region, and 50 cents in the middle-income region (MID). To complete our calibration, we assume a common overall rate of internalization of externalities in the initial equilibrium.[3]

The tax rates we report in Table 12.3 are indirect taxes in the initial data base; we refer to them as pollution taxes, for clarity. In this context, they represent the amount of "emissions fee" charged on the emissions resulting from $1 of output in the benchmark. These constructed benchmark pollution taxes range as high as 1.7% for primary industry in the high-income regions, and as low as 0.1% in the service sectors of the low-income regions (China and MID).

The damages and abatement data were used to generate a standard experiment, whereby emissions fees would be used to internalize fully the (local) environmental externalities. The resulting tax rates (after our experiment) are shown in Table 12.4. What is clear is that fully internalizing the damages in each sector involves raising the tax rates in some sectors and lowering them in others. The procedure we use to generate these tax rates is rather ad hoc, and these tax rates should be interpreted with caution.

Table 12.3. *Constructed Benchmark Pollution Taxes (cents per dollar)*

| Sector | High | Mid | Low |
|--------|------|-----|-----|
| AGR | 0.8 | 0.4 | 0.2 |
| FDM | 0.5 | 0.2 | 0.1 |
| RSC | 1.7 | 0.8 | 0.3 |
| CLO | 0.4 | 0.2 | 0.1 |
| DRT | 1.3 | 0.7 | 0.3 |
| FMN | 0.4 | 0.2 | 0.1 |
| SRV | 0.2 | 0.1 | 0.1 |
| NTS | 0.2 | 0.1 | 0.1 |

Table 12.4. *Constructed Internalizing Pollution Taxes (cents per dollar)*

| Sector | High | Mid | Low |
|--------|------|-----|-----|
| AGR | 2.6 | 1.3 | 0.5 |
| FDM | 0.2 | 0.1 | 0.0 |
| RSC | 2.3 | 1.2 | 0.5 |
| CLO | 2.1 | 1.1 | 0.4 |
| DRT | 4.9 | 2.4 | 1.0 |
| FMN | 1.0 | 0.5 | 0.2 |
| SRV | 0.1 | 0.0 | 0.0 |
| NTS | 0.1 | 0.0 | 0.0 |

## VI    Emissions fees and abatement

When abatement technologies are available, increases in emissions fees typically cause two types of response by firms. First, firms shift their production away from the production of dirty goods and toward cleaner goods. Second, firms tend to use cleaner technologies to avoid some of the taxes. In economic terms, this means using more market inputs to economize on the use of emissions. Thus, when an emissions fee is imposed, we expect to see an increase in the ratio of market inputs to output, and an increase in tax revenues.

It is possible to mimic these changes in the GTAP model, even though the model does not have any explicit abatement technology. This is done by simultaneously shocking technical parameters in the production functions and output tax rates. The idea is to reproduce the same percentage changes in quantities, prices, and input shares in GTAP as would be observed in a model containing an (albeit simple) abatement technology.[4]

## VII   Mapping between the "true" model and GTAP

When we think of abatement, we usually think in terms of using inputs to reduce the emissions associated with a given level of output. As long as the model is reasonably aggregated, a production technology implicitly representing abatement could be summarized as

$$Q = f(X,E), \tag{12.1}$$

where $Q$ is output, $X$ is the quantity of standard market inputs used, and $E$ is the emissions produced. In the simplest case, the "price" of emissions would be the emissions fee charged, and cost covering prices (the unit cost) would be functions of the price of market inputs $(PX)$ and the emissions fee $(PE)$.[5]

If we assume that the input aggregate $X$ has the same functional relation to market inputs as in the original model, and impose a functional form $f()$ on the relation between $Q$, $E$, and $X$, we can represent emissions fee shocks to the true model by shocking two of GTAP's variables, $ao$ and $to$. These are, respectively, a neutral overall productivity shock applied industry by industry, and a change in the power of output taxes.[6]

We considered specifications of $f(X,E)$ that are weighted averages of the Leontief case (no substitution between $X$ and $E$, so abatement occurs only by production shifting) and the Cobb–Douglas case (constant cost share of "abatement" compared to market inputs). The Leontief case is where no abatement (in the sense of lower emissions per unit of output) is possible. Our other discussions will concentrate on a case where abatement is easier than this extreme case, but not as easy as the Cobb–Douglas case (where a 1% increase in the effluent fee would reduce emissions by about 1%).[7]

The details are left to the appendix, where we show how implementation of a given percent increase in an emissions tax can be modeled in GTAP to give the same partial equilibrium output level, tax revenue, input ratios, and emissions effects as the "true" model by using the shocks and associated calculations listed in Table 12.8. Of necessity, these shocks will not yield the same general equilibrium results as the "true" model. For this, one would need the abatement and benefits features to be fully incorporated into the model. However, this method is clearly an improvement over ignoring abatement technologies.

## VIII   Results

The results that follow in Tables 12.5–12.7 represent the effects of implementing the emissions fees under two different assumptions about the production

**Table 12.5.** *Effects on Pattern of Production (% Change)*

|  | AGR | FDM | DRT | FMN | SVC | NTS |
|---|---|---|---|---|---|---|
| *CASE A: No Abatement Substitution* | | | | | | |
| OHI | 0.304 | 0.334 | -1.785 | -1.069 | 0.243 | 0.157 |
| NAM | -0.590 | -0.179 | -1.074 | -0.133 | 0.237 | 0.137 |
| JPN | -0.143 | -0.097 | -0.690 | -0.260 | 0.321 | -0.088 |
| EU | -0.442 | -0.070 | -1.442 | 0.211 | 0.384 | 0.141 |
| MID | 0.002 | -0.171 | 0.619 | -0.692 | 0.005 | -0.016 |
| LOW | 0.153 | -0.270 | 1.896 | -0.728 | -0.375 | -0.132 |
| CHN | 0.115 | -0.204 | 0.999 | -1.745 | -0.210 | -0.083 |
| *CASE B: Abatement Substitution Present* | | | | | | |
| OHI | -0.091 | 0.048 | -1.260 | -1.325 | 0.045 | -0.227 |
| NAM | -0.649 | -0.306 | -0.775 | -0.284 | -0.003 | -0.149 |
| JPN | -0.626 | -0.517 | -0.333 | -0.549 | 0.021 | -0.449 |
| EU | -0.460 | -0.181 | -0.963 | 0.076 | 0.080 | -0.280 |
| MID | -0.163 | -0.388 | 0.930 | -0.872 | -0.221 | -0.302 |
| LOW | 0.117 | -0.396 | 1.887 | -1.022 | -0.530 | -0.324 |
| CHN | 0.067 | -0.402 | 1.017 | -1.971 | -0.367 | -0.363 |

**Table 12.6.** *Welfare Calculations (1992 $US million)*

| Region | Case A: GTAP | Case A: Benefits Present | Case B: Benefits Present |
|---|---|---|---|
| OHI (6.3)[a] | -455.7 | 2,263.1 | 578.4 |
| NAM (5.2) | -811.6 | 43,472.6 | 14,759.8 |
| JPN (8.6) | 1,080.8 | 38,795.9 | 15,713.7 |
| EU (6.5) | -835.5 | 55,512.4 | 20,403.4 |
| MID (4.4) | 172.3 | 21,752.5 | 8,963.9 |
| LOW (1.9) | -297.7 | 3,522.5 | 1,587.6 |
| CHN (3.1) | 1,077.7 | 2,891.3 | 1,815.4 |
| Total | -69.8 | 168,210.3 | 63,822.1 |

[a] Present share of environmental quality in utility, by region.

Table 12.7. *Dollar Value of Environmental Cleanup (1992 $US million)*

| Region | Case A | Case B |
|---|---|---|
| OHI | 3,169.7 | 3,060.2 |
| NAM | 51,328.1 | 49,270.9 |
| JPN | 44,295.7 | 44,780.0 |
| EU | 65,705.0 | 65,334.0 |
| MID | 25,510.3 | 26,444.7 |
| LOW | 4,502.6 | 4,764.9 |
| CHN | 2,173.8 | 2,381.3 |
| Total | 196,685.1 | 196,036.0 |

Table 12.8. *Summary Table*

| Shocks | Leontief | Cobb–Douglas | Weighted |
|---|---|---|---|
| to | $-\beta t$ | 0 | $-\omega_L \beta t$ |
| ao | 0 | $-\beta t$ | $(1-\omega_L)\beta t$ |
| *Emissions* | | | |
| $\dot{e}$ | 0 | $(\beta-1)t$ | $(1-\omega_L)(\beta-1)t$ |
| $\dot{E}$ | $qo$ | $(\beta-1)tqo$ | $\omega_L+(1-\omega_L)(\beta-1)tqo$ |

Notes:

$\beta$ -- cost share of emissions in total cost; $t$ -- proportionate change in emissions tax; $ao$ -- technology shock variable; $to$ -- proportionate change in the power of the output tax; $qo$ -- proportionate change of sectoral output; $\omega_L$ -- weight on Leontief true model; $\dot{e}$ -- proportional change in emissions per-unit output; $\dot{E}$ -- proportional change in total emissions.

process that uses "emissions" and market inputs to produce output. In case A there is no substitution between emissions and market inputs (Leontief). The model shocks used in this case correspond exactly to what someone might do as a first step to analyze the effects of an emissions tax: they calculate a per-unit output tax equal to the emissions fee times the per-unit emissions.

In the other extreme case (Cobb–Douglas), the only model shocks are to the technical parameters (whereby the ratio of market inputs to output is raised to model abatement). A more likely intermediate case applies part of the (Leontief) emissions fee to output, and gives smaller shocks the technological parameters to mimic abatement. This is case B, whereby we assume the abatement process is an (equally) weighted average of Cobb–Douglas and Leontief technologies.

*Sectoral impacts*

The pattern of effects on production (Table 12.5) and patterns of trade are significantly different from one case to another. This is hardly surprising, since the ability to reduce emissions through abatement can reduce the cost disadvantage suffered by firms facing higher effluent fees. The table presents percentage output changes for selected sectors. Because GTAP is a global model, reductions in output in one region tend to be offset by increases in other regions. The biggest changes occur in the dirty industries, where the output tax is largest. In case A output in the "other" high-income economies falls by almost 2% while output in the low-income economies rises by a similar percentage.

Comparison of the results with and without abatement possibilities shows that global output of "dirty" manufacturing is less adversely affected in case B. There are also some sign reversals between the two sets of results, for agriculture and for services output changes in some regions. Thus, specifying one or the other abatement technology affects the qualitative response of the model to a given set of emissions fees.

*Cost of environmental policy*

The welfare evaluation from GTAP does not account for welfare changes corresponding to the improved environmental quality resulting from reduced emissions. In terms of that model, the emissions fees we are evaluating amount to competitive distortions in the market, so that global welfare losses are virtually guaranteed, unless they help offset some other preexisting distortion. Referring to the first column of Table 12.6, we see that world welfare falls by $69.8 million as a result of the introduction of the effluent fees. Four of the seven regions suffer welfare losses.

To take account of the benefits of improved environmental quality, we assume that each consumer has a constant elasticity of substitution (CES) utility function defined over the standard utility aggregate (as in GTAP) plus environmental quality, which is inversely related to the amount of environmental damages done by emissions:

$$\tilde{U} = F(U,Q). \tag{12.2}$$

Here $F$ has the CES functional form, $U$ is the equivalent variation from GTAP, and $Q$ is the environmental quality, defined as follows:

$$Q = \overline{Q} - D, \tag{12.3}$$

where $\overline{Q}$ refers to the "endowment" of environmental quality and $D$ is the damages from emissions.[8] The dollar value of damages is calculated given the emissions per unit output implicit in the specification of the production technology and the assumption that the marginal damage from emissions is constant. Therefore the damages also depend on the pattern of industrial output.

It was necessary to assume a number of values for the CES utility function $F$. In particular, we assumed that the share of initial (benchmark) damages to the endowment of environment quality $(D/\overline{Q})$ is 0.25, while the elasticity of substitution between goods $(U)$ and environmental quality $(Q)$ is 0.50. These assumptions are enough to determine the shares of environmental quality in utility shown in parentheses at the left of Table 12.6. Note that the largest shares are the wealthy countries. These range from 8.6% in the case of Japan, to 1.9% in the low-income economies.

With these parameters, the welfare effects of the emissions fees (adjusted to reflect the benefits of improved environmental quality) are given in the columns under the heading "Benefits Present." In case A, most of the welfare effects are very similar in magnitude to the reductions in environmental damages that result from the emissions fees reported in Table 12.7. Emissions fees reduce environmental damage by roughly 50% in the high-income regions. Given our paramaterization, this implies very high benefits from reduced emissions. The welfare estimates in both cases A and B in Table 12.6 show that all regions benefit from the taxes when environmental benefits are accounted for. Instead of a worldwide loss of $69.8 million, worldwide gains range from (case B) $63,822 million to $168.210 million (case A). Note, however, that if we had used the initial valuation of the damages, we would have concluded that the improvement in environmental quality (measured as the reductions in pollution damage) amounts to almost $200,000 million (Table 12.7), whereas the true gain reported in Table 12.6 is considerably less in *both* cases.

## IX    Qualifications

The calculations we have done suffer from a number of weaknesses that should be noted. First, the paramaterization of the value of general environmental damages (and hence of the benefits from emission reductions) depends on a number of preference parameters on which there is little evidence (particularly at the level of aggregation we are using here.)[9] Depending on the audience to be addressed, it might be preferable to use regular welfare calculations plus a separate "cleanup" calculation, as presented in Table 12.7.

For similar reasons, our calculations assume that the marginal cost of abatement is flatter than real marginal abatement cost curves. In practice the marginal abatement cost curve may become very steep when high levels of abatement are approached.[10] Once again, this can cause our assumed abatement response to be higher than it should be.

If GTAP were to be used regularly for such policy analyses, a preferable alternative to our approach would be to completely incorporate the benefits formulation and abatement technologies, along with corresponding data into the GTAP model.[11] This would remedy the problem of overestimation of benefits, and would improve the reliability of such calculations.

## X    Conclusion

The approach we employed here is still somewhat "back of the envelope," and our policy experiment is largely illustrative. Our intention has been to demonstrate a practical method of using an off-the-shelf model to analyze environmental issues, by supplementing this standard model with a set of outside data and calculations. Although this methodology has some limitations, we feel that it can be useful in circumstances where sufficiently reliable benefits, emissions, and abatement parameters are available to augment GTAP's rich economic and policy data.

### Appendix: Introducing Abatement into GTAP

*GTAP model*

Effectively, we have the following production relation for each good in GTAP:

$$Q = kX$$

Where $X$ is the normal aggregate of inputs with price $Px$ and $x$ refers to the input–output (IO) ratio. The relation between supply prices, market prices and taxes, and the technology shifters in GTAP is as follows:

$$ps = -ao + pm + to,$$

where $pm$ is the proportionate change in the market price, $ps$ is the proportionate change in the supplier's price, $ao$ is the technological change shifter for output, and $to$ is the percentage change in the power of the output tax. The "shocks" needed to implement the emission taxes should be determined such that the following items are identical between the GTAP model and the true model: $pm$, $\dot{x}$ (the rate of change in the input–output ratio), and the per unit tax revenue.

*"True" Cobb–Douglas model*

The true Cobb–Douglas model is summarized as follows:

$$pm = (1 - \beta)px + \beta\dot{t},$$

where $\dot{t}$ is the proportional change in the emissions tax (per dollar of output) and $\beta$ is the share parameter of emission taxes in total costs. (The proportionate change in the emissions tax would be $\dot{\pi}+\dot{\alpha}+\dot{v}$, where $v$ is the valuation of emission damages, $\pi$ is the rate of internalization of damages, and $\alpha$ is the amount of emissions per unit output. But for what follows, we will assume that $\dot{t}=\dot{\pi}$.) As a consequence of the cost shares, the following relations describe the proportionate changes of the per-unit input requirements

$$\dot{x} = \beta\dot{t}, \text{ and } \dot{e} = (\beta-1)\,\dot{t},$$

where $\dot{e}$ is the proportional change in emissions per unit of output.

To get the price change in GTAP to be the same as the price changes in the true model, we get the following:

$$\beta\dot{t} = -ao - to.$$

But note that we will also want

$$\dot{x} = -ao = \beta\dot{t}.$$

Therefore, the only shock to implement a change in emissions tax is to the technology parameter, $ao$. In the Cobb–Douglas case, the power of the (per-unit output) tax in GTAP is always constant at the initial value, and the tax revenue per unit of output changes only because the usage of $X$ in production rises (mimicking substitution of factors for emissions). Therefore, the shocks we implement in the Cobb–Douglas case are:

$$to = 0 \text{ and } ao = -\beta\tau.$$

The proportionate change in emissions per unit of output could be calculated as follows (see also Table 12.8):

$$\dot{e} = (\beta - 1)\,\dot{t}.$$

### Leontief case

In this case, the relation between the proportionate changes in minimum cost and the changes in $\dot{t}$ are as follows:

$$pm = S_x px - S_e \dot{t}.$$

Note that initially $S_x$ will correspond to $(1 - \beta)$ from the Cobb–Douglas case, and $S_e$ will correspond to $\beta$. However, in the Leontief case these shares are not constant. $X$ and $e$ are constant in the true model. As a result, the shocks to $ao$ and $to$ represent a change in emissions tax in the Leontief are:

$$ao = 0 \text{ and } to = -\beta\dot{t}.$$

## NOTES

1. This is not restricted to the popular press. Tobey (1993) talks about environmental regulations "distorting" trade patterns, and Goulder (1993) refers to the distorting effects of a carbon tax.
2. See, for example, Whalley and Wigle (1993) and Jorgensen and Wilcoxen (1993).
3. In other words, we assume that the initial abatement and emissions fees account for 50% of the value of damage done in the economy. We do allow these rates to differ between industries, as is common to most environmental regulatory schemes.
4. There are data on the input mix of the "abatement sector." See for example Nestor and Pasurka (1993). In this simple configuration, the abatement technology for a given sector uses the same input shares as production in that sector.
5. Environmental policies are not frequently set in terms of emissions fees; however, it is relatively straightforward to map between a number of other types of policies and corresponding emissions fees.
6. By the power of the tax, we mean 1 minus the tax rate. (In some cases this refers to 1 plus the tax rate.)
7. If one is fortunate enough to know the approximate reduction in per-unit emissions associated with a given percent tax increase, this information may actually be used to calibrate the model, by revealing the appropriate weighting between the two formulations.
8. The calibration of a utility function with environmental benefits is discussed in more detail in Perroni and Wigle (1994).
9. As a general observation, sensitivity analysis is essential to policy analysis because of the huge parameter uncertainty. Since our purpose here is purely illustrative, we decided not to do sensitivity analysis.
10. Our marginal abatement cost curve has a constant elasticity of marginal abatement cost with respect to abatement.
11. To do so, one would need access to the full GEMPACK software suite.

## REFERENCES

Dean, A., ed. (1993) *The Costs of Cutting Carbon Emissions: Results from Global Models*, Organization for Economic Cooperation and Development, Paris.

Goulder, L. H. (1993) "Effects of Carbon Taxes in an Economy with Prior Tax Distortions: An Intertemporal General Equilibrium Analysis," Stanford University. (Mimeo.)

Jorgensen, D. W., and P. J. Wilcoxen (1993) "The Economic Impact of the Clean Air Act Amendments of 1990," *The Energy Journal*: 14(1):159–182.

Low, P., ed. (1992a) "International Trade and the Environment," International Bank for Reconstruction and Development, Washington, DC.

Low, P. (1992b) "Trade Measures and Environmental Quality: The Implications for Mexico's Exports." In P. Low (ed.), *International Trade and the Environment*, International Bank for Reconstruction and Development, Washington, DC.

Lucas, R. E. B., D. Wheeler, and H. Hettige (1992) "Economic Development, Environmental Regulation and the International Migration of Toxic Industrial Pollution: 1960–88." In P. Low (ed.), *International Trade and the Environment*, International Bank for Reconstruction and Development, Washington, DC.

Nestor, D. V., and Pasurka, C. A. Jr. (1993) "Alternative Specifications for Environmental Control Costs in a General Equilibrium Framework." Economic Analysis and Research Branch, US EPA: Washington, DC. (Mimeo.)

Perroni, C., and R. M. Wigle (1994) "International Trade and Environmental Quality: How Important Are the Linkages?" *Canadian Journal of Economics* 27(3):551–567.

Tobey, J. A. (1993) "Effects of Domestic Environmental Policy on Patterns of International Trade." In M. D. Shane, and H. von Witzke (eds.), *The Environment, Government Policies and International Trade: A Proceedings.* Washington, DC, USDA, Staff Report AGES9314.

Whalley, J., and R. M. Wigle (1993) "Results for the OECD Comparative Modeling Exercise Using the Whalley-Wigle Model." In A. Dean (ed.), *The Costs of Cutting Carbon Emissions: Results From Global Models.* Paris: OECD.

# CHAPTER 13

# Multimarket effects of agricultural research with technological spillovers

*George B. Frisvold*

## I    Introduction and overview

There is an extensive literature on gains from agricultural research. Norton and Davis (1981) and Alston (1993) provide excellent surveys. Relatively few studies formally examine impacts of research in an international context, however. Even fewer have examined the effects of technological spillovers across regions. New technologies may reduce production costs, both in the country where they are developed and in other regions that can adopt these technologies or adapt them to local production conditions.

International spillovers are an important aspect of agricultural research. International research and assistance agencies such as the UN Food and Agriculture Organization (FAO), the World Bank, and the Consultative Group for International Agricultural Research (CGIAR) have missions that include the international dissemination of agricultural technologies. Also, the rise of multinational agricultural input suppliers means that adoption of agricultural innovations will not be confined to particular countries.

Spillovers also have implications for the setting of national research priorities. Because taxpayers incur the costs of domestic public research programs, there is interest in examining the distribution of research gains between the home country and the rest of the world. Research, such as plant breeding for particular production environments may be less transferable to other countries; chemical, mechanical, or processing innovations may be more transferable. National governments may desire to allocate resources to research projects with lower spillover potential to trade competitors; input suppliers or international research agencies may favor wider international adoption of technologies.

This chapter uses the Global Trade Analysis Project (GTAP) model to examine general equilibrium and open economy impacts of agricultural research. Results demonstrate how the size and distribution of net gains from agricultural research depend on (1) the trade position of the innovating country,

(2) technological spillovers, (3) the stage of production in the multistage process where technological change occurs, and (4) the factor bias of technical change.

The approach here differs from most returns-to-research studies that evaluate impacts of technological change in a single-commodity, partial equilibrium setting. Such studies often make two limiting assumptions. First, prices and production of all other commodities are assumed fixed. For example, it would be assumed that changes in the cost of producing corn would not alter market prices of wheat or livestock.[1] In contrast, the applied general equilibrium (AGE) framework allows for endogenous movements of regional prices and quantities in response to technological change.

Second, most studies assume that research results from one region do not affect productivity in others. For example, research to improve wheat yields in Canada would not contribute to increased yields in the US or new food processing technologies developed in Europe would not be adopted elsewhere. An important exception is Edwards and Freebairn (1984), who explicitly considered spillover effects by assuming that domestic research shifts out supply curves of both domestic producers and foreign competitors. Their study, however, considers spillovers in a single commodity, single stage of production setting. This chapter uses the approach of Edwards and Freebairn (1984) to simulate the shocks induced by spillovers. It extends that analysis by considering the full multiregion general equilibrium implications of such spillovers.

The chapter is planned as follows. Section II discusses multimarket effects of agricultural research. The AGE framework is introduced as a natural extension of previous multimarket approaches to assessing these effects. The merits of each approach are discussed. Section III discusses model aggregation and closure. Section IV examines the impacts of crop research with both multimarket and spillover effects. Section V examines the impacts of food processing research. Results of sections IV and V are compared to show how the size, sectoral distribution, and geographic distribution of research gains depend on the stage of production where productivity increases. Section VI examines biased technical change in the food processing sector. The assumption of factor neutrality in technical change often made in computable general equilibrium (CGE) model experiments is not an innocuous one. Changes in prices, sectoral employment, and returns to primary factor owners are highly sensitive to assumptions about the factor bias of technical change. Section VII summarizes major results and suggests directions for future experiments and analysis.

## II     Multimarket effects of agricultural research

### Vertical market linkages

Several studies have examined agricultural production as a multistage process where on-farm production is linked backward to input suppliers and forward to food processors and distributors (Alston and Scobie 1983; Freebairn, Davis, and Edwards 1982, 1983; Mullen, Wohlgenant, and Farris 1988; Mullen, Alston, and Wohlgenant 1989). These studies provide a number of insights about how returns to buyers and sellers at different stages of the production process are affected by the factor bias of technological change as well as the stage of production where innovation occurs. The literature has focused on technological change in markets vertically linked to a single processed animal product, with little attention paid to horizontal linkages to markets for other agricultural commodities or to other regions.[2]

### Horizontal market linkages

Studies of technological change in horizontally linked markets are of two types. In the first, markets for different commodities are horizontally linked when they are substitutes or complements in consumption and/or production. Not only does technological change affect production and consumption in the market where the innovation occurs, but also changes in price in the innovating market lead to changes in prices, production, and consumption in related markets. White and Araji (1991) examined horizontal linkages in the markets for beef and pork. They found that cross-market welfare effects of technological change on consumers were 15–60% as high as own-market effects, depending on which commodity experiences technological change. They also found that producer cross market effects were 37–128% of own-market effects.

The second type of study considers a single commodity in isolation but focuses on linkages between the domestic and world market for that commodity. A number of these make a stylized distinction between open and closed economies (Hayami and Ruttan 1995; de Janvry 1973; Akino and Hayami 1975; Romalho de Castro and Schuh 1977; Renkow 1994). In the open economy case, producers face an exogenous world price. Research-induced cost reductions allow domestic supplies to expand with no impact on world (and domestic) price. In the closed economy case, the commodity is assumed nontradeable and producers face a downward sloping (and usually inelastic) demand curve for crops. A basic result for this type of model is that domestic producers capture (virtually) all the gains from technical change in the open economy case; consumers are the main beneficiaries in the closed economy case. In the latter case, domestic producers may be made even worse off depending on the elasticity of demand and the type of supply curve shift assumed.

Other models employ an excess demand curve to allow domestic production to influence world and domestic price (Oehmke 1988; Edwards and Freebairn 1984; Martin and Havlicek 1977; Sarris and Schmitz 1981; Murphy, Furtana, and Schmitz 1993). The study by Martin and Alston (1994) employs the excess demand method and is rare in that it considers *both* linkages across commodity types *and* linkages between domestic and foreign markets.

*Technological spillovers*

New technologies originally developed in one country are frequently adopted in others. Thus, a country's research may lower costs of both foreign and domestic producers. Spillover benefits can be quite significant. Davis (1991) discusses cases in which spillover benefits exceed those accruing to the innovating country. This result may seem puzzling but can be explained in terms of the relative degree of specialization in production in innovating versus technology borrowing countries.[3]

Edwards and Freebairn's (1984) study was one of the first to examine spillovers for traded commodities. They consider the impact of research that lowers costs of domestically (Australian) produced goods but is also adopted by foreign producers. Research induces a downward shift in both domestic and rest of the world (ROW) supply curves for a commodity. The authors employ a linear, single-commodity trade model to examine how spillovers affect the size and distribution of welfare benefits between consumers and producers, both foreign and domestic. They find that a country's overall welfare gains from cost reductions in commodities it exports (imports) are lessened (increased) when cost reductions spill over to other regions.[4] They also find that producer gains are lessened by spillovers to other regions.

*The AGE framework*

The AGE approach is the most general framework for analysis of technological change. A multiregion AGE model includes all the types of multimarket extensions discussed above as special cases, accounting explicitly for price movements in both horizontally and vertically related markets. Edwards and Freebairn's (1984) approach to modeling spillovers is readily adaptable to an AGE application. This has a number of advantages over partial equilibrium and multimarket approaches. First, the model provides an internally consistent framework to avoid pitfalls of under- or overcounting welfare effects in a multimarket setting [see Alston (1993) for a discussion].

Second, a general equilibrium approach avoids fallacies of composition in the evaluation of the impacts of agricultural research as a whole. Most evaluations of the returns to research examine the impacts of a supply curve shift for a single commodity, holding technology, production, and prices of other commodities fixed. When evaluating impacts of pervasive technological change across multiple agricultural commodities, it is *not* valid to extrapolate from isolated partial equilibrium studies.

Third, the constant elasticity of substitution (CES)–constant elasticity of transformation (CET) specification of technology employed in AGE models provides an exact and theoretically consistent measure of producer gains to research. This is not always the case in returns to agricultural research studies that derive "approximate" welfare measures based on supply functions and supply shifts that are *ad hoc* or inconsistent with profit maximizing behavior.[5] In sum, the AGE framework helps ensure that one is modeling technology or measuring welfare in a comprehensive and theoretically consistent fashion.

Fourth, AGE models specify primary factor markets explicitly. One can thus directly examine impacts of technological change on returns to owners of land, accounting for shifts in land use and differential returns by type of land use. The AGE framework allows one to examine labor movements across sectors. Although impacts of new technologies on rural employment have long been an important policy issue (Cochrane 1958; Owen 1966; Schmitz and Seckler 1970; Brandt and French 1983), most partial equilibrium returns to research studies do not directly measure these impacts.[6]

In spite of the limitations noted above, partial equilibrium analysis of technological change can have a number of advantages over AGE analysis as well. First, there are fewer data requirements and usually more empirical estimates of parameter values and elasticities used in model calibration. Second, models can be run very quickly on small spreadsheet programs. Third, it is often easier to introduce more flexible functional forms or institutional details into simpler partial equilibrium models.

Partial equilibrium and general equilibrium analyses are complementary approaches. Partial equilibrium studies provide valuable insights about what factors (besides general equilibrium effects) matter for evaluating technological change. AGE models can provide information about when it is important to account for intersectoral feedback effects and when a simpler partial equilibrium approach is sufficient. AGE models can also be used to raise broader sets of questions than would be addressed in partial equilibrium analysis.

## III    Model aggregation and closure

Experiments in this chapter are based on a common five-commodity, six-region model using a full multiregion, general equilibrium closure. The commodity–region aggregation is shown in Table 13.1. The multiregion specification allows one to consider open economy effects of technological change. This aggregation also allows for explicit examination of the transmission of effects of technological change among crop, livestock, and processed food sectors of the economy. Crop output is an intermediate input into both livestock and food production; livestock is a major input to the processed food sector. Previous analyses of technological change in multistage production processes have focused on interactions only between the livestock and processed food sectors.

Table 13.1. *Commodity and Regional Aggregation*

| Regional Aggregation | Commodity Aggregation |
|---|---|
| **1. North America (NAM)**<br>    Canada<br>    US | **1. Crops**<br>    Paddy rice<br>    Wheat<br>    Other grains<br>    Nongrain crops |
| **2. Australasia (ANZ)**<br>    Australia<br>    New Zealand | **2. Livestock**<br>    Wool<br>    Other livestock |
| **3. European Union (EU)** | |
| **4. Southeast Asia (SEA)**<br>    Indonesia<br>    Malaysia<br>    Philippines<br>    Singapore<br>    Thailand | **3. Processed Food**<br>    Fisheries<br>    Processed rice<br>    Meat products<br>    Milk products<br>    Other food products<br>    Beverages and tobacco |
| **5. East Asia (EA)**<br>    Japan<br>    Peoples' Republic of China<br>    Hong Kong<br>    Republic of Korea<br>    Taiwan | **4. Mining & Manufactures**<br>    Forestry<br>    Coal<br>    Oil<br>    Gas<br>    Other minerals<br>    Wearing apparel<br>    Lumber and wood products<br>    Pulp, paper, and print products<br>    Petroleum and coal products<br>    Chemicals, rubber, and plastic<br>    Nonmetalic mineral products<br>    Primary iron and steel manuf.<br>    Primary nonferrous metals<br>    Fabricated metal products nec.<br>    Transport industries<br>    Other machinery and equipment<br>    Other manufacturing |
| **6. Rest of World (ROW)** | |
| | **5. Services**<br>    Electricity, gas, and water<br>    Construction<br>    Trade and transport<br>    Other services (private)<br>    Other services (government)<br>    Ownership of dwellings |

## IV    Impacts of crops research

### Focus regions

Three regions are compared: Australasia (Australia and New Zealand), North America (US and Canada), and Southeast Asia. These regions differ with respect to their trade position in crops, the elasticity of demand for their crop output, and the importance of food and agriculture in overall consumption. Table 13.2 highlights some of these differences.

**Table 13.2.** *Economic Characteristics of Three Focus Regions*

| | (ANZ) Australasia | (SEA) Southeast Asia | (NAM) North America |
|---|---|---|---|
| Crop exports / production[a] (%) | 38.3 | 16.2 | 21.6 |
| World trade share in crops[a] (%) | 11.6 | 8.6 | 33.5 |
| General equilibrium own price Demand elasticity for crops[a] | -1.6 | -0.8 | -0.8 |
| Share of crops, livestock and food in consumption budget[a] (%) | 14.1 | 34.0 | 8.4 |
| Share of labor force economically active in agriculture[b] (%) | 6.0 | 53.9 | 2.6 |

[a]  Source: GTAP data base.
[b]  Percentages are for 1988. Source: World Agricultural Trends and Indicators, 1979—89. Agricultural and Trade Analysis Division, Economic Research Service, USDA. Statistical Bulletin No. 815. All other figures are from the GTAP data base.

In Australasia, over 38% of crop production is exported. However, the region accounts for a relatively small percentage of world trade, so that the general equilibrium demand for crops is elastic (Table 13.2). North America represents a "large economy" case where production changes have more of an impact on world prices. This region's crop sector accounts for a third of world trade and faces inelastic demand for crop output. Southeast Asia produces crops primarily for domestic consumption and, like North America, faces inelastic demand for crops. It differs from the other two regions, however, in that food and agriculture account for a greater percentage of employment and consumption. Half of the labor force is economically active in agriculture; food and agricultural products account for one-third of consumption expenditures (Table 13.2).

*Experiment 1: Technical change in a single region with no spillovers*

This experiment (E1) examines the impacts of research that reduce the costs of crop production in a single region with no spillovers to other regions. In other words, other regions cannot make use of the innovating region's research results. The shock applied to the GTAP model is a 2% increase in the output augmentation parameter, *ao*, for the crops sector. The shock is applied in separate experiments to the three focus regions (ANZ, NAM, and SEA). The results of E1, E2, and E3 are presented in Tables 13.3 and 13.4. Table 13.3 presents impacts of technological change on domestic economy and global welfare. Table 13.4 presents a breakdown of impacts of technological change across region.

Table 13.3. *Impacts to Home and Other Regions of Research that Reduces Costs of Producing Crops*[a]

| | E1a ANZ (1) | E1b NAM (2) | E1c EA (3) | E2 ANZ (4) | E2 NAM (5) | E2 SEA (6) | E3a ANZ (7) | E3b NAM (8) | E3c SEA (9) |
|---|---|---|---|---|---|---|---|---|---|
| **Output**[b] *(qo)* | | | | | | | | | |
| Crops | 2.32[c] | 1.55 | 1.72 | 0.02 | -0.15 | 0.58 | -2.19 | -1.66 | -1.10 |
| Livestock | -0.04 | 0.22 | 0.59 | -0.25 | 0.04 | 0.59 | -0.23 | -0.18 | 0.00 |
| Food | 0.16 | 0.16 | 0.90 | -0.22 | 0.03 | 0.85 | -0.38 | -0.13 | -0.05 |
| Manufacturing | -0.11 | -0.05 | -0.26 | 0.20 | 0.04 | 0.07 | 0.31 | 0.08 | 0.32 |
| Services | 0.01 | 0.02 | 0.05 | 0.04 | 0.03 | 0.13 | 0.04 | 0.01 | 0.08 |
| **Output Prices**[d] *(pm)* | | | | | | | | | |
| Crops | -1.82 | -2.02 | -2.05 | -2.78 | -2.42 | -2.98 | -0.96 | -0.40 | -0.93 |
| Livestock | 0.08 | -0.64 | -0.14 | -0.57 | -0.93 | -0.75 | -0.64 | -0.29 | -0.60 |
| Food | -0.09 | -0.30 | -0.55 | -0.44 | -0.48 | -1.01 | -0.35 | -0.18 | -0.46 |
| Manufacturing | 0.06 | 0.04 | 0.07 | -0.09 | -0.03 | 0.00 | -0.15 | -0.07 | -0.07 |
| Services | 0.08 | 0.05 | 0.13 | -0.09 | -0.03 | 0.04 | -0.16 | -0.08 | -0.08 |
| **Factor Prices**[d] *(pfe)* | | | | | | | | | |
| Land in crops | 0.53 | -0.70 | -0.34 | -3.21 | -3.97 | -3.24 | -3.64 | -3.25 | -2.86 |
| Land in livestock | 0.28 | -0.25 | 0.29 | -2.04 | -2.52 | -1.81 | -2.29 | -2.26 | -2.06 |
| Wage rate | 0.10 | 0.06 | 0.22 | -0.09 | -0.01 | 0.11 | -0.18 | -0.07 | -0.11 |
| Capital | 0.09 | 0.06 | 0.21 | -0.05 | -0.03 | 0.16 | -0.14 | -0.08 | -0.05 |
| **Employment** *(qfe)* | | | | | | | | | |
| Crops | 0.38 | -0.53 | -0.39 | -2.44 | -2.56 | -2.06 | -2.74 | -2.02 | -1.65 |
| Livestock | -0.01 | 0.18 | 0.60 | -0.59 | -0.26 | 0.20 | -0.59 | -0.44 | -0.39 |
| Food | 0.15 | 0.16 | 0.89 | -0.20 | 0.02 | 0.89 | -0.36 | -0.14 | -0.01 |
| Manufacturing | -0.11 | -0.05 | -0.26 | 0.22 | 0.03 | 0.12 | 0.33 | 0.08 | 0.37 |
| Services | 0.00 | 0.02 | 0.05 | 0.06 | 0.02 | 0.18 | 0.06 | 0.00 | 0.13 |
| **Land Use** *(qfe)* | | | | | | | | | |
| Crops | 0.14 | -0.10 | -0.08 | -0.69 | -0.33 | -0.18 | -0.80 | -0.23 | -0.10 |
| Livestock | -0.11 | 0.36 | 0.56 | 0.52 | 1.17 | 1.29 | 0.60 | 0.80 | 0.72 |
| **Equivalent Variation** *(EV)* | | | | | | | | | |
| Domestic ($US m) | 199 | 2,585 | 960 | 38 | 2,745 | 886 | -157 | 180 | -57 |
| Total ($US m) | 383 | 4,548 | 1,270 | 23,401 | 23,401 | 23,401 | 23,017 | 18,974 | 22,152 |
| Domestic EV as % of total EV | 52 | 57 | 76 | | | | | | |

Note: Table column heads denote: top row-experiment; middle row-home region; Bottom row-column number.
[a] Technical change is a 2% increase in output-augmentation parameter in crops sector.
[b] All effects are to the home region unless otherwise stated.
[c] All values are percentage changes unless otherwise noted.
[d] All price changes are relative to the numeraire price of savings

**Table 13.4.** *Impacts of Crops Sector Technological Change Across Regions*

| | Region Experiencing Cost Reduction[a] | | | |
|---|---|---|---|---|
| | E1a<br><br>Australasia<br>(1) | E1b<br>North<br>America<br>(2) | E1c<br>Southeast<br>Asia<br>(3) | E2<br>All<br>Regions<br>(4) |
| **Composite Land Price (pm)** | | | | |
| **Index (% Change)** | | | | |
| North America | -0.09 | -0.60 | -0.27 | -3.65 |
| EU | -0.03 | -0.47 | -0.13 | -2.40 |
| Australasia | 0.39 | -0.75 | -0.30 | -2.54 |
| East Asia | -0.08 | -0.82 | -0.18 | -3.16 |
| Southeast Asia | -0.13 | -0.78 | -0.27 | -3.06 |
| ROW | -0.04 | -0.54 | -0.12 | -2.89 |
| **Equivalent Variation (EV)** | | | | |
| **(% Change)** | | | | |
| North America | 7 | 2585 | 17 | 2745 |
| EU | 51 | 628 | 171 | 5651 |
| Australasia | 199 | -42 | -15 | 38 |
| East Asia | 109 | 1216 | 138 | 6471 |
| Southeast Asia | 10 | 1 | 960 | 886 |
| ROW | 7 | 160 | -0 | 7610 |
| **Crop Sector Employment (qfe)** | | | | |
| **(% Change)** | | | | |
| North America | -0.06 | -0.53 | -0.18 | -2.56 |
| EU | -0.04 | -0.45 | -0.12 | -2.52 |
| Australasia | 0.38 | -0.71 | -0.34 | -2.44 |
| East Asia | -0.06 | -0.53 | -0.11 | -2.15 |
| Southeast Asia | 0.08 | -0.47 | -0.39 | -2.06 |
| ROW | -0.03 | -0.37 | -0.08 | -2.24 |
| **World Price (pw)** | | | | |
| **(% Change)** | | | | |
| Crops | -0.04 | -0.43 | -0.15 | -2.72 |
| Livestock | -0.01 | -0.18 | -0.03 | -0.64 |
| Food | -0.01 | -0.13 | -0.04 | -0.65 |

[a] Cost reduction achieved through 2% output augmenting technical change.

This 2% shock is of comparable size to the historic average annual rate of technological progress in US agriculture since the 1950s (1985; Bureau of Labor Statistics n.d.). Many other countries have maintained long-run rates of total factor productivity (TFP) growth close to 2%. Alternatively, the shock may be thought of as the rate at which crop productivity grows *relative* to other sectors. For example, in the US, TFP in agriculture has grown about 1% more per year than in other sectors over the last 15 years. Thus, the 2% productivity shock might represent the amount this productivity differential accrues over two years.

**Australasia.** A number of studies have discussed the impacts of technical change in small open economies (de Janvry 1973; Hayami and Ruttan 1985; Renkow 1994). In the stylized characterization of an open economy, producers face an exogenous world price; domestic and foreign crops, however, are perfect substitutes. Given perfectly elastic output demand, gains from innovation accrue wholly to domestic producers in the form of producer surplus.

The Australasian crop sector is similar but distinct from this stylized characterization. A relatively high percent of domestic crop production is exported (38.3%), but Australasia accounts for only about 11.6% of world crop trade. However, the Armington assumption of foreign and domestic product heterogeneity implies that output demand in the innovating sector will not be perfectly elastic, even for small suppliers of traded commodities. Therefore, welfare gains from research are not completely captured by domestic producers.

Technological change in the Australasian crop sector generates what de Janvry (1973) refers to as a "land price treadmill," in which rising returns to agricultural production are capitalized in land values. A 2% cost reduction in crop production increases crop output by more than 2% but reduces domestic crop price by less than 2%. Agricultural land values rise, with cropland prices rising more than land in livestock production. Land use and employment are shifted away from livestock production toward crop production.

There are also beneficial effects beyond the farm gate. Processed food production increases 0.16% and the associated price falls by 0.09%. Wages rise relative to prices of other purchased commodities. Consumers share gains with producers in the form of lower food prices, and labor enjoys a rising real wage.

Other regions experience significant economic gains (and losses) from innovation in Australasia. Domestic welfare, as measured by Hicksian equivalent variation, rises by over $199 million; foreign benefits are equal to $383 − $199 = $184 million (Table 13.3). Thus, Australasia captures about half of the total welfare benefits from its innovation. Innovation in Australasia has negative impacts on agricultural producers in other regions. Agricultural land prices, and hence producer surpluses, decline in all other regions (Table 13.4). Employment in the crop sector increases in Australasia, yet it declines in all other regions.

**North America.** North America represents a "large economy" case. Here production changes have more of an impact on world prices. Cost reductions of 2% in North American crop production cause world crop prices to fall 0.4% (Table 13.4). This region has a large home market for its crops, exporting less than 22% of domestic output (Table 13.2). At the same time, North America accounts for one-third of world trade in crops. The region thus faces inelastic demand for crops. In this case, technical progress in agriculture generates an "output price treadmill" (Cochrane 1958; Hayami and Ruttan 1985; de Janvry 1973). Crop prices fall more than crop output increases (Table 13.2, column 2). Revenues fall by a greater percentage than costs. The prices of land in both crop and livestock production fall. Land use is shifted out of crop production toward livestock. Labor is released from crop production and moves to other sectors. Consumer prices of food fall, and wages rise relative to the prices of purchased commodities.

Technological progress in agriculture *relative to industry* supplies more output to other sectors and "frees" labor for nonagricultural production. Owen (1966) has referred to this release of output and labor as "the double development squeeze on agriculture" and has referred to technical change in agriculture as a "dynamic intersectoral concealed and cumulative tax on agriculture" (p. 56). The decline in agricultural returns is not a result specific to the AGE framework. Rather, it has to do with the nature of the supply curve shift in the presence of inelastic demand.[7]

Technological change in North America has significant welfare implications for producers and consumers in other regions. The composite price index for land falls 0.60% in North America, and between 0.47% and 0.82% in other regions (Table 13.4). Domestic and foreign consumers are the main beneficiaries of technical change in North American crop production. World welfare increases by over $4.5 billion, but North America receives less than $2.6 billion of this total. Crop sector employment declines about half a percent across all regions. East Asia and the European Union (EU), two net crop importing regions, are both major beneficiaries of technical change in North America; however, welfare in Australasia, a crop exporter, declines.

**Southeast Asia.** Southeast Asia produces crops primarily for domestic consumption and faces inelastic demand for crops (Table 13.2). Food and agriculture account for a large share of employment and consumption compared to the other two regions. These two features result in a distinctly different outcome when crop productivity grows in this region. Specifically, a 2% growth rate increases global welfare by over $1.2 billion, with 75% of this welfare gain captured domestically. The major foreign beneficiaries in terms of equivalent variation (EV) are East Asia and the EU (Table 13.4); Australia and ROW sustain net welfare losses. The composite land price and crop sector employment fall in all regions. In Australasia and North America, these decreases are as big as in Southeast Asia itself. Domestically, crop price falls more than output expands. Labor and land shift out of crop production, and the value of land in crops falls.

Falling crop prices stimulate livestock and processed food production to a much larger extent than the other regions, with food production increasing 0.9%. In the livestock sector, both revenues and land values increase. Labor is pulled from crop and manufacturing sectors toward food and livestock production.

Technical change in crops also has a much larger positive impact on wage rates than in the other regions. Increased crop productivity raises the ratio of the wage rate to the price of processed food by 0.77%. The increase in the wage–food price ratio has important implications for the rural poor. Lower food prices have been argued to redistribute income to poor households effectively because those households spend a relatively large proportion (60–80%) of their income on food (De Franco and Godoy 1993; Lipton and Longhurst 1985; Pinstrup-Anderson 1987). Private household consumption of processed food, and manufactures and services all increases by about 0.4%.[8]

In developing countries the impact of technological change on rural households is complex. First, returns to land holders depend on what type of land they own. Average land values fall, but this average change masks differential returns to different types of land. The price of cropland *declines* by 0.34%, and the price of pasture land *rises* by 0.29%. Rising crop productivity redistributes producer surplus from owners of cropland to owners of pastureland.

Second, smaller-scale, "semisubsistence" producers in developing countries are often net suppliers of agricultural labor, net purchasers of food, and tenants rather than land owners (Hayami and Ruttan 1985; de Janvry and Sadoulet 1987; Renkow 1994). The GTAP model does not disaggregate by household type, yet the aggregate results have interesting implications for poorer rural households. The value of owned cropland and its rental price declines, and the wage–food price ratio appreciates. The results suggest that crop productivity growth can have progressive impacts on rural incomes.[9]

The case of Southeast Asia highlights how general equilibrium analysis provides results quite different from those derived from partial equilibrium analysis. Single-commodity analysis would miss the important stimulus increased crop productivity provides to the livestock and processed food sectors. It would also miss the fairly significant impacts of increased wages and growth in household consumption of nonagricultural products.

### Experiment 2: Effects of technological spillovers

This experiment (E2) considers a case in which research not only reduces costs in the innovating country, but also leads to spillovers that reduce costs in other regions. An increase in the technology augmentation parameter of 2% is equivalent to a downward shift of the unit cost function by 2%, all else equal. In E2 it is assumed that research carried out in one region reduces costs in all regions by 2%. In the terminology of Edwards and Freebairn (1984), the ratio of domestic to ROW cost reduction is 1. This is the simulation strategy employed by those authors.[10]

Alternatively, one may think of the 2% global crop productivity increase as the sum effect of all research activities. Thus, the example considers a worldwide increase in crop productivity *relative to other sectors*. The shock applied to the GTAP model is a 2% increase in the output augmentation parameter, *ao*, for the crops sectors of all six regions simultaneously. The results of global technological progress in crop production are presented in Table 13.3, columns 4–6 and in Table 13.4, column 4.

The impacts of agricultural technological progress on a global scale differ from single-country impacts in a number of important respects. Revenues for both crops and livestock fall in all regions. The movement of resources out of crop production and all agricultural sectors is more pronounced. Land shifts more toward livestock production than in E1. Labor moves out of both livestock and crop sectors in all cases. The presence of spillovers constrains domestic output expansion and makes the fall in food and agricultural prices more pronounced. Spillovers in crop research also make both domestic and foreign land holders worse off. Land in crops falls by more than 3% in the focus regions, and the price of land in livestock falls by more than 1.8% (Table 13.3). The composite price of land falls between 2.4% and 3.6% across regions (Table 13.4).

Spillovers also shift the *relative* gains of technical progress away from the innovating region and toward technology borrowing regions. Spillovers decrease *absolute* welfare gains (EV) in Australasia by over $38 million and in Southeast Asia by $886 million (Table 13.3). In North America, spillover effects actually increase EV by $744.57 million, even though returns to the farm sector decline.

Experiment E2 suggests that the major beneficiaries of pervasive increases in crop productivity are consumers in ROW followed by those in East Asia and the EU. E2 also illustrates the output price treadmill and Owen's (1966) "double development squeeze" operating on a global scale. This also highlights the dilemma of the international agricultural research system created by its very success. Agricultural productivity growth historically has been higher than in other sectors. When this occurs on a global scale, returns to agricultural asset holders decline, labor and capital move out of agriculture, and the world economy becomes less agricultural. As Timmer (1988) notes, "Technical change is also a major factor explaining the rapidly falling share of national income captured by agriculture directly" (p. 297).

E2 also has implications for standard evaluations of the international agricultural system as a whole. Such evaluations tend to survey partial equilibrium studies of impacts of research in a single commodity that suggest innovation in a single commodity increases producer surplus and draws resources into production of that commodity. E2 demonstrates that it is not valid to treat the global impacts of agricultural research as simply the sum of individual-country or -commodity impacts. When agricultural productivity grows relative to nonagriculture on a global scale, producer surplus falls and resources move out of agriculture.

*Experiment 3: Falling behind technologically*

This experiment (E3) consists of three simulations: a 2% output augmenting technical change in the crops sector of all regions except (1) Australasia, (2) North America, and (3) Southeast Asia, respectively. Here, each of the three cases in E3 is compared with E2 to examine what happens when a region does not keep up with others technologically.

**Australasia.** When Australasia keeps pace (E2) with other regions, crop output increases. When other regions increase their relative productivity, however, the region's crop, livestock, and food sectors all contract. Factor prices fall more than in E2, but output prices (particularly crop prices) fall less. Domestic crop prices fall by 1.8% in E1, by 2.8% in E2, but by only 1.0% in E3. This last result may seem counterintuitive. Wouldn't productivity increases in all regions except Australasia have more of an impact on domestic crop prices than a productivity increase in Australasia alone? If domestic and imported crops were perfect substitutes this would be true. However, the Armington assumption implies that imported and domestic crops are imperfect substitutes. Therefore, the associated prices are differentially affected by these two shocks.

When other regions improve their crop productivity relative to Australasia there are a number of negative economy-wide impacts. Domestic equivalent variation actually declines by $157 million. The wage rate also declines relative to the prices of manufactures and services, which account for a large percent of private household consumption.

**North America.** Some impacts of North America falling behind in crop productivity are similar to those in Australasia. Sectoral output and employment contract for crops, livestock, and food. Domestic equivalent variation (EV), although positive, is about $2.5 billion less than E2. Global welfare is over $5 billion less. Wages and capital rental rates fall more and food prices fall less when the region doesn't keep pace. More specifically, failure of the North American crop sector to keep pace technologically reduces returns to domestic labor and capital, reduces global welfare, and leads to relatively higher food prices. These negative consequences are external to agricultural producers, however.

The experiment provides some paradoxical results with respect to agriculture. Returns to agricultural land owners are actually higher when North American crop productivity is stagnant relative to its competitors. Also, in the North American case, more labor moves out of crop and livestock sectors in E2 than in E3. One reason for these results is the large influence North America has on the world crop prices. Additional North American output exerts a strong downward pressure on agricultural prices, revenues, and land rents.[11]

Do these results mean that stagnant productivity is good for North American farmers? Before rushing to this disturbing conclusion, a number of caveats need mentioning. First, assumptions about the Armington elasticities strongly influence overall crop price elasticities. Further sensitivity analysis is needed to test robustness of results to assumptions of import and domestic good heterogeneity. We know, for example, that the long-run elasticities will be larger, thereby increasing the chances of a decline in returns. Second, the simulations assumed that the power of subsidies to crop producers is constant. In many actual commodity programs, such as target price–deficiency payment schemes, the power of the subsidy increases endogenously to maintain producer prices.[12] Third, rural households supply labor that earns a relatively higher wage, and they purchase food that can be obtained more cheaply. Fourth, the demand elasticity for individual crops will be higher than for the aggregate crop sector.

**Southeast Asia.** When Southeast Asia falls behind technologically in crop production, wage rates fall relative to prices for manufactures and services. Domestic welfare declines by over $57 billion relative to a base of no technological change (i.e., compared to E1). Domestic welfare falls by over $940 million compared to the case of keeping pace technologically (i.e., compared to E2). As was the case with Australasia, domestic prices for crops and livestock decline more when the home region reduces costs of crop production than when all other regions reduce their costs.

## V       Impacts of food processing research

This section considers three simulations meant to examine technological competition in food processing:

- E4a: a 1% cost reduction in the North American processed food sector
- E4b: a 1% cost reduction in the processed food sector of all regions
- E4c: a 1% cost reduction in the processed food sector of all regions except North America

Based on estimates from the Bureau of Labor Statistics, the long-run annual rate of cost diminution in the US food processing sector has been about 0.6% per year since the Second World War. Thus, the 1% cost reduction in this experiment is larger than the long-run average annual rate of technological change. Technical change in the food sector has been primarily labor

**Table 13.5.** *Impacts of Research that Reduces Costs of Processed Food Production (cost reduction achieved through labor augmenting technical change)*

| Percent Cost Reduction | E4a | E4b | E4c |
|---|---|---|---|
| in North America | 1% | 1% | 0% |
| in Other regions | 0% | 1% | 1% |
| | (1) | (2) | (3) |
| **Output\* (qo)** | | | |
| Crops | 0.25 | 0.22 | -0.03 |
| Livestock | 0.56 | 0.21 | -0.34 |
| Food | 0.60 | 0.21 | -0.38 |
| **Output Prices(pm)** | | | |
| Crops | 0.09 | 0.05 | -0.03 |
| Livestock | -0.17 | -0.22 | -0.04 |
| Food | -1.05 | -1.09 | -0.04 |
| Manufacturing | 0.03 | 0.01 | -0.02 |
| Services | 0.02 | 0.00 | -0.02 |
| **Factor Prices (pfe)** | | | |
| Land in crops | 0.70 | 0.50 | -0.19 |
| Land in livestock | 0.92 | 0.50 | -0.40 |
| Labor | 0.05 | 0.03 | -0.01 |
| Capital | 0.02 | 0.00 | -0.02 |
| **Employment (qfe)** | | | |
| Crops | 0.32 | 0.26 | -0.05 |
| Livestock | 0.65 | 0.26 | -0.38 |
| Food | -2.43 | -2.81 | -0.38 |
| **Industry Demand (qf)** | | | |
| For crops by livestock sector | 0.56 | 0.21 | -0.34 |
| For crops by food sector | 0.60 | 0.21 | -0.38 |
| For livestock by food sector | 0.60 | 0.21 | -0.38 |
| **Equivalent Variation (EV)** | | | |
| Domestic ($US billions) | 4.99 | 5.08 | 0.11 |
| Total ($US billions) | 5.11 | 27.55 | 22.47 |

\* All impacts are on North America unless otherwise stated.

\* All impacts expressed in terms of percentage change except for equivalent variation.

augmenting (Lee 1986; Connor 1988). In this experiment Harrod-neutral technical change (Chambers 1988) is assumed to reduce costs by 1%.[13] The 1% cost reduction was achieved by shocking the labor augmentation parameter *afe* by 1% divided by labor's cost share in the food sector of a region. Table 13.5 shows the impacts of a 1% cost reduction in the food sector from labor augmenting technical change.

The model assumes that the elasticity of substitution between farm products (crops, livestock) and other inputs is zero in the production of processed food (although any user with access to GEMPACK could easily alter this assumption). Previous studies using multistage production models have shown that the distribution of gains from food processing research between processors, consumers and farmers is sensitive to this assumption (Alston and Scobie 1983; Holloway 1991; Mullen, Wohlgenant, and Farris 1988; Mullen, Alston, and Wohlgenant 1989). Assuming fixed proportions can overstate the benefits to farmers of certain types of processing research.

There are a number of reasons why assuming fixed proportions between farm and other inputs may not be too unreasonable. First, as Freebairn, Davis, and Edwards (1983) note, there is little in the way of econometric evidence to suggest that this elasticity differs much from zero. Second, multistage models make a number of simplifying assumptions that also affect the direction and distribution of welfare impacts that are less empirically or theoretically defensible than the fixed-proportions assumption.[14] The GTAP model is not restricted to using these other assumptions. Third, a main result of sensitivity analysis regarding the substitutability of farm products and other inputs in food processing is that farmers need not benefit from certain types of processing research. As will be shown below, the GTAP model also yields this basic result.

### Technological change in North American food processing with no spillovers

When North America is the sole innovator in processed food, then domestic food, crop, and livestock sectors all expand. Land values rise, and employment increases in the crops and livestock sectors. Labor saving technical change reduces employment in food processing by 2.4%. However, wage rates rise relative to prices of purchased commodities.

The size and distribution of research gains depend crucially on the stage of production where technical change occurs. A 2% cost reduction in North American crop production yields a domestic welfare increase of $2.58 billion and a world welfare increase of $4.55 billion (Table 13.4). About 57% of the welfare gain is captured domestically. In contrast, a 1% cost reduction in North American food production yields a domestic welfare increase of $5 billion and world welfare increase of $5.1 billion, with 98% of the welfare gain captured domestically. Increased crop productivity reduced returns to agricultural land holders, and increased food productivity increased these returns.

A 1% cost reduction in North American food production through labor augmenting technological change appears superior to a 2% cost reduction in North American crop production according to a number of criteria: (1) domestic welfare improvement, (2) global welfare improvement, (3) domestic capture of welfare gains, (4) returns to agricultural producers, (5) maintaining agricultural employment, and (6) raising the ratio of the wage rate to the price of food. Criterion (6) has distributional implications as the poor spend relatively more of their incomes on food.

Three points should be kept in mind, however. First, the comparison is between *gross* benefits of productivity increases. It says nothing about the difficulty or *cost* of achieving those increases. The postwar rate of productivity growth in food processing has been a third of that for crop production. A complete accounting of the relative benefits of each type of research is beyond the scope of this chapter (it would require estimation of the net present value of the research costs needed to achieve such productivity gains). Second, the type of technical change in food processing matters. Agricultural land holders benefit from labor augmenting technical change in food processing, but would not necessarily benefit from other types of change.[15]

The third issue has to do with technological spillovers. Spillovers from crop research could be much lower than those in food processing. Crop breeding research is often tailored to particular agro-climatic conditions. In food processing, mechanical innovations can be readily spread through technology transfer and through expansion of multinational firms. A more accurate comparison of benefits of productivity increases might be argued to be between crop productivity growth with no (or little) spillovers greater than the gross benefits of food research with significant spillovers. We turn now to this comparison.

### Technological spillovers in food processing

The impact of research that reduces unit costs of food production by 1% in North America and all other regions (E4b) is presented in column 2 of Table 13.5. Compared to the case with no spillovers (E4a): (1) North American crop, livestock, and food outputs expand less, (2) agricultural land rents and employment increase less, (3) employment in food processing declines more, (4) domestic food prices fall more, (5) domestic welfare is 3% greater, (6) world welfare is more than five times greater.

Research that reduces food processing costs 1% in all regions yields domestic welfare benefits that are nearly double those obtained from a cost reduction of 2% in crop production. Domestic EV is $5.1 billion in the former case and $2.7 billion in the latter. Global EV increases by $27 billion, with a 1% reduction in food production costs in all regions; it increases by $23 billion with a 2% cost reduction in crop production in all regions.

Spillovers in food processing to other regions reduce gains to land holders relative to what they would otherwise be. However, returns to North American land holders still increase in case E4c, and they decline with cost reductions in North American crop production. Spillovers in processing have a positive impact on overall North American welfare, even though they lessen farm sector benefits.

### Falling behind technologically in food processing

When North America falls behind technologically (E4c = Table 13.5, column 3), domestic production of crops, livestock, and food falls. Land values also fall, and labor moves out of agriculture and food processing. The gross cost of falling behind technologically in the food sector can be measured by comparing the difference in EV between cases E4c (North America keeps pace) with case E4d (all regions but North America reduce costs by 1%). When other regions reduce their costs relative to North America, the cost of falling behind is $5 billion in forgone domestic welfare. In contrast, when other regions reduce their costs of crop production by 2% relative to North America, the cost of falling behind is less than $2.6 billion.

There has been much discussion in the popular press about the need to maintain "competitiveness" as a means of preserving domestic jobs in particular sectors. Column 3 of Table 13.5 shows the case where North America has fallen behind technologically and employment in the food sector declines 0.4%. Keeping pace technologically translates into higher sectoral output but does not translate into higher sectoral employment. When domestic technology keeps pace with foreign competition (column 2, Table 13.5), wages in the whole economy and overall welfare are higher, but employment in food processing declines by 2.8%.

## VI     Biased technological change

AGE studies frequently model technical change as output augmenting and factor-neutral. Table 13.6 compares the effects of a 1% cost reduction in the North American food sector from technical change that is (E4a) labor augmenting, (E5) neutral/output augmenting, (E6) livestock augmenting, and (E7) services augmenting. For factor-biased technical change, the size of the shock was adjusted by the factor cost share to achieve equal rates of cost diminution for each of the experiments.

These experiments seek to demonstrate two points. First, the assumption of factor neutrality in technical change often made in AGE model experiments is not an innocuous one. Prices, sectoral employment, and returns to primary factor owners are sensitive to assumptions about the bias of technical change.[16] Second, increased technological efficiency in the food processing sector may not generate benefits at the farm level.

The effects of labor augmenting technical change were discussed in the previous experiment. Output augmenting technical change leads to a reduction in agricultural (crop, livestock) production and employment and a decline in land values. Livestock augmenting technical change has these same effects but the magnitude is much greater, particularly in the livestock sector. Employment in that sector falls 4.5% and the land price falls 4.8%. The demand for livestock by the food sector declines 4.7%. This has feedback effects to the crops sector, where demand for crops by the livestock sector declines by 3.9%. Increased productivity in the processing sector does not necessarily generate benefits at the farm level and can actually create welfare losses. This has

**Table 13.6.** *Impact of a 1% Cost Reduction in Processed Food Sector Coming from Different Types of Technical Change*

|  | Type of Augmenting Technical Change | | | |
|---|---|---|---|---|
|  | E4a<br>Labor | E5<br>Output | E6<br>Livestock | E7<br>Services |
| **Output** ($q$) |  |  |  |  |
| Crops | 0.25 | -0.25 | -0.65 | 0.23 |
| Livestock | 0.56 | -0.40 | -3.94 | 0.53 |
| Food | 0.60 | 0.48 | 0.38 | 0.58 |
| **Prices** ($pm$) |  |  |  |  |
| Crops | 0.09 | -0.02 | -0.22 | 0.09 |
| Livestock | -0.17 | -0.28 | -0.51 | -0.17 |
| Food | -1.05 | -1.11 | -1.12 | -1.04 |
| Manufacturing | 0.03 | 0.04 | 0.04 | 0.03 |
| Services | 0.02 | 0.03 | 0.04 | 0.03 |
| Land in crops | 0.70 | -0.55 | -2.49 | 0.66 |
| Land in livestock | 0.92 | -0.65 | -4.75 | 0.88 |
| Labor | 0.05 | 0.06 | 0.06 | 0.04 |
| Capital | 0.02 | 0.05 | 0.05 | 0.05 |
| **Employment** ($qfe$) |  |  |  |  |
| Crops | 0.32 | -0.32 | -0.94 | 0.30 |
| Livestock | 0.65 | -0.48 | -4.49 | 0.63 |
| Food | -2.43 | -0.52 | 0.38 | 0.58 |
| **Land Use** ($qfe$) |  |  |  |  |
| Crops | -0.05 | 0.02 | 0.51 | -0.05 |
| Livestock | 0.17 | -0.08 | -1.82 | 0.16 |
| **Industry Demand** ($qf$) |  |  |  |  |
| For crops by livestock sector | 0.56 | -0.40 | -3.94 | 0.53 |
| For crops by food sector | 0.60 | -0.51 | 0.38 | 0.58 |
| For livestock by food sector | 0.60 | -0.51 | -4.67 | 0.58 |
| **Equivalent Variation** ($EV$) |  |  |  |  |
| ($US million) | 4.99 | 5.11 | 5.04 | 4.57 |

important implications given that many farm producer groups impose levies on their members to fund processing research.

Services augmenting technical change simultaneously achieves the goals of increasing employment in food processing, increasing employment in agriculture, and increasing returns to agricultural land holders. However, a 1% unit cost reduction from services augmenting technical change yielded overall welfare gains (EV) of about half a billion dollars (10%) less than equal cost reductions from other types of technical change.

## VII     Conclusions

The experiments in this chapter focused on multimarket and multiregion impacts of technological change in crop and processed food production in the presence of spillovers. A five-commodity, six-region version of the GTAP model was used. Analysis concentrated on three focus regions: Australasia, North America, and Southeast Asia. Major results are summarized below.

First, multimarket effects of technological change in a single region for a single commodity were quite substantial. Foreign welfare gains from domestic cost reductions in crop production ranged from 32% to 92% of domestic gains, depending on the country. Crop cost reductions in a given region reduced agricultural land values in all other regions. Percentage changes in foreign land values were comparable and sometimes larger than changes in the innovating region.

Second, domestic impacts of technological change depend on the importance of crops in trade and the importance of crop production in the region's overall economy. Australia, a small exporting country, faces elastic demand for crops. Cost reductions in crop production increased land values and pulled resources into agriculture. North America, a large exporter, and Southeast Asia, producing primarily for domestic consumption, face inelastic demand for crops. Crop cost reductions in these regions caused agricultural land values and employment to decline. In Southeast Asia, where agriculture accounts for a larger share of employment and consumption expenditures, technological change in crop production generated important general equilibrium effects. A 2% reduction in the unit cost of crop production caused the wage–food price ratio to rise and increased private household consumption of food and manufactures and services.

The chapter examined technological spillovers following the approach of Edwards and Freebairn (1984) which assumes that cost reducing innovations in one region can be adopted by other regions. The simulations illustrated that when all other regions could reduce costs by as much as the innovating region: (1) global welfare rose more than 10 times over single-region cost reductions, (2) relative research benefits shifted away from the innovating region and toward other regions, (3) net research gains shifted from crop producers to consumers, and (4) agricultural land values decline in all regions. Also, spillovers reduced aggregate domestic welfare gains (relative to the no-spillover case) in Australasia and Southeast Asia but increased gains in North America.

Fourth, the impacts of agricultural research as a whole are quite different from the impacts of isolated changes in a single region. When global agricultural productivity grows relative to other sectors, land values fall and agricultural employment declines. Major beneficiaries of agricultural productivity growth on a global scale are consumers in the EU, East Asia, and ROW.

Fifth, the gross benefits of cost reductions in food processing are substantially larger than those for cost reductions in crop production. A 1% cost reduction in the North American food processing sector yielded $5.0 ($5.1) billion in domestic (world) welfare benefits; a 2% reduction in the North American crops sector yielded $2.6 ($4.5) billion in domestic (world) welfare benefits.[17] The costs to North America of falling behind technologically in food processing were also substantially larger than the costs of falling behind in crop production.[18] These results give cause to reiterate the point made by Freebairn, Davis, and Edwards (1982) that greater attention to research and productivity growth beyond the farm gate is warranted.

Sixth, keeping pace technologically with international competition does not necessarily maintain employment in a sector. Two cases compared what happened to domestic sectoral employment when rates of technical change varied across regions. In the first case, all regions but the home region experienced cost reductions. In the second, all regions including the home region experienced the same percentage cost reductions in a sector. In the North American and Southeast Asian crops and North American processed food sectors, more labor left those sectors when they kept pace technologically than when they did not. For the crop sectors this was due in part to the inelastic demand those sectors faced. For processed food, technological change was assumed to be labor-saving in keeping with empirical evidence (Connor 1988).

Finally, the distribution and size of returns from research were sensitive to the factor bias of technical change. Crop and livestock producers do not necessarily gain from all types of cost reductions at the food processing level. Agricultural land holders benefited from labor and services augmenting technical change, but were negatively affected by output and livestock augmenting technical change. Services augmenting technological change achieved multiple goals of raising agricultural prices and land values and increasing employment in food and agriculture sectors. However, a 1% unit cost reduction from services augmenting technological change yielded lower overall welfare gains (EV) (10% less) than equal cost reductions from other types of technical change.

The simulations presented in this chapter are meant as a pedagogical device to demonstrate potential applications of AGE models to the analysis of the size and distribution of returns to agricultural research. AGE models have been widely applied to evaluate the impacts of trade policies, tax policies, and development strategies. Technological change has generally been examined only incidentally in such studies.[19] Analyses of returns to agricultural research have increasingly recognized the importance of extending analyses of multimarket effects vertically (up and down the production chain) and horizontally (across both commodities and regions). One goal of this chapter is to present AGE models as a logical and coherent extension of these multimarket analyses.

This does *not* mean that AGE analysis of technological change is "better" than partial equilibrium analysis. Partial equilibrium studies have several advantages, which include greater ease in modeling sectoral details more explicitly, employing more flexible functional relationships, and bringing larger amounts of econometric evidence to bear on particular parametric specifications. Nevertheless, AGE models remain a little exploited tool in our tool kit to evaluate impacts of agricultural research.

The relatively general experiments presented in this chapter are meant to demonstrate the breadth of issues that may be examined in the GTAP framework. It would be interesting to pursue more precise policy analyses as extensions of this chapter. Two possibilities follow.

1. *Measurement of a general equilibrium net present value of research investment.* The current GTAP model is calibrated to 1992 world economic data. The model could be used to compute the gross research benefits from multifactor productivity growth in crop and livestock sectors from 1991 to 1992 levels attributable to research. One could then use econometric estimates of productivity-research relationships to impute a cost of achieving that level of productivity growth. Results of research costs and benefits could then be used to calculate the net present value of research investment.

2. *Evaluation of changes in agricultural price support and trade regimes on the size and distribution of research benefits.* The current model includes extensive information about subsidies and tariffs in agriculture (and other sectors). Alston, Edwards, and Freebairn (1988); Murphy, Furtan, and Schmitz (1993); Frisvold (1991), and Oehmke (1988) have discussed the theoretical implications of trade barriers and other market distortions on research gains. The model can be employed to examine how returns to research are affected by changes in trade and policy regimes. For example, how might the Uruguay Round Agreement, discussed elsewhere in this volume, affect the returns to different types of research in different regions? Of particular importance is the tariffication of nontariff barriers, which have hitherto inhibited the global transmission of price signals engendered by technological change.

In sum, the analysis of technological change using the GTAP framework is a fruitful area for future research.

## NOTES

1. Important exceptions are White and Araji (1991) and Martin and Alston (1994), which use models of two horizontally linked commodities to examine multimarket effects of research.
2. An exception is Mullen, Alston, and Wohlgenant (1989).

3. Davis (1991) cites the case of forestry research for hot subtropical desert environments, conducted in Australia. Such research is only narrowly applicable across Australian production environments but applies to "a large share of Egypt's production."
4. This result does not necessarily hold in the model presented in this chapter.
5. Log-linear models (Akino and Hayami 1995, Scobie and Posada 1978) assume supply curves pass through the origin of the price–quantity axis. This implies an underlying technology with no shutdown point for firms at any positive output price. Models with inelastic, linear supply functions imply that positive amounts of output would be supplied at nonpositive prices.
6. Schmitz and Seckler (1970) and Brandt and French (1983) do focus on employment effects.
7. For discussion of theoretical conditions and empirical examples of producers losing from technological change, see Duncan and Tisdell (1971), Lindner and Jarrett (1978), Rose (1980), Scobie and Posada (1978), and Wise and Fell (1980).
8. Domestic crop productivity growth increased private household demand for these commodities by about one-fourth as much in Australasia and North America.
9. Both de Janvry and Sadoulet (1987) and Renkow (1994) find such impacts from agricultural productivity growth in models with more disaggregation by household type.
10. Edwards and Freebairn (1984) considered a range of spillover ratios. Davis (1991) notes that interregional spillover rates can exceed unity.
11. Recall that a 2% cost reduction in North American crop production led to a 0.4% reduction in world crop prices (Table 13.4, column 2).
12. An interesting experiment would be to examine the effects of a target price–deficiency payment scheme on the size and distribution of gains and losses from technological change.
13. Harrod-neutral technical change increases the efficiency of labor inputs but leaves the efficiency of other inputs unchanged (Chambers 1988).
14. These include assumptions of (1) linearity of demand and supply functions, (2) supply functions that cut the quantity axis, and (3) parallel supply curve shifts.
15. This point is discussed in more detail in section VI.
16. Coxhead and Warr (1991) examine effects of different types of factor bias using an AGE model of the Philippines. Godoy et al. (1993) compare effects of output augmenting for food versus export commodities in Bolivian AGE.
17. Figures for gains from food research assume labor augmenting technical. However, considering other types of technological change did not alter this qualitative result.
18. The experiments to generate these results assumed that all other regions but North America experienced cost reductions of 2% for crops and 1% for food, respectively.
19. Two interesting exceptions are papers by De Franco and Godoy (1993) and Coxhead and Warr (1991).

## REFERENCES

Akino, M., and Y. Hayami (1975) "Efficiency and Equity in Public Research: Rice Breeding in Japan's Economic Development." *American Journal of Agricultural Economics* 57:1–10.

Alston, J. (1993) "Research Benefits in a Multimarket Setting: A Review," *Review of Marketing and Agricultural Economics* 39:23–52.

Alston, J., G. Edwards, and J. Freebairn (1988) "Market Distortions and the Benefits from Research." *American Journal of Agricultural Economics* 70:281–288.

Alston, J., and G. Scobie (1983) "Distribution of Research Gains in Multistage Production Systems: Comment," *American Journal of Agricultural Economics* 65:353–356.

Ball, V. E. (1985) "Output, Input and Productivity Measurement in U.S. Agriculture, 1948–79," *American Journal of Agricultural Economics* 67:475–486.

Brandt, J., and B. French (1983) "Mechanical Harvesting and the California Tomato Industry: A Simulation Analysis," *American Journal of Agricultural Economics* 65:265–272.

Bureau of Labor Statistics. *Monthly Labor Review*, various years.

Chambers, R. (1988) *Applied Production Analysis: A Dual Approach.* Cambridge: Cambridge University Press.

Cochrane, W. (1958) *Farm Prices: Myth and Reality.* Minneapolis: University of Minnesota Press.

Connor, J. (1988) *Food Processing: An Industrial Powerhouse in Transition.* New York: Lexington Books.

Coxhead, I., and P. Warr (1991) "Technical Change, Land Quality, and Income Distribution: A General Equilibrium Analysis," *American Journal of Agricultural Economics* 73:345–360.

Davis, J. (1991) "Spillover Effects of Agricultural Research: Importance for Research Policy and Incorporation in Research Evaluation Models," *ACIAR / ISNAR Project Papers.* No. 32.

De Franco, M., and R. Godoy (1993) "Potato-Led Growth: The Macroeconomic Effects of Technological Innovations in Bolivian Agriculture." *Journal of Development Studies* 29:561–587.

de Janvry, A. (1973) "A Socioeconomic Model of Induced Innovation for Argentine Agricultural Development," *Quarterly Journal of Economics* 87:410–435.

de Janvry, A., and E. Sadoulet (1987) "Agricultural Price Policy in General Equilibrium Models: Results and Comparisons," *American Journal of Agricultural Economics* 69:230–246.

Duncan, R., and C. Tisdell (1971) "Research and Technical Progress: The Returns to Producers," *The Economic Record* 47:124–129.

Edwards, G., and J. Freebairn (1984) "The Gains from Research into Tradeable Commodities," *American Journal of Agricultural Economics* 66:41–49.

Freebairn, J., J. Davis, and G. Edwards (1982) "Distribution of Research Gains in Multistage Production Systems," *American Journal of Agricultural Economics* 64:39–46.

Freebairn, J., J. Davis, and G. Edwards (1983) "Distribution of Research Gains in Multistage Production Systems: Reply," *American Journal of Agricultural Economics* 65:357–359.

Frisvold, G. (1991) "Emerging Issues in the Allocation of Public Agricultural Research Funds," *American Journal of Agricultural Economics* 73:876–881.

Hayami, Y., and V. Ruttan (1985) *Agricultural Development.* Baltimore: Johns Hopkins University Press.

Holloway, G. (1991) "Distribution of Research Gains in Multistage Production Systems: Further Results," *American Journal of Agricultural Economics* 71:338–343.

Lee, D. (1986) "Interindustry Productivity Changes in U.S. Food Manufacturing, 1958–82," unpublished manuscript; Department of Agricultural Economics, Cornell University, Ithaca, NY, October.

Lindner, R., and F. Jarrett (1978) "Supply Shifts and the Size of Research Benefits," *American Journal of Agricultural Economics* 60:48–58.

Lipton, M., and R. Longhurst (1985) *Modern Varieties, International Agricultural Research, and the Poor.* Washington, DC: The World Bank.

Martin, M., and J. Havlicek (1977) "Some Welfare Implications of the Adoption of Mechanical Cotton Harvesters in the United States," *American Journal of Agricultural Economics* 59:739–744.

Martin, W., and J. Alston (1994) "A Dual Approach to Evaluating Research Benefits in the Presence of Trade Distortions," *American Journal of Agricultural Economics* 74:26–35.

Mullen, J., J. Alston, and M. Wohlgenant (1989) "The Impact of Farm and Processing Research on the Australian Wool Industry," *Australian Journal of Agricultural Economics* 33:32–47.

Mullen, J., M. Wohlgenant, and D. Farris (1988) "Input Substitution and the Distribution of Surplus Gains from Lower Beef Processing Costs," *American Journal of Agricultural Economics* 70:245–254.

Murphy, J., W. Furtan, and A. Schmitz (1993) " The Gains from Agricultural Research Under Distorted Trade," *Journal of Public Economics* 51:161–172.

Norton, G., and J. Davis (1981) "Evaluating Returns to Agricultural Research: A Review," *American Journal of Agricultural Economics* 63:685–699.

Oehmke, J. (1988) "The Calculation of Returns to Research in Distorted Markets," *Agricultural Economics* 2:291–302.

Owen, W. (1966) "The Double Developmental Squeeze on Agriculture," *American Economic Review* 56:43–70.

Pinstrup-Andersen, P. (1987) "Macroeconomic Adjustment Policies and Human Nutrition: Available Evidence and Research Needs," *Food and Nutrition Bulletin* 9:69–86.

Renkow, M. L. (1994) "Technology, Production Environment, and Household Income: Assessing the Regional Impacts of Technological Change," *Agricultural Economics* 10:219 196–231.

Romalho de Castro, J., and G. E. Schuh (1977) "An Empirical Test of an Economic Model for Establishing Research Priorities: A Brazil Case Study." In T. Arndt, D. Dalrymple, and V. Ruttan (eds.), *Resource Allocation and Productivity in National and International Agricultural Research*. Minneapolis: University of Minnesota Press.

Rose, R. (1980) "Supply Shifts and the Size of Research Benefits: Comment," *American Journal of Agricultural Economics* 62:834–844.

Ruttan, V. (1987) "Future Research Evaluation Needs," *Evaluating Agricultural Research and Productivity*, miscellaneous publication 52-1987, Minnesota Agricultural Experiment Station, University of Minnesota.

Sarris, A., and A. Schmitz (1981) "Toward a U.S. Agricultural Export Policy for the 1980s," *American Journal of Agricultural Economics* 63:832–839.

Schmitz, A., and D. Seckler (1970) "Mechanized Agriculture and Social Welfare: The Case of the Tomato Harvester," *American Journal of Agricultural Economics* 52:569–577.

Scobie, G., and R. Posada (1978) "The Impact of Technical Change on Income Distribution: The Case of Rice in Colombia," *American Journal of Agricultural Economics* 60:85–91.

Timmer, C. P. (1988) "The Agricultural Transformation." In H. Chenery and T. N. Srinivasan (eds.), *Handbook of Development Economics*. Amsterdam: North-Holland.

USDA, Economic Research Service (1990) *World Agricultural Trends and Indicators, 1979–89*. Statistical Bulletin No. 815.

White, F., and A. Araji (1991) "Multimarket Effects of Technological Change," *Review of Agricultural Economics* 13:99–107.

Wise, W., and E. Fell (1980) "Supply Shifts and the Size of Research Benefits: Comment," *American Journal of Agricultural Economics* 62:838–840.

PART IV
EVALUATION OF GTAP

# Historical analysis of growth and trade patterns in the Pacific Rim: An evaluation of the GTAP framework

*Mark J. Gehlhar*

## I    Introduction and overview

The product of many model building exercises is often seen as simply another economic model to add to a collection rather than the birth of an important tool capable of generating better information for answering economic questions. The concern that most modeling activity is conducted primarily for the benefit of the economic modeler has been expressed frequently (Dee 1994). Much attention is focused on modeling activity rather than on results generated from models. Are the results generated from applied general equilibrium models (AGE) to be taken seriously? This chapter argues that if results from AGE analyses are to gain greater credibility, further work on model validation is required.

There are many reasons for the current level of skepticism surrounding large-scale modeling efforts. In operationalizing such models, one is required to make many assumptions regarding the data base, behavioral equations, and parameters. This opens AGE-based research to widespread criticism. AGE modelers may find most of these assumptions to be necessary and defensible, yet this provides little assurance of results to consumers – especially those who are already skeptical of large-scale modeling. This author believes that evaluation of a model, solely via the scrutiny of its assumptions, is not a very useful exercise. Of more interest to consumers of AGE results is whether or not a model is capable of producing a proven set of results deemed accurate and reliable. This depends not only on the theoretical assumptions underlying the model, but also on the parameters, data base, and closure employed. Therefore, research aimed at evaluating models based on their predictive performance seems well placed. However, only a few such validation attempts have been made (Kehoe and Sancho 1991; Parmenter, Meagher, and Higgs 1993). The purpose of this chapter is to assess the predictive capability of the

Global Trade Analysis Project (GTAP) modeling framework by performing a "backcasting" exercise.

Despite widespread interest among AGE modelers in issues of computational methods, it is important to bear in mind that this validation exercise is not primarily related to the nature of the computational method employed [see Hertel, Horridge, and Pearson (1992) for a discussion of the latter issue]. In this exercise we seek to test for the economic truthfulness of results as opposed to the mathematical accuracy of solutions alone. Mathematical accuracy of a solution is a necessary, but not a sufficient, condition for obtaining meaningful economic results. Any synthesized data base and fictitious behavioral equations can be used to for testing solution accuracy but would be futile in testing for economic truthfulness.

By performing a "backcasting" exercise, we can evaluate the modeling framework, taken as a whole. If, for instance, the data are regarded as superior but the behavioral equations are poorly specified, the overall performance is likely to be poor. Similarly, good theory combined with poor data is unlikely to bear much empirical fruit. Nothing short of full-blown model simulation, compared with observed outcomes, can provide an assessment of the combined performance of theory data parameter and closure.

Backcasting is a common means of model validation. The advantage of this approach is that the exogenous variables upon which the AGE predictions are conditioned are known. This means that one can focus efforts on how well the model itself performs when compared to the historical record. Choosing an appropriate historical event for comparing model results is critical for this exercise. Since the GTAP model is based on standard, neoclassical theory, it makes sense to choose a backcasting challenge that this theory is capable of explaining. Some historical events are a direct result of rational economic behavior; however, noneconomic events can influence economic variables as well. Embargos, economic sanctions, and catastrophic events such as wars and natural disasters are examples of events not suitable for replication.

Since backcasting requires a complete profile of exogenous shocks and their endogenous consequences, it is difficult to apply this method to specific policy changes. It is often difficult to establish exactly when the policy was announced and when the effects fully materialized [see Kehoe and Sancho (1991) for an exception]. There is also the problem of disentangling these effects from those of other policies. Therefore, this chapter does not focus on policy shocks.

A more obvious economic event is that of growth and structural change in production, consumption, and trade. The fast growing East Asian countries provide the best examples of this type of economic shock. Growth-related changes tend to dominate all other changes for countries in this region, and this process appears to conform well with standard neoclassical growth theory

(Young 1994). It is this growth process for which we choose to perform a historical backcasting exercise of the GTAP model. Starting with the GTAP data base for 1992, a backcasting experiment is conducted whereby individual regions in the model are shocked such that the endowment levels are returned to their original, 1982 levels. The model adjusts to these new endowment levels such that all factor and output markets clear and a new equilibrium is found. The new equilibrium is postulated to depict the 1982 state of the world economy. The difference in export value shares from 1982 to 1992 are calculated and compared with historical changes in these shares in order to evaluate how well the standard GTAP model predicts the dramatic changes in trade composition over this period.

Because of the importance of human capital in the growth of East Asian economies, a modified model is also explored in this chapter. This modified model includes both raw labor and human capital as factors of production. As such, it represents a departure from the structure laid out in Chapter 2.

## II        Historical patterns of growth and trade in East Asia

Much attention has been given to the unprecedented growth that has occurred recently in East Asia. The economies of this region often are referred to collectively as the "growth center of the world." Unlike other parts of the world, these economies continued to grow through the oil crises of the 1970s and the world economic recession in the early 1980s. The dynamic structural changes that occurred in fast growing countries of East Asia have been clearly revealed through an analysis of input–output (IO) tables sponsored by the Institute of Developing Economies (IDE) in Tokyo (Furukawa and Inomata 1993). By making comparisons across different time periods using an international IO system, the dynamics of growth could be observed and analyzed. Specifically, this study examined the changes in bilateral trade, the extent to which developing countries are dependent on foreign inputs of capital goods, the destinations of final demands, and the changing structure of domestic production and trade. In the case of the East Asian developing countries, they relied heavily on foreign inputs for their manufacturing sectors, importing massive amounts of capital goods from the US, Japan, and Europe.

In general, standard trade and development theory (Chenery, Robinson, and Syrquin 1986) suggests that a poor country opening to trade tends to specialize in the export of primary products, although less so the more densely populated the country. If its domestic incomes grow more rapidly than the rest of its partners', production will gradually switch away from primary products to manufactures. The manufactured goods initially exported will be more labor-intensive the more resource-poor or densely populated the country. Since many textile and clothing production activities tend to be intensive in the use of unskilled labor, they would be among the items initially exported by a newly industrializing, densely populated country. In more developed countries where physical capital and human capital are relatively more abundant, real wages tend to be higher, shifting comparative advantage away from labor-intensive sectors. This is indeed the succession of economic activity that is observed among the East Asian countries.

Thailand provides a good example. Historically this country exported primary and agricultural products derived from its rich natural resources. However, as wage rates rose in the newly industrialized economies such as Korea and Taiwan, Thailand gained comparative advantage in light manufactures. The textile and clothing industry became particularly important during the 1980s. Indeed, exports of these products grew so rapidly during this period that they became the country's largest source of foreign exchange earnings. Both Indonesia and the Philippines experienced similar changes during this period. In Indonesia, the decline of world oil prices created strong pressures for structural adjustment in which the primary products sector shrank and light manufacturing grew rapidly.

These developments in Southeast Asia have been mirrored by changes in the more industrialized economies of Taiwan and Korea. The latter have shown declines in the exports of clothing and textiles, with large gains in machinery and equipment. Light manufacturing's share of exports has been rising in the lower-income developing countries, and falling in Korea and Taiwan. In Indonesia, the share of light manufactures was only 2.6% in 1982, but this rose sharply over the ensuing decade, reaching 22.5% in 1992. Throughout the late 1960s and 1970s, light manufactures share had been rising in Korea and Taiwan, but this took a sudden turn downward in the late 1970s. For Taiwan, the share of light manufactures dropped from 32.4% in 1982 to 22.1% in 1992; however, in Thailand the share increased from 11.4% in 1980 to 18.5% in 1992.

Other trends are common to all these East Asian economies. For example, they all expanded their share of machinery, vehicles, and equipment exports over this period. This sector, consisting mainly of differentiated, high-tech finished goods, has been rapidly expanding in the newly industrializing countries. It consisted of only 6.4% of Thailand exports in 1982, but in 1992 it rose to 23.9%. Conversely, agriculture's share of exports for all countries in this region fell during the 1980s. The relative decline in agriculture has traditionally been linked to demand-side factors; however, empirical evidence suggests that factor accumulation and the resulting supply-side pressures may also be important (Martin and Warr 1993; Gehlhar, Hertel, and Martin 1994). These same supply-side forces help explain the extraordinary growth of manufactures in East Asian countries. In addition to factor accumulation, some argue that it was these countries' outward orientation of trade policy, leading to scale economies and improved efficiencies, that generated rapid expansion in manufacturing exports.

What is the primary source of this growth, and can it be accurately represented in the GTAP model? Young (1994) provides compelling evidence on this issue by performing a detailed analysis of historical output growth, factor accumulation, and productivity growth. He concludes that neoclassical theory is well equipped to explain this growth. Specifically, he shows that the combination of factor accumulation, rising labor participation rates, new investment, higher education, and intersectoral transfers of labor out of agriculture to other sectors explain almost all of East Asia's growth in the last two decades. In light of Young's conclusions, it would seem that this provides an ideal situation for conducting a historical validation exercise using GTAP.

It is important to realize that for growth and structural change to occur, appropriate primary factor inputs must be supplied and a demand for output must also exist. Park (1993) summarizes the importance of human capital, stating:

> All the discussion about building of an export base, technological absorptive capacity as well as industrialization in general, seems to revolve around the role of one obvious but all-important factor, namely human capital. Cheap labor alone is not enough. What gives a country its competitive edge is the quality of its labor. Nothing matters more than education. In this regard, it must be recognized that what gives developing countries a potential edge is not cheap unskilled labor, but a skilled workforce, that is managers, professionals, engineers, technicians, scientists and even bureaucrats who are relatively cheap compared to those in developed countries. (p. 57)

For this reason we also explore a modification to the standard GTAP model and data base to break out of human capital as a separate factor of production, thereby enhancing the model's ability to predict the historical changes in trade patterns.

## III    Aggregation of sectors and countries

For purposes of this validation exercise, the 37 GTAP sectors were aggregated into 10 sectors based on similarities in factor shares and similarities of sectoral characteristics (see Table 14.1 for a complete listing of sectors used in this aggregation). Agriculture (AGR) consists of paddy rice, wheat, other grains, nongrain crops, wool, and other livestock. Processed agricultural sectors (PAG) consist of processed rice, meat products, milk products, other food products and beverages, and tobacco. Although processed agriculture does not have to compete for land, its growth is heavily dependent on growth of domestic agriculture, which comprises a large share of intermediate inputs. The other

**Table 14.1.** *Industry/Commodity Grouping*

| Aggregate Groups | Original GTAP Industries |
|---|---|
| **1. Agriculture (AGR)** | |
| | Paddy rice |
| | Nongrain crops |
| | Wheat |
| | Grains, other than wheat & rice |
| | Wool |
| | Other livestock products |
| **2. Processed agriculture (PAG)** | Fisheries |
| | Processed rice |
| | Meat products |
| | Milk products |
| | Other processed food |
| | Beverages and tobacco |
| **3. Fuels and minerals (FMN)** | Coal |
| | Oil |
| | Gas |
| | Petroleum and coal products |
| | Other minerals |
| **4. Clothing and textiles (CTX)** | Textiles |
| | Wearing apparel |
| **5. Other light manufactures (OLT)** | Leather goods |
| | Lumber and products |
| | Pulp paper |
| | Paper and printing |
| | Other manufacturing |
| **6. Chemicals (CHM)** | Chemicals, rubber, and plastic products |
| **7. Machinery-equipment-vehicles (MEV)** | Transport equipment |
| | Machinery and equipment |
| **8. Basic manufactures (BAM)** | Primary iron and steel |
| | Nonferrous metals |
| | Fabricated metal products |
| **9. Nontraded services (NSV)** | Electricity, gas and water |
| | Construction |
| | Ownership of dwellings |
| **10. Traded services (TSV)** | Trade and transport |
| | Other services (private) |
| | Other services (government) |

primary goods sector is fuels and minerals (FMN), which consists of coal, oil, gas, other minerals, and petroleum and coal products.

From the 14 GTAP manufacturing sectors, 5 aggregates were created. These sectors include clothing and textiles (CTX), other light manufactures (OLT), chemicals (CHM), machinery equipment and vehicles (MEV), and basic manufactures (BAM). Of the 6 GTAP service sectors, 2 aggregates were

Table 14.2. *Shocks Used in the Backcasting: Cumulative (reversed) Growth, 1992—1982. (% changes)*

| Regions | Population (1) | Labor Force (2) | Human Capital (3) | Physical Capital (4) |
|---|---|---|---|---|
| US & Canada | -9.03 | -10.87 | -37.64 | -24.60 |
| EU | -3.07 | -8.06 | -34.98 | -23.20 |
| Japan | -4.82 | -7.84 | -41.66 | -41.66 |
| Korea | -10.77 | -20.82 | -67.20 | -66.17 |
| Taiwan | -11.38 | -21.10 | -61.20 | -54.09 |
| Malaysia | -21.51 | -24.10 | -73.04 | -54.66 |
| Thailand | -15.02 | -16.05 | -73.18 | -56.18 |
| Indonesia | -17.25 | -21.56 | -67.57 | -59.14 |
| Philippines | -20.21 | -21.13 | -48.31 | -28.95 |
| ROW | -17.70 | -17.70 | -26.00 | -26.01 |

Sources: Columns 1 and 2: Urban and Nightingale (1993); column 3: Nehru, Swanson, and Dubey (1993); column 4: Nehru and Dhareshwar (1993).

created. These include nontraded (i.e., lightly traded) services (NSV) and traded services (TSV).

Individual countries have grown at different rates, and relative factor proportions have varied across countries. Therefore, the regional aggregation scheme has identified seven *individual* East Asian countries and three regional aggregates. The countries and regions are listed in Table 14.2. Evaluation of results will focus on the six rapidly growing countries in East Asia, where growth-related changes in trade patterns are most obvious. These countries include South Korea, Taiwan, Malaysia, Thailand, Indonesia, and the Philippines. Changes in the composition of export shares are analyzed for these individual countries from 1982 to 1992.

## IV    Modifying the standard GTAP model

In this analysis, an alternative variant of the standard model is also used to shed additional light on directions for improvement of the standard model. This involves a slight alteration in the model's production structure and data base. The standard GTAP model contains only three primary factors of production (agricultural land, labor, and capital). For reasons given above, it is believed that disaggregation of the labor input is important. In fact, some users of the GTAP model/data base have already made such alterations and have found it quite important for their specific applications (McDougall and Tyers 1994; Zhi 1994). Likewise, for this particular application, where attention is focused on sectoral growth and trade, it is also believed that multiple labor types is a critical factor influencing the outcome of a growth shock. To do a thorough job incorporating such information in a multicountry / sector model is a daunting task given the enormous data requirements. As of now, the task is not fully completed. Nevertheless, with the available data one can make a fairly reasonable first cut at the problem.

Labor is broken into two components: human capital and raw labor. Human capital is distinguished from raw labor because of its capability in generating nonrepetitive activity such as strategic decision making, conceptualizing new ideas, and generation of knowledge. Such activity cannot be replicated by nonhuman factors of production, namely physical capital. Raw labor, however, is capable of generating only recurrent or repetitive activity, which technically can be replicated by nonhuman factors of production. This description of human capital follows closely that of Romer (1990). It is the key input to research and development, generating new ideas and products. Countries with greater human capital stocks are capable of introducing more new products, which in turn helps foster growth. Sound empirical evidence shows the importance of human capital and its contribution to growth in cross-country studies (Barro 1991). Individual sectors have different input requirements for human capital, and this factor input adds a new dimension to sectoral differentiation in the model. For example, high-tech or knowledge-intensive manufacturing requires a greater share of human capital than does the assembly of wearing apparel.

Implementation of this particular modification in the standard GTAP model requires an appropriate behavioral specification in the production structure and an appropriate labor payment split between raw labor and human capital. Here it is assumed that human capital and physical capital are complementary inputs (Griliches 1969; Fallon and Layard 1975; Rice 1989). Specifically, these two inputs are nested at the bottom of the CES production function with very limited substitutability ($\sigma = 0.1$). Labor and composite capital (physical and human capital) are substituted in the same manner as in the standard model. This alternative specification is easily implemented via modification of the standard GTAP model. The stock of human capital for individual countries is adopted from Nehru, Swanson, and Dubey (1993), where human capital is measured as an educational stock embodied in the labor force. Since human capital is, by definition, capable of generating critical knowledge and ideas, the stock of tertiary education is the most appropriate proxy for this input. This is believed to be particularly useful in gauging a country's level of development and changes in the stock of its talented professionals.[1] The latter are critical for growth analyses.

In order to split labor payments in the GTAP model, we would ideally like to have data on educational levels and occupation, wage rates, and sector of employment for all labor force participants in the world at a single point in time. Since such data are unavailable, compromises were necessary. In particular, those countries with available data were used as representative members of three types of countries: industrialized, newly industrialized, and developing countries.[2] Data from the US served as representative of industrialized countries. For the US, information on occupational employment by industry and wages and salaries was used to establish the labor shares, by sector. Payments to human capital consist of payments to professionals, paraprofessionals, and technical workers. As stated by the Occupational Employment Statistics Survey, this group of individuals requires substantial educational preparation at the university and postgraduate levels. The largest concentration of this group was found in electrical equipment and machines and transportation equipment industries. Given the high level of product innovations and research and development activity required in these industries, it is not surprising that this sector requires a high share of well-trained individuals. Similar data was also available for Hong Kong (newly industrialized) and China (developing).

Having established employment shares for developed countries, newly industrializing countries, and developing countries, we combined this information with country-specific wage data to convert quantity shares into value shares for countries other than the representative regions. On *value share* basis, machinery, equipment, and vehicles (MEV) is consistently more knowledge-intensive or human capital–intensive than other manufacturing sectors, and clothing and textiles (CLT) is consistently more labor-intensive than all other manufacturing sectors.

## V    Experimental design

The objective of this chapter is to determine to what extent the past is reproducible by the GTAP model. Specifically, can GTAP reproduce the trade patterns as they appeared in 1982, using the 1992 data base as a starting point? Because GTAP is not a growth model, it cannot endogenously determine changes in physical capital, labor force, population, or total factor productivity over time. Therefore, estimates of all relevant growth statistics must be obtained outside the GTAP framework. In particular, four variables must be shocked in this backcasting exercise: population, labor force, human capital, and physical capital. The associated shocks for each country/region over the 1992–1982 period are shown in Table 14.2. Two important assumptions are made in this experiment. First, land is assumed to be in fixed supply between 1982 and 1992. Second, the *ad valorem* equivalent level of policy interventions is left unchanged. That is, lacking further information, we are forced to assume that policy changes produced negligible effects in trade patterns during this period of time.

All regions in the world must be shocked by their corresponding endowment change for the time period. Therefore, it is important to obtain cross-country growth–based rates on the same methodology and definitions. This helps to avoid the problem of obtaining inconsistent or biased growth statistics. (Growth statistics obtained from various single-country studies employing different methodologies would be clearly inappropriate.)

The term "physical capital" is taken in this study to refer to goods that are fixed, tangible, durable, and reproducible. This definition is consistent with the UN classification of gross fixed capital formation. It rules out a country's financial assets (because they are intangible) and natural resources (which are nonreproducible). The estimates of changes in physical capital stocks between 1982 and 1992 were taken from Nehru and Dhareshwar (1993) for all countries in the model. The shocks to human capital were taken from the estimates made by Nehru, Swanson, and Dubey (1993). Specifically, this is a measure of the change in education stock contained in the labor force for individual countries. Shocks for population and labor force were obtained from Urban and Nightingale (1993). Changes in population are directly related to changes in labor force, but differences exist due to demographic changes.

Four experiments are conducted in this exercise. The first (E1a) is a growth experiment with the standard GTAP data base and model with all parameters set at their original values. The second (E1b) is conducted with the standard data base and model, but with the trade elasticities raised by 20% of their original values. This tests the hypothesis that the current Armington elasticities are too small for a 10-year simulation and therefore restrict the trade pattern changes. The third experiment (E2a) uses a data base that breaks out the human capital component in labor. As noted above, human capital is believed to be a factor input that is important in the growth of sophisticated manufactures. Finally, the forth experiment (E2b) uses the combination of both the labor split and the larger trade elasticities.

## VI     Results

The top entries in Table 14.3 (all countries), provide a summary constructed by pooling the results produced from the backcasting exercise for all countries. Because there are 6 individual countries and 7 sectors used in this analysis, there are a total of 42 observations for each experiment. These are used to calculate the statistics found in Table 14.3. Each observation is an export share change calculated by taking the difference between the 1992 value and the 1982 value. Of importance for this analysis is the extent to which the predicted changes produced from the GTAP model correspond to the actual changes that took place in history. We examine two measures of the strength of the relationship between the predicted and actual results. The first is the coefficient of simple correlation. This provides an indication of how well the GTAP model tracks the *direction* of historical change, and is reported in the first pair of columns in Table 14.3. The closer the statistic comes to 1.0, the stronger the correlation is between actual

Table 14.3. *Relationship Between Predicted and Actual Changes in Export Shares*

| Country | Correlation | | Slope | |
|---|---|---|---|---|
|  | Exa[a] | Exb[b] | Exa | Exb |
| **All Countries** |  |  |  |  |
| 1[c] | .71 | .72 | .18 | .21 |
| 2[d] | .77 | .78 | .48 | .55 |
| **Thailand** |  |  |  |  |
| 1[c] | .87 | .88 | .14 | .14 |
| 2[d] | .95 | .96 | .83 | .94 |
| **Malaysia** |  |  |  |  |
| 1[c] | .95 | .95 | .18 | .21 |
| 2[d] | .97 | .97 | .85 | .95 |
| **Philippines** |  |  |  |  |
| 1[c] | .95 | .95 | .23 | .27 |
| 1[d] | .78 | .80 | .31 | .37 |
| **Indonesia** |  |  |  |  |
| 1[c] | .66 | .68 | .19 | .22 |
| 1[d] | .64 | .65 | .13 | .15 |
| **Korea** |  |  |  |  |
| 1[c] | .48 | .54 | .30 | .54 |
| 1[d] | .85 | .85 | .32 | .36 |
| **Taiwan** |  |  |  |  |
| 1[c] | .85 | .82 | .13 | .14 |
| 1[d] | .83 | .84 | .16 | .17 |

[a] The results in this column refer to experiments using the standard trade elasticities.
[b] The results in this column refer to results based on increased trade elasticities.
[c] The results in this row are based on the standard GTAP model.
[d] The results in this row are based on the human capital-augmented model.

and predicted changes. Overall the model performs fairly well in this regard. Of the four experiments, 2b shows the highest correlation of 0.78. This suggests that by adopting a labor split with human capital as a component (experiments 2a and 2b), overall results improve. There is also some indication of a small improvement in the correlation results by increasing the trade elasticities in the GTAP model (experiments 1b and 2b).

The measure of responsiveness of model results, relative to actual changes, is summarized in the slope coefficient reported in the second column of Table 14.3. It represents the coefficient when model predictions are regressed on actual changes. An estimated value of 1 indicates that the magnitude of change in the predicted and actual change is equal. This is an ideal outcome. However, all the slope parameters are less than 1, indicating that the actual changes are consistently greater than the predicted changes. That is, the model is *underpredicting* changes in export shares in East Asia over this period. Like the correlation statistic, there is an improvement, as reported over all countries, by increasing the trade elasticities or making a labor split in the data base. For the standard model, the results appear quite unsatisfactory. The predicted changes are significantly lower than the actual changes, as indicated by the very low slope parameter.

The next part of Table 14.3 displays statistics of the four experiments on a country-by-country basis. This table is helpful for evaluating each individual country's performance in the backcasting experiment. Although the results vary across countries, evidence suggests that the modified version of the model does improve predictive capability. Predictions for some of the Association of South East Asian Nations (ASEAN) countries that were known to have inherent stability in their historical growth patterns performed modifications. Of these, Malaysia and Thailand showed most improvement using the alternative model specification. For Thailand the slope coefficient was 0.14 using the standard model, but it increased to 0.94 using the modified model in conjunction with the increased trade elasticities. Malaysia showed similar improvements in this regard. Korea, Taiwan, and the Philippines also showed some signs of improvement over the standard model predictions either in terms of the slope or correlation coefficients.

Since Indonesia underwent the most radical structural change of any of the countries over this period, it is not surprising that the results are relatively poor. During the period 1982–1992 there was a sudden surge in Indonesian exports of light manufactures, textiles, and wearing apparel that the GTAP model was unable to predict given the very small base it started with in the early 1980s. Many other factors besides factor accumulation contributed to Indonesia's rapid structural change during this period, including a rapid deterioration in oil prices, which is not built into the exogenous shocks to the model.

Overall, the above results suggest that the standard GTAP model has some information content that is relevant to the East Asian experience. This is indicated by the correctness in the *direction of change* of the predicted shares. But the results also point out that the model is missing important economic information pertinent to the evolution of Pacific trade over the 1980s. The sharp improvements in the results generated by the modified version of the GTAP model suggest that separating labor into two components should be a high priority in future work.

## VII    Conclusions

This chapter made three distinct contributions. First, it provided a basic methodology for performing validation exercises with the GTAP model. Second, based on this validation effort, it identified some deficiencies in the standard GTAP model. Third, it tested an extension of the standard model and suggested directions for future improvements in the framework.

Economists will always have to make assumptions in the model-building process, and in doing so they will inevitably face criticism of their decisions. However, it is impossible to evaluate the quality of an empirical model, based solely on its assumptions. In particular, one cannot distinguish the "bad" assumptions from the "not so bad" ones because of the difficulty in determining the effects of the assumptions on the overall results. In this chapter new assumptions were added to an existing model. Like any others, these assumptions are fair game for criticism. The key point is that these new assumptions were evaluated in light of the predictions from the two alternative models. In this case, evidence was produced showing that the new assumptions were indeed beneficial.

Specifically it was shown that by breaking labor into two components–raw labor and human capital–and assuming that capital and human capital are complementary inputs, significantly better predictions in East Asian export share changes could be obtained. It is a fact that human capital accumulation has been an important component in the industrialization of the fast growing East Asian economies. Some sectors are more dependent on this input than others. It is this very information that is missing from the standard GTAP model. However, it cannot be said that the newly created labor share splits are factual themselves. This is because comparable data were not obtained for all countries in the world. This can be rightly criticized. Nevertheless, its addition did result in improved model performance. I believe that the AGE field would benefit significantly from more of this type of model enhancing (as opposed to model building) activity, in conjunction with well-defined validation exercises.

## NOTES

1. This should not suggest that all professionals necessarily make a contribution to growth but that human capital critical for growth is primarily concentrated among professionals within the labor force. Evidence exists suggesting that countries with a higher proportion of engineering college majors grow faster and are strongly positively correlated with investment in physical and human capital, but countries with a higher proportion of law graduates grow more slowly (Murphy, Shleifer, and Vishny 1991).
2. The method and data sources were adopted from Zhi, 1994. Sources include the "U.S. Occupational Employment Statistics Survey (OES) 1990," "Yearbook of Labor Statistics 1992," published International Labor Office, Geneva, and "Hong

Kong 1991 Employment in Manufacturing and other Industries by Major Occupational Group" published by Hong Kong Population Census 1991.

## REFERENCES

Anderson, K. (1987) "On Why Agriculture Declines with Economic Growth," *Agricultural Economics* 1(3):195–207.

Barro, R. J. (1991) "Economic Growth in a Cross Section of Countries," *The Quarterly Journal of Economics* CVI Issue 2, May.

Chenery, H., S. Robinson, and M. Syrquin (1986) *Industrialization and Growth: A Comparative Study.* Oxford: Oxford University Press.

Dee, P. (1994) "General Equilibrium Models and Policy Advise in Australia," paper presented at the IFAC Workshop on Computing in Economics and Finance, Amsterdam.

Fallon, P. R., and G. Layard (1975) "Capital-Skill Complementarity Income Distribution, and Output Accounting," *Journal of Political Economy* 83(2):279–301.

Furukawa, S., and S. Inomata (1993) "Significance of Construciton and Analysis of International Input-Output Tables of Asia Pacific Region." In T. Sano and C. Tamamura (eds.), *International Industrial Linkages and Economic Interdependency in Asia-Pacific Region.* Toyko: Institute of Developing Economies.

Gehlhar, M. J., T. W. Hertel, and W. Martin (1994) "Economic Growth and the Changing Structure of Trade in the Pacific Rim," *American Journal of Agricultural Economics* 76(5):1101–1110.

Griliches, Z. (1969) "Capital-Skill Complementarity," *Review of Economics and Statistics* 51(4):465–468.

Hertel, T. W., J. M. Horridge, and K. R. Pearson (1992) "Mending the Family Tree: A Reconciliation of the Linearization of Levels Schools of Applied General Equilibrium Modeling," *Economic Modeling* 9:385–407.

Kehoe, T., and F. Sancho (1991) "An Evaluation of the Performance of an Applied General Equilibrium Model of the Spanish Economy," Working Paper 480, Federal Reserve Bank of Minneapolis.

Leamer, E. (1984) "Paths of Development in the Three-Factor, *n*-Good General Equilibrium Model," *Journal of Political Economy* 95(3):961–999.

Martin, W., and Warr, P. G. (1993) "Explaining the Relative Decline of Agriculture: A Supply-Side Analysis for Indonesia," *World Bank Economic Review* 7:381–401.

McDougall, R., and R. Tyers (1994) "Asian Expansion and Labour Saving Technical Change: Factor Market Effects and Policy Reactions," *American Journal of Agricultural Economics* 76(5):1111–1118.

Murphy, K. M., A. Shleifer, and R. W. Vishny (1991) "The Allocation of Talent: Implications for Growth," *The Quarterly Journal of Economics* 106(2):503–30.

Nehru, V., and A. Dhareshwar (1993) "A New Database on Physical Capital Stock: Sources, Methodology, and Results," The World Bank, International Economics Department, Washington, DC.

Nehru, V., E. Swanson, and A. Dubey (1993) "A New Database on Human Capital Stock: Sources, Methodology, and Results," Working Paper Series 1124, International Economics Department, The World Bank, April 1994.

Park, S. (1993) "Trade, Interindustry Linkages, and Structural Change in Selected Asia-Pacific Economies." In T. Sano and C. Tamamura (eds.), *International*

*Industrial Linkages and Economic Interdependency in Asia-Pacific Region.* Toyko: Institute of Developing Economies.

Parmenter, B. R., G. A. Meagher, and P. J. Higgs (1993) "Technical Change in Australia During the 1980s: Historical Simulations with a Computable General Equilibrium Model," presented at Conference on Economic Modeling, Goteborg, Sweden, August 1992.

Rice, G. R. (1989) "Complementarity and the Interregional Distribution of Human Capital in U.S. Manufacturing," *Applied Economics* 21(8):1087–1098.

Romer, P. (1990) "Economic Integration and Endogenous Growth," *Quarterly Journal of Economics* 106(2):531–555.

Swaim, P. (1993) "Workforce Education and Training," Agriculture Information Bulletin, Economic Research Service, USDA, No. 664, June.

Urban, F., and R. Nightingale (1993) "World Population by Country and Region, 1950–90 and Projections to 2050." Economic Research Service–USDA, Staff Report No. AGES 9306.

World Bank (1993) "The East Asian Miracle: Economic Growth and Public Policy." Oxford University Press for the World Bank.

Young, A. (1994) "The Tyranny of Numbers: Confronting the Statistical Realities of the East Asian Growth Experience," NBER Working Paper No. 4680, March.

Zhi, W. (1994) "The Impact of Economic Integration among Taiwan, Hong Kong, and China: A Computable General Equilibrium Analysis," unpublished Ph.D dissertation, Department of Agricultural and Applied Economics, University of Minnesota, Minneapolis.

CHAPTER 15

# Implications for Global Trade Analysis

*Thomas W. Hertel*

A decade ago, John Whalley (1986) assessed the state of play in applied general equilibrium (AGE) analysis and summarized his findings in a chapter entitled "Hidden Challenges in Recent Applied General Equilibrium Exercises." At the time, he observed considerable frustration among AGE modelers with the seeming

> necessity to be a jack of all trades. When involved in modelling activity in the applied general equilibrium area, one has to be familiar with general equilibrium theory, to be able to program, to be familiar with data and be able to manipulate and convert it into a model admissible form, to be conversant with literature estimates of key parameters, to have a clear sense of policy issues and institutional structure, and to be able to interpret results. When confronted with this range of activities, it is perhaps not surprising that it becomes difficult for graduate students and others to enter this area." (pp. 38–39)

Although the advent of special purpose programming languages such as GAMS-MPS and GEMPACK have lessened the demands for programming skills, the other problems remain pertinent today. Indeed, with ever greater emphasis on global modeling, data problems have become only more severe.

Whalley goes on to discuss the value of *teams* of researchers, patterned after work in the natural sciences. This is the approach taken by the Impact Project, described in the foreword to this book. It is also the niche that the Global Trade Analysis Project (GTAP) has begun to fill in global trade analysis. By providing a standard data base and modeling framework, it has become possible for economists who are not specialists in AGE modeling to contemplate using the tool to address specific issues of interest without having first to invest an inordinate amount of time in data work and programming. A number of the applications in this book were developed by individuals in precisely these circumstances. Some authors may choose to work further on

364

these questions to improve their analysis in terms of data, parameters, and economic behavior. This process will serve as a *hidden hand* feeding back these improvements and new ideas to GTAP, allowing others to capitalize on them. I believe that this type of cross-fertilization is extremely important to the long-run vitality and credibility of AGE analysis. These individuals also bring new applications ideas. As the software and data base continue to improve, I expect many more examples of this type of cross-fertilization based on GTAP.

### Synopsis

The purpose of this book has been twofold. The first objective was a relatively straightforward one, namely, to document the GTAP framework, including model structure, as well as sources and procedures for constructing the data base and the parameter file. The second objective has been more challenging: to make available to readers a set of significant GTAP applications, along with the tools necessary to replicate them (and explore their sensitivity to key assumptions). As noted by Alan Powell in his foreword, replication is an essential, although oft-neglected, ingredient of empirical economic research. It is one of the best ways to learn about AGE modeling, and a fundamental part of this book.

However, making such applications available for easy replication is no small task. It has required many hours of graduate student time, as well as the expertise of the authors of the software and model. This effort has also benefited greatly from the existence of a "standard model" and a standard set of procedures for implementing applications. Indeed, based on this experience, we have developed a set of guidelines that should greatly facilitate the documentation and replication of future GTAP applications.

Of course, one danger of such an effort is that the standard model will become a straightjacket, unnecessarily limiting applications to what is feasible rather than what is most appropriate. In light of this concern, I am pleased with the diversity and quality of applications that appear in Part III. The Perroni and Wigle application of GTAP to analyze environmental policy offers an excellent example of how the standard model can be adapted to shed light on an important issue. In their case, a few outside calculations are required. However, this is far easier than building a new model from scratch. It can be followed up with further modeling work if deemed necessary.

This brings up an important point. Although the authors of the applications in Part III were required to adhere to the standard model structure, other users need not face this same restriction. Indeed, for those with access to GEMPACK, it is quite straightforward to modify selected equations, as needed, for other applications. Also, since the authors of such modifications have to present only their *changes* to the standard model structure, it is relatively easy to document such work. This frees up more of the methodologically oriented researcher's time for careful attention to the nature of the extensions being undertaken.

Finally, for experienced AGE modelers, with their own, preferred modeling framework, the data base itself will be of greatest interest. It can provide the starting point for applications using different models [e.g., models of trade with imperfect competition; see Francois, McDonald, and Nordstrom (1994); Hertel and Lanclos (1994); Harrison, Rutherford, and Tarr (1995)], or implementations of similar models in different software environments (Lewis, Robinson, and Wang 1995).

### Evaluation and future directions

How does one evaluate an effort such as GTAP? There are several dimensions to this question. One of the main criteria for evaluating the success of AGE-based research efforts in the past has been their ability to generate insights into problems that are too complex to be addressed analytically. In Chapter 7, McDougall and Tyers emphasized the competing nature of income and substitution effects associated with developing country expansion and its impact on relative wages in industrialized economies. Although theoretical outcomes are ambiguous, the evidence they present suggests that the likely empirical effect of this expansion on real wages is positive, but relatively small.

In their chapter on climate change and agriculture, Tsigas, Frisvold, and Kuhn also generate some valuable insights into two, fundamentally empirical, issues. First, because past studies of this problem have been partial equilibrium (PE) in nature, the authors exploit PE closure options in GTAP to obtain estimates of the likely magnitude of the errors in these earlier studies. They find them to be substantial, particularly when only the primary food system is taken into account. Their second insight pertains to the relative importance of carbon fertilization in estimates of the effects on the global food system stemming from a doubling of atmospheric $CO_2$. Omitting this aspect of the problem vastly overstates the adverse consequences of this particular form of climate change for global agriculture. With carbon fertilization effects in place, only two regions experience welfare declines, and global welfare actually rises. Without these effects, all regions lose and the global welfare cost is substantial. This application is also an example of how GTAP may be used to prioritize future research (e.g., obtaining accurate estimates of the $CO_2$ fertilization effect is a high priority).

One of the features that distinguishes many GTAP applications is the emphasis on *experimental design*, which is considered only as an afterthought to many AGE studies. Appropriate experimental design can itself be the source of valuable insights. Whereas most analyses have simply focused on the impact of eliminating the Multifibre Arrangement (MFA), Yang, Martin, and Yanagishima evaluate its interaction with other trade policy instruments. They also show that elimination of the MFA *following* non-MFA Uruguay Round reforms has a stronger effect, because of the tendency of the latter reforms to exacerbate the effect of these bilateral quotas on textiles and wearing apparel.

Experimental design also plays an important role in the Young–Huff chapter on Asia-Pacific Economic Cooperation (APEC) liberalization. Rather than simply examining the impact of a specific type of APEC agreement, those authors choose instead to focus on the *difference* between two alternative strategies for Asia-Pacific free trade. In the first case, liberalization is conducted on a preferential basis. In the second, APEC regions lower trade barriers facing imports from *all* sources. This is currently a topic of heated debate within APEC and the results of these simulations show that a preferential agreement is more attractive for APEC members, unless most favored nation cuts are reciprocated by non-APEC regions.

In some cases the application does not focus on the experimental design issue, but the questions asked, and the comparisons made, may still be new. This is the case with Donald MacLaren's chapter, in which he conducts a series of experiments that have been run many times by others in the context of the Uruguay Round–namely unilateral liberalization of agricultural policies in some of the major exporting regions. However, to date, no one has attempted a serious comparison between what the models have predicted and the negotiating positions of individual countries. This is what makes MacLaren's evaluation of the Cairns Group strategies for agriculture such refreshing reading.

Of course, there are other cases in which we need a general equilibrium model to remind ourselves of something we may already have known, and to demonstrate its importance in the application at hand. George Frisvold's analysis of technological change in agriculture offers a good illustration of this point. There, he shows how the distribution of gains from research depend importantly on the own-price elasticity of demand for the product in question. In the case of agricultural products, which are heavily traded, this depends importantly on the share of the output exported and the relative importance of the innovating country in world output. The GTAP framework offers a consistent vehicle for providing comparisons of these equilibrium elasticities and sorting out their implications for the incidence of technological innovation.

I believe there is considerably more room for interplay between analytical and empirical work based on GTAP. Yang, Martin, and Yanagishima provide an example of how such work might proceed. In their analysis, they find that some of the MFA exporters lose from liberalization of that policy, while others gain. How can one explain this diversity of outcomes? In the appendix to their chapter, these authors show how the local change in welfare for the

MFA exporters may be decomposed into several components. This expression clearly shows that regions with high shares of sales to the restricted market are more likely to lose. That is indeed the case in their results. Future work along these lines could provide a numerical decomposition of the sources of welfare changes. This would go a long way toward increasing the attractiveness of AGE-based studies to other economists.

In the end, the quality of all the insights generated by GTAP hinge critically on the validity of the modeling framework itself. In Chapter 14, Gehlhar points out that this involves a simultaneous test of model, data, parameters, and closure. His effort to validate the GTAP framework by backcasting export shares for East Asian economies over the 1980s represents a pathbreaking attempt to address a major source of criticism of AGE analysis. By choosing an endowment-based shock, he has highlighted the importance of factor intensities in the model. His results show that the standard model lacks sufficient factor detail to reflect accurately these historical changes. When he adds human capital, the predictive performance for these dynamic economies is vastly improved. Gehlhar's work is a good example of how one can take advantage of an existing framework, judiciously building on it in order to address an issue. His research has also put factor intensity information high on the list of priorities for future GTAP data base work. Gehlhar's work also provides a natural lead-in to a discussion of future directions for the GTAP data base.

### Data base

The GTAP data base has proven to be a tremendous resource for AGE researchers. This strong demand is continually demonstrated by the willingness of cash-strapped researchers to purchase it. The uniqueness of this data base is also one of the main reasons that various national and international agencies have stepped forward to join the GTAP Consortium and Advisory Board. There is simply no other publicly available data base that combines bilateral flows and input–output relationships in a microconsistent fashion. The involvement of these agencies will assure the continuity and continued improvement of this data base.

Future data developments will be motivated by the character of applications being demanded. As noted above, interest in growth and trade applications will lead naturally to an upgrade of the factor shares. Similarly, the demand for applications related to European integration is leading to improved coverage of that part of the world in future releases of the data base. Of course, this work must also consider the constraints on availability of secondary data. For this reason, it will be some time before improved coverage of some of the poorest developing countries is possible.

Most of the effort to date has been expended on assembling a globally consistent set of value flows for the GTAP data base. However, in the future, more attention will need to be paid to the behavioral parameters. Given the uncertainty associated with these elasticities, it is important to incorporate information on their *distributions*, as opposed to a single-point estimate. This will open the way to standardized sensitivity analysis, permitting users to place a confidence interval around estimates of particular interest. Current work using Gaussian Quadrature–based procedures (Preckel and Liu 1994) appears quite promising, as it offers a means of greatly economizing on the number of simulations required to provide a full-blown sensitivity analysis.

### Conclusions

The data base is an essential input into GTAP; however, in the long run the most important resource will be the emerging *network of researchers* using the GTAP framework. Contributions from individuals in the network have comprised important ingredients in the annual data updates. These individuals have also played an important role in raising the visibility of GTAP within their respective national and international agencies. To date, most (although not all) of these members of the GTAP network have been participants in one of the annual short courses. It is hoped that publication of this book, combined with the Internet release of the associated software and data, will facilitate a broadening of this network. Consider this your invitation to participate!

### REFERENCES

Francois, J. F., B. McDonald, and H. Nordstrom (1994) "The Uruguay Round: A Global General Equilibrium Assessment," manuscript, GATT Secretariat, Geneva.

Harrison, G. W., T. F. Rutherford, and D. G. Tarr (1995) "Quantifying the Uruguay Round," paper presented at *The Uruguay Round and the Developing Economies* conference, The Work Bank, January 26–27.

Hertel, T. W., and D. K. Lanclos (1994) "Trade Policy Reform in the Presence of Product Differentiation and Imperfect Competition: Implications for Food Processing Activity." In M. Hartmann, P. M. Schmitz, and H. von Witzke (eds.), *Agricultural Trade and Economic Integration in Europe and in North America*. Kiel: Wissenschaftsverlag Vauk Kiel KG.

Lewis, J. D., S. Robinson, and Z. Wang (1995) "Beyond the Uruguay Round: The Implications of an Asian Free Trade Area," *China Economic Review* (6):37–92.

Preckel, P.V., and S. Liu (1994) "Efficient, Independently Weighted Multivariate Quadratures," Purdue University Staff Paper No. 94-21.

Whalley, J. (1986) "Hidden Challenges in Recent Applied General Equilibrium Exercises." In J. R. Piggott and J. Whalley (eds.), *New Developments in Applied General Equilibrium Analysis*. New York: Cambridge University Press.

# Glossary of GTAP notation

*Padma Swaminathan*

## I    Overview

Specification of the GTAP data base and model requires a vast amount of notation. This notation has been carefully chosen to be brief, yet descriptive. This glossary refers to variables used throughout this book. It also corresponds to the GEMPACK representation of the standard GTAP model, GTAP94.TAB, as specified in version 2, April 1995. It lists the sets and subsets, base data, derivatives of the base data, and variables used in the model. We hope that the glossary will be useful for both new and experienced users of the GTAP framework. Some important naming conventions follow.

1. Sets and parameters are denoted in uppercase.
2. The *levels* form of variables in the GTAP are denoted in uppercase. Percentage changes in variables are denoted in lower case (*linearized* form of variables). For instance, $PM(i,r)$ is the market price of commodity $i$ in $r$ in levels form, and $pm(i,r) = [d\ PM(i,r)\ /\ PM(i,r)]*100$ % is the linearized form of this variable.
3. The GTAP data base comprises only value flows (in their levels form). Data base variables are accordingly written in uppercase. These are declared as *coefficients* in the GEMPACK code and are *updated* using percentage changes in the component prices and quantities, after each step in the solution. The data base stores the minimal amount of information. No redundancies are permitted.
4. Derivatives of the data base variables are also in levels form. There are two types of derivatives: value flows and shares. The derivative variables naturally get updated following each update of the data base.
5. The GTAP model consists of a system of linearized equations with all variables appearing in percentage change form. GEMPACK solves

for percentage changes in (endogenous) prices and quantities, thereupon relinearizing the model and solving it once again.

6. Dummy variables to identify zeroes in the base data are always written in uppercase. By including these in the model we avoid reporting meaningless percentage changes in quantity indices corresponding to zero flows.

7. Slack variables appearing in the linearized accounting relationships of the model are always written in lowercase.

8. Percentage changes in some useful derivative variables of trade value flows and income are given different names than their levels counterparts. (GEMPACK is not case-sensitive, so they cannot have the same name.) Although the base data and all the derivatives are automatically updated, they must be called for in separate DISPLAY statements to be viewed. They must also be compared to the initial data base to obtain their percentage change. Therefore, it is handy to give them different names and declare them as percentage change variables. These variables are listed under section D.7.

9. The model also computes changes in regional equivalent variations and trade balances absolute changes in $US 1992 million. Therefore, these variables are written in uppercase.

## II    Glossary

### A    *Sets and Subsets*

#### 1    *Sets*

| | |
|---|---|
| REG | Regions |
| NSAV_COMM | Non-Savings Commodities |
| TRAD_COMM | Tradeable Commodities |
| DEMD_COMM | Demanded Commodities |
| PROD_COMM | Produced Commodities |
| ENDW_COMM | Endowment Commodities |
| ENDWS_COMM | Sluggish Endowment Commodities |
| ENDWM_COMM | Mobile Endowment Commodities |
| CGDS_COMM | Capital Goods Commodities ("cgds") |
| ENDWC_COMM | Capital Endowment Commodity ("capital") |

#### 2    *Subsets*

| | |
|---|---|
| PROD_COMM | $\subset$ NSAV_COMM |
| DEMD_COMM | $\subset$ NSAV_COMM |

| | |
|---|---|
| CGDS_COMM | ⊂ NSAV_COMM |
| ENDW_COMM | ⊂ DEMD_COMM |
| TRAD_COMM | ⊂ DEMD_COMM |
| TRAD_COMM | ⊂ PROD_COMM |
| CGDS_COMM | ⊂ PROD_COMM |
| ENDWS_COMM | ⊂ ENDW_COMM |
| ENDWM_COMM | ⊂ ENDW_COMM |
| ENDWC_COMM | ⊂ NSAV_COMM |

*Example: The 3x3 Economy*

| | |
|---|---|
| REG | = {usa, e_u, row} |
| NSAV_COMM | = {land, labor, capital, food, manufacturing, services, capital goods} |
| TRAD_COMM | = {food, manufacturing, services} |
| DEMD_COMM | = {land, labor, capital, food, manufacturing, services} |
| PROD_COMM | = {food, manufacturing, services, capital goods} |
| ENDW_COMM | = {land, labor, capital} |
| ENDWS_COMM | = {land} |
| ENDWM_COMM | = {labor, capital} |
| CGDS_COMM | = {capital goods} |
| ENDWC_COMM | = {capital} |

**B**   *Base Data*

1   *Value Flows*

A   VALUE FLOWS EVALUATED AT AGENTS' PRICES

$EVOA(i,r)$    value of endowment commodity $i$ output or supplied in region $r$ evaluated at agents' prices

$EVOA(i,r) = PS(i,r) * QO(i,r)$

$\forall i \in ENDW\_COMM$
$\forall r \in REG$

$EVFA(i,j,r)$    value of purchases of endowment commodity $i$ by firms in sector $j$ of region $r$ evaluated at agents' prices

$EVFA(i,j,r) = PFE(i,j,r) * QFE(i,j,r)$

$\forall i \in ENDW\_COMM$
$\forall j \in PROD\_COMM$
$\forall r \in REG$

$VDFA(i,j,r)$    value of purchases of domestic tradeable commodity $i$ by firms in sector $j$ of region $r$ evaluated at agents' prices

$VDFA(i,j,r) = PFD(i,r) * QFD(i,r)$

$\forall i \in TRAD\_COMM$
$\forall j \in PROD\_COMM$
$\forall r \in REG$

$VIFA(i,j,r)$    value of purchases of imported tradeable commodity $i$ by firms in sector $j$ of region $r$ evaluated at agents' prices

$VIFA(i,j,r) = PFM(i,r) * QFM(i,r)$

$\forall i \in TRAD\_COMM$
$\forall j \in PROD\_COMM$
$\forall r \in REG$

$VDPA(i,r)$    value of expenditure on domestic tradeable commodity $i$ by private household in region $r$ evaluated at agents' prices

$VDPA(i,r) = PPD(i,r) * QPD(i,r)$

$\forall i \in TRAD\_COMM$
$\forall r \in REG$

$VIPA(i,r)$    value of expenditure on imported tradeable commodity $i$ by private household in region $r$ evaluated at agents' prices

$VIPA(i,r) = PPM(i,r) * QPM(i,r)$

$\forall i \in TRAD\_COMM$
$\forall r \in REG$

$VDGA(i,r)$    value of expenditure on domestic tradeable commodity $i$ by government household in region $r$ evaluated at agents' prices

$VDGA(i,r) = PGD(i,r) * QGD(i,r)$

$\forall i \in TRAD\_COMM$
$\forall r \in REG$

| $VIGA(i,r)$ | value of expenditure on imported tradeable commodity $i$ by government household in region $r$ evaluated at agents' prices $VIGA(i,r) = PGM(i,r) * QGM(i,r)$ | $\forall i \in TRAD\_COMM$ $\forall r \in REG$ |
| | | |
| $SAVE(r)$ | value of net savings in region $r$ $SAVE(r) = PSAVE * QSAVE(r)$ | $\forall r \in REG$ |
| | | |
| $VDEP(r)$ | value of capital depreciation expenditure in region $r$ $VDEP(r) = PCGDS(r) * KB(r)$ | $\forall r \in REG$ |
| | | |
| $VKB(r)$ | value of beginning-of-period capital stock in region $r$ $VKB(r) = PCGDS(r) * KB(r)$ | $\forall r \in REG$ |

B   VALUE FLOWS EVALUATED AT MARKET PRICES

| $VFM(i,j,r)$ | value of purchases of endowment commodity $i$ by firms in sector $j$ of region $r$ evaluated at market prices | $\forall i \in ENDW\_COMM$ $\forall j \in PROD\_COMM$ $\forall r \in REG$ |
| | $VFM(i,j,r) = PM(i,r) * QFE(i,j,r)$ $= PMES(i,j,r) * QFE(i,j,r)$ | $\forall i \in ENDWM\_COMM$ $\forall i \in ENDWS\_COMM$ |
| | | |
| $VDFM(i,j,r)$ | value of purchases of domestic tradeable commodity $i$ by firms in sector $j$ of region $r$ evaluated at market prices $VDFM(i,j,r) = PM(i,r) * QFD(i,r)$ | $\forall i \in TRAD\_COMM$ $\forall j \in PROD\_COMM$ $\forall r \in REG$ |
| | | |
| $VIFM(i,j,r)$ | value of purchases of imported tradeable commodity $i$ by firms in sector $j$ of region $r$ evaluated at market prices $VIFM(i,j,r) = PIM(i,r) * QFM(i,r)$ | $\forall i \in TRAD\_COMM$ $\forall j \in PROD\_COMM$ $\forall r \in REG$ |
| | | |
| $VDPM(i,r)$ | value of expenditure on domestic tradeable commodity $i$ by private household in region $r$ evaluated at market prices $VDPM(i,r) = PM(i,r) * QPD(i,r)$ | $\forall i \in TRAD\_COMM$ $\forall r \in REG$ |

375

$VIPM(i,r)$    value of expenditure on imported tradeable commodity $i$ by private household in region $r$ evaluated at market prices    $\forall i \in TRAD\_COMM$   $\forall r \in REG$

$$VIPM(i,r) = PIM(i,r) * QPM(i,r)$$

$VDGM(i,r)$    value of expenditure on domestic tradeable commodity $i$ by government household in region $r$ evaluated at market prices    $\forall i \in TRAD\_COMM$   $\forall r \in REG$

$$VDGM(i,r) = PM(i,r) * QGD(i,r)$$

$VIGM(i,r)$    value of expenditure on imported tradeable commodity $i$ by government household in region $r$ evaluated at market prices    $\forall i \in TRAD\_COMM$   $\forall r \in REG$

$$VIGM(i,r) = PIM(i,r) * QGM(i,r)$$

$VXMD(i,r,s)$    value of exports of tradeable commodity $i$ from source $r$ to destination $s$ evaluated at (exporter's) market prices    $\forall i \in TRAD\_COMM$   $\forall r \in REG$   $\forall s \in REG$

$$VXMD(i,r,s) = PM(i,r) * QXS(i,r,s)$$

$VIMS(i,r,s)$    value of imports of tradeable commodity $i$ from source $r$ to destination $s$ evaluated at (importer's) market prices    $\forall i \in TRAD\_COMM$   $\forall r \in REG$   $\forall s \in REG$

$$VIMS(i,r,s) = PMS(i,r,s) * QXS(i,r,s)$$

$VST(i,r)$    value of sales of tradeable commodity $i$ to the international transport sector in region $r$ evaluated at market prices    $\forall i \in TRAD\_COMM$   $\forall r \in REG$   *market prices*

$$VST(i,r) = PM(i,r) * QST(i,r)$$

C    VALUE FLOWS EVALUATED AT WORLD PRICES

$VXWD(i,r,s)$    value of exports of tradeable commodity $i$ from source $r$ to destination $s$ evaluated at world (*fob*) prices    $\forall i \in TRAD\_COMM$   $\forall r \in REG$   $\forall s \in REG$

$$VXWD(i,r,s) = PFOB(i,r,s) * QXS(i,r,s)$$

$VIWS(i,r,s)$    value of imports of tradeable commodity $i$ from source $r$ to destination $s$ evaluated at world (*cif*) prices    $\forall i \in TRAD\_COMM$   $\forall r \in REG$   $\forall s \in REG$

$$VIWS(i,r,s) = PCIF(i,r,s) * QXS(i,r,s)$$

2    Technology, Preference, and Mobility Parameters

| SUBPAR(i,r) | substitution parameter for tradeable commodity $i$ in the CDE minimum expenditure function of region $r$ | $\forall i \in TRAD\_COMM$ $\forall r \in REG$ |
|---|---|---|
| INCPAR(i,r) | income parameter for tradeable commodity $i$ in the CDE minimum expenditure function of region $r$ | $\forall i \in TRAD\_COMM$ $\forall r \in REG$ |
| ESUBVA(j) | substitution parameter between primary factors in the CES value-added nest of the nested production structure of sector $j$ of all regions | $\forall j \in PROD\_COMM$ |
| ESUBD(i) | substitution parameter between domestic and composite imported commodities in the Armington utility/production structure of agent/sector $i$ in all regions | $\forall i \in TRAD\_COMM$ |
| ESUBM(i) | substitution parameter among imported commodities from different sources in the Armington utility/production structure of agent/sector $i$ in all regions | $\forall i \in TRAD\_COMM$ |
| ETRAE(i) | transformation parameter between uses for sluggish primary factor $i$ in the one-level CET production structure in all regions | $\forall i \in ENDWS\_COMM$ |
| RORFLEX(r) | flexibility of expected net rate of return on capital stock in region $r$ with respect to investment (if a region's capital stock increases by 1%, then it is expected that the net rate of return on capital will decline by $RORFLEX\%$) | $\forall r \in REG$ |
| RORDELTA | binary coefficient that determines the mechanism of allocating investment across regions [when $RORDELTA = 1$, investment is allocated across regions to equate the change in the expected rates of return, $rore(r)$, when $RORDELTA = 0$, investment is allocated across regions to maintain the existing composition of capital stocks] | |

377

# C  Derivatives of the Base Data

## 1  Value Flows

**VOA(i,r)**  value of nonsavings commodity $i$ output or supplied in region $r$ evaluated at agents' prices

$$VOA(i,r) = EVOA(i,r) \qquad \forall i \in NSAV\_COMM,\ \forall r \in REG$$

$$VOA(i,r) = \sum_{j\,\in\,DEMD\_COMM} VFA(j,i,r) \qquad \forall i \in ENDW\_COMM,\ \forall i \in PROD\_COMM$$

**VFA(i,j,r)**  value of purchases of demanded commodity $i$ by firms in sector $j$ of region $r$ evaluated at agents' prices

$$VFA(i,j,r) = EVFA(i,j,r) \qquad \forall i \in DEMD\_COMM,\ \forall j \in TRAD\_COMM,\ \forall r \in REG$$

$$VFA(i,j,r) = VDFA(i,j,r) + VIFA(i,j,r) \qquad \forall i \in ENDW\_COMM,\ \forall i \in TRAD\_COMM$$

**VOM(i,r)**  value of nonsavings commodity $i$ output or supplied in region $r$ evaluated at market prices

$$VOM(i,r) = \sum_{j\,\in\,PROD\_COMM} VFM(i,j,r) \qquad \forall i \in NSAV\_COMM,\ \forall r \in REG$$

$$VOM(i,r) = VDM(i,r) + \sum_{s\,\in\,REG} VXMD(i,r,s) + VST(i,r) \qquad \forall i \in ENDW\_COMM$$

$$VOM(i,r) = VOA(i,r)$$

**VDM(i,r)**  value of domestic sales of tradeable commodity $i$ in region $r$ evaluated at market prices

$$VDM(i,r) = VDPM(i,r) + VDGM(i,r) + \sum_{j\,\in\,PROD\_COMM} VDFM(i,j,r) \qquad \forall i \in TRAD\_COMM,\ \forall r \in REG$$

$VIM(i,r)$    value of aggregate imports of tradeable commodity $i$ in region $r$ evaluated at market prices

$$VIM(i,r) = VIPM(i,r) + VIGM(i,r) + \sum_{j \in PROD\_COMM} VIFM(i,j,r)$$

$\forall i \in TRAD\_COMM$
$\forall r \in REG$

$VPA(i,r)$    value of private household expenditure on tradeable commodity $i$ in region $r$ evaluated at agents' prices

$$VPA(i,r) = VDPA(i,r) + VIPA(i,r)$$

$\forall i \in TRAD\_COMM$
$\forall r \in REG$

$PRIVEXP(r)$    private household expenditure in region $r$ evaluated at agents' prices

$$PRIVEXP(r) = \sum_{i \in TRAD\_COMM} VPA(i,r)$$

$\forall r \in REG$

$VGA(i,r)$    value of government household expenditure on tradeable commodity $i$ in region $r$ evaluated at agents' prices

$$VGA(i,r) = VDGA(i,r) + VIGA(i,r)$$

$\forall i \in TRAD\_COMM$
$\forall r \in REG$

$GOVEXP(r)$    government household expenditure in region $r$ evaluated at agents' prices

$$GOVEXP(r) = \sum_{i \in TRAD\_COMM} VGA(i,r)$$

$\forall r \in REG$

$INCOME(r)$    expenditure in region $r$ that equals net income (net of capital depreciation)

$$INCOME(r) = PRIVEXP(r) + GOVEXP(r) + SAVE(r)$$

$\forall r \in REG$

$INC(r)$    initial value of income (expenditure) in the base data in region $r$ stored as a parameter, used in calculating $EV(r)$

$$INC(r) = INCOME(r)$$

$\forall r \in REG$

379

$REGINV(r)$ — gross investment in region $r$ that equals value of output of sector "cgds"

$$REGINV(r) = \sum_{k \in CGDS\_COMM} VOA(k,r) \qquad \forall r \in REG$$

$NETINV(r)$ — net investment in region $r$

$$NETINV(r) = \sum_{k \in CGDS\_COMM} VOA(k,r) - VDEP(r) \qquad \forall r \in REG$$

$GLOBINV$ — global net investment

$$GLOBINV = \sum_{r \in REG} NETINV(r) = \sum_{r \in REG} SAVE(r)$$

$INVKERATIO(r)$ — ratio of gross investment to end-of-period capital stock in region $r$

$$INVKERATIO(r) = \frac{REGINV(r)}{[VKB(r) + NETINV(r)]} \qquad \forall r \in REG$$

$GRNETRATIO(r)$ — ratio of gross to net rate of return on capital in region $r$ [$VOA("capital",r)$ is gross return to capital]

$$GRNETRATIO(r) = \frac{\displaystyle\sum_{k \in ENDWC\_COMM} VOA(k,r)}{\left[\displaystyle\sum_{k \in ENDWC\_COMM} VOA(k,r) - VDEP(r)\right]} \qquad \forall r \in REG$$

$GDP(r)$ — Gross domestic product in region $r$ (trade is valued at world prices)

$$GDP(r) = \sum_{i \in TRAD\_COMM} VPA(i,r) + \sum_{i \in TRAD\_COMM} VGA(i,r) + \sum_{i \in CGDS\_COMM} VOA(i,r) \qquad \forall r \in REG$$

$$+ \sum_{i \in TRAD\_COMM} \sum_{s \in REG} [VXWD(i,r,s) + VST(i,r)] - \sum_{i \in TRAD\_COMM} \sum_{s \in REG} VIWS(i,s,r)$$

$VTWR(i,r,s)$    value of transportation services associated with the shipment of tradeable commodity $i$ from source $r$ to destination $s$ ($fob - cif$ margin)

$\forall i \in TRAD\_COMM$
$\forall r \in REG$
$\forall s \in REG$

$$VTWR(i,r,s) = VIWS(i,r,s) - VXWD(i,r,s)$$

$VT$    value of total international transportation services (sum of $fob - cif$ margins across all commodities and all routes)

$$VT = \sum_{i \in TRAD\_COMM} \sum_{r \in REG} \sum_{s \in REG} VTWR(i,r,s)$$

$VXW(i,r)$    value of exports of tradeable commodity $i$ from region $r$ evaluated at world ($fob$) prices

$\forall i \in TRAD\_COMM$
$\forall r \in REG$

$$VXW(i,r) = \sum_{s \in REG} VXWD(i,r,s) + VST(i,r)$$

$VXWREGION(r)$    value of exports from region $r$ evaluated at world ($fob$) prices

$\forall r \in REG$

$$VXWREGION(r) = \sum_{i \in TRAD\_COMM} VXW(i,r)$$

$VWLDSALES(r)$    value of sales to the world market from region $r$ evaluated at $fob$ prices

$\forall r \in REG$

$$VWLDSALES(r) = \sum_{i \in TRAD\_COMM} \sum_{s \in REG} [VXWD(i,r,s) + VST(i,r)] + NETINV(r)$$

$VXWCOMMOD(i)$    value of exports of tradeable commodity $i$ evaluated at world ($fob$) prices

$\forall i \in TRAD\_COMM$

$$VXWCOMMOD(i) = \sum_{r \in REG} VXW(i,r)$$

$VIW(i,r)$    value of imports of tradeable commodity $i$ into region $r$ evaluated at world ($cif$) prices

$\forall i \in TRAD\_COMM$
$\forall r \in REG$

$$VIW(i,r) = \sum_{s \in REG} VIWS(i,s,r)$$

$VIWREGION(r)$ — value of imports into region $r$ evaluated at world($cif$) prices

$$VIWREGION(r) = \sum_{i \in TRAD\_COMM} VIW(i,r)$$

$\forall r \in REG$

$VIWCOMMOD(i)$ — value of imports of tradeable commodity $i$ evaluated at world ($cif$) prices

$$VIWCOMMOD(i) = \sum_{r \in REG} VIW(i,r)$$

$\forall i \in TRAD\_COMM$

$VXWLD$ — value of worldwide commodity exports evaluated at $fob$ prices

$$VXWLD = \sum_{r \in REG} VXWREGION(r) = \sum_{r \in REG} VIWREGION(r)$$

$PW\_PM(i,r)$ — ratio of world ($fob$) to domestic market prices for tradeable commodity $i$ in region $r$

$$PW\_PM(i,r) = \frac{\displaystyle\sum_{s \in REG} VXWD(i,r,s)}{\displaystyle\sum_{s \in REG} VXMD(i,r,s)}$$

$\forall i \in TRAD\_COMM$
$\forall r \in REG$

$VOW(i,r)$ — value of output of tradeable commodity $i$ in region $r$, evaluated at world ($fob$) prices

$$VOW(i,r) = VDM(i,r) * PW\_PM(i,r) + \sum_{s \in REG} VXWD(i,r,s) + VST(i,r)$$

$\forall i \in TRAD\_COMM$
$\forall r \in REG$

$VWOW(i)$ — value of world supply of tradeable commodity $i$ evaluated at world ($fob$) prices

$$VWOW(i) = \sum_{r \in REG} VOW(i,r)$$

$\forall r \in REG$

## 2  Shares

**SHRDFM(i,j,r)**  share of domestic sales of tradeable commodity $i$ used by firms in sector $j$ of region $r$ evaluated at market prices

$$SHRDFM(i,j,r) = \frac{VDFM(i,j,r)}{VDM(i,r)}$$

$\forall i \in TRAD\_COMM$
$\forall j \in PROD\_COMM$
$\forall r \in REG$

**SHRDPM(i,r)**  share of domestic sales of tradeable commodity $i$ used by private household in region $r$ evaluated at market prices

$$SHRDPM(i,r) = \frac{VDPM(i,r)}{VDM(i,r)}$$

$\forall i \in TRAD\_COMM$
$\forall r \in REG$

**SHRDGM(i,r)**  share of domestic sales of tradeable commodity $i$ used by government household in region $r$ evaluated at market prices

$$SHRDGM(i,r) = \frac{VDGM(i,r)}{VDM(i,r)}$$

$\forall i \in TRAD\_COMM$
$\forall r \in REG$

**SHRIFM(i,j,r)**  share of aggregate imports of tradeable commodity $i$ used by firms in sector $j$ of region $r$ evaluated at market prices

$$SHRIFM(i,j,r) = \frac{VIFM(i,j,r)}{VIM(i,r)}$$

$\forall i \in TRAD\_COMM$
$\forall j \in PROD\_COMM$
$\forall r \in REG$

**SHRIPM(i,r)**  share of aggregate imports of tradeable commodity $i$ used by private household in region $r$ evaluated at market prices

$$SHRIPM(i,r) = \frac{VIPM(i,r)}{VIM(i,r)}$$

$\forall i \in TRAD\_COMM$
$\forall r \in REG$

**SHRIGM(i,r)** — share of aggregate imports of tradeable commodity $i$ used by government household in region $r$ evaluated at market prices

$$SHRIGM(i,r) = \frac{VIGM(i,r)}{VIM,(i,r)}$$

$\forall i \in TRAD\_COMM$
$\forall r \in REG$

**FMSHR(i,j,r)** — share of imports in the composite for tradeable commodity used by firms in sector $j$ of region $r$ evaluated at agents' prices

$$FMSHR(i,j,r) = \frac{VIFA(i,j,r)}{VFA(i,j,r)}$$

$\forall i \in TRAD\_COMM$
$\forall j \in PROD\_COMM$
$\forall r \in REG$

**PMSHR(i,r)** — share of imports in the composite for tradeable commodity $i$ used by private household in region $r$ evaluated at agents' prices

$$PMSHR(i,r) = \frac{VIPA(i,r)}{VPA(i,r)}$$

$\forall i \in TRAD\_COMM$
$\forall r \in REG$

**GMSHR(i,r)** — share of imports in the composite for tradeable commodity $i$ used by government household in region $r$ evaluated at agents' prices

$$GMSHR(i,r) = \frac{VIGA(i,r)}{VGA(i,r)}$$

$\forall i \in TRAD\_COMM$
$\forall r \in REG$

**CONSHR(i,r)** — budget share of the composite for tradeable commodity $i$ in private household expenditure in region $r$ evaluated at agents' prices

$$CONSHR(i,r) = \frac{VPA(i,r)}{PRIVEXP(r)}$$

$\forall i \in TRAD\_COMM$
$\forall r \in REG$

$MSHRS(i,r,s)$    market share of source $r$ in the aggregate imports of tradeable commodity $i$ in region $s$ evaluated at market prices

$$MSHRS(i,r,s) = \frac{VIMS(i,r,s)}{\displaystyle\sum_{r \in REG} VIMS(i,r,s)}$$

$\forall i \in TRAD\_COMM$
$\forall r \in REG$
$\forall s \in REG$

$SVA(i,j,r)$    share of endowment commodity $i$ in value-added of firms in sector $j$ of region $r$ evaluated at agents' prices

$$SVA(i,j,r) = \frac{VFA(i,j,r)}{\displaystyle\sum_{k \in ENDW\_COMM} VFA(k,j,r)}$$

$\forall i \in ENDW\_COMM$
$\forall j \in PROD\_COMM$
$\forall r \in REG$

$REVSHR(i,j,r)$    share of endowment commodity $i$ used by firms in sector $j$ of region $r$ evaluated at market prices

$$REVSHR(i,j,r) = \frac{VFM(i,j,r)}{\displaystyle\sum_{k \in PROD\_COMM} VFM(i,k,r)}$$

$\forall i \in ENDW\_COMM$
$\forall j \in PROD\_COMM$
$\forall r \in REG$

$FOBSHR(i,r,s)$    share of $fob$ price in the $cif$ price for tradeable commodity $i$ exported from source $r$ to destination $s$

$$FOBSHR(i,r,s) = \frac{VXWD(i,r,s)}{VIWS(i,r,s)}$$

$\forall i \in TRAD\_COMM$
$\forall r \in REG$
$\forall s \in REG$

$TRNSHR(i,r,s)$    share of transport price in the $cif$ price for tradeable commodity $i$ exported from source $r$ to destination $s$

$$TRNSHR(i,r,s) = \frac{VTWR(i,r,s)}{VIWS(i,r,s)}$$

$\forall i \in TRAD\_COMM$
$\forall r \in REG$
$\forall s \in REG$

385

## D   *Variables*

### 1   *Quantity Variables*

| | | |
|---|---|---|
| $QO(i,r)$ | quantity of nonsaving commodity $i$ output or supplied in region $r$ | $\forall i \in NSAV\_COMM$ <br> $\forall r \in REG$ |
| $QOES(i,j,r)$ | quantity of sluggish endowment commodity $i$ supplied to firms in sector $j$ of region $r$ | $\forall i \in ENDWS\_COMM$ <br> $\forall j \in PROD\_COMM$ <br> $\forall r \in REG$ |
| $QDS(i,r)$ | quantity of domestic sales of tradeable commodity $i$ in region $r$ | $\forall i \in TRAD\_COMM$ <br> $\forall r \in REG$ |
| $QXS(i,r,s)$ | quantity of exports of tradeable commodity $i$ from source $r$ to destination $s$ | $\forall i \in TRAD\_COMM$ <br> $\forall r \in REG$ <br> $\forall s \in REG$ |
| $QST(i,r)$ | quantity of sales of tradeable commodity $i$ to the international transport sector in region $r$ | $\forall i \in TRAD\_COMM$ <br> $\forall r \in REG$ |
| $QFE(i,j,r)$ | quantity of endowment commodity $i$ demanded by firms in sector $j$ of region $r$ | $\forall i \in ENDW\_COMM$ <br> $\forall j \in PROD\_COMM$ <br> $\forall r \in REG$ |
| $QVA(j,r)$ | quantity index of value-added (land labor composite) in firms of sector $j$ in region $r$ | $\forall j \in PROD\_COMM$ <br> $\forall r \in REG$ |
| $QF(i,j,r)$ | quantity of composite tradeable commodity $i$ demanded by firms in sector $j$ of region $r$ | $\forall i \in TRAD\_COMM$ <br> $\forall j \in PROD\_COMM$ <br> $\forall r \in REG$ |
| $QFD(i,j,r)$ | quantity of domestic tradeable commodity $i$ demanded by firms in sector $j$ of region $r$ | $\forall i \in TRAD\_COMM$ <br> $\forall j \in PROD\_COMM$ <br> $\forall r \in REG$ |

| Symbol | Index | Description |
|---|---|---|
| $QIW(i,r)$ | $\forall i \in TRAD\_COMM$, $\forall r \in REG$ | quantity of aggregate imports of tradeable commodity $i$ demanded by region $r$ using cif prices as weights |
| $QXW(i,r)$ | $\forall i \in TRAD\_COMM$, $\forall r \in REG$ | quantity of aggregate exports of tradeable commodity $i$ supplied from region $r$ using fob prices as weights |
| $QIWREG(r)$ | $\forall r \in REG$ | volume of merchandise imports demanded by region $r$ |
| $QXWREG(r)$ | $\forall r \in REG$ | volume of merchandise exports supplied by region $r$ |
| $QIWCOM(i)$ | $\forall i \in TRAD\_COMM$ | volume of global merchandise imports of tradeable commodity $i$ |
| $QXWCOM(i)$ | $\forall i \in TRAD\_COMM$ | volume of global merchandise exports of tradeable commodity $i$ |

| | | |
|---|---|---|
| *QXWWLD* | volume of world trade | |
| *QOW(i)* | quantity index for world supply of tradeable commodity $i$ | $\forall i \in TRAD\_COMM$ |
| *QT* | quantity of global transport services supplied | |
| *QCGDS(r)* | quantity of capital goods sector supplied in region $r$ | $\forall r \in REG$ |
| *QSAVE(r)* | quantity of savings demanded in region $r$ | $\forall r \in REG$ |
| *GLOBALCGDS* | quantity of global supply of capital for net investment | |
| *KSVCES(r)* | quantity of capital services in region $r$ | $\forall r \in REG$ |
| *KB(r)* | quantity of beginning-of-period capital stock in region $r$ | $\forall r \in REG$ |
| *KE(r)* | quantity of end-of-period capital stock in region $r$ | $\forall r \in REG$ |
| *POP(r)* | population in region $r$ | $\forall r \in REG$ |
| *QGDP(r)* | quantity index for GDP in region $r$ | $\forall r \in REG$ |
| *WALRAS_DEM* | quantity demanded in the omitted market (equals global demand for savings) | |
| *WALRAS_SUP* | quantity supplied in the omitted market (equals global supply of new capital goods composite) | |

## 2 *Price Variables*

| | | |
|---|---|---|
| *PS(i,r)* | supply price of nonsavings commodity $i$ in region $r$ | $\forall i \in NSAV\_COMM$ $\forall r \in REG$ |
| *PM(i,r)* | market price of nonsavings commodity $i$ in region $r$ | $\forall i \in NSAV\_COMM$ $\forall r \in REG$ |
| *PMES(i,j,r)* | market price of sluggish endowment commodity $i$ supplied to firms in sector $j$ of region $r$ | $\forall i \in ENDWS\_COMM$ $\forall j \in PROD\_COMM$ $\forall r \in REG$ |
| *PFE(i,j,r)* | demand price of endowment commodity $i$ for firms in sector $j$ of region $r$ | $\forall i \in ENDW\_COMM$ $\forall j \in PROD\_COMM$ $\forall r \in REG$ |

| | | |
|---|---|---|
| $PVA(j,r)$ | price of value-added in sector $j$ of region $r$ | $\forall j \in PROD\_COMM$ <br> $\forall r \in REG$ |
| $PF(i,j,r)$ | demand price of composite tradeable commodity $i$ for firms in sector $j$ of region $r$ | $\forall i \in TRAD\_COMM$ <br> $\forall j \in PROD\_COMM$ <br> $\forall r \in REG$ |
| $PFD(i,j,r)$ | demand price of domestic tradeable commodity $i$ for firms in sector $j$ of region $r$ | $\forall i \in TRAD\_COMM$ <br> $\forall j \in PROD\_COMM$ <br> $\forall r \in REG$ |
| $PFM(i,j,r)$ | demand price of imported tradeable commodity $i$ for firms in sector $j$ of region $r$ | $\forall i \in TRAD\_COMM$ <br> $\forall j \in PROD\_COMM$ <br> $\forall r \in REG$ |
| $PP(i,r)$ | demand price of composite tradeable commodity $i$ for private household in region $r$ | $\forall i \in TRAD\_COMM$ <br> $\forall r \in REG$ |
| $PPD(i,r)$ | demand price of domestic tradeable commodity $i$ for private household in region $r$ | $\forall i \in TRAD\_COMM$ <br> $\forall r \in REG$ |
| $PPM(i,r)$ | demand price of imported tradeable commodity $i$ for private household in region $r$ | $\forall i \in TRAD\_COMM$ <br> $\forall r \in REG$ |
| $PG(i,r)$ | demand price of composite tradeable commodity $i$ for government household in region $r$ | $\forall i \in TRAD\_COMM$ <br> $\forall r \in REG$ |
| $PGD(i,r)$ | demand price of domestic tradeable commodity $i$ for government household in region $r$ | $\forall i \in TRAD\_COMM$ <br> $\forall r \in REG$ |
| $PGM(i,r)$ | demand price of imported tradeable commodity $i$ for government household in region $r$ | $\forall i \in TRAD\_COMM$ <br> $\forall r \in REG$ |
| $PPRIV(r)$ | price index for private household expenditure in region $r$ | $\forall r \in REG$ |
| $PGOV(r)$ | price index for government household expenditure in region $r$ | $\forall r \in REG$ |

| Symbol | Description | |
|---|---|---|
| $PFOB(i,r,s)$ | world (*fob*) price of tradeable commodity $i$ exported from source $r$ to destination $s$ (prior to including transport margin) | $\forall i \in TRAD\_COMM$ $\forall r \in REG$ $\forall s \in REG$ |
| $PCIF(i,r,s)$ | world (*cif*) price of tradeable commodity $i$ imported from source $r$ to destination $s$ (after including transport margin) | $\forall i \in TRAD\_COMM$ $\forall r \in REG$ $\forall s \in REG$ |
| $PMS(i,r,s)$ | market price by source of tradeable commodity $i$ imported from source $r$ to destination $s$ | $\forall i \in TRAD\_COMM$ $\forall r \in REG$ $\forall s \in REG$ |
| $PIM(i,r)$ | market price of aggregate imports of tradeable commodity $i$ in region $r$ | $\forall i \in TRAD\_COMM$ $\forall r \in REG$ |
| $PIW(i,r)$ | world price of aggregate imports of tradeable commodity $i$ in region $r$ | $\forall i \in TRAD\_COMM$ $\forall r \in REG$ |
| $PXW(i,r)$ | price index for aggregate exports of tradeable commodity $i$ from region $r$ | $\forall i \in TRAD\_COMM$ $\forall r \in REG$ |
| $PIWREG(r)$ | price index of merchandise imports in region $r$ | $\forall r \in REG$ |
| $PXWREG(r)$ | price index of merchandise exports from region $r$ | $\forall r \in REG$ |
| $PIWCOM(i)$ | price index of global merchandise imports of tradeable commodity $i$ | $\forall i \in TRAD\_COMM$ |
| $PXWCOM(i)$ | price index of global merchandise exports of tradeable commodity $i$ | $\forall i \in TRAD\_COMM$ |
| $PXWWLD$ | price index of world trade | |
| $PR(i,r)$ | ratio of domestic market price to market price of imports for tradeable commodity $i$ in region $r$ | $\forall i \in TRAD\_COMM$ $\forall r \in REG$ |
| $PW(i)$ | world price index for total supply of tradeable commodity $i$ | $\forall i \in TRAD\_COMM$ |
| $PSW(r)$ | price index received for tradeables produced in region $r$ including sales of net investment to the global bank | $\forall r \in REG$ |

| | | |
|---|---|---|
| $PDW(r)$ | price index paid for tradeables used in region $r$ including purchases of savings from the global bank | $\forall r \in REG$ |
| $TOT(r)$ | terms of trade for region $r$ <br> $TOT(r) = [PSW(r) \ / \ PDW(r)]$ | $\forall r \in REG$ |
| $PT$ | price of global transport services supplied | $\forall r \in REG$ |
| $PCGDS(r)$ | price of investment goods in region $r$ [equals $PS(\text{``cgds''}, r)$] | $\forall r \in REG$ |
| $PSAVE$ | price of composite capital good supplied to savers by global bank | |
| $RENTAL(r)$ | rental rate on capital stock in region $r$ [equals $PS(\text{``capital''}, r)$] | $\forall r \in REG$ |
| $RORC(r)$ | current net rate of return on capital stock in region $r$ | $\forall r \in REG$ |
| $RORE(r)$ | expected net rate of return on capital stock in region $r$ | $\forall r \in REG$ |
| $RORG$ | global net rate of return on capital stock | |
| $PGDP(r)$ | price index for GDP in region $r$ | $\forall r \in REG$ |

## 3 Policy Variables

| | | |
|---|---|---|
| $TO(i,r)$ | power of the tax on output (or income) of nonsavings commodity $i$ in region $r$ | $\forall i \in NSAV\_COMM$ <br> $\forall r \in REG$ |
| $TF(i,j,r)$ | power of the tax on endowment commodity $i$ demanded by firms in sector $j$ of region $r$ | $\forall i \in ENDW\_COMM$ <br> $\forall j \in PROD\_COMM$ <br> $\forall r \in REG$ |
| $TFD(i,j,r)$ | power of the tax on domestic tradeable commodity $i$ demanded by firms in sector $j$ of region $r$ | $\forall i \in TRAD\_COMM$ <br> $\forall j \in PROD\_COMM$ <br> $\forall r \in REG$ |
| $TFM(i,j,r)$ | power of the tax on imported tradeable commodity $i$ demanded by firms in sector $j$ of region $r$ | $\forall i \in TRAD\_COMM$ <br> $\forall j \in PROD\_COMM$ <br> $\forall r \in REG$ |

| | | |
|---|---|---|
| $TPD(i,r)$ | power of the tax on domestic tradeable commodity $i$ demanded by private household in region $r$ | $\forall i \in TRAD\_COMM$ <br> $\forall r \in REG$ |
| $TPM(i,r)$ | power of the tax on imported tradeable commodity $i$ demanded by private household in region $r$ | $\forall i \in TRAD\_COMM$ <br> $\forall r \in REG$ |
| $TGD(i,r)$ | power of the tax on domestic tradeable commodity $i$ demanded by government household in region $r$ | $\forall i \in TRAD\_COMM$ <br> $\forall r \in REG$ |
| $TGM(i,r)$ | power of the tax on imported tradeable commodity $i$ demanded by government household in region $r$ | $\forall i \in TRAD\_COMM$ <br> $\forall r \in REG$ |
| $TXS(i,r,s)$ | power of the tax on exports of tradeable commodity $i$ from source $r$ to destination $s$ (levied in region $r$) | $\forall i \in TRAD\_COMM$ <br> $\forall r \in REG$ <br> $\forall s \in REG$ |
| $TMS(i,r,s)$ | power of the tax on imports of tradeable commodity $i$ from source $r$ to destination $s$ (levied in region $s$) | $\forall i \in TRAD\_COMM$ <br> $\forall r \in REG$ <br> $\forall s \in REG$ |
| $TX(i,r)$ | power of the variable export tax on exports of tradeable commodity $i$ from region $r$–destination-generic | $\forall i \in TRAD\_COMM$ <br> $\forall r \in REG$ |
| $TM(i,r)$ | power of the variable import tax (levy) on imports of tradeable commodity $i$ in region $s$–source-generic | $\forall i \in TRAD\_COMM$ <br> $\forall r \in REG$ |

## 4  Technical Change Variables

| | | |
|---|---|---|
| $AO(j,r)$ | output augmenting technical change in sector $j$ of region $r$ | $\forall j \in PROD\_COMM$ <br> $\forall r \in REG$ |
| $AFE(i,j,r)$ | primary factor $i$ augmenting technical change in sector $j$ of region $r$ | $\forall i \in ENDW\_COMM$ <br> $\forall j \in PROD\_COMM$ <br> $\forall r \in REG$ |

| | | |
|---|---|---|
| $AF(i,j,r)$ | composite intermediate input $i$ augmenting technical change in sector $j$ of region $r$ | $\forall i \in TRAD\_COMM$<br>$\forall j \in PROD\_COMM$<br>$\forall r \in REG$ |
| $AVA(j,r)$ | value-added augmenting technical change in sector $j$ of region $r$ | $\forall j \in PROD\_COMM$<br>$\forall r \in REG$ |
| $ATR(i,r,s)$ | technical change in the transportation of tradeable commodity $i$ from source $r$ to destination $s$ | $\forall i \in TRAD\_COMM$<br>$\forall r \in REG$<br>$\forall s \in REG$ |

## 5    Dummy (0, 1) Variables

| | | |
|---|---|---|
| $D\_EVFA(i,j,r)$ | 0, 1 variable for identifying zero expenditures in $EVFA(i,j,r)$<br>$D\_EVFA(i,j,r) = 0$<br>$D\_EVFA(i,j,r) = 1 \ \forall \ EVFA(i,j,r) > 0$ | $\forall i \in ENDW\_COMM$<br>$\forall j \in PROD\_COMM$<br>$\forall r \in REG$ |
| $D\_VFA(i,j,r)$ | 0, 1 variable for identifying zero expenditures in $VFA(i,j,r)$<br>$D\_VFA(i,j,r) = 0$<br>$D\_VFA(i,j,r) = 1 \ \forall \ VFA(i,j,r) > 0$ | $\forall i \in TRAD\_COMM$<br>$\forall j \in PROD\_COMM$<br>$\forall r \in REG$ |
| $D\_VXWD(i,r,s)$ | 0, 1 variable for identifying zero expenditures in $VXWD(i,r,s)$<br>$D\_VXWD(i,r,s) = 0$<br>$D\_VXWD(i,r,s) = 1 \ \forall \ VXWD(i,r,s) > 0$ | $\forall i \in TRAD\_COMM$<br>$\forall r \in REG$<br>$\forall s \in REG$ |
| $D\_VST(i,r)$ | 0, 1 variable to identify zero expenditures in $VST(i,r)$<br>$D\_VST(i,r) = 0$<br>$D\_VST(i,r) = 1 \ \forall \ VST(i,r) > 0$ | $\forall i \in TRAD\_COMM$<br>$\forall r \in REG$ |

## 6    Slack Variables

$profitslack(j,r)$ — slack variable in the ZEROPROFITS equation [this is exogenous as long as output, $QO(j,r)$, is endogenous]    $\forall j \in PROD\_COMM$  $\forall r \in REG$

$cgdslack(r)$ — slack variable in the RORGLOBAL equation [this is exogenous as long as output of capital goods, $QO("cgds",r)$, is endogenous]    $\forall r \in REG$

$endwslack(i,r)$ — slack variable in the MKTCLENDWM and ENDW_SUPPLY equations [this is exogenous as long as primary factor rental rates, $PM(i,r)$ and $PME\text{-}S(i,j,r)$, are endogenous]    $\forall i \in ENDW\_COMM$  $\forall r \in REG$

$tradslack(i,r)$ — slack variable in the MKTCLTRD equation [this is exogenous as long as price of tradeable, $PM(i,r)$, is endogenous]    $\forall i \in TRAD\_COMM$  $\forall r \in REG$

$incomeslack(r)$ — slack variable in the REGIONALINCOME equation [this is exogenous as long as regional household income, $Y(r)$, is endogenous]    $\forall r \in REG$

$saveslack(r)$ — slack variable in the SAVINGS equation [this is exogenous as long as savings, $QSAVE(r)$, is endogenous]    $\forall r \in REG$

$govslack(r)$ — slack variable in the GOVERTU equation [this is exogenous as long as real government purchases, $UG(r)$, is endogenous]    $\forall r \in REG$

$walraslack$ — slack variable in the WALRAS equation [this is exogenous as long as price of savings, $PSAVE$, is endogenous as is the case in a *standard GE closure*. When any one of the GE links is broken, this is swapped with $PSAVE$, the numeraire price, thereby forcing global savings to equal global investment]

7    *Value and Income Variables*

| | | |
|---|---|---|
| $vxwfob(i,r)$ | percentage change in value of exports of tradeable commodity $i$ from region $r$ using *fob* weights [is identical to the linearized form of $VXW(i,r)$] | $\forall i \in TRAD\_COMM$ <br> $\forall r \in REG$ |
| $vxwreg(r)$ | percentage change in value of merchandise exports from region $r$ using *fob* weights [is identical to the linearized form of $VXWREGION(r)$] | $\forall r \in REG$ |
| $vxwcom(i)$ | percentage change in value of global merchandise exports of tradeable commodity $i$ using *fob* weights [is identical to the linearized form of $VXW\text{-}COMMOD(i)$] | $\forall i \in TRAD\_COMM$ |
| $viwcif(i,r)$ | percentage change in value of imports of tradeable commodity $i$ into region $r$ using *cif* weights [is identical to the linearized form of $VIW(i,r)$] | $\forall i \in TRAD\_COMM$ <br> $\forall r \in REG$ |
| $viwreg(r)$ | percentage change in value of merchandise imports into region $r$ using *cif* weights [is identical to the linearized form of $VIWREGION(r)$] | $\forall r \in REG$ |
| $viwcom(i)$ | percentage change in value of global merchandise imports of tradeable commodity $i$ using *cif* weights [is identical to the linearized form of $VIW\text{-}COMMOD(i)$] | $\forall i \in TRAD\_COMM$ |
| $vxwwld$ | percentage change in value of worldwide commodity exports using *fob* weights [is identical to the linearized form of $VXWLD$] | |
| $valuew(i)$ | percentage change in value of global supply of tradeable commodity $i$ using *fob* weights [is identical to the linearized form of $VWOW(i)$] | $\forall i \in TRAD\_COMM$ |
| $vgdp(r)$ | percentage change in value of GDP in region $r$ [is identical to the linearized form of $GDP(r)$] | $\forall r \in REG$ |
| $y(r)$ | percentage change in regional household income in region $r$ [is identical to the linearized form of $INCOME(r)$] | $\forall r \in REG$ |
| $yp(r)$ | percentage change in private household expenditure in region $r$ [is identical to the linearized form of $PRIVEXP(r)$] | $\forall r \in REG$ |

395

8    *Utility Variables*

| | | |
|---|---|---|
| $U(r)$ | per capita utility from aggregate household expenditure in region $r$ | $\forall r \in REG$ |
| $UP(r)$ | per capita utility from private household expenditure in region $r$ | $\forall r \in REG$ |
| $UG(r)$ | aggregate utility from government household expenditure in region $r$ | $\forall r \in REG$ |

9    *Welfare Variables*

| | | |
|---|---|---|
| $EV(r)$ | equivalent variation in region $r$, in \$US million (positive figure indicates welfare improvement) | $\forall r \in REG$ |
| $WEV$ | equivalent variation for the world, in \$US million (positive figure indicates welfare improvement) | |

10    *Trade Balance Variables*

| | | |
|---|---|---|
| $DTBAL(r)$ | change in trade balance of region $r$, in \$US million (positive figure indicates increase in exports exceeds increase in imports) | $\forall r \in REG$ |
| $DTBALi(i,r)$ | change in trade balance for tradeable commodity $i$ in region $r$, in \$US million (positive figure indicates increase in exports exceeds increase in imports) | $\forall i \in TRAD\_COMM$ $\forall r \in REG$ |

# Index